São Tomé and Príncipe

the Bradt Travel Guide

Kathleen Becker

www.bradtguides.com

Bradt Travel Guides Ltd, UK
The Globe Pequot Press Inc, USA

edition
I

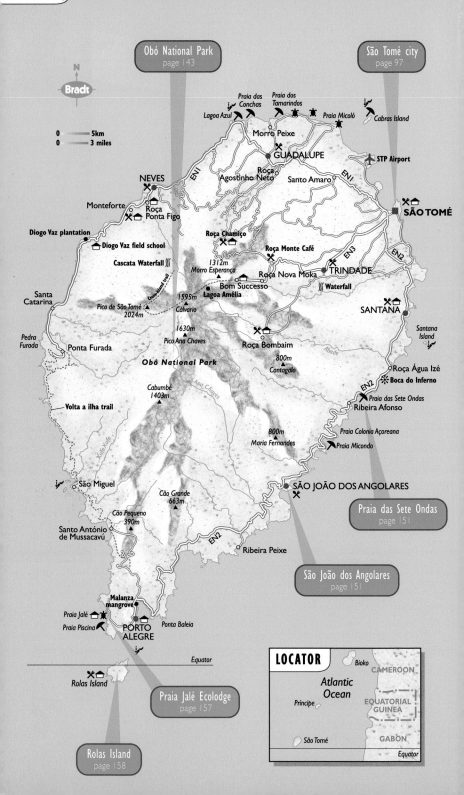

SÃO TOMÉ

Obó National Park
page 143

São Tomé city
page 97

N

Bradt

| 0 | 5km |
| 0 | 3 miles |

Praia das
Conchas

Praia dos
Tamarindos

Lagoa Azul

Praia Micoló

Cabras Island

Morro Peixe

GUADALUPE

STP Airport

Roça
Agostinho Neto

Santo Amaro

NEVES

Monteforte

Roça
Ponta Figo

SÃO TOMÉ

ENI

ENI

Ouro

Diogo Vaz plantation

Diogo Vaz field school

Roça Chamiço

Cascata Waterfall

Roça Monte Café

1312m
Morro Esperança

Roça Nova Moka

TRINDADE

EN3

EN2

Santa
Catarina

1595m
Cálvario

Bom Sucesso

Waterfall

SANTANA

Pico de São Tomé
2024m

Lagoa Amélia

Santana
Island

Pedra
Furada

Ponta Furada

1630m
Pico Ana Chaves

Obó National Park

Roça Bombaim

800m
Cantagalo

Roça Água Izé

Boca do Inferno

EN2

Cabumbé
1403m

Ana Chaves

Volta a ilha trail

Xufe-Xufe

Abade

Praia das Sete Ondas

Ribeira Afonso

800m
Maria Fernandes

Praia Colonia Açoreana

Praia Micondo

São Miguel

Cão Grande
663m

SÃO JOÃO DOS ANGOLARES

Praia das Sete Ondas
page 151

Cão Pequeno
390m

Santo António
de Mussacavú

EN2

São João dos Angolares
page 151

Ribeira Peixe

Malanza
mangrove

Praia Jalé
Praia Piscina

PORTO
ALEGRE

Ponta Baleia

Equator

Praia Jalé Ecolodge
page 157

Rolas Island

LOCATOR

Bioko

CAMEROON

Atlantic
Ocean

Príncipe

EQUATORIAL
GUINEA

São Tomé

GABON

Equator

Rolas Island
page 158

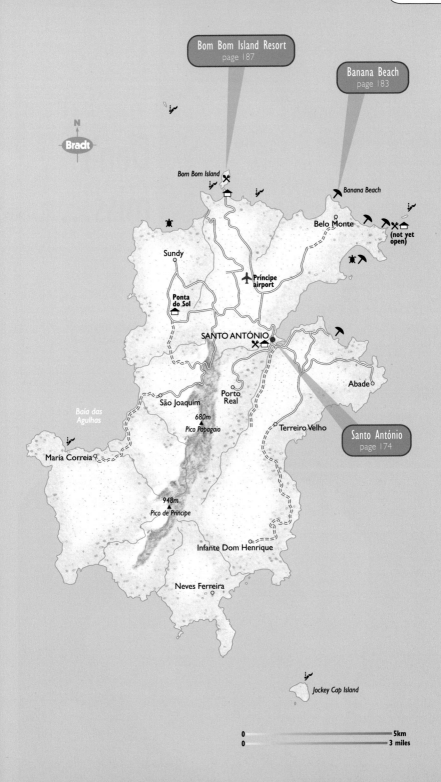

Bom Bom Island Resort
page 187

Banana Beach
page 183

Bradt

N

Bom Bom Island

Banana Beach

Belo Monte

(not yet open)

Sundy

Príncipe airport

Ponta do Sol

SANTO ANTÓNIO

Abade

São Joaquim

Porto Real

Baía das Agulhas

680m
▲ Pico Papagaio

Terreiro Velho

Maria Correia

Santo António
page 174

948m
▲ Pico de Príncipe

Infante Dom Henrique

Neves Ferreira

Jockey Cap Island

0   5km
0   3 miles

São Tomé and Príncipe

Don't miss…

Superb Beaches
Banana Beach, Príncipe
(CW) page 183

Cocoa plantation
Cracking open a cocoa pod
(CW) page 6

Birdwatching
Blue-breasted
kingfisher
(NB) page 32

**Diving among
pristine
coral reefs**
Hawksbill turtle
(WF) page 82

**Meeting the
people**
Smiling children,
São Joaquim
Plantation, Príncipe
(KB) page 12

top left   **Santo António Church, Príncipe** (CW) page 181

top right   **Statue of first Portuguese to discover the islands, National Museum, São Tomé** (KB) page 117

left   **Building engulfed by tree roots, Santo António, Príncipe** (KB)

top   **National Museum, São Tomé**
(CW) page 117

above   **Presidential Palace, São Tomé**
(CW) page 118

right   **Colonial architecture in downtown São Tomé** (RD)

Pico Cão Grande monolith
(IM) page 3

AUTHOR

Kathleen Becker is a German-Irish travel writer, radio journalist and translator who over the past fifteen years has reported from various European countries, the Americas and Africa. She has written a travel guide to London and co-authored guides to the literary landscapes of Norfolk and British detective fiction. Now based in Lisbon, Kathleen speaks half a dozen languages and is secretly chuffed that some Lisboners take her for a Brazilian! (Most just think she is mad for travelling around the city by bike.)

AUTHOR'S STORY

These two islands have so much more to offer than their tiny size would suggest. To write this guide I spent months hiking among its dense rainforests, lounging on empty beaches, visiting crumbling colonial plantation houses, climbing extinct volcanoes (sweating for Britain, or Bradt, rather), and tasting roasted cocoa beans as well as some of the best chocolate in the world. What's more, the destination is, as yet, largely undiscovered. One out-of-season British traveller told me he didn't meet a single other tourist in the three weeks he was out there. But the buzz of change is unmistakable in São Tomé and Príncipe: ecotourism and investment are beginning to take root. One only hopes the natural beauty of the islands will be preserved.

On a separate note, moving to Portugal has allowed me to see the islands through a kind of reverse prism: the country that previously ruled São Tomé and Príncipe for 500 years is home to many Santomeans, but lots live in near-slum conditions, and among many is a longing for their lost Africa. This book is as much for them as it is for the adventurous traveller dabbling with the idea of exploring these African islands. As I said, research was a huge amount of fun, but if the shy ossobó bird could finally show its face next time I visit that would be nice, thanks …

PUBLISHER'S FOREWORD   *Hilary Bradt*

The first Bradt travel guide was written in 1974 by George and Hilary Bradt on a river barge floating down a tributary of the Amazon. It was followed by *Backpacker's Africa*, published in 1979. In the 1980s and '90s the focus shifted away from hiking to broader-based guides to new destinations – usually the first to be published on those places. In the 21st century Bradt continues to publish these ground-breaking guides, along with guides to established holiday destinations, incorporating in-depth information on culture and natural history alongside the nuts and bolts of where to stay and what to see.

Bradt authors support responsible travel, with advice not only on minimum impact but also on how to give something back through local charities. Thus a true synergy is achieved between the traveller and local communities.

* * *

Bradt has always championed the 'little' places, pretty spots that tend to fly beneath the tourist radar – and are often all the more rewarding for it. São Tomé and Príncipe squarely fits the bill. Together the two islands form Africa's second-smallest country, but what they lack in size they make up for in charm. This is a destination that drips with colour, from its turquoise waters and deep green foliage to the bright clothes worn by the people themselves. Furthermore, Kathleen presents its attractions with a relish that makes this book a vivid portrait of a truly enticing country.

First edition published July 2008
Bradt Travel Guides Ltd, 23 High Street, Chalfont St Peter, Bucks SL9 9QE, England
www.bradtguides.com
Published in the USA by The Globe Pequot Press Inc, 246 Goose Lane,
PO Box 480, Guilford, Connecticut 06475-0480

Text copyright © 2008 Kathleen Becker; Extract (translation: KB) from Miguel Sousa
Tavares *Equador* printed with kind permission by Bloomsbury, London, who are publishing
their translation (by Peter Bush) in 2008; Recipe on page 76 courtesy of João Carlos Silva
and Oficina do Livro (translation: KB)
Maps copyright © 2008 Bradt Travel Guides Ltd; special thanks to Marcelin Ouangraoa,
Burkina Faso
Illustrations copyright © 2008 Individual photographers and artists
Editorial Project Manager: Emma Thomson

ISBN-13: 978 1 84162 216 3
British Library Cataloguing in Publication Data
A catalogue record for this book is available from the British Library

Photographs Camilla Watson (CW), Inna Moody (IM), Kathleen Becker (KB), Nigel Blake (NB),
Réne Dechaine (RD), Water Frame (WF)
Front cover Smiling woman (CW; www.camillawatson.com)
Back cover Praia dos Tamarindos beach (KB)
Title page Saotomean woman (CW), Porcelain rose (CW), Male greenthroat parrotfish (WF)

Illustrations William V Clarke **Maps** Steve Munns
Typeset from the author's disc by Wakewing
Printed and bound in Malta by Gutenberg Press Ltd

Acknowledgements

A big thank you to Bibi Braunstein and Luis Manuel Beirão from the Navetur agency in São Tomé for making things happen in the country, and to Julian Earwaker in the UK, Zé Bruno Parrinha in Portugal, and Marie and John O'Donoghue in Ireland for love and support. Thanks to Asterio Seca, an unflappable telecom whiz, sunny Bernardino Leite, José Spencer, Luis Mario Almeida, Maria João Pombo, Nora Rizzo and Jean-Louis Testori in São Tomé; Gerhard Seibert, who knows much more about the country than fits into the meticulously researched doorstopper he has written about it; Reto Scherraus for good ideas, and linguist Tjerk Hagemeijer and poet Conceição Lima in London; Dominique Gallet in France; and to all the travellers who shared tips, experiences and pictures with me – in particular Leon Debell and Richard Jamieson in the UK, trekking companions *extraordinaires* in the Príncipe rainforest, Camilla Watson in London/Lisbon, Sorin Lisker in Israel, Helmut and Karin from Munich, masters of the Pico de São Tomé, all the STP researchers and bloggers, as well as Emma Thomson, Adrian Phillips, Deborah Gerrard, and others in the Bradt office. And a special thanks to the countless Santomeans who gave me a warm welcome – in the hope of a brighter future for everyone.

In memoriam Sophie Warne, who first discovered São Tomé and Príncipe for Bradtpackers.

FEEDBACK REQUEST

The author would be delighted to hear about your own experiences in São Tomé and Príncipe. Any useful information/updates will be used in new editions of the guide to help other travellers. The best and most detailed updates will receive a free copy of the next guide. Email the author, in English, French, German, Portuguese, Spanish or Italian, at kathleenbecker@t-online.de.

Contents

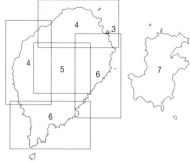

LIST OF MAPS

Introduction

'*Amiiiiiga!*' Friend! 'Taxi?' These bright yellow taxis are everywhere – so many zoom around the central market square of São Tomé, they show up on Google Earth. But wasn't life here supposed to be *léve-léve* calm, easy-going, relaxed? Escaping from the clinch of yellow fenders into the maze of the market building leads you straight into the rich colours of São Tomé: neat piles of green limes, red chilli pepper, yellow turmeric, dark grey charcoal, herbs and plantains, and the metallic shimmer and glassy stare of a swordfish in a bucket. Further afield, you'll find more colours: the waxy pink of the porcelain rose, the turquoise of a coastal bay, the rainbow of clothes spread to dry across the stones along one of the many rivers, and the luscious greens of the trees, plants and ferns of the rainforest that covers three quarters of the islands – nourished by rivers, waterfalls, and the tropical downpours of the rainy season. The forest creeps down to sandy beaches, white, golden, graphite-grey, where you are unlikely to meet a single tourist – but maybe a fisherman who'll sell you a fish from his catch. Freshly grilled fish 'belly', the sides of the Atlantic sailfish, is only one of the taste sensations of the archipelago; the delicious stickiness of the jackfruit, the acidity of a coffee cherry and the aromatic bitterness of a toasted cocoa bean are others. A hundred years ago, this archipelago was one of the world's biggest producers of cocoa; today, the faded glory and tumble-down charm of the plantations tell the story of the decline of colonial rule and the mono crops that sustained it. Rest your hiking feet on the creaking wraparound balcony of a restored plantation house, clutching a cold beer by candlelight, and you are in the middle of a living history lesson – on the story of west Africa, colonialism and the slave trade, and the crops that shaped these islands: sugar cane, coffee and, most of all, cocoa. Chocolate from 'the cocoa islands' is starting to appear on the shelves of supermarkets abroad; however, only one gourmet brand is actually produced here. Most Santomeans, working for a monthly wage many expats spend on a night out, certainly can't afford this luxury.

In Africa's second-smallest country, political power and business are concentrated around the capital and the northeast of main São Tomé island. In the poorer south, phallic basalt outcrops rising hundreds of metres out of the oil and coconut palms, shrouded in mist, create a certain Lord of the Rings atmosphere. And really, this is Middle Earth: São Tomé and Príncipe is the closest landmass to where the meridian, the line of zero longitude running through Greenwich in London, crosses the zero latitude, in other words, the equator. The equatorial archipelago's diverse habitats include rocky reefs covered in sea fans, hiding places for colourful parrotfish and snappers, grumpy-looking moray eels and majestic barracudas – and five species of turtles. São Tomé and Príncipe is one of west Africa's most important nesting sites for marine turtles; each winter they come to lay their eggs on the small strips of sand separating the Atlantic from the dense rainforest. Two dozen endemic bird species are starting to attract birdwatchers from all over the world, tick-lists in hand. Over the centuries, the arrival of slaves and 'contract workers' from the Congo basin, Angola, Cape Verde and Mozambique created a unique ethnic and cultural blend of musical and dramatic traditions, and a deliciously varied cuisine. Over half the population continue to live on one dollar a day, among mutterings of speculation about where exactly those millions of dollars went that the government received for the oil discovered in Santomean territorial waters. So far nobody has actually seen a drop of the black stuff, but if and when it starts flowing, *petróleo* is supposed to solve all the problems...

Some people will breezily tell you that you can see all of Príncipe in one day. You can of course, if you zoom along the island's few kilometers of tarred road in a jeep. However, you can spend weeks here and not see every corner of this spectacular island. In the 'city' of Santo António, the rainforest keeps trying to impose its grip on the crumbling colonial houses; a handful are restored in pretty colours, of others, only a stark façade is left. Maybe because of the splendid isolation of the island, experiences stay in your mind even more clearly: wonderful meals on the deck at the Bom Bom Island four-star resort, frugal picnics of biscuits and corn rolls atop an unknown waterfall, looking down across the indented coastline – or the spaghetti dinner with luke-warm beer at Belo Monte plantation, the shadowy silhouettes of our guide's siblings dancing by the light of a candle (on the wall) to *kizomba* tunes from the battery-powered stereo. The next morning we look down over Banana Beach, perfectly curved around turquoise waters. On Príncipe, the transition from beach paradise to rain-soaked misery can be quick. Retracing the steps of a scientist who had reported sand sharks feeding at the mouth of a particular river on an isolated beach in the southwest of the island involved a lot of walking, a lot of machete work to clear the path, a lot of aggressive mosquitoes, a lot of rain, more rain ... so it is six o'clock and nearly dark when we finally stumble down to the beach. We have barely finished wading through the river, water up to our hips, when we suddenly see them: a pair of sand sharks, elegant fins slicing the water at the river mouth. As it turns out, my hammock got left behind, so the evening's entertainment consists of flapping a sopping Gore-Tex jacket over the campfire in the rain, trying to dry-grill my legs at the same time. I snuggle up to the unconvincing fire, piling all the soaked wood within my reach onto it, too wet and cold to sleep. The next day, my walking socks have gone, quietly consumed by the fire in the night. *Caca–ôôô!* is, I think, the expression the *Santomense* use for this kind of thing.

A touch of mystery, farce even, clung to my departure from the archipelago. Spending hours having my African braids rearranged, I manage to miss the plane from Príncipe back to São Tomé. But wait, the air force plane from São Tomé is due in, I can get that! But then no, a bird has wrecked the turbine, the plane can't take off, and I'm stuck on the island for two more days. Funnily enough, I heard the 'bird-in-turbine' story again, not long afterwards, when I was due to travel home. This time though, it turned out to be the sound of my airline folding. Over a hundred people were left stranded, amidst the constantly changing rumours that are so typically Santomean. (I did get off the island, only four days late.) So, São Tomé and Príncipe is certainly not a tropical 'all-included' paradise, but you won't be short of good stories to tell!

Part One

GENERAL INFORMATION

Islands Two main islands: São Tomé, Príncipe; Ilhéu das Rolas (straddling the equator, inhabited), and several uninhabited islets: Ilhéu das Cabras, Ilhéu de Santana, Ilhas Tinhosas, Ilhéu de Caroço

Location Atlantic Ocean, approx 250km off the west African coast; the two main islands are about 150km apart

Size 1,001km^2 (São Tomé 854km^2, Príncipe 142km^2, Ilhéu das Rolas 3km^2)

Status Independent republic

Government Multi-party democracy

Population 160,000 (estd 2008): Creole, Capeverdian/Angolan descent, Angolar, mixed-race

Life expectancy 68 years

Capital São Tomé, on São Tomé island (population c55,000)

Economy Cocoa, tropical flowers, coconuts, tourism

Religion Roman Catholic (80%), Protestant (15%)

Currency Santomean dobra ($), € widely used, US$

Exchange rate US$1 = 15,000$, £1 = 30,000$, €1 = 23,000$ (July 2008)

International telephone code +239

Time GMT

Electricity supply 220V round, European two-pin sockets

Flag Two black stars on a horizontal three-band of green-yellow-green and a red isosceles triangle on the left

Public holidays: 1 January, 3 February, 1 May, 12 July, 6 September, 30 September, 26 November, 21 December, 25 December. See also page 79.

1

Background Information

GEOGRAPHY AND CLIMATE

São Tomé and Príncipe lie in the Gulf of Guinea, some 250km east of Gabon on the African mainland. At 1,001m², the archipelago is the second smallest country in Africa after the Seychelles; it is roughly three quarters the size of Greater London, or a third of Rhode Island state. Nicknamed the 'centre of the world', it is the closest landmass to the point in the Atlantic where the imaginary line of the equator crosses the zero meridian. The larger island, São Tomé, has a surface area of around 854km² and lies 250km off the Gabonese coast. At 142km², Príncipe, some 150km to the northeast and 225km off the coast of Equatorial Guinea, is about nine times smaller. Both islands are crisscrossed by rivers; on São Tomé most rivers have their source in the Obô national park, around the Pico de São Tomé. The islands' soil is fertile, thanks to their geologic make-up. São Tomé and Príncipe form part of the 1,200km Main Cameroon Line volcanic chain, stretching southwest from Lake Chad on the African mainland and including Bioko (previously called Fernando Pô), Príncipe and São Tomé down to Annobón (previously called Pagalu; both Bioko and Anobón now belong to Equatorial Guinea). Geologically and biologically, São Tomé and Príncipe are young, consisting mainly of hard undersaturated basalt lava – the Holocene shield volcano – that is reflected in the landscape of greatly eroded, precipitous mountains and dramatic **phonolithic rock towers** rising up vertically out of the rainforest of the south: the mighty Cão Grande, or *Pico Caué* (633m), and its smaller counterpart, Cão Pequeno. Phonolite is much more resistant to weathering and erosion than basalt; these volcanic plugs or dikes were created by the phonolite intruding into a basaltic volcano, and the softer surrounding basalt subsequently eroding away. Most of the time these phallic-looking towers are shrouded in mist, *leite de voador* ('flying fish milk'); getting a clear shot of Cão Grande has defeated more than one photographer. **Volcanic activity** stopped earlier here than on the other Gulf of Guinea islands. The oldest part of the archipelago is the Ilhéu das Cabras off the northern coast of São Tomé, at some 13 million years of age. The most recent dated volcanic rock is 0.1 million years old, and the basaltic cinder cones, mainly in the southeast of São Tomé, only formed around 100,000 years ago. On Príncipe, volcanic activity stopped earlier, some 15.7 million years ago; the island is much more deeply eroded, resulting in spectacular phonolitic rockscapes on a small surface area, seen particularly well along the southern coast.

At each side, the islands' rocky flanks plummet down to a depth of 3,000m below sea level, with most of the continental shelf around Príncipe – the archipelago was never part of the African mainland. This separate evolution and zoogeographical isolation accounts for the high level of **endemism**: many plant and bird species can only be found here, making the islands a paradise for wildlife lovers, birdwatchers and botanists. While the equatorial climate means

3

maximum average daily temperatures of 27°C to 29°C, there is a massive **difference in rainfall** across these small islands. The dry savannah area in the rain-shadow to the northeast of São Tomé island, including the capital, only receives around 60cm of rain per year, whereas the mountainous southern and western parts of the island, in the path of the mainly southwesterly winds, receive about 6m. Of the two islands, Príncipe has the wetter climate, again with the south of the island receiving a lot more rain than the north. Most rain falls in March and April.

HISTORY

The human history of São Tomé and Príncipe probably begins on **21 December 1470**, when the Portuguese seafarers Pedro Escobar and João de Santarém discovered the island they were to call São Tomé after the feast day of Saint Thomas (in the official saints' calendar, the day has since been moved to 3 July).

A replica of the *padrão* stone pillar that marked all Portugal's territories still stands above the beach where Escobar and Santarém landed, and the men themselves are commemorated by over-life-size sandstone statues outside the National Museum in São Tomé. On 17 January the following year, Escobar and de Santarém discovered a smaller island further north, which they called Santo Antão, after that day's saint. There has been a heated debate on whether the archipelago was populated before the Portuguese arrived. Given the proximity to the west African coastline, it is conceivable that there might have been settlers coming over by boat, and the issue is of great importance to nationalists seeking to establish a Santomean identity independent from the Portuguese settlers. However, to date, no archaeological evidence has been found to prove that early African settlers overcame the considerable navigational challenge, and the scientific consensus today is that the islands were indeed virgin territory when the Portuguese arrived. São Tomé's first administrator, João de Paiva, began populating the island when he took office in 1485, undeterred by the first settlers in the northwest succumbing to disease. **Sugar cane** was introduced in 1493, starting the 'sugar cane cycle'. Príncipe began to be settled in 1500. As early as 1515–17, the Portuguese king Dom Manuel I gave the slave men and women of the first settlers, and their common children, their freedom, manumitting them by the *Carta de Alforria*; this also freed their mixed-race (*mestiço*) children. Later, the slaves of the original settlers were freed, too. *Alforria* is where the name *forro* comes from, used for the majority ethnic group on São Tomé island and also the national creole, spoken by some 85% of *Santomense*. This is the source of the *forros'* feeling of superiority, as descendants of free Africans.

In the 15th and 16th centuries, the islands exported sugar cane, wood and pepper, and became a major **trading post** of the **transatlantic slave trade**. But there were many revolts against the colonialisers, starting in 1517. In 1553, Yon Gato, a blind planter, led a raid against the colonial powers with a group of slaves; today, one of the main squares in São Tomé town bears his name. Legend has it that around this time a ship bearing Angolan slaves was shipwrecked on Sete Pedras, a small group of tall sharp rocks some 5km off the southeastern coast. This gave rise to the widely propagated misconception that those who managed to swim ashore founded the Angolares community along the southeastern coast, around what is today the town of São João dos Angolares (see box, page 154). Today, 90% of the fishermen are Angolares, and they have their own language and culture. What is known is that Angolar slaves escaped to the deep rainforest to join communities of runaway slaves, *quilombos*, and descended on the town of São João dos Angolares and plantations to take chicken, goats and bananas – and women. In 1585 they burned down part of the city of São Tomé.

In **1595**, the leader of the most successful slave uprising, Amador, was captured, hung and quartered by the Portuguese. Today, **Rei Amador** is celebrated as a hero of the national struggle and commemorated by a fictitious likeness on all dobra banknotes, by a large bust outside the Historical Archive in São Tomé town and by a commemorative day on 4 January. From the turn of the 17th century, the colony was further weakened by pirate and corsair raids, starting in 1599, when São Tomé town was sacked by a Dutch fleet. This marked the beginning of two centuries of decline on the islands, during which the people sustained themselves with the cultivation of corn, manioc, yams, vegetables, citrus fruit and sugar cane spirit. In 1641, the Dutch came back, conquered São Tomé, razed over 70 sugar mills and occupied the island for over seven years. In 1709, São Tomé was attacked by the French. Yielding a much inferior product, sugar cane cultivation was moved across to the better soil and more stable political conditions of Portuguese's largest colony, Brazil. Due to ongoing troubles and raids, the island's capital was transferred from São Tomé to Santo António on Príncipe in 1753. It was nearly a hundred years (1852) before the capital was transferred back to São Tomé. Thus it was to the island of Príncipe that João Baptista da Silva introduced coffee (see box, page 130) from Brazil in 1787. And the smaller island was also the first to see the crop that was to make São Tomé's name: cocoa (see box, page 8). The introduction of these cash crops marked the **second colonisation** of the islands by the Portuguese.

The first wave of settlers had been sustained by convicts, as in the face of rampant malaria, the Portuguese king was finding it difficult to find settlers willing to colonise these faraway islands. In the second half of the 19th century however, the Portuguese started to gradually dispossess the *forros*, through land purchases, but also fraud. By the end of the 19th century, 90 % of the land was in the hand of Portuguese planters. The labour-intensive cocoa and coffee plantations needed vast numbers of workers, provided by slave labour from the African mainland. After the **abolition of slavery** in **1875**, tens of thousands of contract workers, *serviçais* ('servants'), mainly from Angola, and later Cape Verde and Mozambique, and indentured labourers continued to cultivate the monocrops, often in conditions virtually indistinguishable from slavery. Workers were rounded up, given a contract they could not read, had their documents taken and promised a return passage that after years of hard labour would then not materialise, as workers had to pay for their own food and lodgings. In the context of slavery (and the latter contract work, in many respects, different only in name), few of the original African traditions – dances, rituals, songs, stories – of the people forcibly brought to the islands survived intact, but were forged into an emerging **creole nation**, a cultural blend of the majority *forros*, traditionally occupying the higher positions in society, the *serviçais* contract labourers and their descendants born on the islands called *tongas*. One of the cultural legacies slavery has left in Santomean society, is a preference to working for themselves, to their own timetable, an attitude which still hampers the development of a modern work ethic.

Despite the country's geographic isolation, in the wake of burgeoning **independence movements** across colonial Africa, Santomeans, politicians and students had started to organize resistance, centring their efforts in nearby Gabon. An early turning point came in 1953, with the '**Massacre of Batepá**'. The events of 2–3 February 1953 mark a turning point in the islands' colonial history and the birth of Santomean nationalism. Against the background of the

On São Tomé and Príncipe, the larger plantation estates (*roças*), set up by the Portuguese for the production of cocoa and coffee, were their own self-contained, self-sufficient universes, operating largely outside the colonial administration's remit. The verb *roçar* in Portuguese means to clear land of forest, and the cleared land would stretch up the hill from the sea, to allow for the high altitude needed for arabica coffee. There would be the house of the administrator (*casa do patrão/administrador*), the quarters for administration and book-keeping, coffee and cocoa driers (*secadores*), the workers' quarters (*sanzalas*), a workshop and a nursery. The larger *roças* had beautiful hospitals; at one point there were over 20 on the islands. A large plantation, such as Água Izé or Rio do Ouro (now Agostinho Neto), would have had 20–30 satellites (*dependências*), connected by a network of railways which transported the beans to town, from where they would be shipped to Lisbon – where many plantation owners lived as absentee landlords. Many beaches still have the sad remnants of a pier sticking out to sea, and in the grounds of the plantations themselves railway tracks are sometimes just visible still under the grass or forest growth. Around the turn of the 20th century, there were some 800 plantations on the islands. The *serviçais* from Cape Verde, Angola and Mozambique would work a six-day week; breaking the monotony only with the songs, dances and traditions of their homelands. With independence in 1975, the world of the *roças* changed forever. The 2,000 or so Portuguese residents left, in fear of reprisals, taking with them the know-how to run the plantations. On 30 September 1975, two dozen larger plantations were nationalised, to great popular enthusiasm. However, with lack of investment, know-how and experience, production dipped drastically and the buildings and facilities fell into disrepair. Plantations were later regrouped into *empresas* but, in the face of volatile world market prices and internal corruption, they could not compete with cheap cocoa from other producing countries, such as the Ivory Coast. Today, most *roças* belong to the state, but are leased out to private individuals or consortia for business ventures. The majority seem slightly forlorn, as most buildings are dilapidated, not connected to the national grid, and few people are in work. All operate small-scale coffee production for private consumption. Agostinho Neto is maybe the most impressive; Água Izé is great for photography. Monte Café used to be the biggest producer of coffee, a role now taken on by Nova Moca, whilst another, much smaller plantation, São José, is exporting tropical flowers. A visit to any small plantation, off the beaten track in particular, gives a fascinating insight into a bygone era, much present still in the Portuguese psyche, and a good opportunity to glimpse the legacy of colonialism, not to mention wonderful photography opportunities: ferns and palm trees reclaiming the land, slowly obliterating the traces of human intervention. The plantations are usually open to visit, though the owner's house is sometimes guarded; there is no system of guided tours locally. Arranged tours focus mainly on Agostinho Neto and Água Izé but, if you are visiting on your own, informal guides are easy to come by and can show you around. On a tour, it can feel slightly exploitative to visit for five minutes, crowded in by curious children demanding sweets or a little money, take pictures and zoom off again, as the locals do not gain anything from living on a tourist attraction. So if you have the chance, wander around and buy a drink or biscuits from one of the shops, or some street food. The larger plantations often also have a *cantina* or *loja* where you can try the local food. If you don't mind roughing it a bit, it is always worth asking whether it is possible to stay the night. In a smaller plantation, ask for the community leader, *responsável*. On São Tomé, plantations such as São João, Bombaim or Monteforte have successfully been turned over to rural tourism, a trend starting in Príncipe too.

ongoing **labour problem on the plantations** under the new colonial governor (1944–53) Carlos Gorgulho, whose prestige rested on logistical construction and other projects (airports, stadium, cinema), achieved using forced labour, rumours that *forros* would be conscripted by force to work on the plantations led to protests. On 3 February, in Batepá, just north of Trindade (a stronghold of *forro* nationalism), an officer was killed with a machete. During the repression that followed, *forros* were rounded up, some burnt alive trying to hide in a cocoa drier, and many taken to a forced labour camp at Fernão Dias. Prominent *forros* such as Salustino Graça and sympathetic white planters were deported to Príncipe. Physical and psychological torture was used, with the notorious former prisoner Zé Mulato, from the Ponta Figo plantation, the most feared. In one of the most notorious incidents, of the 46 people crammed into a cell intended to hold only ten, only 18 survived the night. It remains unknown how many died in total; the often-cited figure of 1,032 deaths is taken to be largely symbolic as the last two digits reference the day and month of the beginning of the massacre: 3/2/1953. A young teacher, Alda Graça Espírito Santo (see page 26), took notes from survivors – and went on to become one of the country's foremost politicians and poets. Indirectly, the Massacre of Batepá' led to the formation of the **CLSTP** (Comité de Libertação de São Tomé and Príncipe) in 1960, the forerunner of the MLSTP liberation party, recognized by the UN and the Organisation of African Unity. Today still, every year, the day is commemorated by youth marches, speeches and storytelling at Fernão Dias and debates in the media ruminate on the significance and the legacy of 1953.

DECOLONISATION Portugal was the first colonial world power and the last to release its colonies into independence. In the Portuguese **Estado Novo** ('new state'), under the dictatorship of António Oliveira Salazar (1933–70) and Marcello Caetano (–1974), the colonies were vital to Portugal's existence and role on the international stage, a small country hemmed in – by Spain on one side, and the Atlantic Ocean on the other. The church saw its role as the civilising arm of the Portuguese nation. In 1968, the socialist and anti-colonialist Mário Soares was exiled to São Tomé for several months; already in custody, he was called in and told to pack his bags as he was leaving for São Tomé the next day. Once here, he was constantly followed around the island's pot-holed roads by 22 agents of the Portuguese secret police PIDE (who had started operating on the island in 1953 to investigate the causes of the massacre of Batepá), who were trying to isolate the dangerous subversive from the population and the country's independence movement, which at that time was coordinated by exiled leaders Miguel Trovoada and Manuel Pinto da Costa. When Salazar was replaced by Marcello Caetano in September 1968 (following a brain haemorrhage), Soares was allowed to leave in November. In 1972, Pinto da Costa, freshly returned from East Berlin with a PhD in economics, was elected general secretary of the MLSTP (the successor to the CLSTP) in Santa Isabel (Malabo). After the fall of the dictatorship on 25 April 1974 in the army-led **Carnation Revolution**, Soares went on to become prime minister (1976–8 and 1983–5) and president (1986–96) of the new democracy. Decolonisation was triggered by the bloodless coup in Portugal; at that point, colonial wars (from 1961) in Angola, Guinea-Bissau and Mozambique had already cost thousands of lives. On 5 September 1974, a demonstration in São Tomé and Príncipe demanded independence for the archipelago; only two deaths occurred and these were unrelated to the demonstration. Whilst unrest had started much earlier, in November of that year, the treaty of Algiers was signed between the Portuguese government and the representatives of the *Movimento de Libertação de*

Few people know that São Tomé and Príncipe were the first African countries to cultivate cocoa. Cocoa was introduced from the Lower Amazon basin to Príncipe first (the Simaló plantation) in 1820, while Brazil was fighting its war of independence, by the Brazilian chief-captain João Baptista Silva (died 1837; his bones are kept in a wooden box in the National Museum in São Tomé). Over the following 150 years, the monoculture of cocoa on the 'Chocolate Islands' has been more of a curse than a blessing, but given the trend towards gourmet and single-estate chocolate, together with the possibilities of rural tourism, cocoa could be turned to good use for the archipelago's tourism industry. I met a French couple on honeymoon who were inspired to travel to São Tomé by a chocolate wrapper! Cocoa, *Theobroma cacao*, originates in the Americas and only grows in a very limited geographical zone: around ten degrees to the north and south of the equator. The 'food of the Gods' performs best at an altitude of up to 700m. Today, a third of the islands is covered in cocoa trees, *cacaoeiros*. The cocoa and coffee trees are of a similar height: if you can't see whether they have pods or berries, you can easily distinguish them by their leaves: those of the coffee tree are a shiny dark green, those of the cocoa tree turn in part various colours. Cocoa was initially only introduced into the country as a decorative plant, before its potential as a cash crop was discovered. As for coffee, the story of cocoa cultivation in São Tomé and Príncipe starts in Príncipe. Cocoa took 30 years to reach the bigger island, when the Brazilian João Maria de Sousa e Almeida (died 1869), Gomes' godchild, started cultivating cocoa at the Água Izé plantation in 1852; he was the first mixed-race baron of any Portuguese colony. Both coffee and cocoa need shade; for this, fast-growing flame trees were imported from South America, *erythrinas* with beautiful orange flowers that are visible everywhere around the plantations.

With the **abolition of slavery** in 1876 in Portugal, the problem of labour rose ever more urgently. In the early 20th century, the islands were one of the top cocoa producers in the world, but persistent reports of contract workers being employed in conditions of effective slavery were beginning to impact on the colony. In 1908, William

São Tomé and Príncipe (MLSTP), accepted by the UN as the sole representatives of the Santomean people. The treaty paved the way for **independence**, proclaimed on 12 July 1975. Don't be surprised, however, if some of the older Santomeans will tell you that things were *much* better during colonial times: there was power, there was drinking water, there were proper bus services, and less poverty and disease.

POLITICS AND SOCIETY

Some say that 'STP' stands for *Somos Todos Primos* ('we are all cousins'), reflecting the family-style dynamics of a small-island population. Santomean politics are indeed based around people and kinship rather than issues, and a number of high-profile *forro* families – Gomes, Graça, Tiny, Pinto da Costa, Trovoada – continue to form the local elite. This cosy – or claustrophobic, if you like – situation has repercussions for the islands' politics, economy, judiciary and the media.

When the **Democratic Republic of São Tomé and Príncipe** was founded on **12 July 1975**, with independence from Portugal, the country became a one-party state led by the liberation party MLSTP, with **Manuel Pinto da Costa** (1937–) its first president and **Miguel Trovoada** (1936–) its first prime minister. Da Costa and Trovoada were leading a nationalised (and, from 1979 onwards, centrally planned) economy, with its own secret service and repression of dissent.

Cadbury himself came over to São Tomé in person to investigate. Despite his Quaker faith and humanitarian concern, he did not have much regard for the native population, but his book, *Modern Slavery*, resulted in a **boycott** of Santomean cocoa in 1909 by British and German chocolate producers – Cadbury Brothers in Bournville/Birmingham, Rowntree in Bristol, and Stollwerck in Cologne, Germany. Britain's motives were maybe not completely altruistic, as cocoa from São Tomé was in direct competition with the cocoa from their own colony, the Gold Coast, today's Ghana. The story of the colonial rivalry between Portugal and Britain is told in fictionalised form in Miguel Sousa Tavares' romance *Equador* (see page 27).

Today, the islands' most famous cocoa comes from **Príncipe** (see *Terreiro Velho*, page 183). The pods, sprouting directly from the purplish-grey trunk in a range of beautiful colours – burgundy, orange, green, yellow, red – are harvested using a curved knife on a long pole. The pods are opened with a machete, to extract the around 40 fatty seeds (beans) encased in a fresh white acidic-sweet pulp. Kids on the plantations love to suck this; try it, it is delicious. A good breaker can open up to 500 pods an hour. Then, the most important part of the process begins: fermentation. The beans, still covered by the pulp, have to be moved regularly in their wooden crates for about six days while the juice drains away ('sweating'). Then, the beans are spread out on long *secadores*, solar drying racks, protected from the rain by plastic covers and regularly moved using little rakes. Then the tiny stem is removed, by hand. To make one pound of chocolate, some 400 beans are needed. On today's markets, cocoa fetches around US$1,900 per ton. Over half of Santomean cocoa is bought by the Dutch. The plantation workers themselves could never afford to buy the chocolate, and have probably never tasted it either, let alone the Mars and Snickers bars in the shops. There are some organic cocoa plantations in the north, but no fairtrade ventures as yet. The only producer actually making chocolate on the islands is the Italian Claudio Corallo, but with the trend towards vintage chocolate, 'São Tomé' chocolate bars are beginning to appear in shops all over the world. In 2007, worldwide demand for chocolate was forecast to grow by 15% over the following five years.

Marxist-Leninist doctrines and jargon flourished. The **flag** – two black stars on a horizontal three-band of green-yellow-green and a red isosceles triangle on the left echoes the pan-African colours of Ethiopia.

The country's **motto** *Unidade – Disciplina – Trabalho* ('Unity – Discipline – Work') features on the Santomean **coat-of-arms**: a palm tree topped by a blue star and flanked by a black kite to the left, representing São Tomé, and a grey parrot to the right, representing Príncipe. However, despite the backing of aid from fellow Socialist states such as the Soviet Union, Cuba, neighbouring Angola and East Germany, São Tomé and Príncipe's economy struggled from the start. Soon, against the background of collapsing cocoa prices on the world markets, low productivity and internal **power struggles**, the party leadership became increasingly dogmatic and repressive, cutting off the island state even more from the outside world. Political change started as early as 1983–4, but the island's isolation became untenable with the advent of *perestroika* in Gorbachev's Soviet Union in the late 1980s, and the crumbling of old alliances. Seeing its economic fortunes wane with the downward course of its Socialist allies, the party engaged in dialogue and change to attract western donors, and in 1991 São Tomé and Príncipe became a **multi-party democracy**, in a bloodless transition – as one of the first countries in Africa! In the first, largely free and fair, multi-party elections, the Santomeans elected **Miguel Trovoada president**. With the exception of a couple of years, the non-affiliated party, now called MLSTP/PSD, was to hold on to this post for the next decade. Elected for five years, for a maximum of two terms, the president has a prominent role in Santomean politics. In the first **regional elections** in December 1992, the MLSTP (Partido Social Democrático) took six out of seven districts. 1995, the year that Príncipe (Pagué) was given self-government, was marred by an (unrelated) shortlived and bloodless **military coup**.

At the **2001 presidential elections**, wealthy businessman Fradique de Menezes ('Fradique', see box page 11) was elected president, beating the MLSTP/PSD's Manuel Pinto da Costa, then party leader and former head of state (1975–91). Another military coup in 2003 was again short-lived – in São Tomé, even the coups are léve-léve – and did not involve any bloodshed: when President Fradique de Menezes was in a conference in Nigeria, members of the military seized their opportunity. In protest at what they saw as a fake 'democracy' built on vote-buying, amongst deteriorating living conditions for both the general population and the army (at that point, the military had not been paid for months), Alércio Costa and Major Fernando Pereira led half of the country's 400 soldiers plus over a dozen former mercenaries to detain government ministers in the barracks. The coup was universally condemned, and without external support, after a week, order was restored. The Nigerian president Olusugun Obasanjo accompanied Fradique on his way back to show support. However, the issue of oil (see box page 16) and the distribution of potentially big revenues, was already looming large in the background.

At the legislative elections in March 2006, the MDFM/PCD alliance (*coligação*) won 23 of the 55 seats in the National Assembly, beating the fathers of Santomean independence and former communists of the MLSTP/PSD. This ended the awkward cohabitation situation with the MLSTP/PSD – at that point Fradique's presidency had been plagued by conflicts with six different governments for five years.

During my first visit, in the summer of 2006, I had the chance to observe two elections in a row. On the streets, the campaigns were accompanied by lots of palm-wine fuelled dancing, T-shirts showing Fradique de Meneze's moustachioed face and brightly coloured traditional skirts with party prints on them, trucks with huge sound systems strapped onto them doing the rounds of the islands, lots of free beer and *bulawé* drums, and raunchy dancers. At the **presidential elections** of July 2006 Fradique de Menezes was re-elected president, winning around 60% of the vote. The candidate for ADI (*Acção Democrática Independente*, Independent Democratic Action), businessman Patrice Trovoada (1962–), son of former president Miguel Trovoada, but a controversial figure, tainted by accusations of illegal arms trading and other shady deals, challenged Fradique de Menezes for the presidency party and won 38% of the vote. By Santomean standards, the 65% was not high.

Fradique's party also went on to dominate the **regional elections** of August 2006 (the first since 1992) and, with its Secretary General, Tomé Vera Cruz, provided the country's new **prime minister.** Vera Cruz' training as an electrical engineer should have come in handy in solving the ongoing energy crisis in the country, but 2007, in the words of President Fradíque de Menezes, turned out to be one of the 'most difficult' years for the young nation in recent history, despite the pardon of the country's debt (see page 18) and successes in combating malaria. In July 2007, STP was in the news again – if only really in the lusophone media – for the wrong reasons: an elite police unit, Angolan-trained 'ninjas', protesting for not receiving a promised bonus pay, seized the main police headquarters, taking the police commander and other officers hostage, but releasing them shortly afterwards. **Political instability** remains one of the constants of Santomean

Born in 1942 in the Água Telha neighbourhood of Madalena to a Portuguese father (a supervisor for the Vale Flor company on the Rio do Ouro – today Agostinho Neto – plantation), and a Santomean *mestiço* mother, Fradique de Menezes is a shrewd businessman as well as a very determined politician. With his frizz of greying hair and moustache, jovial 'Fradique' has been very successful in projecting a popularist image as 'one of the people'. Despite not coming from one of the traditional influential families, Fradique is certainly now one of the country's wealthiest men, with a fleet of cars parked at his house on the Quinta da Favorita, near Trindade. Fradique received all his higher education from the age of 12 onwards in Portugal and experienced the colonial wars first-hand during his military service in 1965 in Mozambique – fighting on the side of the Portuguese. Studying psychology in Belgium – incidentally, the country with the highest per-capita chocolate consumption – he met his first wife, chocolate dynasty heiress and teacher Miriam Lampert; he brought her to São Tomé in the 1980s, where they taught French at the local secondary school. The couple had no children, but his wife founded a children's charity, before dying of malaria in 1993. Affiliating himself initially with the MLSTP and MLSTP/PSD, Fradique joined the ADI (Action for Democratic Independence) party (founded in 1992) in 1994. By that time, he was buying most of the island's cocoa and as owner of the CGI company effectively has a monopoly in the import of cement. To be able to stand for president in 2001, de Menezes had to renounce his Portuguese citizenship. He founded a new party, *Movimento Democrático Força de Mudanza* or, some said, the 'Movement for the Defense of Fradique de Menezes'. A law limiting the powers of the presidency was passed in early 2003. However, the attempted coup later that year left de Menezes in a stronger position, and his 2006 re-election with 60% of the vote showed that most Santomeans seem to credit him with the business nous to manage the country's potentially huge oil wealth.

public life, as do liberally-spread rumours and mutually-traded accusations of corruption. When in early 2008, parliament refused to approve the annual budget (*orçamento*), the government was brought down. Amidst **popular discontent** following shortages of staple foods such as rice, sugar and cooking oil, as well as spiralling energy costs, Prime Minister Vera Cruz stepped down, accusing the opposition of making the country 'ingovernable' at an important juncture in its development, on the cusp of the awaited oil flow. At this point, for example, the ANP (Agência Nacional de Petróleo) body governing the national oil resources had been without leadership for months and there was a threatening conflict between the World Monetary Fund and the government about changes to the oil revenue laws. ADI's Patrice Trovoada assumed the post of prime minister of the country's 12th constitutional government in February 2008, illustrating yet again the circular nature of Santomean politics. As of early 2008, the MDFM, PCD and ADI together held 34 of the parliament's 55 seats, the MLSTP/PSDFM/PSD opposition, led by Rafael Branco, 20. Branco now heads the new government, formed in June 2008, as after only three months a vote of no confidence toppled Trovoada's government. If you should be on the islands during one of these periodic crises, you will notice however, that the vast majority of the population remains unfazed by developments, life continuing much the same as before.

Elections are of course the one time when politicians do like to engage the population. São Tomé and Príncipe has an endemic culture of political favouritism and vote-buying. While the ballot is secret and, despite a few minor irregularities, elections are generally considered free and fair, the practice of **banho** ('bath'), giving presents and favours for votes, is deeply engrained. Around election time, all of a sudden, a fleet of brand-new motor bikes will appear on the streets, a reward for successfully mobilising votes. There is also a dispiriting history of development aid being channelled into personal pockets. In 1996, for instance, 18 brand-new Renault cars for the new MLSTP/PSD/ADI government turned out to have been paid for by the World Bank's structural adjustment credit of over US$3 million, while there was no money to fix the generators and sort out the constant energy provision problems of many of the capital's neighbourhoods. More than ten years later, a local deputy complained to me that foreign donors do not supervise how the money is spent. In 2004, the **corruption scandal** around the **GGA** (Gabinete de Gestão de Ajudas) food aid agency brought down Prime Minister Maria das Neves. In 2007, the corruption-monitoring organization Transparency International placed São Tomé and Príncipe at joint position 118 out of 179 evaluated countries, the first time the country was ranked. Ministers accused of corruption are often given prestigious postings abroad, or return to government a bit later down the line, as happened during Fradique's cabinet reshuffle in late 2007. As few politicians and public servants are put on trial for corruption, let alone convicted, a sense of general impunity prevails.

On the diplomatic level, São Tomé and Príncipe joined the United Nations shortly after independence and is a member state of **PALOPS** (*Países Africanos de Lingua Official Portuguesa*) countries with Portuguese as official language. With the foundation of **CPLP** (*Comunidade dos Povos de Lingua Portuguesa*) in 1996, tiny São Tomé and Príncipe joined Angola, Brazil, Cape Verde, Guinea-Bissau and Mozambique in a community of 200 million Portuguese-speaking people. In terms of development, Cape Verde, the island state further north along the African west coast is seen as the model to follow. The country of origin of thousands of contract labourers who chose to stay on at independence rather than return to their drought-stricken home is now a successful tourist destination. Portugal remains an important partner in commerce, aid and cultural co-operation, but in 2007 Fradique de Menezes joined other African leaders in rejecting the European Union's offer of Economic Partnership Agreements, arguing the tiny country was not ready to open itself up to the Common Market. Among the Gulf of Guinea states, traditionally, Angola has been a close ally in terms of financial, logistical and military assistance, but since the emergence of the joint oil exploration with Nigeria, the most populous country in Africa has been successfully vying for influence, promising infrastructural, social and cultural investments. Taiwan has been an important partner since 1997, when Miguel Trovoada swapped Beijing for Taipeh.

The overall **human rights** situation in the country is good. However, the judiciary suffers from long delays in sentencing; prisoners often remain in jail without judgement. People's faith in the justice and political system has been eroded amongst accusations and counter-accusations of the 'blue bag', *saco azul*, of corruption. While the police service is currently being reformed, impunity is a problem many people have commented on to me. In terms of diplomacy, **relations with the US** are excellent: Voice of America radio transmitters since the early 1990s, and joint military exercises in the Gulf of Guinea (a strategic zone due to its oil wealth) for years. The US recently installed a radar system to monitor the territorial waters.

PEOPLE

One of the best things about São Tomé and Príncipe is the **lack of tribal, ethnic or religious strife**. The Santomeans (*Santomense*) are the fruit of a dynamic ethnic mix. The Portuguese colonialists traditionally mixed more with the native population than the English; there is a saying that whereas the English and French colonisers made enemies, the Portuguese made children. Like other Portuguese colonies, such as Angola or Mozambique, São Tomé and Príncipe have a very diverse society. The dominant sector, both in terms of numbers and prestige, are the *forros*, descendants of freed slaves or the product of relationships between Portuguese and local women (*filhos da terra*). They traditionally disdained manual work on the plantations, and in 1953 the rumour of imminent conscription brought on demonstrations, triggering the massacre of Batepá (see page 5).

Mixed-race *Santomense* are called *mulattos* or *bobos* ('yellows'); in contrast to other creole societies they do not necessarily occupy higher positions in society. Prominent mulattos include: President Fradique de Menezes, current prime minister Rafael Branco and Attorney General Roberto Raposo. *Tongas* are the descendants of African workers born in São Tomé and Príncipe. Those born on Príncipe are known as *minuiê*, but sometimes called *moncós* in a disparaging manner. On Príncipe most of the population (90%) have Capeverdian heritage. Whites of all nationalities are called *brancos/brancas* or, as I was called in a couple of villages in the south: *colomba*. If you spend a while on the islands, you get used to calls of '*Branco/a, branco/a!*'

São Tomé's rich ethnic mix also contains a **Jewish** element. In 1493, in an attempt to populate the island and to 'whiten the race', around 1,000 Jewish children aged between two and ten years of age were shipped to São Tomé by order of Dom Manuel I. Their parents had fled to Portugal a year earlier, when Spain expelled all Jews, but were not able to pay the extortionate poll tax demanded for crossing the border. Three years later, the Jews were expelled from Portugal too. In São Tomé, the children were converted to Catholicism and put to work on the plantations. Many of them succumbed to malaria and other tropical diseases, but some 600 survived and intermarried with members of the creole community. Today, there are few traces of their passing; there is no known Jewish community on the islands, but an international conference in 1995 was the starting point for more research on this little-known part of the island's history. With the arrival of many **Nigerians** on the oil trail, there has been a fear that Nigerians, indeed far more astute business people than the *Santomense*, are 'taking over', some buying property on the island without even visiting the country. There is also a Chinese element to the rich Santomean mix, as evidenced by family names such as Ten Jua or Chong.

With a median age of 16 years (2006 est) and some 45% of Santomeans under 15, São Tomé and Príncipe is a young society. The urban youth who can afford it wear American-style sportswear, topped with baseball caps, and talk to the world via MSN Messenger.

EDUCATION

The official literacy rate of 75% is wildly optimistic considering how many people I witnessed struggling with scribbling their names. Until 1952, there were no grammar schools on the islands. Today, the Liceu Nacional in the capital has 4,000 students, studying up to grade 11, age 17; in Príncipe, pupils can only study up to grade 9, and many only get a few years' basic schooling. With children working on the plantations or lacking the money for books, absenteeism is a problem. School uniforms cost money: their introduction for higher education was very controversial. Only about 85% of children go to school – as evidenced by the kids selling necklaces or cakes in the street – and only 80% in Príncipe; where over 25% of students drop out before the fourth grade. Since 1996, São

Tomé and Príncipe has had a higher-education polytechnic, offering baccalaureate degrees. In the late 19th century, São Tomé sent more black students to study in Portugal than any other Portuguese colony. Today, unrest amongst young people is growing, out of frustration with the limited number of study grants to go abroad, and there are stories of nepotism networks ensuring that the few available places go to friends and relations of influential families. Partly in response to this, the private Lusíadas University opened in 2007, offering degrees in business administration and law.

WOMEN

In politics and the judiciary, women occupy a fairly prominent position. A former minister of trade, Maria das Neves (MLSTP/PSD) served as prime minister from 2002 to 2004; though much loved by low-income citizens, she had to step down amongst accusations of corruption. Women currently occupy five of the seats (9%) in parliament. In recent memory, during the government of Prime Minister Maria das Neves, the president of the Supreme Court and the governor of the Central Bank were both female, the Secretary of State of Trade and Commerce, the deputy prime minister/Minister for Planning and Finance, and the Minister for Education, Culture, Youth and Sports were female. The head of the Treasury and Financial Directorate is a woman, as is the president of the Supreme Court. Other women occupy senior positions in the more traditionally female sectors of health and culture. Historically, many topographical names, many beaches, plantations and mountains bear the names of women, such as Ana de Chaves, who gave her name to the bay of São Tomé, to its second-highest peak and to a river. In colonial times, many Portuguese settlers had local lovers, euphemistically called *lavadeiras*, 'washer women'. You will notice that in discussions of colonialism, most Portuguese remain proud of their policy of mixing, of 'making children', unlike the more segregationist British or French attitude. Today, despite the **fertility** rate going down, women have an average of five children, and still shoulder a large workload in a male-dominated society. Market traders (*palaiês*), all women, have an important role and manage large budgets. In the fishing community, women have considerable power, though some of the market fishwives are feared for their sharp tongue and rough manners. The taboo surrounding **domestic violence** in São Tomé and Príncipe is being lifted, and the topic is now discussed in the media and portrayed in community drama. Men often complain of their partners' jealousy, maybe not unfounded, given Santomean men's perceived track record as two-timing *bandidos*. Only about 10% of 15–24-year-old women have comprehensive and correct knowledge of **HIV/AIDS**. Official figures put the rate of infection at around 2%, but this probably hides a higher, increasing rate. The immune system deficiency virus carries an immense stigma still, as one local woman found who spoke to local television about her condition. Even with her back turned to the camera, she was identified in her community and ostracised, as was one of her children, also HIV positive. Fearing the stigma, infected patients refuse to go to the clinic to pick up retro-viral medication and infected mothers refuse to use formula milk. Despite the imaginatively painted panels you see showing the benefits of condoms, and their availability for free or at a symbolic price, only a third of Santomeans use them regularly. Often women defer to their partner's unwillingness to use a condom – 'one should not eat a banana with its skin', as a popular saying goes – or feel using them would make them seem immoral. The level of sexual education is very low and, while sexual banter is a fixture of Santomean culture, discussing disease and prevention still carries a taboo. Meanwhile, in the capital, prostitution is common in hotels and along the capital's Água Grande canal. A recent story in the newspaper involved a local businessman looking for a girl who was surprised to find his own daughter waiting for clients. Some of them, but not all, use condoms, and many are young – *catorzinhas*, literally 'little/sweet 14-year-olds'. Already, Santomeans working in the neighbouring Gulf of Guinea states with higher rates of infection, such as Equatorial Guinea, Cameroon and Gabon, are putting themselves at risk. If and when the oil rush takes off, more prostitution and higher infection rates will follow. Under-age sex is common. The official age for marriage on São Tomé and Príncipe is 14 for girls, 16 for boys. Many young women have their first pregnancy at 14; abortions are illegal, but do take place, using traditional healers. **Homosexual** acts are banned.

ECONOMY

São Tomé and Príncipe's main cash crop for export is still **cocoa**, bringing in US$5 million a year. Most families live by subsistence farming, bringing in the produce from their yard (*quintal*) to market. As there is not much diversity, most yield the same crops (bananas, papayas, tomatoes, limes, cocoyam, etc), and competition is intense. There are some 50 small and medium-sized enterprises, plus several hundred micro-enterprises, such as restaurants, tailors, shoemakers and carpenters. **Privatisation** since the early 1990s has been slow, hampered by inefficiency, bureaucracy and political meddling. In the fishing industry, a sector with potential growth, attempts are being made to install refridgeration and introduce sanitised handling conditions – most fish today is preserved by salting and drying. Palm oil production is being encouraged. **Diversification** is the buzzword, encouraged by NGOs and often carried out by Portuguese investors. In the face of logistical challenges, **tourism** is slow to grow, though there are some encouraging sustainable and community-oriented ventures alongside major investments by the Portuguese Pestana group amongst others.

Two **free-trading zones** are set to add to STP's portfolio of economic activities. One *zona franca* service hub, with a surface area of 17 hectares, is being built just behind the airport on São Tomé island, offering duty-free trading, off-shore business centre/banking, health and leisure facilities for the local elite and expats. A deep-sea port is vaguely envisaged for the Morro Carregado area around Fernão Dias further west along the northern coastline. On Príncipe, a second free-trading zone, earmarked for the Baía das Agulhas, is now being shelved in favour of tourism development. Whilst good news for jobs, commercial logistics and investment – drinking water is finally arriving at the surrounding coastal villages – there were fears that the construction and running of the port would cause lasting damage to the environment.

It would be a risky strategy for Santomeans to pin their hopes exclusively on *petróleo*, **oil** (see box, pages 16).

DEVELOPMENT In the Human Development Index 2007, São Tomé and Príncipe came in at number 123, out of 175 states surveyed, rising three places. In the same year, life expectancy was 57 for men and 60 for women. Statistics paint a brighter picture than for many other African countries (over the past few years the IMF has been recording economic growth), but since independence the economy and social indicators have gone down. The country is very rich in fresh water but, due to degraded reservoirs and pipes, only some 20% of *Santomense* have access to clean drinking water, and only around 15% of the population have access to a latrine, meaning that, effectively, most defecate in the open air, with dire consequences for public health. One thousand under-

Gerhard Seibert, researcher at the CEA/ISCTE, Lisbon

Speculations about onshore oil resources in the archipelago already existed in colonial times. However, as exploration drillings in the north of São Tomé island in 1989 were negative, it was presumed that oil could only exist offshore in the country's territorial waters, close to the already discovered offshore oil reserves of Nigeria and Equatorial Guinea. Motivated by this assumption, the small US company Environmental Remediation Holding Corporation (ERHC) became the first company to develop the country's oil sector. The development of oil in São Tomé and Príncipe started in May 1997 when the country signed its first oil agreement with ERHC. At that time nobody in São Tomé's weak and corrupt administration had any expertise in oil dealings. The company helped the local government to delineate its 200-mile Exclusive Economic Zone (EEZ) and claim its maritime boundaries. In 1998 São Tomé and Príncipe signed a second agreement with Mobil (now ExxonMobil) on the execution of seismic surveys. Plagued by financial problems at home, ERHC was not in a position to meet its contractual obligations. Consequently, in 1999 the country's government unilaterally rescinded the contract. In turn, ERHC lodged a request for arbitration at the International Chamber of Commerce in Paris. The problem was only solved when in early 2001 ERHC was taken over by Chrome Energy Corporation, owned by the Nigerian businessman Emeka Offor. In exchange for a new agreement with ERHC the company's new owner withdrew the request for arbitration. Around the same time the Norwegian Petroleum Geo-Services (PGS) signed an agreement on seismic surveys with the government.

Aware of the importance of an internationally recognised EEZ, São Tomé and Príncipe had signed bilateral agreements on the delineation of its maritime borders with Equatorial Guinea (1999) and Gabon (2001). However, sea border negotiations with Nigeria failed, because Abuja refused to accept a boundary based on equidistance between the continent and the archipelago. Instead, in February 2001 Nigeria and STP established a Joint Development Zone (JDZ) in the waters disputed by the two countries. A Joint Development Authority (JDA) in Abuja manages the 28,000km^2/10,819 sq miles JDZ. The two countries share the JDZ's profits and costs, in the proportions of Nigeria 60% and São Tomé and Príncipe 40%.

Foreign experts and the local opposition considered São Tomé's oil agreements with ERHC, Mobil and PGS as prejudicial to the country's national interests, because they allowed the foreign companies far-reaching financial advantages against inadequate returns. The International Monetary Fund (IMF) blamed the government for a lack of transparency and demanded an independent analysis of all oil dealings. Consequently the government hired US legal experts. Presenting their highly critical assessment in April 2002, they considered the agreements with ERHC and PGS extremely one-sided, since the government received little in return for what it gave to the companies. In the opinion of the experts only the agreement with Mobil approached similar agreements elsewhere in the international oil industry. As a result São Tomé and Príncipe demanded the renegotiation of all oil agreements. Officially the anomalies detected by the US experts were attributed to the inexperience of the country's negotiators. At the same time persistent rumours circulated that bribes paid to office-holders in São Tomé might have been instrumental in the process.

In early 2003 renegotiated contracts were consecutively signed with ExxonMobil, PGS, and ERHC. The new agreements with ExxonMobil and PGS were more favourable to São Tomé and Príncipe than the previous ones. In contrast, foreign analysts considered the new agreement with ERHC excessively generous to the Nigerian company. Nevertheless, the renegotiated agreements paved the way for the first licensing round of nine blocks of the JDZ in October 2003. Twenty oil companies submitted 33 bids for eight of the blocks. ChevronTexaco offered the highest bid of $123 million for Block 1. Half of the bidders were Nigerian companies with uncertain financial and technical capacities. Finally, in spring 2004, only Block 1 was licensed to ChevronTexaco (51%), ExxonMobil (40%), and the Nigerian Energy Equity Resources (9%). Reportedly, to avoid assigning the blocks to companies with uncertain capacities, Blocks 2–6 were put into a new bidding round in December 2004, while Blocks 7–9 were withdrawn from the auction. By that time the London-based Equator Exploration had acquired the rights owned by PGS.

In April 2005, the announcement of the five block awards to different consortiums, including small Nigerian oil companies with dubious capacities, provoked accusations of irregularities and a lack of transparency in São Tomé. Consequently, the Oil Committee of the National Assembly asked the local Attorney General to investigate the block awards. The investigation report of the Attorney General submitted in December 2005 confirmed the allegations of irregularities in the second licensing round, including vague selection criteria and the awarding of blocks to companies with doubtful technical and financial capacities. Unimpressed by the conclusions of the report, in March 2006 the JDA signed production-sharing contracts with the consortiums that had been awarded Blocks 2, 3 and 4. The signing of the respective contracts for Blocks 5 and 6 was postponed. Altogether São Tomé received signature bonus shares of some $49 million for Block 1 in 2005 and $28.5 million for Blocks 2, 3 and 4 in 2006. Due to ERHC's bonus-free options in the three last blocks, the Nigerian company was exempted from paying signature bonuses of nearly $52 million, a considerable loss for São Tomé and Príncipe.

In early 2006 ChevronTexaco drilled the first exploration well located at a depth of 1,700m in Block 1. The results of the drilling were disappointing; although the company announced the discovery of oil, the deposits were not commercially exploitable. The news provoked some frustration in São Tomé and certainly dampened the initial enthusiasm about the country's oil perspectives. In early 2007, the Swiss company Addax and the Chinese Sinopec, which, together with ERHC and other companies, possess the concessions for Blocks 2 and 4, announced exploration drillings in the two blocks starting in the second half of 2008. After having reassessed seismic surveys conducted by PGS from 2001 to 2003, in mid-2007 the company British Geological Survey identified 18 potential ultra-deep locations containing hydrocarbons in the country's own EEZ. New licensing rounds for blocks in the JDZ and the EEZ have been announced for 2008.

While São Tomé and Príncipe still awaits the first discovery of oil, the country has with foreign assistance adopted important anti-corruption legislation for the oil sector. Together with the World Bank and the Earth Institute of Columbia University in New York, local lawmakers elaborated a regulatory law of oil revenue management. This oil revenue management law, unanimously approved by the National Assembly in late 2004, provides for the creation of a National Oil Account, the sound management and allocation of funds, the establishment of a Permanent Reserve Fund for future generations, annual audits of the oil accounts and the implementation of checks and transparency principles. In October the same year, the government created a National Oil Agency (ANP; www.anp-stp.gov.st) as the regulating body of the country's oil industry. The agency executes the instructions of the simultaneously established 15-member National Petroleum Council (CNP). As early as June 2004 Presidents Obasanjo and de Menezes signed the Abuja Joint Declaration on transparency in the JDZ. All information to be made public according to the declaration would appear on the website of the JDA (www.nigeriasaotomejda.com). At the time of writing at least, this has not been done accordingly. São Tomé's leaders have on various occasions promised sound management, transparency, accountability and the investment of the possible future oil wealth for the benefit of the entire people. However, for the time being, nobody knows if the country's leaders really have the political will to meet their promise and if the country has the institutional capacity to implement the complex oil legislation.

fives die each year of infectious diseases like bacterial diarrhoea, typhoid fever and malaria, the biggest killer, and the mortality rate for children under five has remained unchanged (118) between 1990 and 2005. The cholera epidemic of 2005/6, the first outbreak of cholera for 15 years, due to dilapidated pipes on a privatised plantation, resulted in three deaths. Whilst there is no hunger, due to the richness of the land, there is very real poverty, and the children with protruding bellies you see everywhere illustrate the lack of balanced nutrition. Over half of the population lives on less than one dollar per day, the official measure of poverty. Meanwhile, the population is growing at an annual rate of over 3%, standing currently at around 160,000, and projected to be 208,000 by 2025. Pressure on resources is growing, as more and more Santomeans leave the impoverished plantations for the capital, which is already home to 55,000 people. Unemployment, whilst difficult to measure, probably runs at about 50%. In 2007/8, the cost of living went up yet again – the high rates for water and an unreliable electricity service infuriating the locals – as did crime. The government is often perceived as talking and not doing much. A Santomean woman explained the system using the, originally Mozambican, image of *cabritismo*: the *cabra*, goat, of the people is tied to the stack in the middle by a short cord and can only graze what it can reach, whereas the government, grazing on a long cord, is free to take all it likes.

With US$239 per head per year, São Tomé and Príncipe receives one of the highest amounts of **aid** per capita in the world, and 80% of the national budget is made up of external aid. Some 80 non-governmental organisations (NGOs) are said to operate on these small islands; you'll see many jeeps with 'Cooperação Japonesa' or school buses 'Donated by the Republic of China (Taiwan)' rumbling around the pot-holed streets, and highly paid consultants tapping into their laptops, working on project evaluations and audits in the country's few air-conditioned spaces. Unfortunately, projects are often not coordinated well amongst the agencies. In the media, Cape Verde is touted as the model to follow: a country that was once so poor that many couples were only too willing to come to São Tomé to work in harsh conditions to escape famine at home, but that today has wisely invested its foreign aid. In early 2007, after granting partial debt relief over the years and encouraging the implementation of a tax reform and combat corruption, the World Monetary Fund and World Bank pardoned the vast majority of São Tomé and Príncipe's debt of US$327million under the **Highly Indebted Poor Countries** (HIPC) initiative. The country is hoping to see a pardon of the remainder. Taiwan continues to be a major donor, having invested an estimated US$100 million in the first ten years of diplomatic relations being established in 1997, financing, for instance, an information technology centre to drive the computerisation of the public administration services. (While mainland China was holding back for years, it is now also entering the oil sector.) The leader of the MLDSP-PSD opposition party, veteran politician Rafael Branco has however spoken out against Taiwan-supported prestige projects such as a planned multi-million dollar international conference centre; this was since replaced by an electricity plant. The **United Nations**, who have a fairly active office in the capital, are funding social assistance programmes through their Population Fund, investing in poverty reduction, health and women's rights (2008–2011) with over US$2 million. Visitors talking to Santomeans will notice that a certain culture of dependency has resulted in much talk of 'the government's' responsibilities to support and help and a certain lack of initiative, born out of a paralysing mix of lack of capital, distrust of empty promises of the past, and Santomean *léve-léve*.

RELIGION

The vast majority of Santomeans are **Christian**, with around 80% Roman Catholic and 15% Protestant (growing). Many little shops will have names such as 'Deus Quer' or 'Fe-em-Deus' suggesting a God-fearing society. However, the moral teachings of the traditional church – such as monogamy – don't really interfere with the Santomean way of life, and never have, back to the Catholic priests not observing celibacy in early colonial times. **Polygyny** is the norm: men have several women, often cohabiting with a main woman but keeping other lovers and contributing to the upkeep of children. The 'shocking' statistic that the rate of births outside marriage is the highest in the world is down to the fact that few couples marry. Pope John Paul II's sermon during a nine-hour visit in 1992 had little impact. A man with four women is seen as a great guy, *fofo*; for women, the morals don't work quite in the same way. In the years since the opening up of the country, increasingly, pentecostal churches offer a counterpoint to the establishment. At weekends, you can often hear gospel songs emanating from places of worship. The Portuguese Maná church has been one of the most successful; sometimes you can see full-body immersion baptisms on the beach next to the museum in São Tomé, with blaring music. The most visible and active faith is the Switzerland-based New Apostolic Church, which started proselytising here in the early 1980s. In addition to this, there are Seventh-Day Adventists, who own the oldest Protestant church on the island and are very involved in development work; a growing number of – fairly determined – Jehovah's Witnesses; a growing community of about 200 Muslims; and a similar number of the Baha'i faith. Relations between the religious groups are amicable, though the aggressive money-soliciting of some new churches is now criticised in the media. In the towns and villages, patron saints are venerated on their feast day with celebrations lasting days and involving processions, dancing, traditional music, food and drink stalls, and *Tchiloli*. The feast day of São Isidro in Ribeira Afonso at the end of January kicks off the saints' season, followed by São Pedro, the fishermen's patron saint at the end of January, and so it goes on. With a society as mixed as this, animist traditions that believe in the unity of body and soul, and the existence of souls in plants and animals, remain strong and exist alongside Christian rituals. For instance, many Santomeans follow the common magical ritual of *Pagá dêvê* ('pay what you owe', based on the assumption that a problem, such as bed-wetting with children, represents an open debt from a former life that has to be paid off), leaving carved votive figurines near rivers, or believe that rain that falls on the third of May (*Chuva de Três de Maio*) is divine benediction for the fertilisation of the fields and collect this sacred water in containers to drink or to wash in. Practitioners of witchcraft are often members of a major religion. Herbal concoctions are used against the evil eye (*mau olhar*) to make men faithful; and, careful – if you drink a tea made of certain leaves, you might stay on São Tomé forever! Healers (*curandeiros*) are called in to dispel a curse, exorcise a spirit or to cast a spell on a rival. **Djambi** is a spirit-possession cult with the aim of curing illness through communicating with the ancestors, where the healer, the patient and the onlookers enter a state of trance, induced through dance and psychotropic drugs; some participants even cut themselves. With a bit of determination and asking around, it should be possible to get yourself invited to a *djambi*.

CULTURE

MUSIC Music is the surround sound of Santomean society, the soundtrack to life and love, work and emigration, joys and daily deprivations. In the popular quarters, the *kizomba* beats start early in the morning; even the poorest houses have a stereo, and

Tjerk Hagemeijer, Lisbon

Considering the geographical size of the country, São Tomé and Príncipe exhibits an unexpectedly rich linguistic diversity. The official language and the language of prestige, (European) Portuguese, used in administration, education and daily life, is spoken by almost all the inhabitants of both islands. However, especially due to the historical coexistence with creole, the Portuguese language spoken on the islands shows several specific grammatical and lexical traits compared with standard European Portuguese.

The mother tongue of practically all speakers is either Portuguese or one of the creole languages described below. Many speakers are bilingual, speaking both Portuguese and one (or sometimes more) of the creole languages. It is therefore common to find people switching between creole and Portuguese during conversations. Although there are no official sociolinguistic data, Portuguese tends to be used more in and around São Tomé town and among younger speakers.

The three local creole languages spoken on the islands, *Lungwa Santome*, *Lunga Ngola* and *Lung'iye*, do not have the status of official language. They lack, for instance, an official orthography and are not used for administrative and educational purposes. Thus, the creoles are essentially confined to informal environments, such as music, family relations, folk tales, even though radio and television do sometimes broadcast in two of the creoles, namely *Santome* and *Lung'iye*.

The main creole in terms of number of speakers has several designations, namely *Lungwa Santome* (lit. 'language of São Tomé'), *Santome*, *fôlô* or *forro* (historically derived from (*carta de*) *alforria* 'letter of manumission', a document granting freedom to slaves), *Lungwa Tela* (literally 'language of the country') and *dioletu* (dialect), and is widely spoken and/or understood on both islands, even though it was originally the language of the *forro* population on São Tomé. Typical areas of *Santome* speakers are the districts Água Grande (around the capital), Mé-Zochi and Lobata. *Santome* is the only creole that has enjoyed some written tradition, with the first examples of writings in this language dating from the second half of the 19th century. A collection of different types of writings in Santome can be found in *Coroa do Mar* (1998) ('Crown of the sea'), by Carlos Espírito Santo (see page 212).

The designations *Angolar*, *Ngola* or *Lunga Ngola* ('Angolares' Language') refer to the creole language spoken by the Angolares, a closed community that arguably descends from 16th-century runaway slaves with significant nuclei of speakers in the southern part of São Tomé, especially in the coastal areas of the Caué and Lembá districts. However, the fishing tradition of male Angolares resulted in the spread of the community to other coastal areas of São Tomé. Whilst there are still many thousands of speakers, their number may tend to decrease and in the future put *Angolar* at risk of language death due to the spread of the speech community and consequent language contact with other languages, especially *Santome* (through intermarriages, for instance), and increasing exposure to Portuguese (through the media, education, etc).

On the island of Príncipe, a very small community of no more than a few hundred persons still speaks *Lung'iye* (literally 'language of the island'), a language that might well disappear within a few generations, subject to a process of substitution with Capeverdian creole. Unlike *Santome* and *Ngola*, it is nowadays hard to find people actually speaking this creole in daily life. (See box page 170.)

In addition to the local creoles, it is worth mentioning *Fa d'Ambô* ('speech of Ano

thumping music will follow you around everywhere. Once I saw a father holding a mobile playing a tune to the ear of his baby. You might have heard *Sodade*, the famous ballad of Capeverdian emigration popularised by Cesária Evora, expressing the emigrants' longing for the homeland (...*esse caminho longe, esse caminho para São*

Bom'), the creole spoken on the small island of Pagalu (Equatorial Guinea). This island, lying to the south of São Tomé, was a Portuguese possession until 1777, when it became Spanish territory (Annobón), until the independence of Equatorial Guinea. *Santome*, *Angolar*, *Lung'iye* and *Fa d'Ambô* descend historically from a common root, a contact language that came into existence on São Tomé by the end of the 15th century, when the island was permanently settled by the Portuguese. This contact language, which evolved directly into *Santome*, must have stabilised during the 16th century and is the result of contact between the Portuguese and slaves from the African mainland. These slaves were first predominantly recruited in the Niger delta area (Nigeria), with a special role for the old kingdom of Benin (not to be confused with the country of Benin). Quickly, however, slaves from Bantu areas, especially the Congo and Angola, became more dominant, particularly when the island of São Tomé shifted from self-sufficiency to a sugar cane plantation society, around 1520.

Despite the fact that most of the vocabulary of the four creoles has its roots in (old) Portuguese, although strongly modified by the phonological rules of African languages, there are also a substantial number of words in the creoles that can be traced back to the African continent, and particularly to the languages spoken in the regions indicated above, namely Edo (Edoid), Kikongo and Kimbundu (Bantoid). *Lung'iye* preserved more linguistic features and vocabulary that can be assigned to the Nigerian delta area, whereas *Angolar* exhibits significant amounts of Bantu lexicon, presumably because the early runaway community started absorbing large numbers of Bantu speakers that fled from the rough labour conditions at the sugar cane plantations throughout the 16th century. Despite these lexical particularities, the three creole languages on São Tomé and Príncipe, as well as *Fa d'Ambô*, are structurally very similar and all reflect more clearly the impact of Nigerian rather than Bantu languages. Due to the diffusion of the early contact language in time and space, the three creole languages are nowadays not mutually intelligible. The structure of the creoles, very distinct from Portuguese, reflects the strong impact of African languages during its formative period.

In addition to the local creole languages, São Tome and Príncipe has a significant speech community of Capeverdian creole speakers. This creole, originally spoken on the Capeverdian islands, is genetically unrelated to the above creoles. It was the Capeverdian contract labourers in the 20th century who brought along their own creole language, which still constitutes a means of affirmation for the Capeverdian community on the islands. The majority of Príncipe's inhabitants, for example, are of Capeverdian descent. There is also 'Tonga' Portuguese, a language variety that can still be heard on, for instance, the plantations of Monte Café and Agostinho Neto, where mostly Umbundu-speaking contract labourers from Angola developed a new linguistic code based upon Portuguese. Due to the impact of Portuguese and the unstable nature of this variety, however, Tonga Portuguese is bound to disappear in the near future.

Despite the lesser prestige of the local creole languages, there is a growing interest in their preservation. In fact, the promotion of the creole languages has been stated on the government's programme, although this has not translated into significant developments. The exception was the first International Colloquium on the National Languages, held in October 2001 in São Tomé. There is a need to adopt official policies towards the creole languages in order to prevent the disappearance over time of this important piece of cultural patrimony and national identity.

Tomé? …this long way to São Tomé). In colonial times, slaves and later contract workers would use song lyrics to criticise their masters. Flutes and *sacaia*, a small calabash or woven basket filled with grains – you can buy them at the Roça de São João (see page 152) – would accompany the *socopé* and *puita* dances. Today, these old styles are struggling to survive, but some groups try to keep the tradition alive; contact English-speaking Edson Andreza (✆ *905013;* e *edyblack5@ hotmail.com*). Edson belongs to a group of young people performing traditional dances in the capital; they are glad of a donation to finance the costumes, etc. A very popular percussion tradition you will encounter during creole nights (*noites crioulas*), election campaigns and as a tourist attraction, is *bulaué*.

In the 1980s, some bands toed the party line, making propaganda music extolling the virtues of the new one-party state and the bright future. In the 1990s, with the opening up of the country, Santomean musical taste became more open to new influences. The style of popular music you are still most likely to encounter during fairs and religious feasts is *Nacional*, where all generations take to the dance floor. The band **Sangazuza** still rule the roost; they and their rivals **África Negra** tour a lot on the islands. There is always music at popular *festas*; check what's on during your visit on the tourist board website. Príncipe has had to invite combos from São Tomé since the demise of África Verde. Today, *zouk* from the Antilles, *kadançe* from Cape Verde and Angola and *kizomba* from Angola rule the dance floor, reflecting the younger generation's preference for the earworm beats and easy lyrics of Loony Johnson and Haylton Dias. *Zouk* and *kizomba* have also been adapted to *forro* and Capeverdian creole. One of the most venerated and charismatic local *kizomba* singers, **Camilo Domingos**, of Capeverdian descent and also very successful in Angola, died young. One of his most popular songs is *A Menina Fala d'Amor* ('The Girl Talks about Love'). Lisbon-based *zouk* singer **Juka** regularly visits his home country to perform; he was brought in, for instance, to sing for Fradique de Menezes' election campaign in 2006. Popular clubs (*discotecas*), often no more than a wooden shack with a few strobe lights, are a way of life, a place to meet and celebrate and to forget daily worries. First-time visitors might be surprised how sensual the dancing is – bodies rub up very close to each other and seem to move very very slowly, particularly during the *tarachinha*, even though this Angolan dance has a fast beat. Western women struggling with the moves and the closeness might be told to 'relax', which is, of course, no great help. Dancing on your own, European-style, is not really done and can feel awkward; men assume that you are waiting to be invited to dance. While Santomean men are generally free to dance with whoever they like, women going to a club with their boyfriends are often only allowed to dance with them. Clubs sometimes have live shows by popular singers with a new album out; look for posters and listen to the grapevine.

FINE ARTS There was no real tradition of painting on the islands until the early 20th century; over 30 years after independence, the economic situation sometimes makes it difficult for some artists even to afford paint and brushes. Born in 1894 on Roça Laranjeiras near Santana, Pascoal Viana de Sousa e Almeida Vilhete, **Sum Canalim**, became famous for his naïve, ethnographic paintings of the *Tchiloli*, *Danço Congo* and *Sócopé* ('only-with-foot'). One of the painters heavily influenced by Sum Canalim was **Protásio Dias Xavier Pina** (1960–99) from Príncipe, whose naïve murals representing the islands' landscapes or traditional dancing are shown in various spaces in São Tomé, including the airport and the Residencial Avenida. There is a great buzz in the **contemporary arts** scene at the moment. A new generation of very talented painters living and working in São Tomé (or painting Santomean themes from their Portuguese bases) create work that you can find on sale at the only art gallery in the capital (see page 118). Visitors interested in purchasing work can also try contacting artists through their national organisation, **AAPLAS** (✆ *223596*). One of the most popular painters is the Angolar painter and musician **João Carlos (Nezó;**

see page 153), whose distinctive stylised works hang in the CST phone centre in São Tomé and the Pestana resort on the Ilhéu das Rolas. The abstract oil/acrylic paintings by one of the youngest artists, **René Tavares**, make him a universal painter (✆ *912445/222489;* e *kito-rivas@ifrance.com*). **Olavo Amado's** (see page 152) paintings lead the viewer to guess people and figures through a blurred mist of soft colour tones and three-dimensional collage elements (✆ *225135;* e *amado79olavo@hotmail.com; http://br.geocities.com/olavo_amado*), whilst **Eduardo Malé's** dynamic figures in a contemporary context seem to speak up for the times coming to São Tomé (*maleeduardo@hotmail.com;* ✆ *918919/+ 351 968242562*). **Guillerme Carvalho** and **Bruno Spagnol** (see page 111) create beautiful images with sand from the islands' multi-coloured beaches. **Armindo Lopes** paints and sculpts iconographic African figures, and the abstract paintings of cultural promoter and TV chef **João Carlos Silva** give a taste of richly flavoured colours. **Dário Quaresma Vaz Alves de Carvalho** presents an African take on Cubism, whilst **Adilson Castro's** powerful colours painted on treated wood with doors and small sculpted figures in geometric compositions speak up for symbolism. Living and working in Santana (see *Santana*, page 149), **Osvaldo dos Reis** uses exuberant colours and playfully energetic geometry to represent timeless Santomean scenes. Also watch out for **José Manuel Mendonça (Zemé), Kwame Souza** and **Oswaldo Gomes. Geane Castro's** metal animal sculptures made out of recycled pieces reveal the creative potential in simple objects, while **Aurélio Silva's** expressive wood sculptures tap into the spiritual, votive traditions of African art. The vibrant photo-paintings of the island by French artist **Tony Soulié** are available through Amazon (*www.amazon.com*) and www.fnac.fr. A metal-framed print costs US$160; standard prints around €30.

LITERATURE In a largely illiterate society with no bookshops or daily newspaper, oral tradition has always played a major role. Stories featuring animals, such as the clever *tartaruga* (turtle), always after food and his own advantage, and spiritual entities, such as the devil, are told by the *griot* (storyteller). The hunt for food plays a major role in these stories, which also often contain a grotesque or sexually scurrilous element. *Contági* are based on real events, and are told to keep the memory of historical events, such as the traumatic events of 1953, alive for future generations. There are *sóia* stories that must only be told at night. Today, storytelling is losing ground to TV soap operas. **Poetry** is the dominant form of literary production; the beauty of the islands has inspired several poets, most of whom lived the greater part of their lives in Portugal. Bohemian poet-philosopher **Francisco Stockler** (see box page 25), a Santomean teacher reared in Lisbon, wrote much of his wry, self-deprecating ironic poetry in *forro* creole. In recent time, **Mé Sossô** (pseudonym for José Luis Martinho, 1952–) continues this strand, appropriating the image of the 'prodigal son', who travels the world without ever knowing about the death of his family members. A recurrent motif in the romantic poetry of **Caetano Costa Alegre** (1864–1890) is the dichotomy between a fatalistic resignation to the alienation born from the colour of his skin and its valorisation. Inspired by Costa Alegre, the essence of the work of Príncipe-born militant poet **Marcelo da Veiga** (1892–1976), who became an activist and member of parliament, is crystallised in the image of the *Ossobó*, the elusive solitary cuckoo of the forest and the name of his major collection. His poem 'Evocação' (Ilha do Príncipe) indeed 'evokes' a nostalgic past 'when the island was ours' with 'fine plantations, distant', where, on feast days 'there were no invitations, everyone went', 'canoes without sails / that opened flight like birds wth oars only...'. Born on São Tomé, **Herculano Levy** (1889–1969) in his poems, infused with sadness

CONCEIÇÃO LIMA (1962–): AFRO-INSULARITY

Translated by Russell G. Hamilton

On the islands they left a legacy
of hybrid words and sorrowful plantations
rusted sugar mills breathless prows
resonant aristocratic names
and the legend of a shipwreck on Sete Pedras

Arriving from the North they cast anchor here
by mandate or by chance in the service of their king:
navigators and pirates
slave traders thieves contrabandists
common folk
also rebel outcasts
and Jewish children
so tender that they faded
like sun-dried ears of corn

The ships brought
compasses trinkets seeds
experimental plants heinous acidities
a stone monument as pallid as wheat
and other cargo without dreams nor roots
because all of the island was a port and a road
with no return
all of the hands were pitchforks and hoes

And alive they became stuck on the rocks
like scabs--every coffee tree now breathes
a dead slave.

And on the islands remained
incisive arrogant statues on street corners
more than a hundred churches and chapels
for a thousand square kilometres
and the insurgent syncretism of nativity residences.
And there remains the palatial cadence of the *Ussuá* Creole dance
the aroma of garlic and olive oil
in traditional clay pots
and in the *calulú* the bay leaf mixed with palm oil
and the fragrance of rosemary
and basil from family gardens

And to the ticking of insular clocks were cast
Spectres – implements of the empire
in a structure of ambiguous clarities
and secular condiments
patron saints and demolished fortresses
inexpensive wines and shared auroras

At times I think of their livid skeletons
their fetid hair on the sea shore

Here, on this fragment of Africa
where, facing South,
a word dawns on high
like a banner of distress.

FRANCISCO STOCKLER (1840–84)

Translated from Forro by Don Burness

Sun Fâchicu Estoclê	Mr Francisco Stockler
Tómá cádjá fé lóça d'ê	Made out of a prison his plantation
Chimiá báná, chimiá cáfê,	He planted banana, he planted coffee
Forchi só cu çá di pádêcê.	But he is only wealthy in suffering.

FRANCISCO JOSÉ TENREIRO (1921–63): ISLAND NAMED AFTER A SAINT (1942)

Translated by Don Burness

Land!
of plantations of cocoa of copra of coffee
of coconut palms extending as far as the eye can see
until they reach the sea
The sea blue like the most pleasing sky in all the world!

Where the pure yellow and round sun shines on the backs
of men of women their nerves excited
in a cadence magical yet human: threshing dreaming planting!

Where the women whose arms are stouter and more bent than
limbs of the *ocá*
are black like the coffee they gather
working along side their men in muscular labor!
where the little kids watch their parents in a daily rhythm
letting the flavour the warm sap of the ripe *safú* fruit
flow down their moist chins!

Where the star-filled nights
and a full moon round like a fruit
the blacks the kids the extended family
- even the white man and his mulatto lover -
come to the *sócópé* at the lady's place
to hear the guitar played by the vagabond musician
singing to the music!

And the sea echoes the sound…
Where despite the gunpowder in the white man's unlit ship
where despite the sword and multicolored flag
proclaiming power proclaiming force
proclaiming the empire of the white man
this is the land of men singing life
unknown to the white man
this is the land of *safú* of *sócópé*
of the mulatto woman
– ui! Fetish of the white man! –
this is the land of the black man
loyal strong and valiant like no other!

and desire, frequently returns to plantation life, the *obô* forest and the *Ossobó* bird that lives its treacherous life there. The poetry of the *mulatto* geographer, deputy of the Portuguese National Assembly and author of ethnographic essays on his home country, **Francisco José Tenreiro** (1921–63, see box page 25) was infused with themes of creole identity, pitching a proud and angry Panafrican *négritude* against colonial oppression, but blending in sensual, fertile Santomean imagery; today, his portrait hangs in the National Library in São Tomé. In poems such as '*A ilha te fala*', **Maria Manuela Margarido** (1925–2007) evoked the sensuous sounds and smells of her native Príncipe with arresting yet subtle images: 'The island speaks to you / of wild roses / with petals / of abandonment and fear…', while the poems and dramatic works of **Fernando de Macedo** (1927–2006) focus on Angolar history, giving voice to a marginalised part of Santomean society. Macedo, a Portuguese writer who stylised himself as the descendant of the last Angolar king, celebrates the landscape and the force of tradition in the 'Fortunate Islands'.

Born in 1926 into the prominent Espírito Santo family from Trindade, Alda Graça Espírito Santo is the *grande dame* of Santomean politics and culture. Studying in Lisbon in the 1940s, Alda encountered everyday racism – 'We were called "monkey", and all the rest of it,' she recalls – but also made friends with the prime movers of the Luso-African independence movements, such as Amilcar Cabral from Cape Verde and Agostinho Neto from Angola. Back on the island, working as a primary school teacher, a coincidence brought her into contact with a Portuguese lawyer, who had come to the island to take depositions of the 1953 massacre. (Alda's mother, a primary school teacher, was also imprisoned.) One of her best-known poems, 'Where are the Men Hunted Down in this Wind of Madness?', commemorates these events, a fierce lament and demand for justice: 'Blood falling in drops on the earth / men dying in the forest / and the blood dripping, dripping… of the people thrown out to sea…'. The only writer of note to remain on the islands in colonial times, she is venerated by many; a waitress at a café once described her to me as like a 'saint' for her people. As Minister of Culture, she wrote the national anthem, *Independência Total*, and is today president of the Writers' Union UNEAS. A lifetime of political activism has fed into political poems with a Marxism-based outlook, inspired by hope. A new voice, carrying on some of Alda Graça's themes, is London-based **Conceiçao Lima** (1962– ; see box page 25), a journalist former producer with the BBC, some of whose poems have been translated into English. Equally, the poetry of physician, activist and former guerrilla fighter in Angola, **Tomás Medeiros** is suffused with images of war and exhortations of '*camaradas*' and '*companheiros*'; in '*Aquí estamos*'; '…Here we are with our black back against the sun, / fertilising the soil with our hoes, / with the song of the sun in our breasts without wearying / and the telluric cry that comes from the volcanoes.' **Maria Olinda Beja** (1946–) explores themes, in the words of **Inocência Mata**, the Lisbon-based Príncipe-born authority on Santomean cultural expression and the editor of current anthology *Bendenxa* (see page 212), of *mestiço* mysticism, identity, exile and the poet's place in the world ('Sometimes I go looking for myself / all over the island…'). One of the few Santomean born-and-bred poets actually continuing to live on the island is lawyer **Aíto Bonfim** (1955–) working with strong, aggressive even, political images.

While most 'Santomean' **novelists** also spent most of their life in Portugal, the universe of the plantation looms large in their work. The stories of **João Maria Viana de Almeida** (1903– ?) explored the issue of *mulatto* identity in Santomean society in a tone of mocking irony. **Sum Marky** (1921–2003) was the adopted name of a writer born on São Tomé to Portuguese parents, whose atmospheric novels are still read today. The events of 1953 were already in the background of novels such as *Vila Flogá* (1960) and *No Altar da Lei* (1962) – the latter had him arrested by

The setting: young Lisbon dandy Luís Bernardo Valença has just arrived on the island to take over as governor, with a delicate political mission (see page 211).

…His aim was to do an initial tour of the important plantations on São Tomé island and then go on to Príncipe. This was not a quick task: although the island was small, it only had a few dozen kilometres of open roads where you could circulate in a horse-drawn carriage. Most of the plantations had to be visited on horseback or by boat. Navigating along the coast was in fact, the easiest way to get from the city to the plantations because the *roças* were located mainly in the coastal areas, from where they advanced into the *mato*, as far as deforestation and plant cultivation had reached. The interior of the island was still virgin jungle, just as the Portuguese had found it in the 1400s, with volcanic peaks reaching towards the sky like needles. The highest of them all was the Pico de São Tomé, at 2,042 metres' high. But it was only rarely that you could see the top, eternally drowned in clouds and fog. This densely wooded central zone that takes up the majority of São Tomé's surface area is the kingdom of the obô – the forest – an inextricable dense labyrinth of giant trees: jackfruit, *ocás*, lianas, *micondó* and *marupiões* trees, mango trees, begonias. Underneath those, around them, desperately climbing above them, straining with the vital effort to reach the light above that eternal liquid cover in suspension, lived the creepers, the *lemba lemba*, the *corda d'água*, the *corda pimenta* and the climbing lianes. Deep in the forest, hanging from the tree branches, ready to let herself drop onto a man passing inadvertently underneath, lived the terrible black cobra, whose bite was the kiss of death, quick and cruel. The old people would say that the only man that ever escaped death from a black cobra was a black fugitive from the Monte Café plantation that now lived in Angolares with one arm missing. When he felt the snake's teeth in his arm, he reacted with the speed of lightning, with two precise and swift strikes of his machete. With the first one, he cut his enemy's neck, with the second, he cut off his own arm below his shoulder – and he survived. Because the *obô* forest is a ghostly territory, where the fugitive black slaves would run to, in a moment of madness, because of a crime committed on a *roça*, or simply in the insane desire for liberty, the forest would readily welcome them, making them free in its liquid shady hug of death. No-one else in their right mind would venture further than a few steps into that opaque and submersed universe…

Salazar's security police – but are at the very heart of his last novel *Crónica de uma Guerra Inventada* (1999). Sum Marky's novels are hard to come by now, but he was given a ceremonial burial with all honours on the 54th anniversary of the Massacre of Batepá in 2007. The novels and short stories of **Fernando Reis** (*Roça, Soiá*), born in the Ribatejo province of Portugal, indulge in atmospheric descriptions of plantation life; he also anthologised traditional stories. The *Rosa de Riboque* collection of stories by former minister of culture **Albertino Bragança** explores life in the capital's popular quarter. In recent years, Portuguese journalist Miguel Sousa Tavares had a runaway success with the atmospheric *Equador* (see box above), and a couple of contemporary French writers have started to be inspired by the islands to highly original fiction and travelogues, blending Santomean culture and contemporary themes, such as the oil issue.

PERFORMANCE/DRAMA

Danço Congo São Tomé's most popular dramatic representation, Danço Congo, has a frenetic rhythm, and is performed for religious or popular celebrations in the

With thanks to Françoise Gründ and Paulo Alves Pereira

Tchiloli or, as it is more commonly called, *tragédia*, is a dramatic spectacle unique to São Tomé. 'The Tragedy of the Marquis of Mantua and the Emperor Charlemagne' tells the story of a quest for justice in a vibrant performance, blending European costumes and music with African elements, various registers of the Portuguese language, medieval and contemporary literature and votive imagery. Whilst performances may be adapted to suit place, occasion and audience, the basic chronology remains the same. Dom Carloto (Prince Charles), son of the emperor Charlemagne, and his best friend Valdevinos (Baldwin), the nephew of the Marquis de Mântua, an important vassal of Charlemagne, are out hunting. Dom Carloto, who has designs on Baldwin's wife Sibilla, tricks Baldwin into the dense forest and kills him. The sound of the fanfare announces the entrance of eight musicians, playing *pitu* bamboo flutes and *bombo* drums and shaking *sacaias* filled with shells and seeds. Their dance steps, variations on the waltz, quadrille and contradanse, accompany the beginning of the action, as sometimes the scene of Dom Carloto killing Valdevinos, witnessed by a hermit, is not played out.

Enter one of the key figures: Ganelão, Ganelon of Mayence, Charlemagne's brother-in-law, dressed in white with a gilded riding coat and an elaborate bicorne hat on his head. He commences his dance. The High Court of Charlemagne and his entourage, often elevated and draped with colourful fabrics, is at one end, and the Lower Court of the Mantuans, as vassals of Charlemagne, at the other. Charlemagne, wearing a red robe and a crown made of tin foil topped by a brass cross and a white cotton-wool beard, evokes a medieval figure, though this creole incarnation has little to do with the first emperor in 9th-century Europe.

Two more masked men in black: the Dukes Amão (Armand) and Beltrão (Bertrand), appear followed by the group of the Marquis of Mântua, a French nobleman, dressed in black, his sister Ermelinda, mother of Valdevinos, and his niece Sibilla, Valdevinos' widow. They take turns to dance around the small coffin containing the bones of Valdevinos, which marks an invisible barrier between the two camps. Sibilla, expressing her grief twirling round and round, her black skirt ballooning, presents a dramatic image of mourning.

One of the highlights of a *tchiloli* performance is the apparition of Renaud of Montauban (Reinaldo de Montalvão), also a nephew of Charlemagne, but affiliating himself in the play with the Mântuas. Clad entirely in black, with a crucifix sown into his cloak and a thick black wig with a braid and beard, he begins his spellbinding dance, twirling around his stick, menacing in his anarchic movements. Meanwhile, around the performance area there is a constant coming and going of spectators, eating and drinking, encouraging the actors and expressing support and disgust.

Dom Carloto meanwhile marches with rigid steps, reminiscent of a marionette, and wearing a fedora-style hat. The Justice Minister, in military uniform, golden epaulettes and weighty chain of office across his chest, disarming Dom Carloto, demands the death penalty. Dom Carloto pleads not guilty. Using contemporary Portuguese business language, the Justice Minister telephones the count/defence lawyer, who arrives with his attaché case, sunglasses and white gloves, also effecting a marionette-like dance. The Empress, wearing a large pink crinoline and a crown above her transparent veil and white mask, pleads pity for her son. The appearance of Algoz – a figure dressed in red whose identity is unclear: the devil, a fool, the executioner? – and his duel with Renaud of Montauban, elicit a strong response from the public. Another high point of suspense is reached with the appearance of the page Mosca, holding a letter written by Dom Carloto to Roland, asking for help and admitting his guilt. Amidst much running and commotion, the letter is intercepted by Ganelon and presented to indict Dom Carloto. It is suggested that it was indeed Ganelon behind the scheme all along, to get closer to the throne. There is, however, a general reconciliation scene at the end.

In the *tchiloli*, the participants are all male, even when playing the female roles (the Empress, her maids, Ermelinda and Sibilla), and the roles are hereditary. Masks made from wire, reminiscent of fencing masks, work like a uniform. The rest of the costume is made up of elaborate headgear, sunglasses, mirrors sown onto the costumes (against the evil eye), ribbons, batons, and kneesocks. The music, with its different motifs for Charlemagne and the Mantuans, respectively, follows the heptatonic scale common in Western music, rather than the pentatonic scale characteristic of the Gulf of Guinea region.

How did this spectacle get to São Tomé, and why has it been so successful here? It has traditionally been assumed that the text was brought to São Tomé by Balthasar Dias, a blind poet from Madeira (another Portuguese possession) in the mid-16th century, building his 4,000 verses in iambic tetrameter on the 12/13th-century Carolingian cycle of historical legends, and the late 11th-century *Chanson de Roland* telling of Roland's death through Ganelon's treachery, and medieval troubadour romances (the text in Old Portuguese can be found in Fernando Reis' *Povô Floga, O Povo Brinca*, see page 213). However, recent research suggests that the text reached the island only in the late 19th century, in the wake of a renaissance of the 'cordel literature' (literally 'string') pamphlets, telling the story of Charlemagne's rebellious vassal in Portugal. Even the etymology of the word *tchiloli* is not clear. The *tchiloli*'s social function is thought to reflect the need for a burial on plantations connecting with beliefs of slaves from the continent and as a vehicle for satire and criticism of the colonial powers, as the Marquis of Mantua's demands for justice suggest a society of equals, entitled to justice. Today, in the face of issues such as corruption and impunity, this demand still resonates with many Santomeans.

Catching a *tchiloli* performance should not be too difficult for travellers visiting in one of the dry seasons; they are usually put on for saints' days. On Príncipe, *tchiloli* performers come over for the St Laurent's festivities in mid-August. Today, there are about nine *tragédias* on São Tomé island. The best-known and most prestigious group is Formiguinha de Boa Morte; another popular one is from Caixão Grande, both suburbs of the capital.

The *tchiloli* has changed over time, as have costumes; today, faces powdered white with manioc flour and sunglasses often supplant the wire masks, the language is updated to include some *forro* or even English words, the politics of the day find their way into the text, and the performance time is often now reduced to around two hours. In the current difficult economic situation, the lack of funds for costumes etc remains a problem. The Formiguinha *tragédia* has travelled to theatre festivals in Europe to introduce Western audiences to this unique Santomean form of dramatic expression. Meanwhile, the fascinating subtexts of this repository of African burial rites, ancestor worship, political expression and exploration of justice keep folklorists and researchers busy.

For more information, contact the head of Formiguinha, Armâncio Alves Carvalho (✆ 926116), who plays the role of the Marquis de Mântua. Senhor Carvalho lives in Boa Morte but works at an office next to the Água Grande Policlinic in town. If you take a taxi out to Boa Morte, ask for *o kinté*, or *o sitio onde se faz a tragédia*, and people will probably be happy to show you; it is only a few hundred metres off the main road (only accessible by 4x4). The rectangle of earth is surrounded by a few traditional wooden houses bedecked with palm fronds, banana trees and washing lines. Taking the little path going off at the top right-hand side leads you to the sanctuary, the little chapel dedicated to Saint John (São João) where on important occasions, such as the saint's feast day on 27 January, tradition dictates that the soil has to be doused with palm wine to honour the ancestors. Formiguinha's Jorge Espírito Santo, who plays Sibilla, speaks English and can probably be found working at the Pestana Hotel in the capital.

dry season by two dozen all-male dancers wearing elaborate and colourful costumes with frilly trains and ribbons, balloon trousers, knee-high socks and huge headdresses (*capacetes*), wire constructions with fluttering strips of paper. The story can be performed with variations: the owner of a *roça* leaves the plantation to his incompetent sons, *bobos* (literally 'fools') and their wives – wearing large masks. The bobos call in the *capitão* (captain) for help. A big party on the plantation ensues, with the *bobos* fooling around and interacting with the audience around them. To the sound of flutes, the seed-filled *sacaia* and the clanging of iron bells, the dancers march in rows of two, stomping fiercely on the ground, and rasping a stick up and down a hollowed-out stick of bamboo or sugar cane. The frenetic choreography is led by the captain, who can be seen throwing his decorated bamboo stick high up in the air and catching it again. The two singing angels (*anzu cantá*) helping him are said to represent the ancestors. The captain, however, is a traitor who calls in the sorcerer, *feiticeiro* (*fitxicêlu* in creole), to help him usurp power. Dressed in red, the sorcerer arrives with his assistant: the *zuguzugu*. Another central figure is the **Opé Pó** (*pé-pau*, 'wooden foot') on stilts, who comes accompanied by the angel (*anzo mole*). After a fierce struggle for power, the angel is murdered by the *zuguzugu*. Most Danço Congo troupes however don't enact this scene, for fear that if the person playing the angel closes his eyes when playing the death, he will die for real. When the sorcerer and his assistant are chased away, the captain calls in the devil (*diabo*), dressed in black, who is also chased away. Finally, the angel is resurrected, and there is a big reconciliation scene at the end. The action, which can last several hours but is often condensed to about 90 minutes, has been read in many different ways, as denouncing vice and corruption and the pretentions of high office, or as a parable of colonisation and loss of identity, order and disorder. In 1919, the Danço Congo was banned by the colonial authorities, worried by the performance's aggressive character and semiotics (devil killing angel). In the mid-sixties, the Portuguese changed their minds, supporting new groups. Today, it is widely performed, and the troupe you are most likely to encounter is the fabulous Aliança Nova company from Neves (*contact Urbano,* ❧ *916673*), an Angolares town in the north of São Tomé island. Their sorcerer is in his nineties! Another active group is Macunjá Consol from Ribeira Afonso. While possibly older than both the *Tchiloli* (see box, page 28) and the Auto de Floripes (see box, page 171) from Príncipe, in terms of costumes and music, the Danço Congo has a lot in common with these other unique cultural manifestations.

NATURAL HISTORY AND CONSERVATION

TREES AND PLANTS The dense rainforest of the islands is home to about 900 species of vascular **plants,** 130 of which are endemic: on São Tomé 14%, on Príncipe 11%. The most interesting plant family is the *Rubiaceae*, ie: flowering plants containing over 10,000 species (coffee is one of them). The flower that is most associated with the country is the **porcelain rose**, a tropical pink flower with waxy stems and petals; it grows wild and is also cultivated at some plantations. In the interior of São Tomé island, giant white **begonias**, the rigid stems of bright-red monkey flowers and **bamboo** rods as thick as arms line the path. For number and diversity, **tree ferns** have no equal on the African continent: there are over 150 of them. The archipelago's plant world still holds many mysteries for botanists in terms of geographic distribution – for instance, why is the *Grammitis nigrocincta* fern found only on Príncipe and Madagascar? – and every scientific expedition yields new species, species thought to be extinct and species under threat. The magnificent trees with massive trunks have a multitude of uses: in construction of the traditional Santomean plank houses on

The rainforest is a natural pharmacy; herbalists use many plants and tree barks. For example, the roots of the wild ginger, *gengibre*, are used to treat various conditions, from colic to impotence and asthma. Papaya, *mamão*, contains papaine, aiding digesting, and carpaine, acting as a depressant on the nervous system. The bark of the wild quinine tree contains an anti-malarial agent, quinidine. *Folha d'amina* serves as a natural painkiller against headaches; the liquid is drawn out through little holes in the bark. A stomach-calming tea can be made from the bark of the wild cinnamon tree, *canela*. There is a huge body of local knowledge, and though some studies have been carried out no plants are commercially exploited as yet. An ethno-pharmacological project involving the University of Coimbra in Portugal, the Santomean Ministry of Health, as well as 40 local traditional healers, has been working for 15 years cataloguing local medicinal plants. However, as a new plant syrup developed by the foremost traditional healer in the country is claiming to 'put the virus to sleep'. HIV activists fear such claims will result in a more relaxed attitude to prevention, amongst rising incidence of HIV/AIDS.

stilts, canoe-building and in traditional medicine (see box above). Forest covers about 90% of the islands.

On the beaches, **coconut palms** reach right down to the fringes of the beaches. **Oil palms** are cultivated for the palm oil used abundantly in the local cuisine. In the towns, **almond trees** and **bread fruit** trees line the streets, **banana** plantations and fields of **sugar cane** abound. The most conspicuous tree on the plantations are the imported fast-growing **flame trees**, with their bright orange flowers, giving shade to the cocoa and coffee plants (**shade forest**). In the dry plains of the northern part of São Tomé, that are burned regularly in the dry season, **acacias**, **tamarinds** and **baobabs** are dotted around the grasslands and the fields of millet and sugar cane. **Primary forest** (*obô*) still covers about a quarter of the islands, and it is for the protection of this sensitive and species-rich area that the **Obô National Park** was established, covering some 300km² across both islands. Most of the **lowland rainforest** (0–400m) was cleared in the first half of the 20th century, to make way for cocoa cultivation. Containing populations of every endemic species, this type of forest is now restricted to small areas in southwestern and central São Tomé. **Upland primary rainforest** (400–800m) is confined to the centre of São Tomé island, around the source of the Xufe Xufe and Ana Chaves rivers and south of Lagoa Amélia. For the lay person it is not that easy to distinguish between primary forest and mature **secondary forest** (*capoeira*), which represents about 30% of the islands' forest cover and is reclaiming crumbling plantations. At higher levels, between 800m and the top of the Pico de São Tomé around 2,000m you find beautiful **montane** and **mist forest** with mighty endemic trees, such as the *Afrocarpus mannii* yellowwood stretching their branches towards the sky or smaller trees like *Cratispermum montanum*, whose bark is used in a fortifying drink for swordfish hunters and as an aphrodisiac – there are many of these around. These areas (Lagoa Amélia/Calvário), receive very few hours of daily sunshine.

Orchids

With special thanks to Faustino Oliveira and Dr Tariq Stevart

The queen of plants finds perfect conditions in the lush rainforest, with a high number of endemic species. To date, 129 species of orchid are known on the archipelago, of which 101 are on São Tomé and 64 on Príncipe. Both in numbers of species and in terms of frequency, orchids are the most important amongst the spontaneous plants on the islands. Tropical orchids are classified according to the supporting organism. Three quarters of orchids on São Tomé and Príncipe are **epiphytes** (ie: they live on trees), a third are **terrestrial,** planting their roots in or on the soil, and only a few are **lithophytic**, rooting themselves on rock; some orchids combine the two modes

On São Tomé, the botanical gardens at **Bom Sucesso** are the best base for orchid-themed walks (contact Faustino Oliveira or Lucio (see page 82); the arboretum houses nearly all species from the islands. To the untrained eye, out of season they don't seem much to look at, but in the flowering season (winter) they exhibit their full beauty. *Angraetum doratophyllum* has lovely delicate white flowers with a hooked spur, *Cribbia confusa* has small, strongly scented greenish-orange flowers (both are available from cultivation over the internet). The prolongation of the Lagoa Amélia trail towards Morro Porvaz and Chamiço (not often undertaken) yields mountanous orchids, amongst them endemic epiphytes such as *Chamaeangis thomensis*, *Polystachya parivlora* and *Cribbia thomensis*. The most commonly found terrestrial orchid is *Cheirostylis lepida*. Climbing towards Pico de São Tomé from Bom Sucesso, the mountain crests display a rich variety. Escadas is a good spot for epiphytes such as *Liparis gracilenta* covering the tree bark. The Mesa Pico Pequeno, an hour-and-a-half's walk from the summit, on the way down towards Cascata and Manual Morais is another, and easier to get to. Guides are needed as the paths can change and the information contained in Oliverira/Tariq's authoritative study (see page 214) should not be used as a hiking reference. Last not least, few people realise that the vanilla plant is also an orchid!

On Príncipe, it is the southeast (only accessible with a guide) which is of most interest to orchid lovers. One of the most commonly found species (also available in cultivation) is *Cyrtorchis acuminata*, with broad leaves and large waxy-white flowers.

BIRDS The birdlife of the islands is exceptionally unique. Of the over 120 species recorded on São Tomé and Príncipe, some 28 are endemics. Of the 20 São Tomé species, 14 occur only on that island ('single-island endemics'); of the 11 on Príncipe, five only occur there. The first species you are likely to encounter are black kites circling above Ana de Chaves Bay at São Tomé town, called falcons – *falcãos* by the locals. For reasons of space, only the English name (and occasionally the local creole name) is given in this section – the creole names, often onomatopoetic, are the ones you are most likely to hear. Birdwatchers should bring their own binoculars and bird book; if you're lucky, some guides know the French names; consider photocopying our glossary (see page 191) to take with you. The easiest birds to spot in the lowlands of São Tomé and Príncipe are the black kite (*falção*), hovering over the harbour looking for scraps of fish, and the cattle egret (*garça*). There are few cattle on the island, but this all-white bird with a yellow beak lives both around beaches and at higher altitude. One of the best-loved and most easy to spot (though now threatened) **endemics** is the São Tomé oriole, commonly known as *papa-figo* (it is on the 5,000-dobra note). This large black bird, with a pronounced red beak and yellow-tipped tail, lives in the forest and plantations up to an altitude of 1,300m and responds to imitation of its distinctive call. Others to look out for are the São Tomé scops owl, São Tomé spinetail, starlings, drongo seed-eaters, São Tomé green pigeon and São Tomé bronze-naped pigeon. The threatened São Tomé short-tail is a resident endemic and, according to the undisputed authority on São Tomé and Príncipe birds, Patrice Christy, 'the greatest ornithological enigma of São Tomé'. The emerald cuckoo with a yellow belly, the **ossobó**, has a prominent role in Santomean culture and appears on the 10,000 dobra banknote. On forest hikes, you are likely to hear its call, thought to

The rarest bird on the islands is the endemic São Tomé grosbeak. Last seen in the late 19th century, around São João dos Angolares and in the southwest of the island, the dark chestnut-black bird, with reddish-brown underparts, a strong parakeet-style beak and bullish head, had been eluding birdwatchers and was considered extinct by some ornithologists ever since. It was only in 1991 that it was spotted again, along a ridge above the Xufe-Xufe river in the southwest, by the British ornithologist David Sargeant. The only known taxidermy specimen in the world is in the British Museum collection in Tring; the two others perished in a fire at a Lisbon museum. The first ever photograph of this bird was taken in 2006; see it on the www.ggcg.st site. Surprisingly, Norberto Vidal (see *Local tour operators*) can literally guarantee you will see one on a week-long trip to the remote southwest. So take him up on it!

announce rain – I heard its call several times on a hike around the Ponta Figo plantation – but the bird itself is very hard to see.

Príncipe has its own six endemics: the Príncipe glossy starling, the Príncipe speirops, the Príncipe sunbird, the Dohrn's thrush-babbler and the Príncipe weaver – all easily seen along the roadside in the north or walking along the river from Santo António to Bela Vista.

Top Birdspots

North The savannah zone to the north of São Tomé, around the town of Guadalupe, and the coast road from Diogo Nunes to Praia das Conchas is home to introduced species such as the red-winged bishop; the common waxbill is indeed common there, and it is also the main habitat of the bronze mannikin. Blue waxbills – their local name, *suín-suín*, is onomatopoeic, suggesting their chant – are easy to spot even in the shrubs and gardens of the capital of São Tomé, but the main habitat of this small cream-blue bird is here and in the grass along the side of the western coast road down to Santa Catarina. Other common birds are swifts, the white-winged widow bird, the golden-backed bishop, fire-crowned bishop and Vitelline masked weaver. In the dry lowlands of the northwest, also look for the endemic São Tomé bronze-naped pigeon.

Bom Sucesso/Lagoa Amélia (Interior) The botanic gardens of Bom Sucesso and the dry crater lake of Lagoa Amélia are great sites for easy birdwatching. An easy-to-spot endemic is the São Tomé weaver, to be found at Nova Moca and Lagoa Amélia. The higher primary forest around Lagoa Amélia is also a good place to go looking for two threatened species: the elusive maroon pigeon and the São Tomé scops owl (common in the forests; it responds to its call). The (threatened) São Tomé white-eye lives mainly on the edge of primary forests. If you're climbing the Pico de São Tomé, look out for the giant sunbird.

South The rivers and streams of the **east coast road** are good places for birdwatching. The best place to spot the endemic dwarf olive ibis is around the **Roça São João** on the southeastern coast, where it feeds, silently, on the forest floor. A dull olive-brown colour with blackish belly and flesh-coloured legs and short flesh-orange bill, sometimes hunted for their tasty meat, these birds are shy. Hard-core birdwatchers will want to head for the **Xufe Xufe river** area in the southwest, where all 20 island endemics occur, including the elusive São Tomé fiscal shrike, glossy black with a white broken line across the wing, a yellow-orange throat, chin, breast and belly, and a long tail. This area is considered the second-most important forest area for threatened bird species in the Afrotropical and Malagasy region. The giant weaver nests around Santo António, while the beautifully coloured giant sunbird is most easily found in primary forest above the river.

Southern forests of Príncipe While birders are usually able to tick off all six island endemics on a wander from the capital to Bela Vista or around the Bom Bom Island resort, spending a night camping in the forest gives the advanced birder the chance to see the Príncipe thrush, African grey parrot (see illustration, page 192), and Príncipe olive ibis, and this is also the habitat of a small owl that still hasn't been seen by outsiders. The southern shores offer the opportunity to see the Príncipe seedeater.

Identifying **sea birds** can be tricky as colour range is generally narrow, the plumage of juveniles is often drab, and native species mix with migrants. The Sete Pedras rocks in the south have a nesting colony of bridled terns. With its long white double queue, the white-tailed tropicbird is one of the most conspicuous sea birds; its white plumage is marked by a black V, and it has a yellow beak. They are easy to see in gracious flight around **Jockey's Cap** islet (Ilhéu Boné de Jóquei) off Príncipe. Both brown noddies and white-capped noddies as well as brown boobies nest and feed around the Pedra da Galé off Príncipe. The **Ilhas Tinhosas** offer large colonies of sooty terns. Amongst the **shore birds**, the most common migrants are the large whimbrel (*Numenius phaeopus*), with its curved beak, and the winter visitor common greenshank (*Tringa nebularia*), with its distinctive 'barking' cry when taking off, as well as the common sandpiper (*Actitis hypoleucos*). The rivers and the island's one major mangrove are the haunts of the malachite kingfisher with its metallic plumage, and the African cormorant.

REPTILES There are two dozen species of reptiles, most of them endemic. Two endemic **frogs** are Africa's largest tree frog and a tiny brown puddle frog. The endemic *Lygodactylus thomensis* gecko can be identified by its yellow eye-band.

MARINE LIFE
With thanks to Peter Wirtz, of the Centre for Marine Science, University of Algarve
The Gulf of Guinea is one of the world's hotspots of marine biodiversity. In terms of species present, this area of the Gulf is similar to the Caribbean, if with slightly less variety. Despite lying so close to the African continent, the fish fauna of the islands has its own particularities. Amongst the about 230 species recorded so far, many are endemic (such as the *Thalassoma newtoni* parrotfish) and the waters are still largely unexplored. Fish fauna are of particular interest because, at the latitude the islands are on, the easterly flowing Equatorial currents link the western and eastern Atlantic. It is not just invertebrates (sea slugs, etc) that present a mix of the two regions; many of the species found here are 'amphi-Atlantic'. The best-represented families are Carangidae, Serranidae, Gobiidae and Scombridae. The fish market can give you an idea of the most commonly seen fish: the horse-eye jack, various types of spear fish, as well as yellowfin tuna, with its greenish back, golden-yellow flanks and belly. Divers can look for snappers, sweetfish, stingrays, octopus, sea horses, turtles, fan coral, moray eels and giant sea slugs. Around the islands, the bottom of the sea shows high relief, as much so as the surface you see above the sea. This 'upswelling' brings in many smaller fish that in turn attract the big game fish. The littoral (surrounding fringe) is very narrow, and São Tomé island is separated from the neighbouring Gulf of Guinea islands and the mainland by depths of up to 2,000m. The fish fauna also shows some similarities with the western Indian Ocean.

The Gulf of Guinea has fewer species than the Caribbean and **coral** cover, at under 10%, is relatively low. The most abundant hard coral is great star coral (*Montastraea cavernosa*), in mid to deeper areas in particular, followed by the golden cup coral (*Tubastraea aurea*), its orange-glowing polyps opening up at night. A recent expedition found that **Ilhéu das Cabras/Kia** had the highest fish density and species richness of the sites studied. As the underwater world around Príncipe is even less disturbed by dragnets, the marine fauna here is even more amazing. It is a favourite habitat of **billfish:** predators including marlin, sailfish and swordfish. Blue marlins can weigh over 750kg, but take about 30 years to reach 450kg. Atlantic blue marlins travel thousands of miles for their food; the waters off Príncipe are said to have some of the best marlin fishing in the world. The best time to see them is July to September. The most common billfish, the Atlantic sailfish, *peixe andala*, has huge sail-like dorsal fins. The best time to see them is September to December. On the market or the beach in São Tomé you often see Atlantic swordfish, pulled by their long flat bill. Swordfish can reach weights of over 500kg and dive down to a depth of over 600m.

Watching **flying fish** (popular in Santomean cuisine) propel themselves like rockets out of the water by their tail-fins to whir across the waves for up to 400m is a fascinating sight. In the dry season the *peixe voador* or *peixe apanhá* is caught using straw matting. One of the most appreciated fish is the flying gurnard, *concón*, which gets its name from the sound it makes when taken out of the water.

The largely unexplored coastal waters bear many surprises and mysteries still. A National Geographic Society expedition in 2006 recorded nearly 60 new fish, ten of these from species never before described. One of them was a near-blind shrimp lobster living in symbiosis with a goby fish, the first goby-shrimp symbiosis to be found in the eastern Atlantic. Although the exact dynamics of the relationship are not clear, the goby guards the shrimp's nest against predators while living in the tunnel dug by the shrimp. One very strange type of fish to be found on São Tomé and Príncipe is the **mudskipper**. *Cucumbas* are the only fish on earth that can 'walk' – on their webbed fins – and stay out of water for hours, thanks to their ability to store water in their gills and to breathe through their skin. They can be seen near the Bom Bom Island resort on Príncipe and along the Papagaio river in the capital, Santo António, and generally at stagnant ponds of water near beaches, like at Praia Micoló.

Turtles São Tomé and Príncipe has the most diverse range of **sea turtles** (*tartarugas*) in central Africa, with four of the five species nesting here. Sea turtles belong to the most ancient reptile family (*Chelonidæ*), and have been around for around 200 million years. Marine turtles migrate several thousand kilometres from their foraging grounds to their nesting sites where they deposit several clutches of eggs between October and February, mainly at night. Today, they are all endangered.

The **green turtle**, *mão grande*, weighs up to 230kg. Its carapace, around 120cm long, is green-grey in colour, with occasional olive brown, yellow or dark streaks and spots; it is dome-shaped in front, flattening out towards the back. The upper parts of the green turtle's small rounded head are greenish or yellowish; its underside is yellowish-white, and it has a single visible claw on each flipper. It only eats plants: seagrass and algae. Its preferred nesting beaches have dense vegetation and a gentle slope down to the water. Green turtles have a very developed sense of orientation; a female green turtle born on a Santomean beach can cross the Atlantic and return 20 years later to nest on the same beach! The **olive ridley** (*tatô*, only nesting on São Tomé, not Príncipe) is the smallest (weight 35–50kg) and has a wide heart-shaped carapace (around 75cm long), olive-green to brown in colour, with a hump. The olive ridley's toothless jaw resembles a beak; it feeds on shellfish, mollusk, jellyfish and algae. Olive ridleys lay their eggs on the top of sand banks, preferring open beaches with a gentle slope. Unlike the other species which lay eggs only every two to three years, olive ridleys tend to reproduce every year. The omnivorous **hawksbill**, *sada*, critically endangered because of the popularity of its shell for crafts and jewellery, has a serrated amber carapace of up to 90cm long, mottled with dark and light spots and streaks, and a small head with a hawk-like beak. When laying their eggs – up to 200 – hawksbills prefer small isolated beaches bordered by thick overhanging vegetation to shelter their nests. The most impressive of them all is the **leatherback**, also critically endangered. It is huge – up to 180cm long, and weighing in at an average of 500kg; the local name for leatherbacks is *ambulância*, 'ambulance'. Leatherbacks' carapace is a thick layer of fat and tiny bones covered with a bluish-black skin with white spots; also, they have no horny scales or claws. Feeding mainly on shellfish and jellyfish, they can dive as deep as 1,000m. On São Tomé and Príncipe, leatherbacks nest on beaches with a shallow slope to make it easier for the female to haul her bulk to the nesting site. The **loggerhead turtle**, with a brown-orangey carapace and on average 70–90cm long, has been seen in the waters around São Tomé, and seen mating, but not yet observed nesting.

The **turtle tracks** you see in the sand vary: symmetrical (green and leatherback turtle), where the fore and hind legs move together, and asymmetrical (olive ridley and hawksbill), where diagonally opposite limbs move together. The nests of olive ridleys are about 40cm deep, leatherbacks' nests are on average 70cm deep. Depending on the species, the female drops 80–130 eggs into the incubation chamber of the flask-shaped nest; the eggs' soft shell membrane stops them from cracking. Luckily for turtle tourists, during egg laying the females are not sensitive to disturbance and may be observed from fairly close up. After laying their eggs, the turtles fill in the nest, shovelling sand, compacting it with their flippers, and camouflaging the nest by sweeping sand across the area. When the turtles return to the sea, they orient themselves by the light; all artificial lights, including photo flash, need to be turned off so as not to confuse them. The sex of the hatchling is determined by the temperature during the middle period of incubation. If the temperature in the nest is above the 'pivotal' temperature (depending on the species, between 28–30°C or 82–86°F), there will be more female hatchlings; if it is below this temperature, there will be more male hatchlings. After several weeks, the hatchlings leave the eggshell. Using their caruncle (temporary egg tooth), the hatchlings break open the egg membrane and wiggle out of the shell. They then take four to five days to dig their way up through the sand and emerge. The hatchlings race down the beach to the water and start swimming straight away.

The turtle has a special place in Santomean **folklore**, as a heroic creature that by clever and astute actions manages to outfox its opponents; the turtle is indeed seen as the equivalent to the fox in Western fairytales. Always hungry, *Senhor Tartaruga* (Sum Tataluga, in *forro*) is usually trying to work out new ways of finding food – if need be, behind the back of his family. In *forro* culture, the *tataluga* is however also a symbol of courage and resistance; accordingly, the *forro* expression *cloçon tataluga* (heart, *coração*) refers to a fearless person. However, turtles and their eggs are still cooked and eaten by many Santomeans – the meat of the olive ridley, in particular, is popular – while hawksbill turtle scales are turned into crafts items, such as bracelets, hair clips, combs or boxes. An adult turtle yields about 2kg of usable shell. São Tomé and Príncipe is a signatory to both CITES (Convention on International Trade in Endangered Species of Wild Fauna and Flora) and CMS (Convention on the Conservation of Migratory Species of Wild Animals), but lacks the means and political will to enforce either. You don't see whole conserved

ON TURTLE PATROL

Every night between September and April, Hipólito Lima patrols the 4km stretch of beach from Morro Peixe to Praia Micoló, protecting and marking egg-laying turtles, checking the hatchlings, disguising nests, and carrying buckets of turtle eggs back to the incubator. Tonight, when Elísio Neto, MARAPA's turtle patrol coordinator, and I get to Morro Peixe on his motorbike, the sea is too rough still for the turtles to venture onto the beaches, so we join Hipólito for a dinner of cooked bananas and fish, with cool beers from the village store. Just as well, because, as it turns out, turtle patrols take time. The strong moonlight makes it easier to see, but unfortunately more unlikely for turtles to risk coming out. At the top of Praia Governador, Hipólito digs a tiny grey olive ridley hatchling out of its nest, carefully disguised by the volunteers. The miniature turtle squirms between Hipólito's fingers, but it is still too early for this one; all its brothers and sisters are waiting below in the sand for the opportune moment to be released back into the sea, so Hipólito puts it back in. Elísio and Hipólito shine their torches across some tracks, showing that a turtle did come crawling out of the sea, but changed her mind and went back in. Making our way through the low shrubs bordering the beaches, Elísio and Hipólito tell me funny *tartaruga* stories. Goats mill around the broken pier of the Fernão Dias plantation, near the monument commemorating the tragic events of 1953. There, clearly, are tracks coming up from the sea, but then they suddenly stop. 'An element of the local population got to this one,' says Hipólito, matter-of-factly. Sometimes the patrol apprehends the *tartarugeiras*, but as it is not illegal to hunt turtles in São Tomé, there is nothing they can do to stop them. We wade through the river and cross the endless shell-strewn stretch of Praia Micoló, finally resting for half an hour before the 4km walk back to Morro Peixe. I am walking on autopilot, with my eyes practically shut, and bitterly regretting not taking more water with me, when at last, at half past one in the morning, back on Praia Governador, Hipólito and Elísio point out an olive ridley busily sweeping a space with her hind flippers, her head half hidden under a twig. The turtle is measured and marked; her scales are counted, as are her eggs: 128 in all. Hipólito digs them all out, arranging them in a bucket, to be taken to the incubator, where they will be safe from dogs, crabs – and humans. In the incubator patch, the eggs are put into an artificial nest of exactly the same depth as the natural one. When we get back to the capital, exhausted, it is four in the morning.

It is estimated that only 1% of turtles that reach the sea will survive to grow to maturity and reproduce.

turtles for sale anymore, as happened in the early 1990s, but turtle meat and eggs are openly on sale at São Tomé market. The only way to diminish this trade is to **refuse to buy turtle crafts** and be sure to tell the vendors why. Export is legal; however, most countries, including the EU, the US, Australia and New Zealand, prohibit the import of tortoiseshell goods. In 2000, the Tatô Project successfully retrained tortoiseshell artisans to work in fishing, tourism or to use other materials – wood, coconuts, cowhorn – but, with few project funds available, it is difficult to make the living turtle worth more financially than a dead turtle. In São Tomé, the MARAPA conservation and fishing organisation looks after turtle projects and the burgeoning 'turtle tourism'. MARAPA discourages tourists from paying locals to liberate turtles if they see them being caught, as it encourages the practice even more. There is a good display on turtles and their protection in the museum in São Tomé town. The stretch of beach between **Praia Micoló** and **Morro Peixe** is probably the most famous for turtles on São Tomé; all four species come here to lay eggs. In the south of the island, there is an incubation centre near Praia Jalé and there are two successful turtle projects on Príncipe. The nesting season lasts for several months, and the nesting process itself has seven phases that can last between one and three hours: crawling up the beach, sweeping the chosen area clear, digging the nest, laying the eggs, filling in the nest, camouflaging it, and returning to the sea. What seems like sea turtles' 'tears' during the nesting process is in fact a salty fluid secreted by a salt gland behind the eye to keep its eyes free of sand. It is during nesting that the turtles are most vulnerable. Natural threats include water entering a nest built too close to the water, erosion, wild dogs and pigs feeding on the eggs, and sea birds and crabs eating the hatchlings. Apart from being hunted for their meat, eggs and carapace, man-made threats include plastic bags thrown into the sea – leatherbacks confuse them with jellyfish and can asphyxiate. To protect the turtles, every year tens of thousands of eggs are taken out to be incubated in one of the incubation centres.

ENVIRONMENT As there is hardly any industry, the waters around São Tomé and Príncipe are pristine, around Príncipe in particular. Yet, the Gulf of Guinea islands that the archipelago is part of, exceptionally rich in endemic species, were named in a 2002 conservation report as number two in a list of ten threatened coral reef hotspots. **Fishing stocks** are starting to suffer from foreign fleets trawling in Santomean waters. One of the aims of the new radar system set up by the US in the Gulf of Guinea is to stop this. The US Navy are also engaged in mapping the ocean floor around the islands. In the face of the ongoing energy crisis and, according to local media, some of the highest energy prices in the world, **renewable energy** projects (wind and solar) are starting up, with German and Spanish co-operation. The Portuguese Soares da Costa construction group began building a dozen new 'mini' hydro-electric power plants in 2008, suggesting that lessons have been learnt from from previous 'mega' projects that turned out to be impossible to maintain. These will take Santomean electricity production from the current 10 megawatts (mainly generated by the capital's thermic plant, dependant on imported diesel) up to 40 megawatts. For the time being, visitors will continue to see the many small shops lining Santomean streets illuminated by (imported) candles. It might not look like it, but **forest conservation** is a vital issue on the islands. In the past, large areas of **lowland forest** were cleared for cocoa plantations. Today, partial land privatisation has brought the division of farm plots and more tree clearance. Some exotic species are threatening to upset the ecological balance: in the case of the forest snail, for instance, the exotic species is putting pressure on the endemic one. Illegal logging of tropical hardwood continues, especially around the 'end of the road' in the north of the island, whilst Santomeans use the trees for charcoal for cooking and to carve their dug-out canoes. Export is technically prohibited now. Luckily, the **primary forest**, which has the highest number of endemic species, is difficult to access. The forest is as yet unprotected, but a new law on protected areas and the protection of threatened species is currently awaiting final ratification. ECOFAC is rightly thinking of introducing an entrance fee for the Obô National Park that stretches across the two islands, but continuous funding problems are hampering conservation. At the moment, the only real demarcation of the park is a wooden entrance sign near Bom Sucesso on São Tomé. Because tourism is growing and the road network is being extended in the east and west of São Tomé, species will be pushed deeper into the forest. Deforestation, erosion and exhaustion of the soil are issues. Also, sometimes sand is diverted from the beaches for use in construction. Twenty-six tree species are considered vulnerable. A few **birds,** such as the dwarf olive ibis, *galinhola de São Tomé*, and the maroon pigeon, are shot to be eaten. Currently, ten bird species are threatened, with the dwarf olive ibis, the São Tomé fiscal shrike and the São Tomé grosbeak 'critically endangered' on BirdLife International's Red List. In the past, many grey parrots, one of the world's most popular pet birds, and featuring on the dobra coins, were trapped and captured for the international pet trade; it is thought that on Príncipe some 100 trappers supplement their income with the sale of grey parrots, giving them the local *cacharamba* firewater to drink to keep them quiet on the boat journey across the sea. A rehabilitation centre on Príncipe for confiscated parrots is planned. In 2006, São Tomé and Príncipe adopted the UNESCO Convention on Wetlands, which will protect the seabird-colony on Ilhas Tinhosas, a breeding site for over 300,000 migratory waterbirds on just 24ha (under threat from seabird harvesting by fishermen), the Malanza mangrove and the highland wetland crater of Lagoa Amélia.

In São Tomé in particular, **litter** is becoming an increasing problem, sitting in heaps along the roadside and starting to spoil some of the northern beaches close to town. In the capital, more effort is now being made to clean up the streets, but there is no real understanding of environmental issues and its link with tourism. An open-air dump close to a residential area continuously emits a cloud of toxic smoke that is worrying health officials and occupying the media. Despite well-meaning painted signs sponsored by local environment agencies, beer and soft-drink bottles are often left on the beach after a picnic. I know of only one recycling inititative, involving liqueur bottles. As access to sanitary installations is limited, many locals defecate in the *mato*, the forest, or on the beach.

2

Practical Information

WHEN TO VISIT

While you can visit the islands at any time of the year, the most popular time is during one of the two dry seasons, either between June and September, or around January/February. Temperatures on the islands hover around 27°C/80°F all year round, but the summer months of the long dry season, *gravana*, are the best time for hiking and birdwatching. August visitors in particular have a good chance to catch popular saints' feast days and cultural events, where the streets are thronged with stalls, open-air discos and entertainment; don't miss the unique *tchiloli* and Danço Congo dramatic performances. Every other summer (around mid-June–mid-July), in even years, the Bienal cultural festival takes place in the capital. Mid-August, around the St Laurent's festivities, is an ideal time to visit Príncipe, to catch the colourful spectacle of the Auto de Floripes, the biggest celebration on the smaller sister island. To see humpback whales migrating, you have to come between August and October. Another good option is the short dry season, *gravanita*, which lasts from around mid-January to mid-February, including carnival celebrations which are a good opportunity for seeing traditional dances. This period is good for birdwatching too, as the birds are sporting their mating plumage. Between November and March, visitors may watch marine turtles laying their eggs and hatchlings being returned to the sea between September and April. Divers will find best visibility between December and March. However, January, February and March are the hottest months of the year, with the dry and dusty winds blowing sand from the Sahara into the Gulf of Guinea, often clouding the scenery in a 'Harmattan' haze, locally called *bruma seca*. In the rainy season between October and May, hiking becomes tricky on muddy terrain and the air is heavy with humidity, bringing out the mosquitoes, but photographers will find better light, blue skies and brighter contrasts. Days can be a mixed bag: you might get rain in the morning, then a beautiful afternoon, with blue skies and the air feeling fresh after the tropical downpour, then a more cloudy evening with some rain, or a string of days where it only rains in the afternoons and evenings. The rainy season is best for orchid-spotting, but if you want to see orchids and still be comfortable hiking, a lot of the species growing above 800m are still in flower in January. This is also the start of the saints' days season, beginning with São Isidro in Ribeira Afonso on the main island in late January, and on Príncipe, on 17 January, with the celebrations of the discovery of the island on Saint Anthony's Day.

HIGHLIGHTS AND ITINERARIES

Hike through dense rainforest to discover the crumbling colonial splendour of plantations; go beach-hopping and birdwatching. Rough it at an ecolodge; go back in time at a plantation house; and relax at Bom Bom Island resort on Príncipe. Taste slow-cooking Santomean specialities and the citrus freshness inside a cocoa pod. Admire majestic tropical flowers and a pristine underwater world. Stand on the equator mark; climb the Pico de São Tomé; and catch performances of the medieval Charlemagne cycle in the rainforest. Replace with elements from other itineraries as preferred.

ONE WEEK

Day 1: One-day walk of São Tomé town, overnight in the capital
Day 2: Drive north (Lagoa Azul), plantation visit (Agostinho Neto), crab lunch at Neves, drive to end of road, overnight Roça Monteforte
Day 3: Beach day at Club Santana (visit Água Izé plantation on the way), overnight Club Santana
Day 4: Drive to Bom Sucesso, exploring the plantations of Monte Café and Nova Moca, overnight Bom Sucesso
Day 5: Early-morning birdwatching, walk to Lagoa Amélia, overnight in the capital
Day 6: Head south via Roça de São João (lunch), swim at Praia Piscina, overnight at Praia Jalé ecolodge
Day 7: Malanza mangrove canoe tour, catch boat to Rolas Island for lunch and visit equator mark, drive back to capital, stop at Roça de São João for coffee and to pick up souvenirs, visit local *discoteca* in São Tomé town

TWO WEEKS

Day 1: One-day walk of São Tomé town, overnight in the capital
Day 2: Drive north (Lagoa Azul), visit Agostinho Neto plantation, crab lunch at Neves, drive to end of road, overnight Monteforte plantation
Day 3: Drive back to capital and on to Bom Sucesso, exploring the plantations of Monte Café and Nova Moca, overnight Bom Sucesso
Day 4: Early-morning birdwatching, explore botanical collection, walk to Lagoa Amélia, overnight Bom Sucesso
Day 5: Hike to Bombaim plantation
Day 6: Beach day at Club Santana, overnight Club Santana
Day 7: Drive south from Santana via Roça São João (lunch), overnight Praia Jalé eco-lodge
Day 8: Day trip to Rolas Island, visit to equator mark and lunch, overnight Praia Jalé écolodge
Day 9: Back to capital, visiting Água Izé plantation on the way
Day 10: Fly to Príncipe, afternoon sea birding trip or half-day exploring the plantations, overnight Bom Bom Island resort (or budget option)
Day 11: Early-morning birdwatching, relaxing/snorkelling or walk around Santo António, overnight Bom Bom Island resort (or budget option)
Days 12/13: Fly back to São Tomé with a couple of days to spare for onward connection home (beach day, souvenir shopping)
Day 14: Visit Roça de São José, explore area (plantations) and pick up flowers to take home

If no trip to Príncipe planned, replace with three-day cycling tour, Pico de São Tomé, or snorkelling trip to Ilhéu das Cabras and diving baptism.

THREE WEEKS

Day 1: One-day walk of São Tomé town, overnight in the capital
Day 2: Drive north via Lagoa Azul, visit plantation (Agostinho Neto), crab lunch at Neves, overnight in the capital

Days 3/4:	Two-day cycling tour (or kayak trip to Ilhéu das Cabras plus organised day trip)
Day 5:	Drive to Bom Sucesso, exploring the plantations of Monte Café and Nova Moca, overnight Bom Sucesso
Day 6:	Early-morning birdwatching and exploring botanical collection, walk to Lagoa Amélia, overnight Bom Sucesso
Days 7/8:	Climb Pico de São Tomé with one night camping and overnight at Bombaim plantation
Day 9:	Drive south via Roça de São João (lunch), overnight Praia Jalé ecolodge
Day 10:	Day trip to Rolas Island, with visit to equator mark and lunch, snorkelling, overnight Rolas
Day 11:	Relax, back to capital, stopping at Sete Ondas beach and/or Água Izé plantation on the way, overnight capital
Day 12:	Beach-hopping along the coast from Praia Micoló, overnight capital
Day 13:	Fly to Príncipe, relax at Bom Bom Island resort, overnight Bom Bom
Day 14:	Early-morning birdwatching, full-day guided visit to plantations
Day 15:	Relax, sea-birding boat trip or visit to Santo António, overnight Santo António or Bom Bom
Day 16:	Climb Pico de Papagaio or visit Banana Beach, overnight Santo António or Bom Bom Island resort
Days 17:	Explore the rainforest south of the island with guide, overnight at Bom Bom ecocamp (if up and running) or camp with guide
Days 18/19:	Fly back to São Tomé with a couple of days to spare before connection home (beach day/souvenir shopping)
Day 20:	Visit to Roça São José, explore/hike around area (plantations) and pick up flowers to take home

TOUR OPERATORS

Given the high air fares, it often works out cheaper, even for independent-spirited travellers who prefer to organise everything themselves, to book a package, eg: a diving package, with an extension of a week or two. You could sort out the rest once you're there, either through a local operator such as Navetur (see *Local travel agencies*, page 100), or by yourself for a lower price, especially if you are resourceful, maybe speak a bit of Portuguese and make some local friends. A tour operator will organise your visa, arrange a pick-up at the airport, and assist you with any problems. For people travelling on their own, signing up for a few excursions provides ready-made travel companions.

UK

Audley Travel New Mill, New Mill Lane, Witney, Oxon, OX29 9SX; ☎ 01993 838500; e cate.mackenzie@ audleytravel.com; www.audleytravel.com. Upmarket agency, using 'Country Specialists', who have experience of the places they are selling; can offer tailor-made trips to STP both as an extension to a Gabon tour & as a separate destination.

Birdquest Two Jays, Kemple End, Stonyhurst, Lancs, BB7 9QY; ☎ 01254 826317; e birders@birdquest.co.uk; www.birdquest.co.uk. Birdquest's groups of hardcore international birders hit STP in July/August, as an extension of their

Gabon trip, guided by Nik Borrow, one of the foremost authorities on STP birds. Detailed trip reports on website.

Destination-Cape Verde Madeira House, 37 Corn Street, Witney, Oxon, OX28 6BW; ☎ 01993 773269; e mail@destination-capeverde.co.uk; www.destination-capeverde.co.uk. Portugal/Cape Verde specialist offering 5 different packages, from 7-night stay at 2 different plantation houses (£223, HB) to a 14-night relaxing tour of all 3 island resorts (£836). The packages exclude flights; the company can book those for you, for a £15 fee.

Farside Africa 16 Dean Park Mews, Edinburgh, EH14 1ED; ☎ 0131 3152464; e info@farsideafrica.com; www.farsideafrica.com. Small Scottish company who can organize anything from camping in the rainforest to a stay at the top-notch Bom Bom Island resort. Good web content, plus voluntary carbon-offsetting initiative.

Greentours Leigh Cottage, Gauledge Lane, Longnor, Buxton, Derbyshire, SK17 0PA; ☎ 01298 83563; e enquiries@greentours.co.uk, www.greentours.co.uk. This company's predominantly UK clients are less driven than Birdquest's & more interested in a rounded natural history experience, again as an extension of Gabon. Detailed trip reports on request.

Sao Tomé Travel 14 Market Pl, Hornsea HU18 1AW; ☎ 01964 536 191; e sales@saotometravel.co.uk; www.saotometravel.co.uk.

Tim Best Travel 4 Cromwell Place, London, SW7 2JE; ☎ 020 7591 0300; e info@timbesttravel.com; www.timbesttravel.com. Catering to the top end of the market, the company is beginning to work with STP as an add-on to Gabon, but can also organise a tailor-made trip.

Undiscovered Destinations Saville Exchange, Howard St, North Shields, Tyne & Wear, NE30 1SE; ☎ 0191 2962674/from the US/Canada: 1 800 3153846; e info@undiscovered-destinations.com; www.undiscovered-destinations.com. This small, friendly adventure travel agency specialising in pioneering destinations offers a 9-day tour (starting from £1,690, inc flights & some meals; land-only rate £750), taking in the Bombaim plantation, hiking to Bernardo Faro, the east coast, the southern beaches, a trip to the equator & the northeast, or tailor-made itineraries inc the Bom Bom Island resort. You can also visit STP as part of a 16-day Gabon/STP package, or combine STP with another up-and-coming destination & former Portuguese colony: Angola. Departures every Wed from London, min 2 people.

Wildlife Worldwide Long Barn South, Sutton Manor Farm, Bishops Sutton, Airesford, SO24 0AA; ☎ 0845 130 6982/01962 737630; e sales@wildlifeworldwide.com; www.wildlifeworldwide.com. Award-winning operator; stay at Bom Bom Island resort as either an extension to Gabon or a separate trip.

US

Bushtracks 824 Healdsburg Av, Healdsburg, CA 95448; ☎ 1 800 9008689; e info@bushtracks.com; www.bushtracks.com. Tailor-made trips, inc a 12-day rainforest adventure to Central African Republic/Gabon/Príncipe, through family-run Africa experts supporting conservation & educational projects. A 4-day Príncipe extension to their National Geographic Gabon trip (www.nationalgeographicexpeditions.com) costs US$1,800 (3 departure dates per year).

Journeys International Inc 107 Aprill Drive, Suite 3, Ann Arbor, MI 48103; ☎ 1 800 2558735; e info@journeys.travel; www.journeys-travel. Ecotourism operator offering STP as an extension to their annual Gabon safari.

Undiscovered Destinations (see UK) ☎ 1 800 3153846.

World Travel Agency 5444 Westheimer Rd 125, Houston, TX 77056; ☎ 713 6211000; e sburlet@carlsontravel.com; www.agencewta.com. Resort holidays at Club Santana.

AFRICA
Angola
World Travel Agency Av 4 de Fevereiro, N° 39 RC Luanda; ☎ 02 310972/02 311252; f 02 31 0717; e tour@wtangola.com; www.agencewta.com. Club Santana resort holidays.

Cameroon
Equatorial Tours BP 15709, Douala; ☎ 9995 58 01/7476 56 15; f 33425531; e info@ equatorialtours.com; www.equatorialtours.com. Packages and individual itineraries (adventure tours/honeymoons), leaving from Gabon and Douala and using upmarket hotels.

Gabon
Africa's Eden B P 99, Port Gentil; ☎ 564818; f 54819; e info@africas-eden.com; www.africas-eden.com The former Operation Louango (see Netherlands).

Mistral Voyages Immeuble Diamant, BP 2106, Libreville; ☎ 760421/761222; f 747780; e info@ecotourisme-gabon.com; www.tourisme-gabon.com. Established agency with offices in Port-Gentil & São Tomé, & head office in Marseille (see France opposite). Can also book flight tickets to São Tomé & on to Príncipe.

Nigeria

Aero Contractors Aero Lagos International Airport Office, Room 2058, 2nd Floor, Murtala Mohammed International Airport; ☎ 01 2711512/08023929301; e reservations.intl@acn.aero; www.acn.aero. Nigerian airline selling packages to Pestana Equador resort, Residencial Avenida small city hotel & the upmarket Omali Lodge Hotel. Sat departures.

South Africa

Birding Africa 4 Crassula Way, Pinelands 7405, Cape Town; ☎ 21 5319148; e info@birdingafrica.com; www.birdingafrica.com. Whilst STP is offered as an extension to their regular Gabon birdwatching expedition (trip report on website), they are happy to tailor-make an expedition.

Rockjumper Birding Tours PO Box 13972, Cascades 3202; ☎ 33 3940225; e info@rockjumper.co.za; www.rockjumper.co.za. This birdwatching specialist will be offering STP again as an extension to their August Gabon trip from 2009, inc 3 nights' camping on São Tomé & a stay at Bom Bom Island resort on Príncipe, but if you want, you can book the STP leg only & arrange your own flights.

EUROPE
Belgium

Odysseus Plaslaar 34, 2500 Lier; ☎ 03 4910460; e info@odysseus.be; www.odysseus.be. Luxury travel (Bom Bom Island resort).

Vitamin Travel Rue Van Artevelde 48, 1000 Bruxelles; ☎ 02 5127464; e info@vitamintravel.be. Partner agency of Terres d'Aventure in France (see *France*, below).

France

Club Aventure 18, rue Séguier, 75006 Paris (with branches in Lyon and Geneva, Switzerland); ☎ 0826 882080; www.clubaventure.fr. Departures throughout the year, with min 2 clients travelling. 9-day trips with plenty of trekking, staying mainly at plantation houses.

Mistral Voyages 111 Rue du Commandant Rolland, 13008 Marseille; ☎ 04 91547371; e info@mistralvoyages.com; www.sao-tome.st. 7-night stays in a variety of hotels/residencials/resorts, or 4 themed trips, including an island-hopping circuit, where you get to visit both the main islands & the equator island. Wed departures from various European cities (Brussels, Geneva, Paris, Lyon, London…). Tailor-made itineraries available too. Partner agencies on São Tomé and in Gabon (Libreville, Port Gentil).

Nomade 40 Rue de la Montagne Ste-Geneviève, 75005 Paris; ☎ 0825 701702; e infos@nomade-aventure.com; 43 Rue Peyrolières, 31000 Toulouse, ☎ 0825 701702; e toulouse@nomade-aventure.com; www.nomade-aventure.com. 9-day tours ('dynamique' or 'tranquille'), from €1,750, with stays at Monteforte, Bombaim & São João plantations, treks from Monteforte to Neves, boat trips to the capital & through the mangrove, exploring the plantations of Monte Café, Água Izé, equator mark, Praia Jalé ecolodge, plus traditional music. Guaranteed departures with a minimum of 3 travellers.

Terra Incognita 36 Quai Arloing, 69256 Lyon Cedex 09; ☎ 04 72532490; e ti@terra-incognita.fr; www.terra-incognita.fr. Luxury tailor-made trips, arranged through Africa's Eden.

Terres d'Aventure 30 Rue Saint Augustin, 75002 Paris; ☎ 0825 700825 (for all French branches); e infos@terdav.com; www.terdav.com. Interesting 9-day programme from €2,370 all in, with 6 days of trekking, staying at the plantations of Bombaim, Monteforte, São João and at the Praia Jalé ecolodge, and including a boat trip along the southwest coast, as well as a trek along the mouth of Rio Grande. Also tailor-made packages for groups.

Vie Sauvage 24 Rue Vignon, 75009 Paris; ☎ 01 44510800; e info@viesavage.fr; www.viesauvage.fr. Wildlife/photosafari specialist currently offering the Omali Lodge Hotel on São Tomé as a beach extension to their Gabon programme.

Voyageurs du Monde 55 Rue Ste Anne, 75002 Paris (various other branches), ☎ 0892 235656; www.vdm.com. Two 9-day trips, one based at small town hotel Avenida (from €1600), one at Club Santana resort (from €2,000). A minimum of 2 people is required. Normally, clients travel via Lisbon, but a stay in Gabon, with passage via Libreville, can be organised too.

World Travel Agency 144 Bd Haussmann, 75008 Paris; ☎ 01 53537300; e infos@world-travel-agency.net; www.agencewta.com. 7 nights at Club Santana. Occasional promotional prices.

Zig-Zag Randonnées 54 Rue de Dunkerque, 75009 Paris, ☏ 01 42851393; e informations@ zig-zag-randonnees.com; www.zigzag-randonnees.com. 'Sur la piste des plantations' packages, 9-day (from €1,800) & 16-day (€2,100), excellent for keen walkers who also want to discover São Tomé's culture & history.

Germany

Cobra Verde Bauernreihe 6a, 27726 Worpswede; ☏ 04792 952124; e kontakt@cobra-verde.de; www.cobra-verde.de. Pioneers of STP travel offering relaxing beach holidays, two 8-day São Tomé circuits, & a 16-day trip to both islands, with the option of an additional beach week.

Ivory Tours Schnieglinger Str 4, 90419 Nürnberg; ☏ 0911 3938520; e info@ivory-tours.de; www.ivory-tours.de/www.divingsaotome.de. Africa/diving specialist offering a 9-day trip with flexible dates throughout the year (min 2 people), from €1,990 to €2,190. Typically, this will include 3 nights in the capital (in upmarket hotels), with an English-speaking programme: a half-day visit of the town & 2 day trips (to Bom Sucesso/São Nicolão waterfall & the northern beaches), before you go on to Ilhéu das Rolas for diving & other activities (birdwatching, boat tours, walks, sailing, African dance workshop, volleyball). You can book an additional week on Rolas.

One World – Reisen mit Sinnen Roseggerstr 59, 44137 Dortmund; ☏ 0231 5897920; e oneworld@reisenmitsinnen.de; www.reisenmitsinnen.de. Award-winning 16-day 'São Tomé Discovery' package, travelling on foot, by bike & jeep with stays at various plantations & 3 days on Príncipe (staying at the Pensão Palhota and exploring the island on foot), from €2,890 (min 6 people). A second option is 1 week exploring ST island, plus a week relaxing on Rolas. German-language tour leader. Offset the carbon emissions of your trip (3,760kg!) with a voluntary payment to a climate protection project.

Quetzal Tours Dänenstr 15, 10439 Berlin; ☏ 030 24628793; e info@quetzal-tours.de; www.quetzal-tours.de. Wildlife specialist, offering a beach week at Club Santana or Omali Lodge as an extension of their Gabon tour.

TUI Star Schweinberger Reisewelt Huchenfelder Hauptstr 127; 75181 Pforzheim; ☏ 07231 788547; e info@schweinberger.de; www.schweinberger.de. Tailor-made 8-day tours, based around a choice of city hotels, plus an optional week at the beach, through another STP pioneer.

Italy

Latitude Zero Via Giovanni XXIII No 10, 22072 Cermenate (Como); ☏ 333 4396719; e flavio@latitudezero.it; www.latitudezero.it. For the 2004 'Latitude Zero Equatorial Challenge', a group of Italians & Portuguese attempted to drive the circumference of São Tomé in 4x4s. The team never did make it all around the island, but it gave organiser Flavio Pedraglio the inspiration to introduce Italian travellers to STP: 2-week trips, based in the capital, with nature hikes, beach trips, etc. Holidays combining STP with Angola are planned.

Netherlands

Africa's Eden Sonsbeekweg 26, 6814 BC Arnhem; ☏ 026 3705567; e info@africas-eden.com; www.africas-eden.com. Ecotourism operator offering STP as a week-long programme directly (departures from Lisbon with TAP) or as an extension to their Gabon programme (departures from Port Gentil and Libreville in Gabon, or Douala in Cameroon with Africa's Connection – SCD Aviation), with 3 days on each island.

Kilroy Travels Singel 413 (Naast de UB), 1012 WP Amsterdam; ☏ 0900 0400636/+31 36 8222203; www.kilroytravels.nl. Student travel specialist, with offices in Denmark, Sweden, Finland, Norway; can only book TAP flights.

Portugal

Abreu ☏ 707 201840; e directo@abreu.pt; www.abreu.pt. Portugal's biggest tour operator has over 80 branches across Portugal selling 9-day packages, combining stays at Omali Lodge, Bom Bom Island resort, Club Santana & Pestana Equador Island Resort on Rolas. Other major operators, such as **Mundovip** (www.esoperadores.com), **Soltrópico** (www.soltropico.pt) or **Tagus** (☏ 707 220000; e telesales@viagenstagus.pt; www.taguseasy.pt.) and **Entremares** (www.entremares.pt), work with the same hotels. These packages are bookable through travel agents, eg: **Atlântida Viajens** Av Columbano Bordalo

Pinheiro, 61B, 1070-061 Lisbon; ☏ 21 7228210; e geral@atlantidaviajens.pt; www.atlantidaviagens.pt. **Terra Africa** ☏ 21 7514855; e reservas@terraafrica.pt (mind their very sensitive spam filter, you might have to try geral@terraafrica.pt or phone); www.terraafrica.pt. Owned by the Pestana group. Two packages: a 2-centre stay combining Pestana Equador resort & Residencial Avenida, Miramar or Club Santana, starting from €1,290, & a 1-week stay in the

capital only, with the same hotel options, starting from €1,100 per person/dbl room; flights with TAP. New from 2008: summer packages with Euroatlantic Airways, with stays at the Rolas resort & the brand-new 5-star Pestana Equador hotel in the capital, bookable through the company or any travel agent in Portugal & abroad. Unfortunately for independent travellers, an additional week spent on your own attracts a €400 supplement and you haven't bought your accommodation yet.

Spain

Viajes Dragontours Serreta 17, Cartagena / Avda Doctor Meca 28, Puerto de Mazarron; Comercial, 30, Urb Camposol (Mazarrón); ☏ 902 194 766; e info@dragontours.net; www.dragontours.net.

Packages with a wide selection of accommodation, arranged locally through the Navetur agency, so there is any choice of activities and type of holiday.

Sweden

Check out www.islandsresort.se

Switzerland

A&M Africa Tours Postfach, 8712 Stäfa; ☏ 01 9267979; e travel@africatours.ch; www.africatours.ch. Tailor-made itineraries, from Bom Bom Island resort holidays to rainforest camping and plantation stays, by knowledgeable and enthusiastic operator.
Terres d'Aventure – Néos Voyages 50 Rue des Bains, 1205 Genève; ☏ 022 3206635;

e geneve@neos.ch & 11 Rue du Simplon, 1006 Lausanne; ☏ 021 6126600; e lausanne@neos.ch; www.terdav.com. Swiss partner of French company (see *France* above).
World Travel Agency 19 Quai du Mont Blanc, 1201 Genève; ☏ 022 7411482; e mary.aubry@wta.ch; www.agencewta.com

RED TAPE

ENTRY REQUIREMENTS You need: a **passport** that is valid for another 3–6 months (check with the visa-issuing authority) after your return date, a return ticket, a **visa** (see below), and a **yellow fever vaccination** certificate. You will need to show the latter before you go through passport control. If you haven't got one or have lost the document, you can (and will have to) have the vaccination done there and then, for €20.

VISAS Unless you are a citizen of São Tomé and Príncipe, you will need a visa (*visto*). Currently, most European residents, apart from the Portuguese, the French and the Italians, have to obtain their visa through the embassy in Brussels. São Tomé and Príncipe has no diplomatic representation in the UK, despite old contacts circulating on the internet. In the US, the São Tomé and Príncipe embassy is a one-man show, and unless you live in NYC, it might save you hassle to go through a visa service (eg: *www.traveldocs.com*). Australians, New Zealanders, South Americans and the rest of the world can apply to any São Tomé and Príncipe embassy; I would recommend the one in Brussels, which is very professionally run. South African citizens obtain their visas from the São Tomé and Príncipe embassy in Angola or Gabon. Note that even applicants for a tourist visa are asked to provide a 'reference' in São Tomé; just put: 'Direcção Nacional do Turismo, Av 12 de Julho, CP 40, São Tomé, tel: 00 239 221542'.

If you are using a **tour operator** in your country or locally, they will take care of your visa. For instance, Navetur or Mistral can email you a form to fill in for a 'permission letter' sufficient to obtain a pre-arranged visa payable at the airport (€60 if you are from a country with a visa-issuing São Tomé and Príncipe representation, €50 otherwise). In addition, Navetur also requests a photocopy/scan of the first four pages of your passport. Be careful: you might hear through the grapevine that you should be OK to get a visa on arrival if there is only one or two of you. This might have happened in the past – the airlines have a duty to take you back to your country of origin and risk a fine, but in practice don't always check visas – but the law has been tightened, and tourists arriving without a visa have been sent back, and no offer of paying a fine will help. Don't take the risk. Visitors from a country without any São Tomé and Príncipe diplomatic representation can obtain a permission letter by applying to the **Department of Immigration** (Av 12 Julho; \f 22 26 95; at airport: \ 22 11 48), justifying the reasons, in Portuguese (currently, the officer in charge is Lt Col António Paquete de Sousa). You can apply for more than one person at once, but you need to post/fax this request well in advance (turnaround is at least a week), show the return fax on arrival, and pay €55. This process might be formalised in the future; again, for the time being, there is no real reason to take this route; the safest option is to go through Brussels. The immigration services, *Serviço de Migraçao e Fronteiras* is also where, once in the country, extensions to your visa can be requested fairly easily.

Ⓔ EMBASSIES AND CONSULATES

ABROAD

USA (Permanent mission to the United Nations) 460 Park Av (between 57th & 58th St), 11th Flr, New York, NY 10022; \ 212 317 0644; f 212 317 0624; e stpun@verizon.net. Residents of the Americas should contact the ambassador, Domingos Ferreira, for an electronic application form. If you are in a hurry, better ring to make sure he is available. Fill in the form & FedEx in your passport, a passport photo, a self-addressed prepaid courier envelope (& an official letter stating the purpose of travel if you need a business visa). A visa takes 2 working business days; fees have to be paid by money order. A single-entry tourist visa of up to 3 months costs US$65, a business visa US$85; add US$5 if you need it on the same day. If you can take in your documents personally (or get a friend to do it for you) the ambassador might be able to issue the visa there and then.

Angola (embassy) 173 Rua Eng. Armindo de Andrade, Mira-Mar, Luanda; \ 222 328663/222 329013; f 222 326624; e emb-stp.ango@snet.co.ao

Austria (consulate) Margarethengürtel 1a–3a, 1050 Wien; \ 01 545165350; f 01 6643553120; e gerhard.schiesser@schiesser.at. No visa service.

Belgium (embassy for most European citizens) Square Montgomery, 175 Av de Tervuren, 1150 Brussels; \ 02 7348966; f 02 7348815; e ambassade@saotomeeprincipe.be. The very

professionally run embassy in Brussels can email you a form to fill out. You will usually need to take in or post (registered) your passport (valid up to 3 months after your return), 1 passport picture, your yellow fever certificate, plus a self-addressed envelope with your details. For a business visa you will need to provide a letter from your company. The visa, turnaround 48hrs, costs €40, urgent (same-day) €50, & is usually valid for up to 30 days; however, it is not a problem to request a longer validity. Payment is by electronic transfer; add €6 to cover the postage.

Canada (honorary consulate) Pierre Mantha, FCA, 2, Westmount Square, Suite 200, Montreal, Québec, H3Z 2S4; \ 514 9890395; f 514 9891572; e pierre.mantha@vdn.ca. No visa service; apply to the embassy in New York.

France STP has two (very active) honorary consulates in France; both can issue a visa.
(consulate) 111 Rue du Commandant Rolland, 13008 Marseille; \ 04 91375802; f 04 91539572; e consulat@sao-tome.st; www.sao-tome.st. The dynamic consul, Jean-Pierre Bensaïd, is the owner of Mistral Voyages and is involved in various initiatives supporting the country and fostering Franco-Santomean links.
(consulate) 144 Bd Haussmann, 75008 Paris; \ 01 42896724; f 01 42563693; e consulat.saotome@wanadoo.fr; www.consulat-

SaoTome-Principe.fr (English, French, Portuguese). Linked to Club Santana.

Gabon (embassy) Bd de la Mer, BP 489, Libreville; ☎ 721527; f 721528

Germany Neither of the honorary consulates can currently issue visas, though this is planned for the future.
(honorary consulate) Marcusallee 9, 28359 Bremen; ☎ 0421 1736186; f 0421 1736198; e rbo@germanlashing.de
(honorary consulate) Nymphenburger Str 118, 80636 München; ☎ 089 1295388; f 089 187773; e christine.oesterlein@steuerzahler-bayern.de; www.sao-tome.com

Hungary (consulate) Szasz Karolz u 1, Budapest 1027; ☎ 01 2667572; f 01 2667574; e titkarsag@diplomatamagazin.hu. No visa service.

Italy (consulate) Via Cavour 44, 00184 Roma; ☎ 06 47823867; f 06 48930692; e info@saotomeprincipe-roma.it; www.saotomeprincipe-roma.it. The honorary consulate for Rome & the Lazio region can issue a visa & is also active in humanitarian relief work (collecting donations for medical instruments). If you live in northern Italy, contact Flavio (www.latitudezero.it, see *Tour Operators*), who can hand-deliver your documents for you.

Netherlands (consulate) Minervalaan, 90 III, 1077 PL Amsterdam; ☎ 020 6391756; f 020 6391259; e consulaat.saotome@minervalaan.nl. Visa service; make an appointment by phone with Mrs C.A.M. Mentink.

Portugal You can get your visa from both the embassy & the consulates. There are several consulates (including Albufeira, Funchal & Coimbra), but as the contact information is volatile, it's best to phone Lisbon for details.
(embassy) Av Almirante Gago Coutinho, 26–A–r/c, 1000-017 Lisbon; ☎ 21 8461917/8; f 21 8461895; e embaixada@emb-saotomeprincipe.pt; www.emb-saotomeprincipe.pt. A same-day visa for STP is available. The salmon-brown building next to a BP petrol station is a 5min walk from Areeiro metro station. You cannot apply by post. Bring your passport, 1 passport picture & €49 between 09.30 & 12.30 (better by 11.30), pick up a form, fill in your details (inc your address in STP) & you can walk away with the visa after an hour or so. The cost is only €39 if you can wait for around a week for your passport to be sent to you by post. If you are looking for a place to wait, cross the Avenida, go straight for a few metres & take a right, there's a nice café, Manuel Cazador, on the left-hand side.
(consulate) Av de Boa Vista, 4100-130 Porto; ☎ 22 6093436; e consulado.stp-porto@mail.telepac.pt. An emergency visa, available within 48hrs, costs €48, otherwise €40. You need to bring 2 passport pictures & you have to both deliver your documents & pick up your visa in person; there is no postal service.

Spain (consulate) C/General Diaz Portier 49-2°, 28001 Madrid; ☎ 911211783; f 915777989; e brunet@inypsaimc.com. Same-day visa service; bring or send in your passport, 2 passport photos, plus €50 in cash.

Sweden (consulate) Gräsåkersvägen 41 F, 178 36 Ekerö, Stockholm; ☎ 08 56033986/708490703; f 08 490773; e jan.lage@globalnet.net. No visa service.

Taiwan (embassy) 18 Chi-lin Road, 3rd floor, Taipeh; ☎ 02 28766824; f 02 28766964; e stpw@ms69.hinet.net

IN SÃO TOMÉ You should not have much reason to contact your embassy. If you do, accredited embassies (with the exception of Portugal and France) are on the African mainland, in Gabon, Angola or Cameroon. The honorary consuls (usually, local businessmen) should be able to direct you, but they are not always available. Most countries' embassy details are on the internet.

UK (honorary consulate) Praça da Independência; ☎ 241100/903227; f 221372; e joaolimagomes@yahoo.com. João Gomes works from the office with the STP & Union Jack flags at the corner of Rua Moçambique. ⊕ 07.30–12.00 & 14.00–17.00 Mon–Fri. The Ambassador is based in Angola: Rua Diogo Cão 4, CP 1244, Luanda, Angola; ☎ +244 222 334582/out-of-hours emergency ☎ +244 222 334582; f +244 222 333331; e ppa.luanda@fco.gov.uk

USA (diplomatic mission) Pinheira; ☎ 225519; f 223406; e ipinto@sto.ibb.gov. Some 5km out of town, on the Voice of America (☎ 223400) site. The accredited embassy is in Libreville: Bd du Bord de Mer, BP 4000, Libreville, Gabon; ☎ 0762003/4/emergencies: 07380171; f 0745507/0768849; http://usembassy.state.gov/libreville

Angola (embassy) 353 Av Kwame Nkrumah; ☎ 222376/224169; f 221362; e info@embang.st,

2

www.embangola.st. A common reference point on this long street.

Australia Contact the Australian High Commission in Nigeria: 5th Floor, Oakland Center, 48 Aguiyi Ironsi St, Maitama District, Abuja; ✆ +234 413 5226; f +234 413 5227

Brazil (embassy) 20 Av 12 Julho; ✆ 226062/45; f 226895; e embrasil@cstome.net

Canada Contact the High Commission in Cameroon, Rue Natchigal & Independence (CP 572), Yaoundé; ✆ +11 237 2232311; f +11 237 2221090; e yunde@international.gc.ca

Cape Verde (consulate) Rua Damão; ✆ 221075, f 221954

Gabon (embassy) Embaixada da República do Gabão, Rua Damão; ✆ 224434; f 224437

France (embassy) Bairro Quinta Santo António; ✆ 222266/224208; f 221792; e frederic.merlet@diplomatie.gouv.fr. Next to the TVS TV station.

Germany (consulate) Honorary Consul Manuel Lima Nazaré (✆ 903306) is currently setting up an office above the Instituto Camões; meanwhile, you can also get hold of him through the Padaria Moderna bakery on Rua 3 de Fevereiro (✆ 223217; f 226574; e pamoderna@live.com).

Italy (consulate) Av 12 de Julho; ✆ 222236/222934; e corallo@cstome.net. Chocolate maker Claudio Corallo doubles up as consul.

Netherlands (consulate) Rua de Moçambique, ✆ 222685/222084/908457; f 221254; e farmacabral@cstome.net. Honorary consul: Abilio Afonso Henriques. Contact the embassy in Angola: Edificio Secil, Av 4 de Fevereiro No 42, 6th floor, Luanda; ✆ +244 222310686; f +244 222310966; e lua@minbuza.nl

Nigeria (embassy) Av Kwame Nkrumah; ✆ 225404/5; f 225406; e nigeria@cstome.net. Next to the UN building

Portugal (embassy) Av 12 de Julho; ✆ 221130/224997; f 221190; e eporstp@cstome.net. Near the (currently closed) Miramar Hotel

South Africa Contact the embassy in Gabon: South African Embassy, Les Arcades Building, 2nd Floor, 142 Rue de Chavannes, Centrville/BP 4063, Libreville; ✆ +241 77 4530/1; f +241 77 4536

Taiwan (diplomatic mission) Av 12 Julho/Bairro Banco Mundial; ✆ 222671/223529; f 221376; e rocstp@cstome.net Near the National Museum.

GETTING THERE AND AWAY

✈ **BY AIR** The most common route for Western travellers is through **Lisbon**, using the Portuguese national airline **TAP**. From the African continent, the points of entry are Libreville, the capital of Gabon, Lagos (Nigeria), Accra (Ghana) and also Douala (Cameroon), Luanda (Angola) and Port Gentil (Gabon). Generally, book early, and, as the flight situation can change very quickly, it is probably best to start your research by sending an email to Navetur (see page 100). TAP's monopoly and high prices have been challenged in the past (by Air Luxor, which went bust in 2006) and, more recently, the new national company **STP Airways**, operated by Angolan national carrier **TAAG**. At the time of writing, TAAG planes were suspended from flying in European airspace due to safety concerns, requiring a change of plane in Luanda, and **Euroatlantic Airways**, the Portuguese charter carrier majority-owned by the Pestana group (that owns three hotels on São Tomé and Príncipe), was taking over operations, running on a Monday during the summer months. These flights can unfortunately only be purchased with a Pestana package (Pestana São Tomé, Rolas Island, see page 47). There is the possibility to extend your stay by a week and do your own thing, but you pay a €400 supplement for the privilege!

Round-trip prices start at €870 with TAP – second class gets booked up very quickly. If you are travelling from outside Portugal, it might be cheaper to book your tickets separately, coming in to Lisbon with a budget airline; however, if there's a delay with your incoming flight, without a TAP through-ticket you lose the right to take the next available flight the following week. In any case, make sure on the return flight that you don't cut it too fine between arriving back in Lisbon and your onward connection, as I heard about one traveller being denied her onward flight to Madrid after a delay coming back from São Tomé, with the argument that her flight was in fact operated by the White company. The latest news (spring 2008) was that a smaller plane was going to be used on this route, with a detour via Senegal, possibly on both legs. Always get the latest information from Navetur.

It is also possible to connect at Libreville (Air France) or Accra (BA has a daily flight), but overnight stops are required for both connections. In the future, there might be more connections to Lisbon, Johannesburg and Paris, even Houston, but at the time of writing this was still the proverbial pie in the sky. At least, a threatened TAP boycott of São Tomé due to the bad state of the runway was averted in early 2007, when the Taiwanese government paid for the repairs.

Consider **combining** a holiday in São Tomé and Príncipe with **Lisbon** or **Cape Verde**. The city landscapes couldn't be more different, but there are many fascinating historical and cultural ties between São Tomé and Príncipe and both the seat of the former colonial power and the arid archipelago, also an ex-colony of Portugal and now a popular tourist and property investment destination, with its own Bradt guide to its name, too. From the UK, there are now direct flights to Sal from London Gatwick and Stansted airports, as well as from Manchester with TAP and Astraeus (*www.flystar.com*). The national Capeverdian carrier TACV (*www.tacv.cv*) has flights from London Stansted and Boston, as well as European, Brazilian and African hubs.

If you are passing through Lisbon airport travelling light (maybe because your luggage didn't make it from London Gatwick, as in my case), be prepared for locals to ask you while you wait in the check-in queue whether you could check in a crate or suitcase for them. At my first visit, after turning down ten requests, I finally gave in and checked in cooking oil and clothes for a couple of families. The security risk might be minimal but be aware that anything you carry for other people is your own responsibility entirely, as well as being illegal.

The most important thing is that you pack a piece of **on-board luggage** (keeping within the required dimensions), containing everything you cannot do without for 10 days. If you are going to go snorkelling or trekking, pack everything you need for this, along with your malaria protection and other medication or relevant cosmetics (subject to current restrictions on what you can take: buy cosmetics miniatures; if you wear contacts, starter packs for contact lens fluids up to 100ml are allowed). If your luggage stays in Europe, you might have to wait days for information, constantly phoning TAP at your own cost and having to deal with a robotic 'We do not have this information'-style information policy. The office in town is of limited help. The maximum compensation you are entitled to is only US$100. To get this, you will have to send in the receipts for bills you incurred as a result of the delay (e *faleconosco@tap.pt*). So make sure you have adequate travel insurance to make up for the shortfall. Delayed baggage appears to be a common problem; I heard the same story from travellers starting their journey in London, Berlin, Milan and Amsterdam. One English couple I met never actually got their luggage in the entire two weeks of their holiday – a fate they bore with admirable grace – while a trunk with diving kit from Germany took five weeks to get to the island. The only scheduled European airline losing more baggage than TAP is British Airways.

When you leave the country, you have to pay a **departure tax** before checking in. The counter is at the front of (outside) the airport building. You can pay 260,000$, US$21 or €18, but have the exact amount ready; if you hand over a €20 note, for example, you are not likely to get any change back.

From Lisbon

TAP Portugal Chapter House, 22 Chapter St, London, SW1P 4NP; ☎ 0845 6010932; f 020 79323611; www.flytap.com. Lisbon–São Tomé: Dep: Wed 23.30 — arr: Thu 05.30. São Tomé–Lisbon: Dep: Thu 07.00 — arr: 13.00.

STP Airways/TAAG This new company, the successor of Air São Tomé and Príncipe, started in early 2007, as a practically virtual company, operating with Angolan state airline TAAG planes, making the flights dependent on the (frequently delayed) connection from the Angolan capital Luanda (see page 53). With the suspension of TAAG planes over European airspace in summer 2007, the flight stopped temporarily, but was resumed, using a South African Airlines charter to get to Luanda, & a TAAG plane for the Luanda–STP leg. At the time of writing, STP Airways had sold its planes to Euroatlantic Airways, but if it gets the ST–Lisbon route off the ground again, tickets will be available through local agencies. TAAG (UK) 259–269 Old Marylebone Rd, Winchester House, Suite GF1, London NW1 5RA; ☎ 020 7170 4343 (you might have to try several times); e airline@taag118.co.uk (but it's better to phone) TAAG (Portugal) Av do Brasil 31A, 1700-062 Lisbon; ☎ 21 3575899; e reservas@taag.pt

UK–Lisbon There is a fair amount of competition on this route, so take your pick. Leave enough time – ideally an overnight stay or even a few days to explore Lisbon. Be aware that if your onward ticket to São Tomé is with TAP and you miss your connection, you are only protected to take the São Tomé flight the following week if you've come in with TAP, otherwise, the minimum payment is US$135. Double-check the prices of two separate tickets against through-tickets. Whilst TAP maintains it is not cheaper to buy the two legs individually, some travellers have told me otherwise. Some of the following services are seasonal.

Bmibaby ☎ 0871 2240224; www.bmibaby.com. Birmingham–Lisbon 3 times a week (Sun, Tues, Thurs) with British Midland's budget subsidiary.
British Airways ☎ 0870 850 9850; www.ba.com. 3 daily flights from London Heathrow, starting at £110 rtn.
TAP Portugal ☎ 0845 601 0932/020 793 2600; www.flytap.com. The Portuguese national airline flies daily from London Heathrow & London Gatwick.
Easyjet ☎ 0905 821 0905; www.easyjet.com. The no-frills carrier flies from London-Luton, London Gatwick, Bristol (4 times a week) & Liverpool (3 times a week).
Monarch ☎ 0870 040 5040; www.flymonarch.com. Budget flights to Faro (4hrs by train from Lisbon)

from London-Gatwick, London-Luton, Birmingham & Manchester.
Thomsonfly ☎ 0870 190 0737; www.thomsonfly.com. Manchester–Faro (4hrs by train from Lisbon) several times a week. Faro departures, with varying frequencies, also from Belfast, Bristol, Cardiff, Coventry, Doncaster Sheffield, East Midlands, Edinburgh, Glasgow, Humberside, Leeds, London Gatwick and London Stansted & Newcastle. Also London Gatwick–Sal (Cape Verde) on Tues, which would suggest exploring the Cape Verde Island for a couple of days/10 days before connecting with the Fri TAAG service to São Tomé (via Accra).

From Ireland
TAP ☎ 01 656 9162; www.flytap.com. TAP's Dublin–Lisbon route is fairly expensive & only runs via London Heathrow or London Gatwick.
Aer Lingus ☎ 0818 365000; www.aerlingus.com. The Irish national carrier offers reasonable fares & a daily early-morning Dublin–Lisbon flight.

Ryanair ☎ 0818 303030; www.ryanair.com. The Irish budget airline flies twice daily from Dublin to Porto. Portugal's second city is a short metro hop plus a comfortable 3hr train ride from Lisbon's Santa Apolonia station; Porto is well worth a visit in its own right; a round trip on an open ticket costs about €60 (www.cp.pt)

Getting to Lisbon from other countries For a full and easy-to-use current list of Lisbon's airport (*www.ana.pt*) connections, search www.wikipedia.org for 'Portela Airport'.

From Europe TAP fly to Lisbon direct from many European cities: Barcelona, Bologna, Budapest (via Prague), Frankfurt, Munich, Madrid, Paris, Prague, Venice, Zagreb, as do Lufthansa (Frankfurt, Munich), Alitalia (Rome-Fiumicino), Air France, KLM (Amsterdam), SAS (all Scandinavian hubs), Iberia (Madrid), etc.

More and more budget carriers are adding Lisbon to their route network, eg: Germanwings (Cologne, Stuttgart), LTU (Düsseldorf), Easyjet (Basel, Berlin-Schönefeld, Geneva, Milan-Malpensa, Paris-CDG), Centralwings (Krakow).

From the US and Canada Various carriers belonging to the Star Alliance network (*www.staralliance.com*) fly to Lisbon from the US. TAP has a daily direct New York (Newark)–Lisbon overnight service (and sometimes, special offers), and Continental Airlines has one daily overnight flight from New York (Newark). From Canada, Air Transat flies from both Montreal and Toronto, and the Azorean airline SATA has competitive fares from Toronto (and Boston) via the Azores. Remember that on flights from North America the rules on taking liquids on board are stricter than when flying from within Europe.

TAP Portugal ☎ 1 800 2217370; f 9738546859; e tapusa@tap.pt; www.flytap.com
Air France ☎ 1 800 237 2747; www.airfrance.us. Flights to Lisbon for the TAP or STP Airways connection, or to Libreville for the Air Service connection. Air France can book you a through ticket from US airports to São Tomé.

Air Transat ☎ 1 888 TRANSAT; www.airtransat.com
Continental Airlines ☎ 1 800 231 0856; www.continental.com
SATA Boston ☎ 508 677 0555; Toronto ☎ 416 5157 188; ☎ (Portugal): +351 296 209 720; www.sata.pt
US Airways ☎ 1 800 4284322; www.usairways.com

From the African mainland

From Angola There are two flights every week from the capital, Luanda, to São Tomé, one TAAG flight, and one operated by TAAG for STP Airways. Round trip fares from Luanda start at €190.

Apart from Lisbon, TAAG connects Luanda with Paris, Harare (Zimbabwe), Johannesburg (SA), Lusaka (Zambia), Brazzaville, Kinshasa, Point Noir (DRC), Windhoek (Namibia), Rio de Janeiro (Brazil), and Sal (Cape Verde). A code-shared BA/TAAG flight from the UK leaves London Heathrow every Thursday at 21.00 and arrives in Luanda Friday at 05.25, connecting with the STP Airways Luanda–ST flight two days later, Sunday at 07.30.

TAAG Angola Rua da Missão, 123, PO Box 79, Luanda; (skype) ☎ 222 333 235/(skype from Portugal) ☎ 222 334 854; f 222 337 338; e taagangola@aol.com; www.taagangola.pages.web.com (with more contact
numbers). Luanda–São Tomé: Dep: Thu 06.30 – arr: 08.20, São Tomé–Luanda: Dep: Fri 17.00 – arr: 18.50
STP Airways Luanda–São Tomé: Dep: Sun 07.30 – arr: 08.20. São Tomé–Luanda: Dep: Mon 16.00 – arr: 18.50

From Cameroon SCD Aviation, sister company of operator Africa's Eden runs flights from the commercial capital of Cameroon. For contact, see below (From Gabon).

From Gabon The Gabonese capital Libreville is the hub for African connections, and since 2007, travellers coming into Libreville from London or Paris with Air France, or combining a trip to Gabon with São Tomé and Príncipe, have had the choice of two onward connections. Libreville-based **Air Service** (*no direct contact*) connects the Gabonese capital with São Tomé three times a week (return trip from €380). Book your ticket through Mistral Voyages or Navetur. You can book a through ticket to São Tomé with Air France, but you will need to stay overnight in Libreville. The closest hotel to the airport is the **Atlantique**, just across the road from the terminal building, on the beach (☎ *+241 732480; f 732436; e reservation@hotelatlantique.com; www.hotelatlantique.com*). An en-suite/AC room costs about US$125. A cheaper option is the **Tropicana** (☎ *+241 731531/32; f 736574*) some

800m further south (a CFA2,000 taxi ride away, CFA4,000 at night), also on the beach, also with en-suite/AC rooms (US$28), plus a nice bar and outside restaurant. Book early.

Libreville–São Tomé:	São Tomé–Libreville:
Dep: Wed 11.30 – arr: 11.45	Dep: Wed 12.15 – arr: 14.30
Dep: Thu 16.20 – arr: 15.15	Dep: Fri 15.45 – arr: 17.30
Dep: Sun 14.45 – arr: 15.15	Dep: Sun 15.45 – arr: 17.30

A new company, Africa's Connection – SCD Aviation (see page 46), operating to international standards, has scheduled and chartered flights to all major capitals in west central Africa, including Libreville, Port Gentil and Douala, the economic capital of Cameroon. As the schedules are liable to change, they are not published on the website, you'll have to phone or send an email.

Europe/US to STP via Gabon Due to the stopover in Libreville, this is only a good idea if you are planning to combine a trip to São Tomé and Príncipe with seeing Gabon. From London, Air France flies to Libreville via Paris CDG on Tuesdays, Thursdays, Fridays and Sundays, leaving Heathrow at 06.40, for the 10.55 connection to Libreville. Whilst the Eurostar to Paris is the greener option, if there is a delay, without an Air France through-ticket from London, you will have to pay a supplement to get on the next day's flight. Since 2007, private airline Gabon Airlines has been connecting Paris CDG with Libreville Sunday, Tuesday, Thursday (arriving very early the next morning), with competitive rates starting at €880 round trip, and with some onward flights to Pointe Noire in the Congo. You can buy your ticket in the UK, Gabon, Paris, and a few other countries (see website). The direct onward connection to ST with Air Service is on Wednesday. All in all, unless TAP flights are completely booked up, even for travellers based in France, the pricing and the potential stopover required probably makes Paris–Libreville–ST less attractive than Paris–Lisbon–ST.

Air France UK ☎ 0870 1424343; www.airfrance.co.uk
Air France US ☎ 1 800 237 2747; www.airfrance.us

Gabon Airlines UK agent: Jetair ☎ 01293 566080; e reservations.gb@gabonairlines.com, www.gabonairlines.com

From Ghana TAAG also connects Ghana's capital Accra and São Tomé; BA flies daily to Accra from London Heathrow, arriving in the evening.

Accra–São Tomé: Dep: Fri 14.35 – arr: 16.05   São Tomé–Accra: Dep: Thu 09.15 – arr: 10.45

From Nigeria With the expected oil wealth and the exploitation of the Joint Development Zone between the two countries, more flights from Nigeria are likely, possibly even direct flights to Príncipe.

Aero Contractors Aero Lagos International Airport Office, Room 2058, 2nd Floor, Murtala Mohammed International Airport; ☎ 01 2711512/08023929301; e reservations.intl@acn.aero; www.acn.aero. STP office: Rua Santo António do Príncipe; ☎ 227284/skype: 906543; f 227281. This reputable Nigerian private carrier operating a Lagos–São Tomé route once a week is unfortunate to share its name with the North Carolina-based company accused of carrying out rendition flights for the CIA… Navetur can book an 'Aero' ticket for you (round trip Lagos–ST–Lagos from €550/US$700), or you can book online (prices start from around NGN90,000/US$710). Lagos–São Tomé: Dep: Sat 12.30 – arr: 1.30. São Tomé–Lagos: Dep: Sat 14.30 – arr: 17.30

From South Africa Currently, there are no direct flights, but private airline Interair flies Johannesburg–Libreville on Mondays, with a chance of an increased frequency in the future, from around 5,000 rand. As the next Air Service connection is not until Tuesday, you have to stop overnight in Libreville (see page 53). South African Airways charge from around 8,850 Rand for their twice-weekly flights, round trip. US travellers wanting to combine visiting South Africa with São Tomé and Príncipe can use SAA, too, departing from New York JFK or Washington Dulles Airport. Fares start at around US$1,650 (breaking up the fare into individual legs is cheaper than a through-ticket!), requiring a two-day stopover.

Interair Private Bag 8, PO Box JHB International Aiport 1627; ✆ 011 6160636; f 011 6160930; e info@interair.co.za; www.interair.co.za. Johannesburg–Libreville: Dep: Mon 09.15 – arr: 14.20, Libreville–Johannesburg: Dep: Wed 13.25 – arr: 20.30

South African Airways UK ✆ 0870 747 1111; e customerservice@long.flysaa.com; www.flysaa.com Johannesburg–Libreville: Dep: Wed, Fri: 11.50, dep: 12.25 (summer).– arr: 15.55 (winter), Libreville–Johannesburg: Dep: Thu, Sat 00.20 – arr: 06.25
South African Airways US ✆ 0861 359722; e saausa@flysaa.com; www.flysaa.com

Local airline offices in São Tomé

São Tomé Airport/Aeroporto de São Tomé ✆ 221877
SCD Aviation c/o Omali Lodge Hotel (see page 102); ✆ 222350. 24-hour reservations, also by phone: reservations with credit card.
TAAG Av Giovani; ✆ 222593/241150; f 221823/222701; e taagstp@cstome.net. The Angolan airlines also handle tickets for STP Airways. Cash payments only.

TAP Av 12 Julho, CP 414; ✆ 222307, f 221528; e tapstp@cstome.net; ⏰ 07.45–15.30 Mon–Fri. Office of the Portuguese national airline. If you have a problem, ask for Senhora Adalvira; she is very helpful. The manager's name is Natasha d'Alva. The winter schedule 2008 might change to Thu/Fri.

BY SEA There are cargo boats from Libreville, but they are overloaded, uncomfortable and dangerous – nobody I've spoken to recommends this way of travelling.

✚ HEALTH *with Dr Felicity Nicholson; special thanks to Dr Gian Meyer & Bibi Braunstein*

People new to exotic travel often worry about tropical diseases, but it is accidents that are most likely to carry you off. With the increase in traffic, road accidents are becoming more common in São Tomé and Príncipe, so be aware and do what you can to reduce risks. Try to travel during daylight hours, always wear a seatbelt, and refuse to be driven by anyone who has been drinking.

PREPARATIONS Preparations to ensure a healthy trip to São Tomé and Príncipe require checks on your immunisation status: it is wise to be up-to-date on tetanus, polio and diphtheria (now given as an all-in-one vaccine, Revaxis, that lasts for 10 years), and hepatitis A. Immunisations against meningococcus and rabies may also be recommended. Proof of vaccination against **yellow fever** is mandatory for entry into São Tomé and Príncipe. The World Health Organisation (WHO) recommends that this vaccine should be taken for STP by those over nine months of age, although proof of entry is only officially required for those over one year of age. If the vaccine is not suitable for you, then obtain an exemption certificate from your GP or a travel clinic. Immunisation for cholera is not usually recommended for STP unless there is a local outbreak and you are working in poorer areas. The oral vaccine (Dukoral) offers around 75% of coverage for cholera and comprises two doses given at least one to six weeks apart and at least one week before entry for those aged six or over. Younger children require three doses and get less sustained protection.

Hepatitis A vaccine (Havrix Monodose or Avaxim) comprises two injections given about a year apart. The course costs about £100, but may be available on the NHS in the UK; it protects for 25 years and can be administered even close to the time of departure. **Hepatitis B** vaccination should be considered for longer trips (two months or more) or for those working with children or in situations where contact with blood is likely. Three injections are needed for the best protection and can be given over a three-week period if time is short to those aged 16 or over. Longer schedules give more sustained protection and are therefore preferred if time allows. Hepatitis A vaccine can also be given as a combination with hepatitis B as 'Twinrix', though two doses are needed at least seven days apart to be effective for the hepatitis A component, and three doses are needed for the hepatitis B.

The newer injectable **typhoid** vaccines (eg: Typhim Vi) last for three years and are about 85% effective. Oral capsules (Vivotif) are currently available in the US (and soon in the UK); if four capsules are taken over seven days it will last for five years. They should be encouraged unless the traveller is leaving within a few days for a trip of a week or less, when the vaccine would not be effective in time. Meningitis vaccine (ideally containing strains A, C, W and Y, but if this is not available then A+C vaccine is better than nothing) may be recommended for travellers, especially for trips of more than four weeks and if you are working with local people (see *Meningitis*, page 66).

Experts differ over whether a **BCG vaccination** against tuberculosis (TB) is useful in adults: discuss this with your travel clinic.

In addition to the various vaccinations recommended above, it is important that travellers should be properly protected against malaria. For detailed advice, see page 57.

Ideally you should visit your own doctor or a specialist travel clinic (see page 58) to discuss your requirements if possible at least eight weeks before you plan to travel.

PROTECTION FROM THE SUN The incidence of skin cancer is rocketing as Caucasians are travelling more and spending more time exposing themselves to the sun. Keep out of the sun during the middle of the day and try building up exposure gradually from 20 minutes per day. Be especially careful of sun reflected off water and wear a T-shirt and lots of waterproof suncream when swimming; snorkelling often leads to scorched backs of the thighs and shoulders, so wear bermuda shorts and a T-shirt if you're going for more than a quick dip. Sun exposure ages the skin and makes people prematurely wrinkly; cover up with long, loose clothes and wear a hat when you can. Don't forget sun cream. In the capital of São Tomé, the Intermar supermarket (see *Shopping*) sells various sunscreens up to factor 30, but if you need one with a higher sunblock factor, bring your own. Thanks to the Santomean haze, the sun does not have a relentless feel to it, but don't forget you are on the equator. For my light skin I've found a factor 30, transparent non-stick spray (such as Garnier Ambre Solaire Clear Protect) ideal, rather than a sticky cream. The glare and the dust can be hard on the eyes, too, so bring UV-protecting sunglasses and, perhaps, a soothing eyedrops.

MALARIA IN STP with *Philip Briggs*
Although diminishing on both islands (on Príncipe in particular), *paludismo* is still the biggest killer of children under five. The rates of infection are steadily going down; thanks to an intensive fumigation campaign inside houses, and education on

impregnated mosquito nets, with many donated or sold at a symbolic price. A few years ago, São Tomé hospital had to cram two children into one bed, now there are far fewer cases. In Príncipe, the incidence of malaria is lower still; a survey carried out in 2006 on thousands of people found only a few dozen cases. The anopheles mosquito that transmits the parasite is most abundant near marshes and still water, where it breeds, and the parasite is most prolific at low altitudes. Malaria-carrying mosquitoes tend to live in the walls of houses, and a campaign to spray houses with permethrin is gradually covering the whole island. The ambitious plan is to carry out three rounds of *fumigação/pulverização*, then test the whole population and treat the positive cases, thus gradually eliminating the disease. In mid-altitude locations, malaria is largely but not entirely seasonal, with the highest risk of transmission occurring during the rainy season. Those heading for moist and low-lying areas, such as the capital and along the coast, and of course anyone spending long periods deep in the forest, are at high risk throughout the year, but the danger is greatest during the rainy season. Even if this does not apply to you, all travellers to central Africa should assume that they will be exposed to malaria and should take precautions throughout their trip.

Malaria prevention There is not yet a vaccine against malaria that gives enough protection to be useful for travellers, but there are other ways to avoid it; since most of Africa is very high risk for malaria, travellers must plan their malaria protection properly. Seek current advice on the best antimalarials to take: usually mefloquine, Malarone or doxycycline. If mefloquine (Lariam) is suggested, start this two-and-a-half weeks (three doses) before departure to check that it suits you; stop it immediately if it seems to cause depression or anxiety, visual or hearing disturbances, severe headaches, fits or changes in heart rhythm. Side effects such as nightmares or dizziness are not medical reasons for stopping unless they are sufficiently debilitating or annoying. Anyone who has been treated for depression or psychiatric problems, has diabetes controlled by oral therapy or who is epileptic (or who has suffered fits in the past) or has a close blood relative who is epileptic, should probably avoid mefloquine.

In the past doctors were nervous about prescribing mefloquine to pregnant women, but experience has shown that it is relatively safe and certainly safer than the risk of malaria. That said, there are other issues, so if you are travelling to São Tomé and Príncipe while pregnant, seek expert advice before departure. Bear in mind that the information in Europe in particular about the various types of malaria in the country is neither exact nor current. You might consider phoning the Taiwanese Mission in the capital for the most up-to-date information.

Malarone (proguanil and atovaquone) is as effective as mefloquine. It has the advantage of having few side effects, can be started the day before travel and need only be continued for one week after returning. However, it is expensive and because of this tends to be reserved for shorter trips. Malarone may not be suitable for everybody, so advice should be taken from a doctor. The licence in the UK has been extended for up to three months' use and a paediatric form of tablet for children is also available, prescribed on a weight basis.

Another alternative is the antibiotic doxycycline (100mg daily). Like Malarone it can be started one day before arrival. Unlike mefloquine, it may also be used in travellers with epilepsy, although certain anti-epileptic medication may make it less effective. In perhaps 1–3% of people there is the possibility of allergic skin reactions developing in sunlight; the drug should be stopped if this happens. Women using the oral contraceptive should use an additional method of protection for the first four weeks when using doxycycline. It is also unsuitable in pregnancy or for children under 12 years.

Chloroquine and proguanil are no longer considered to be effective enough for São Tomé and Príncipe, but may be considered as a last resort if nothing else is deemed suitable.

All tablets should be taken with or after the evening meal, washed down with plenty of fluid and, with the exception of Malarone (see above), continued for four weeks after leaving.

Despite all these precautions, it is important to be aware that no anti-malarial drug is 100% protective, although those on prophylactics who are unlucky enough to catch malaria are less likely to get rapidly into serious trouble. In addition to taking anti-malarials, it is therefore important to avoid mosquito bites between dusk and dawn (see *Avoiding insect bites*, page 63).

There is unfortunately the occasional traveller who prefers to 'acquire resistance' to malaria rather than take preventive tablets, or who takes homeopathic prophylactics thinking these are effective against this killer disease. Homeopathy theory dictates treating like with like so there is no place for prophylaxis or immunisation in a well person; bona fide homeopaths do not advocate it. Travellers to Africa cannot acquire any effective resistance to malaria, and those who don't make use of prophylactic drugs risk their life in a manner that is both foolish and unnecessary.

Malaria: diagnosis and treatment Even those who take their malaria tablets meticulously and do everything possible to avoid mosquito bites may contract a strain of malaria that is resistant to prophylactic drugs. Untreated malaria is likely to be fatal, but even strains resistant to prophylaxis respond well to prompt treatment. Because of this, your immediate priority upon displaying possible malaria symptoms – including a rapid rise in temperature (over 38°C), and any combination of a headache, flu-like aches and pains, a general sense of disorientation, and possibly even nausea and diarrhoea – is to establish whether you have malaria, ideally by visiting a clinic.

Diagnosing malaria is not easy, which is why consulting a doctor is sensible: there are other dangerous causes of fever in Africa, which require different treatments. Even if you test negative, it would be wise to stay within reach of a laboratory until the symptoms clear up, and to test again after a day or two if they don't. It's worth noting that if you have a fever and the malaria test is negative, you may have typhoid or paratyphoid, which should also receive immediate treatment.

Travellers to remote parts of São Tomé and Príncipe would be wise to carry a course of treatment to cure malaria, and a rapid test kit. With malaria, it is normal enough to go from feeling healthy to having a high fever in the space of a few hours (and it is possible to die from falciparum malaria within 24 hours of the first symptoms). In such circumstances, assume that you have malaria and act accordingly – whatever risks are attached to taking an unnecessary cure are outweighed by the dangers of untreated malaria. Experts differ on the costs and benefits of self-treatment, but agree that it leads to over-treatment and to many people taking drugs they do not need; yet treatment may save your life. There is also some division about the best treatment for malaria, but either Malarone or Coarthemeter are the current treatments of choice. Discuss your trip with a specialist either at home or in São Tomé and Príncipe. An apparently very efficient Taiwanese herbal medicine (commercial name Arisunate) is for sale locally. It has no side-effects, but cannot be used for prophylaxis.

TRAVEL CLINICS AND HEALTH INFORMATION A full list of current travel clinic websites worldwide is available from the International Society of Travel Medicine on www.istm.org. For other journey preparation information, consult www.tripprep.com. Information about various medications may be found on www.emedicine.com. For information on malaria prevention, see www.preventingmalaria.info. If you want to do your bit for world health, consider getting back to the above-mentioned institutions to help mapping of the types of malaria in this little-known country.

UK

Berkeley Travel Clinic 32 Berkeley St, London W1J 8EL (near Green Park tube station); ✆ 020 7629 6233

Cambridge Travel Clinic 48a Mill Rd, Cambridge CB1 2AS; ✆ 01223 367362; e enquiries@ travelcliniccambridge.co.uk; www.travelcliniccambridge.co.uk. ⏱ 12.00–19.00 Tue–Fri, 10.00–16.00 Sat.

Edinburgh Travel Clinic Regional Infectious Diseases Unit, Ward 41 OPD, Western General Hospital, Crewe Rd South, Edinburgh EH4 2UX; ✆ 0131 537 2822; www.mvm.ed.ac.uk. Travel helpline (0906 589 0380) ⏱ 09.00–12.00 weekdays. Provides inoculations & antimalarial prophylaxis, & advises on travel-related health risks.

Fleet Street Travel Clinic 29 Fleet St, London EC4Y 1AA; ✆ 020 7353 5678; www.fleetstreetclinic.com. Vaccinations, travel products & latest advice.

Hospital for Tropical Diseases Travel Clinic Mortimer Market Bldg, Capper St (off Tottenham Ct Rd), London WC1E 6AU; ✆ 020 7388 9600; www.thehtd.org. Offers consultations & advice, & is able to provide all necessary drugs & vaccines for travellers. Runs a healthline (✆ 0906 133 7733) for country-specific information & health hazards. Also stocks nets, water purification equipment & personal protection measures.

Interhealth Worldwide Partnership House, 157 Waterloo Rd, London SE1 8US; ✆ 020 7902 9000; www.interhealth.org.uk. Competitively priced, one-stop travel health service. All profits go to their affiliated company, InterHealth, which provides health care for overseas workers on Christian projects.

Liverpool School of Medicine Pembroke Pl, Liverpool L3 5QA; ✆ 0151 708 9393; f 0151 705 3370; www.liv.ac.uk/lstm

MASTA (Medical Advisory Service for Travellers Abroad) Moorfield Rd, Yeadon, Leeds, West Yorkshire, LS19 7BN; ✆ 0113 238 7500; www.masta-travel-health.com. Provides travel health advice, anti-malarials & vaccinations. There are over 25 MASTA pre-travel clinics in Britain; call or check online for the nearest. Clinics also sell mosquito nets, medical kits, insect protection & travel hygiene products.

NHS travel website www.fitfortravel.scot.nhs.uk. Provides country-by-country advice on immunisation & malaria, plus details of recent developments, & a list of relevant health organisations.

Nomad Travel Store/Clinic 3–4 Wellington Terrace, Turnpike Lane, London N8 0PX; ✆ 020 8889 7014; travel-health line (office hours only) ✆ 0906 863 3414; e sales@nomadtravel.co.uk; www.nomadtravel.co.uk. Also at 40 Bernard St, London WC1N 1LJ; ✆ 020 7833 4114; 52 Grosvenor Gardens, London SW1W 0AG; ✆ 020 7823 5823; & 43 Queens Rd, Bristol BS8 1QH; ✆ 0117 922 6567. For health advice, equipment such as mosquito nets & other anti-bug devices, & an excellent range of adventure travel gear. Clinic also in Southhampton.

Trailfinders Travel Clinic 194 Kensington High St, London W8 7RG; ✆ 020 7938 3999; www.trailfinders.com/travelessentials/travelclinic.htm

Travelpharm The Travelpharm website, www.travelpharm.com, offers up-to-date guidance on travel-related health & has a range of medications available through their online mini-pharmacy.

Irish Republic

Tropical Medical Bureau Grafton Street Medical Centre, Grafton Bldgs, 34 Grafton St, Dublin 2; ✆ 1 671 9200; www.tmb.ie. A useful website specific to tropical destinations. Also check website for other bureaux locations throughout Ireland.

USA

Centers for Disease Control 1600 Clifton Rd, Atlanta, GA 30333; ✆ 800 311 3435; travellers' health hotline (fax service) 888 232 3299; www.cdc.gov/travel. The central source of travel information in the USA. The invaluable *Health Information for International Travel*, published annually, is available from the Division of Quarantine at this address.

Connaught Laboratories Pasteur Merieux Connaught, Route 611, PO Box 187, Swiftwater, PA 18370; ✆ 800 822 2463. They will send a free list of specialist tropical-medicine physicians in your state.

IAMAT (International Association for Medical Assistance to Travelers) 1623 Military Rd, 279, Niagara Falls, NY 14304-1745; ☎ 716 754 4883; e info@iamat.org; www.iamat.org. A non-profit organisation that provides lists of English-speaking doctors abroad.

International Medicine Center 915 Gessner Rd, Suite 525, Houston, TX 77024; ☎ 713 550 2000; www.traveldoc.com

Canada
IAMAT Suite 1, 1287 St Clair Av W, Toronto, Ontario M6E 1B8; ☎ 416 652 0137; www.iamat.org

TMVC Suite 314, 1030 W Georgia St, Vancouver BC V6E 2Y3; ☎ 1 888 288 8682; www.tmvc.com. Private clinic with several outlets in Canada.

Australia, New Zealand, Singapore
IAMAT PO Box 5049, Christchurch 5, New Zealand; www.iamat.org
TMVC ☎ 1300 65 88 44; www.tmvc.com.au. Clinics in Australia, New Zealand & Singapore, including: *Auckland* Canterbury Arcade, 170 Queen St, Auckland; ☎ 9 373 3531

Brisbane 75a, Astor Terrace, Spring Hill, QLD 4000; ☎ 7 3815 6900
Melbourne 393 Little Bourke St, 2nd floor, Melbourne, VIC 3000; ☎ 3 9602 5788
Sydney Dymocks Bldg, 7th floor, 428 George St, Sydney, NSW 2000; ☎ 2 9221 7133

South Africa and Namibia
SAA-Netcare Travel Clinics Sanlam Building, 19, Fredman Drive, Sandton, P Bag X34, Benmore, JHB, Gauteng, 2010; www.travelclinic.co.za. Clinics throughout South Africa.

TMVC NHC Health Centre, Cnr. Beyers Naude & Waugh Northcliff; PO Box 48499, Roosevelt Park, 2129 (Postal Address); ☎ 011 888 7488; www.tmvc.com.au. Consult website for details of other clinics in South Africa & Namibia.

Switzerland
IAMAT 57 Chemin des Voirets, 1212 Grand Lancy, Geneva; www.iamat.org

PERSONAL FIRST-AID KIT A minimal kit contains:

- A good drying antiseptic, eg: iodine or potassium permanganate (don't take antiseptic cream)
- A few small dressings (Band-Aids)
- Suncream
- Insect repellent; anti-malarial tablets; impregnated bed-net or permethrin spray
- Aspirin or paracetamol
- Antifungal cream (eg: Canesten)
- Ciprofloxacin or norfloxacin, for severe diarrhoea & a product to re-establish the intestine flora, such as ultralevure
- Tinidazole for giardia or amoebic dysentery (see below for regime)
- Antibiotic eye drops, for sore, 'gritty', stuck-together eyes (conjunctivitis)
- A pair of fine pointed tweezers (to remove hairy caterpillar hairs, thorns, splinters, coral, etc)
- Alcohol-based hand rub or bar of soap in plastic box
- Condoms or femidoms
- Digital thermometer if you are in more remote areas
- Antihistamine for allergic reactions to insect bites
- Sterilising hand spray/wet wipes – useful in between counting dobras to pay for food and touching your food to eat it

COMMON MEDICAL PROBLEMS

Travellers' diarrhoea Travelling in São Tomé and Príncipe carries a risk of getting a dose of travellers' diarrhoea; perhaps as many as half of all visitors will be affected and the newer you are to travel, the more likely you will be to suffer. By taking precautions against travellers' diarrhoea you will also avoid typhoid, cholera, hepatitis, dysentery, worms, etc. Travellers' diarrhoea and the other faecal-oral diseases come from getting other peoples' faeces in your mouth. This most often happens from cooks not washing their hands after a trip to the toilet, but even if the restaurant cook does not understand basic hygiene you will be safe if your food has been properly cooked and arrives piping hot. I remember plenty of lukewarm plates of rice, so if in doubt, ask for your food to be re-heated (*faz favor, pode aquecer mais um pouco?*). Even if this presents some hassle for your waiter/waitress, the locals do usually realise that a tourist's stomach, *barriga*, is more vulnerable. The maxim to remind you what you can safely eat is:

PEEL IT, BOIL IT, COOK IT OR FORGET IT.

This means that fruit you have washed and peeled yourself, and hot foods, should be safe but raw foods, cold cooked foods, salads, fruit salads which have been prepared by others, ice cream and ice are all risky. Ask for your drink without ice, *sem gelo*. That said, plenty of travellers and expatriates enjoy fruit and vegetables, so do keep a sense of perspective: food served in a fairly decent hotel in a large town or a place regularly frequented by expatriates is likely to be safe. If you are struck, see below for treatment.

Water sterilisation It is much rarer to get sick from drinking contaminated water but it happens, so try to drink from safe sources such as mineral water. Water should have been brought to the boil (even at altitude it only needs to be brought to the boil), or passed through a good bacteriological filter or purified with iodine; chlorine tablets (eg: Puritabs) are also adequate although theoretically less effective and they taste nastier.

Treating travellers' diarrhoea It is dehydration that makes you feel awful during a bout of diarrhoea and the most important part of treatment is drinking lots of clear fluids. Sachets of oral rehydration salts give the perfect biochemical mix to replace all that is pouring out of your bottom but other recipes taste nicer. Any dilute mixture of sugar and salt in water will do you good: try Coke or orange squash with a three-finger pinch of salt added to each glass (if you are salt-depleted you won't taste the salt). Otherwise make a solution of a four-finger scoop of sugar with a three-finger pinch of salt in a 500ml glass. Or add eight level teaspoons of sugar (18g) and one level teaspoon of salt (3g) to one litre (five cups) of safe water. A squeeze of lemon or orange juice improves the taste and adds potassium, which is also lost in diarrhoea. Drink two large glasses after every bowel action, and more if you are thirsty. These solutions are still absorbed well if you are vomiting, but you will need to take sips at a time. If you are not eating you need to drink three litres a day plus whatever is pouring into the toilet. If you feel like eating, take a bland, high carbohydrate diet. Heavy greasy foods will probably give you cramps.

If the diarrhoea is bad, or you are passing blood or slime, or you have a fever, you will probably need antibiotics in addition to fluid replacement. A dose of norfloxacin or ciprofloxacin repeated twice a day until better may be appropriate (if you are planning to take an antibiotic with you, note that both norfloxacin and ciprofloxacin are available only on prescription in the UK). If the diarrhoea is greasy and bulky and is accompanied by sulphurous (eggy) burps, one likely cause

2

Dr Jane Wilson-Howarth

Long-haul air travel increases the risk of deep vein thrombosis. Although recent research has suggested that many of us develop clots when immobilised, most are resolved without us ever having been aware of them. In certain susceptible individuals, though, clots form on clots and when large ones break away and lodge in the lungs this is dangerous. Fortunately this happens in a tiny minority of passengers.

Studies have shown that flights of over 5½ hours are significant, and that people who take lots of shorter flights over a short space of time can also form clots. People at highest risk are:

- Those who have had a clot before – unless they are now taking warfarin
- People over 80 years of age
- Anyone who has recently undergone a major operation or surgery for varicose veins
- Someone who has had a hip or knee replacement in the last three months
- Cancer sufferers
- Those who have ever had a stroke
- People with heart disease
- Those with a close blood relative who has had a clot

Those with a slightly increased risk:

- People over 40
- Women who are pregnant or have had a baby in the last couple of weeks
- People taking female hormones, the combined contraceptive pill or other oestrogen therapy
- Heavy smokers
- Those who have very severe varicose veins
- The very obese
- People who are very tall (over 6ft/1.8m) or short (under 5ft/1.5m)

is giardia. This is best treated with tinidazole (four x 500mg in one dose, repeated seven days later if symptoms persist). Some people react to malaria with diarrhoea, so most doctors will expect you to have taken a malaria test before you come to their consultation, just to be sure that hypothesis can be eliminated.

Mosquito bites Whether or not you are taking malaria tablets, it is important to protect yourself from mosquito bites (see *Malaria in São Tomé and Príncipe* and *Malaria prevention*, pages 000), so keep your repellent stick or roll-on to hand. Be aware that no prophylactic is 100% protective but those on prophylactics who are unlucky enough to catch malaria are less likely to get rapidly into serious trouble. It is easy and inexpensive to arrange a malaria blood test.

Dengue fever This mosquito-borne disease may mimic malaria but there is no prophylactic medication available to deal with it. The mosquitoes that carry this virus bite during the daytime, so it is worth applying repellent if you see any mosquitoes around. Symptoms include strong headaches, rashes, excruciating joint and muscle pains, and high fever. Dengue fever lasts only for a week or so and is not usually fatal. Complete rest and paracetamol are the usual treatment; plenty of fluids also help. Some patients are given an intravenous drip to prevent dehydration. It is especially important to protect yourself if you have had dengue fever before, since a second infection with a different strain can result in the

A deep vein thrombosis (DVT) is a blood clot that forms in the deep leg veins. This is very different from irritating but harmless superficial phlebitis. DVT causes swelling and redness of one leg, usually with heat and pain in one calf and sometimes the thigh. A DVT is only dangerous if a clot breaks away and travels to the lungs (pulmonary embolus). Symptoms of a pulmonary embolus (PE) include chest pain that is worse on breathing in deeply, shortness of breath, and sometimes coughing up small amounts of blood. The symptoms commonly start three to ten days after a long flight. Anyone who thinks that they might have a DVT needs to see a doctor immediately who will arrange a scan. Warfarin tablets (to thin the blood) are then taken for at least six months.

PREVENTION OF DVT Several conditions make the problem more likely. Immobility is the key, and factors like reduced oxygen in cabin air and dehydration may also contribute. To reduce the risk of thrombosis on a long journey:

EXERCISE BEFORE AND AFTER THE FLIGHT
- Keep mobile before and during the flight; move around every couple of hours
- Drink plenty of water or juices during the flight
- Avoid taking sleeping pills and excessive tea, coffee and alcohol
- Perform exercises that mimic walking and tense the calf muscles
- Consider wearing flight socks or support stockings (see www.legshealth.com)
- Ideally take a meal each week of oily fish (mackerel, trout, salmon, sardines, etc) ahead of your departure. This reduces the blood's ability to clot and thus the DVT risk. It may even be worth just taking a meal of oily fish 24 hours before departure if this is more practical.

If you think you are at increased risk of a clot, ask your doctor if it is safe to travel.

potentially fatal dengue haemorrhagic fever. The good news is that whilst dengue fever cannot be discounted, it has not recently been reported on São Tomé and Príncipe.

Avoiding insect bites As the sun is going down, don long clothes and apply repellent on any exposed flesh. Pack an insect repellent containing at least 50-55% DEET (roll-ons or sticks are the least messy preparations for travelling). You also need either a permethrin-impregnated bednet or a permethrin spray so that you can 'treat' bednets in hotels. Permethrin treatment makes even very tatty nets protective and prevents mosquitoes from biting through the impregnated net when you roll against it; it also deters other biters. Otherwise, retire to an air-conditioned room, burn mosquito coils or sleep under a fan. Coils and fans reduce rather than eliminate bites. Travel clinics usually sell a good range of nets, treatment kits and repellents.

Mosquitoes and many other insects are attracted to light. If you are camping, never put a lamp near the opening of your tent, or you will have a swarm of biters waiting to join you when you retire. In hotel rooms, be aware that the longer your light is on, the greater the number of insects will be sharing your accommodation.

Aside from avoiding mosquito bites between dusk and dawn, which will protect you from elephantiasis and a range of nasty insect-borne viruses, as well as malaria, it is important to take precautions against other insect bites. During the day it is wise to wear long, loose (preferably 100% cotton) clothes if you are pushing through scrubby country; this will keep off ticks and also tsetse and day-biting *Aedes* mosquitoes which may spread viral fevers, including yellow fever. São Tomé and Príncipe is thought to have *Aedes aegypti* mosquitoes that are not as yet carriers of dengue fever, but given the lack of serum diagnostic facilities, it is difficult to say with certainty.

Tsetse flies hurt when they bite and it is said that they are attracted to the colour blue; locals will advise on where they are a problem and where they transmit sleeping sickness.

Tumbu flies or putsi are a problem where the climate is hot and humid. The adult fly lays her eggs on the soil or on drying laundry and when the eggs come in contact with human flesh (when you put on clothes or lie on a bed) they hatch and bury themselves under the skin. Here they form a crop of 'boils' each with a maggot inside. Smear a little Vaseline over the hole, and they will push their noses out to breathe. It may be possible to squeeze them out but it depends if they are ready to do so as the larvae have spines that help them to hold on.

In putsi areas either dry your clothes and sheets within a screened house, or dry them in direct sunshine until they are crisp, or iron them.

Jiggers or sandfleas are another flesh-feaster, which can be best avoided by wearing shoes. They latch on if you walk barefoot in contaminated places, and set up home under the skin of the foot, usually at the side of a toenail where they cause a painful, boil-like swelling. They need picking out by a local expert. The *larva migrans* hookworm sometimes hitches a ride with STP tourists. Transmitted by water contaminated with dog faeces and accompanied by an annoying itch, as the 'geography worm' burrows map-like tracks under the skin, the parasite is treated with either an ethyl choloride spray or carbon dioxide freezer spray (used for warts). If neither is to hand, mix a few crushed thiabendazole tablets with a bland skin cream and apply it to the area for 12 hours under a waterproof dressing. Be sure to bring a soothing medicated gel for mosquito bites; I know of only one place in São Tomé that occasionally sells anything like that (Economax supermarket in the capital, see *Shopping*), and it's not very effective. A gel such as Fenistil is also good for sunburn.

Bilharzia or schistosomiasis

with thanks to Dr Vaughan Southgate of the Natural History Museum, London

Bilharzia or schistosomiasis is a disease that commonly afflicts the rural poor of the tropics. Two types exist in sub-Saharan Africa – *Schistosoma mansoni* and *Schistosoma haematobium*. It is an unpleasant problem that is worth avoiding, though it can be treated if you do get it. The most risky shores will be close to where people use water, wash clothes etc.

It is easier to understand how to diagnose it, treat it and prevent it if you know a little about the life cycle. Contaminated faeces are washed into the body of water, the eggs hatch and the larva infects a certain species of snail. The snails then produce about 10,000 *cercariae* a day for the rest of their lives. The parasites can digest their way through your skin when you wade, or bathe in infested fresh water.

Winds disperse the snails and *cercariae*. The snails in particular can drift a long way, especially on windblown weed, so nowhere is really safe. However, deep water and running water are safer, while shallow water presents the greatest risk. The *cercariae* penetrate intact skin, and find their way to the liver. There male and female meet and spend the rest of their lives in permanent copulation. No wonder you feel tired! Most finish up in the wall of the lower bowel, but others can get lost and can cause damage to many different organs. *Schistosoma haematobium* goes mostly to the bladder.

Although the adults do not cause any harm in themselves, after about 4–6 weeks they start to lay eggs, which cause an intense but usually ineffective immune reaction, including fever, cough, abdominal pain, and a fleeting, itching rash called 'safari itch'. The absence of early symptoms does not necessarily mean there is no infection. Later symptoms can be more localised and more severe, but the general symptoms settle down fairly quickly and eventually you are just tired. 'Tired all the time' is one of the most common symptoms among expats in Africa, and bilharzia, giardia, amoeba and intestinal yeast are the most common culprits.

Although bilharzia is difficult to diagnose, it can be tested at specialist travel clinics. Ideally tests need to be done at least six weeks after likely exposure and will determine whether you need treatment. Fortunately it is easy to treat at present.

Avoiding bilharzia

- If you are bathing, swimming, paddling or wading in fresh water which you think may carry a bilharzia risk, try to get out of the water within ten minutes.
- Avoid bathing or paddling on shores within 200m of villages or places where people use the water a great deal, especially reedy shores or where there is lots of water weed.
- Dry off thoroughly with a towel; rub vigorously.
- If your bathing water comes from a risky source try to ensure that the water is taken in the early morning and stored snail-free, otherwise it should be filtered or Dettol or Cresol added.
- Bathing early in the morning is safer than bathing in the last half of the day.
- Cover yourself with DEET insect repellent before swimming: it may offer some protection.

Skin infections Any mosquito bite or small nick in the skin gives an opportunity for bacteria to foil the body's usually excellent defences; it will surprise many travellers how quickly skin infections start in warm humid climates and it is essential to clean and cover even the slightest wound. Creams are not as effective as a good drying antiseptic such as a spray, dilute iodine, potassium permanganate (*permanganato de Potassio*; a few crystals in half a cup of water), or crystal (or gentian) violet (*cristales de violete de genciano*). One of these should be available in pharmacies. The most common problem with insect bites on the islands comes from something as banal as scratching yourself with dirty nails (women in particular) and getting infected wounds, often on the ankles. Hand hygiene and self-control work well. If the wound starts to throb, or becomes red and the redness starts to spread, or the wound oozes, and especially if you develop a fever, antibiotics will probably be needed: flucloxacillin (250mg four times a day) or Augmentin (250–500mg three times a day). For those allergic to penicillin, erythromycin (500mg twice a day) for five days should help. See a doctor if the symptoms do not start to improve in 48 hours.

Fungal infections also get a hold easily in hot moist climates, so wear 100% cotton socks and underwear and shower frequently. An itchy rash in the groin or flaking between the toes is likely to be a fungal infection. This needs treatment with an antifungal cream such as Canesten (clotrimazole), which is sold in pharmacies. If this is not available try Whitfield's ointment (compound benzoic acid ointment) or crystal violet (although this will turn you purple!).

Eye problems Bacterial conjunctivitis (pink eye) is a common infection in Africa; people who wear contact lenses are most open to this irritating problem. The eyes feel sore and gritty and they will often be stuck together in the mornings. They will need treatment with antibiotic drops or ointment, difficult to obtain in São Tomé and Príncipe; consider bringing one from home. Lesser eye irritation should settle with bathing in salt water and keeping the eyes shaded. If an insect flies into your eye, extract it with great care, ensuring you do not crush or damage it, otherwise you may get a nastily inflamed eye from toxins secreted by the creature. Bring your own contact lens solution; include a couple of starter packs (under 100ml) in your hand luggage in case of lost baggage. Better even, unless you wear hard/gas-permeable lenses, are dailies that can be disposed of on a daily basis.

Prickly heat A fine pimply rash on the trunk is likely to be heat rash; cool showers, dabbing dry, and talc will help. Some people react well to Lauroderm in powder (used for babies' nappy rash/diaper skin), which can be found at local pharmacies. Treat the problem by slowing down to a relaxed schedule, wearing only loose, baggy, 100% cotton clothes and sleeping naked under a fan; if it's bad you may need to check into an air-conditioned hotel room for a while.

OTHER MEDICAL ISSUES

Meningitis This is a particularly nasty disease as it can kill within hours of the first symptoms appearing. The telltale symptoms are a combination of a blinding headache (light sensitivity), a blotchy rash and a high fever. Immunisation protects against the most serious bacterial form of meningitis and the tetravalent vaccine ACWY is recommended for central Africa, but if this is not available then A+C is better than nothing. Other forms of meningitis exist (usually viral) but there are no vaccines for these. When meningitis occurs on São Tomé and Príncipe, no analysis is made of the particular type; treatment is purely by antibiotics. Local media normally report localised outbreaks. A severe headache and fever should make you run to a doctor immediately. There are also other causes of headache and fever, one of which is typhoid, which can occur in travellers to central Africa. Seek medical help if you are ill for more than a few days.

Tropical amoeba This is a tiny organism, transmitted through faeces. Often, there are no symptoms at all, but amoebae can cause dysentery or a liver abscess up to a year after travel. Stay alert to changes in your body/health after your return.

Safe sex The risks of sexually transmitted infection are high in São Tomé and Príncipe, whether you sleep with fellow travellers or locals. About 80% of HIV infections in British heterosexuals are acquired abroad. If you must indulge, use condoms or femidoms, which help reduce the risk of transmission. If you notice any genital ulcers or discharge, get treatment promptly since these increase the risk of acquiring HIV. In São Tomé and Príncipe, where HIV rates are low still, syphilis and gonorrhea, as well as candida and trichomonad infections, are more cause for concern. Although there is a family planning organisation in the capital, the morning-after pill is only intermittently available.

If you do have unprotected sex, visit a clinic as soon as possible; this should be within 24 hours, or no later than 72 hours, for post-exposure prophylaxis for HIV.

Rabies Rabies is not normally present in São Tomé and Príncipe, but animal or bat bites should always be assessed carefully.

Snakes and spiders Apart from a bee or wasp crawling into your drink can, the only real wildlife hazard present on the islands is the black cobra (*Naja melanoleuca*), originally introduced to combat the rats eating the cocoa pods. The *cobra preta*'s neurotoxic (nerve-destroying) venom results in paralysis if not immediately treated. First symptoms are paralysis of the eye muscles (usually the eyelid dropping), with the danger then of respiratory arrest, which cannot be treated on

There is no general phone number for medical emergencies. Most villages have a first aid post, but these *postos de saúde* do not have much equipment and can only deal with small injuries. In an emergency, head straight for the hospital. Apart from the central hospitals in the capitals of both islands (proper A&E services only in São Tomé), there is one in São João dos Angolares in the south of São Tomé island, and in Neves in the north, but neither is equipped to deal with major injuries. The only pharmacies (*farmácias*) are in both capitals and Trindade. You will probably need some Portuguese, although you may manage in French or English. There are about 40 doctors practising on São Tomé and Príncipe, amongst them a number of competent Cuban doctors. Few medical staff speak English, but most will have some French, others some Spanish or German from training in Cuba or the former eastern Germany. I've been given unreliable medical advice on both islands. Add to that the hazards of communicating in a foreign language, and it is probably best to bring somebody who can translate for you, or to find an English-speaking medic; on São Tomé this means the Taiwanese Medical Mission in the capital. Divers should note: there is no decompression chamber on the island. Although there is one in Libreville, Gabon, 250km away, evacuation takes many hours – so don't run any risks. Diving accidents are always due to human error. Commonly required medicines such as ibuprofen, antiseptic sprays and common antibiotics are widely available in pharmacies, but bring a high-strength (50%) DEET insect repellent stick/spray (better bring two), also a good cream/gel (*pomada*) for insect bites (I've only found one on sale once); and if you have sensitive teeth, bring your own toothpaste. Treatments for malaria are best bought in advance – in fact it's advisable to carry all malaria-related tablets on you, and only rely on their availability locally if you need to restock your supplies. Air conditioning often brings on an irritated throat through dry air, abrupt changes in temperature and dirty filters. On my first visit, I picked up a throat problem that stayed with me for two months and eventually turned into tonsillitis – don't do as I did and self-medicate willy-nilly with antibiotics; go and see a doctor. And remember to drink lots of water; if you are feeling thirsty, you are already starting to get dehydrated. Mineral water is widely available; using a platypus water dispenser while hiking is a great way of accessing water without having to stop and take your daypack off. If you are on any medication prior to departure, or you have specific needs relating to a known medical condition (for instance if you are allergic to bee stings or you are prone to attacks of asthma), then you are strongly advised to bring any related drugs and devices with you. For minor conditions, consider trying traditional medicine.

the islands. The juvenile black cobra is completely black, the adult has yellow-white scales at the front. It is fairly common in the southern and eastern parts of São Tomé island; on a six-hour forest walk I saw two: a juvenile, her head aggressively raised, and an adult one, around 1.8m long, sunbathing – plus a headless adult dangling from the hands of a palm wine worker. Locals will usually kill black cobras immediately as, if bitten, their chances of getting to the hospital in time (within 30–120 mins) for the antivenom are slim. Even so, according to local guides, this will only delay death for a couple of days – probably due to the fact that the hospital in São Tomé held the wrong antivenom for years; by the time you visit, the correct one should be in place. Don't panic though: while there are many stories involving the black cobra (people chopping off their arm with their machete in order to survive), hikers being bitten are unheard of, and deaths by cobra bite are very rare on the island as a whole.

African ticks are not the prolific disease transmitters they are in the Americas, but they may spread Lyme disease, tick-bite fever and a few rarities. Tick-bite fever is a flu-like illness that can easily be treated with doxycycline, but as there can be some serious complications it is important to visit a doctor.

Ticks should ideally be removed as soon as possible as leaving them on the body increases the chance of infection. They should be removed with special tick tweezers that can be bought in good travel shops. Failing that you can use your finger nails: grasp the tick as close to your body as possible and pull steadily and firmly away at right angles to your skin. The tick will then come away complete, as long as you do not jerk or twist. If possible douse the wound with alcohol (any spirit will do) or iodine. Irritants (eg: Olbas oil) or lit cigarettes are to be discouraged since they can cause the ticks to regurgitate and therefore increase the risk of disease. It is best to get a travelling companion to check you for ticks; if you are travelling with small children, remember to check their heads, and particularly behind the ears.

Spreading redness around the bite and/or fever and/or aching joints after a tick bite imply that you have an infection that requires antibiotic treatment, so seek advice.

Tour guides do not carry the antivenom. If it makes you feel safer, you can order the (expensive) Saimr polyvalent snake antivenom from Saimr (*Modderfontein Road 1, 2131 Sandringham, South Africa;* \ *+27 11 5318600;* f *11 5318616;* e *cillaf@savp.co.za; www.savp.co.za/default.htm*) and donate it to the hospital when you leave. Be aware though that the antivenom cannot simply be injected into a muscle, it has to be injected intravenously, diluted in short infusions under supervision for allergic reactions that may occur. It also has to be kept cool, which is impossible in the south of the island. Happily, the black cobra never made it to Príncipe, nor to the Ilhéu das Rolas. See www.africanreptiles-venom.co.za/snake_courses_snake_handling_c.html.

Like all snakes, black cobras rarely attack unless provoked. Wear stout shoes and not too tight clothing, including long trousers in the forest, watch your step and look where you're putting your hands. A guide will alert you to any danger. If bitten, snakes will dispense venom in only about half of their bites. Keeping this fact in mind may help you to stay calm. Many so-called first-aid techniques do more harm than good: cutting into the wound is harmful; tourniquets are dangerous; suction and electrical inactivation devices do not work. The only treatment is antivenom. In case of a bite that you fear may have been from the black cobra:

- Try to keep calm – it is likely that no venom has been dispensed.
- Prevent movement of the bitten limb by applying a splint.
- Keep the bitten limb BELOW heart height to slow the spread of any venom.
- If you have a crepe bandage, bind up as much of the bitten limb as you can, but release the bandage every half hour.
- Evacuate to a hospital which has antivenom – in São Tomé and Príncipe, only the capital.

And remember:

- NEVER give aspirin; you may offer paracetamol, which is safe.
- NEVER cut or suck the wound.
- DO NOT apply ice packs.
- DO NOT apply potassium permanganate.

The brown *samangungú* tarantula is one of the largest spiders in Africa, but you don't come across many: I saw one once ambling across the road in Santo António on Príncipe, and another near the Pico de São Tomé. Locals will tell you that the *samangungú* might jump you if they feel attacked. If you are bitten, you mustn't drink water; left untreated, the bite will be painful, but that's all. Wash any bite with soap and water or similar, protect against infection and monitor for changes/anaphylactic reactions (breathing difficulties/chest pains). There are a couple of nasty, beautiful fire worms on the islands, and very few scorpions: you'd have to go and seek them out in the cracks of a basalt wall near Lagoa Azul. *Aliança* is a tiny yellow ant whose small size stands in no proportion to the painfulness of its bite. Watch out for sea urchins (*ouriços*); the spines of the big *ouriço gallo* can give you fever. On beaches, you might get your toes pinched by one of the many crabs; consider bringing water sandals or buying some cheaply in the market. The only shark in these waters to be a bit wary of is the tiger sand shark, who likes to feed at river mouths and, incidentally, is the only shark known to adjust its buoyancy by 'burping'.

Toxic plants At contact with the innocuous-looking *folha ganhoma*, a type of nettle called *lochiga* locally, the skin will come up in harmless but painful blisters. Guides can point it out to you and will often chop it with their machete. One traveller I met had a leaf attach itself to her upper arm; when peeled off, it left the skin scarred for a week. The locals use palm oil, but a wash and an antiseptic is probably a better idea. A string of tiny sticky leaves but which can cause a slight reaction on the skin is the *pega-pega*. If you are travelling with small children, watch the tropical plants in resort gardens; ask locally which are toxic.

Marine dangers Before assuming a beach is safe for swimming, always ask local advice. It is always better to err on the side of caution if no sensible advice is forthcoming, since there is always a possibility of being swept away by strong currents or undertows that cannot be detected until you are actually in the water. Accidents due to undercurrents and human error have been reported from Club Santana, Ilhéu das Rolas, and due to violent waves and human error from Bom Bom and Jalé, as well as from Praia Piscina (very sudden violent waves). On the last two beaches, caution is important, as, unless you are part of a group, you are likely to be on your own there.

Snorkellers and divers should wear something on their feet to avoid treading on coral reefs, and should never touch the reefs with their bare hands – coral itself can give nasty cuts, and there is a danger of touching a venomous creature camouflaged against the reef. On beaches, never walk barefoot on exposed coral. Even on sandy beaches, people who walk barefoot risk getting coral or urchin spines in their soles or venomous fish spines in their feet.

If you do tread on a venomous fish, soak the foot in hot (but not scalding) water until some time after the pain subsides; this may be for 20–30 minutes in all. Take the foot out of the water to top up; otherwise you may scald it. If the pain returns, re-immerse the foot. Once the venom has been heat-inactivated, get a doctor to check and remove any bits of fish spine in the wound.

CRIME AND SECURITY

Generally, São Tomé and Príncipe is a very safe place indeed for travellers. There is very little violent crime; armed robberies and rapes are rare still. Where else in Africa can you walk around the streets of the capital at practically any time of the day or night, the only danger a raspy throat from answering so many questions? *Não temos fronteira*, you'll hear as an explanation, we have no border – nobody can just jump onto the next plane to immunity. There has however been a rise in petty crime. Mobile phone theft was hardly heard of a few years ago; unfortunately, today, nicking *telemóveis* has become common. You won't get mugged for a mobile phone, but don't leave it unattended for opportunists to take advantage. I had two cellphones stolen, one on each island, and both times from inside a bag, the thieves leaving money and other things behind. Discos and beaches are the most common place for this to happen; a beach that might look completely deserted to you might not be. Lock your valuables in the car; if you don't have one, carry your money/mobile phone in a waterproof pouch (available from outdoor stores back home, not on the islands) that you can sling over your neck and take into the water. Other possibilities might be to pay locals a few dobras to look after your things, or to hide them under palm leaves or suchlike. If you do have a *telemóvel* stolen, people will probably suggest you go to the National Radio station, to appeal for information; unless you are staying on for a while, I wouldn't bother though. If you are planning to claim on your travel insurance, go to the police to try and obtain a report for your insurance; if you are not planning to claim, again, I wouldn't bother. If you want to report a crime to the police, take your passport and a Portuguese-speaker with you, and draw up a short text in Portuguese and English beforehand, detailing what happened, and ask the duty officer, *chefe de serviço*, for a stamp and signature, so you have something in black and white: 'I need this for the insurance company': *preciso disso para o seguro*. One other precaution: if you give people lifts, move much-coveted items such as torches out of sight – and temptation. The general phone number for the police (24 hours) is ☎ 222222. If you go out at night, be aware that with the exception of a couple of places in the capital, there is usually no provision for left items in clubs; people leave their belongings in their cars or carry a handbag. Even in the most isolated fishing village, if you leave your daypack in somebody's house while you go out on a boat, for instance, it's best to bring a little padlock.

WOMEN TRAVELLERS Women travellers should have no problem apart from gentle harassment, hissing and hailing in the street. I have felt perfectly safe moving around at all hours; even the most persistent chat-ups or drunken ramblings were never threatening. However, exercise the usual caution in an unfamiliar place and be aware that especially as a white woman on your own you are seen as a potential adventure, or, if you are staying longer, even a potential second or third *mulher*. A friendly chat or a desire to learn about the country and its culture is easily misconstrued as romantic interest. Expect to be repeatedly asked the following: whether you are travelling on your own (*sozinha*), where you are staying (*onde estás hospedada?*), whether you have a *namorado* (boyfriend) or a *marido* (husband; to be married is *casada*) and where the boyfriend/husband is, plus how many children (*filhos*) you have. Santomean men like to tell women travellers without children that they must at least have one! If you are asked for your phone number (*contacto*) and give it out, in my experience hardly anybody, men or women, actually calls; it seems more of a friendly ritual to type your number into their mobile phone memory. Wearing a ring will ensure a quieter life; even better might be to invent a jealous, *muito cumento*, Santomean boyfriend, *namorado Santomense*. In line with things being more rough and ready on Príncipe, some men there have a tendency to try and boss women travellers around, assuming, for instance, that giving you a lift somewhere stakes some kind of claim on you, and lecture you on how impolite it is not to then stay glued to their table. If this kind of thing happens, just thank them politely for the lift/drink and walk away. More worryingly, two female students were harassed on a beach trip organised by two male acquaintances; trust your instincts. Again on Príncipe, a passing motorbike rider once shouted at me to go back to my own country, whilst in a couple of villages in the south of São Tomé some kids called me *colomba*, a derogatory term for white colonials. However, these were the only times I encountered anything resembling hostility. This is the advice from a long-term expat: 'Do think about the way you dress; the local dresscode changes from place to place, from situation to situation, from social group to social group. Take a look around; you may want to look twice as sexy as the local girls, but be prepared to be treated as twice as cheap too.'

WHAT TO TAKE

[] denotes either optional items or things that not all travellers will need, but that are difficult/impossible to get on the islands

- Adapter (3-to-2 pin from UK, US 2-pin-to-European 2-pin from the US)
- Plenty of memory cards/rolls of film & batteries
- Waterproof dry bag/case for keeping your camera dry hiking/on the water
- Strong mosquito repellent (2x)
- Mosquito-bite relief gel
- Sunscreen
- Permethrin spray for mosquito nets
- Head torch (2x if you are planning to do a lot of hiking)
- [Contact lens solution/glasses]
- [Platypus/camelback hydration pack for hiking]
- Binoculars for birdwatching
- Hiking boots with a good grip
- Small padlock
- Small dry bag to keep car keys/mobile safe when swimming
- Water-/windproof matches
- Photos of family to show
- Small fold-out map of the world to show where you live
- Small presents: notebooks, pens, picture books, Portuguese-English phrasebooks/mini dictionaries
- Photocopies of passport with visa, yellow fever certificate, credit cards, flight tickets

$ MONEY

The official currency on São Tomé and Príncipe is the dobra ($). One dobra equals 100 *cêntimos*. There are notes of 5,000 (purple), 10,000 (green), 20,000 (red) and 50,000 (brown), and coins of 100, 200, 500, 1000 and 2000 dobras. The dobra is not traded on international markets, but you can convert online on most currency converter websites (eg: *www.xe.com*), or the useful site of the Central Bank of STP (*www.bcstp.st*). Economists are recommending the dobra be pegged to the euro (as in Cape Verde). In 2008, the rate of inflation was running at around 25%, with the price hike in essential consumer goods such as cooking oil and rice affecting the population badly; no wonder you will frequently hear that life is a bit *complicado*, or *difícil*, 'difficult'. An agricultural worker takes home under 300,000$, an office clerk about 500,000$; at the big hotels, waiters earn US$30 a month, receptionists around US$200. The current minimum wage is around 450,000$; a recent study for the FMI recommended setting it at 1,000,000$.

As regards travellers, the **euro** is much more common than the US$ and is the **lead currency** now. Generally, wherever prices are displayed in euros or dollars, you pay more. There are a number of banks in the capital and one on Príncipe.

PRICE OF EVERYDAY GROCERIES

	$
Local snack (bar/restaurant)	15,000–55,000
Fish & bananas (lunch/dinner)	35,000–150,000
Pizza	55,000–150,000
Small piece of jackfruit	2,000
500g tomatoes from the market	20,000
Bread	5,000
Palm wine	400
Beer	15,000–25,000
Coca cola	10,000–20,000
Coconut on the beach	1,000–3,000
Cooking oil	40,000
1.5l bottle of mineral water	50,000
Imported butter	55,000
Imported cheese	40,000–300,000
Imported wine	60,000–1,000,000
Príncipe biscuits	10,000
Imported biscuits	35,000
Gourmet Santomean chocolate	60,000–300,000
500g Santomean coffee	40,000–450,000
500g gourmet Santomean coffee	90,000–500,000

Credit cards are still hardly used. In inimitable *Santomense* style, the day the National Investment Bank launched the first Santomean American Express card, after two years of preparations and negotiations, the bank's assets were frozen under suspicion of fraud. The only hotels on the island where guests can pay by credit card are the Miramar, La Provence, Omali Lodge, Pestana Equador/São Tomé; and on Príncipe, only at the Bom Bom resort. There has been talk of ATM machines coming to both São Tomé and Príncipe for a while, but so far there is only one in the capital, which dispenses only dobras, and for the time being only to account holders with Ecobank, a Togo-based operation with 450 branches in 22 African countries. More relevantly for travellers, at the **Banco Internacional de São Tomé and Príncipe**, again in the capital, you can use your Visa/Master/Diners debit/credit card to arrange a **money transfer** in about 10 minutes, with your passport. If you are staying for longer, it is quite easy to open a BISTP account. Just bring a photocopy of your passport (if you are opening the account on Príncipe, have one ready in your luggage, as you might not find a working photocopier). You will be issued with cheques that you can use in some, but not all, shops and restaurants on the islands. If you don't have a Visa/MasterCard, but have an account with BISTP and a contact in Portugal, the BISTP offers a cheap way of transferring money called *Transferência Expresso*. This might be a life-saver if you should find yourself stranded on Príncipe, without ATMs, facilities for wiring money, nor ways of accessing money with your debit/credit card. The *Transferência Expresso* procedure is explained in a leaflet you can pick up from the BISTP branch in both islands. In theory, it's simple: somebody in Portugal pays in money at any Caixa Geral de Depósitos (CGD) branch (*www.cgd.pt*), Caixa Geral de Depósitos holding 27% of BISTP shares. The money has to be paid to BISTP, account number 0001.027355.330, with your name and own BISTP account number added below. To confirm the transfer and activate the money, the branch or yourself has to send a fax or email to BISTP in São Tomé (**f** +239 222427; **e** bistp@cstome.net); it is best to do both. The money will be available in anything between three and 24 hours. Unfortunately, in practice, the *Transferência Expresso* was a struggle every time, as staff at Portuguese Caixa Geral branches have often never heard of this service; the person sending you the money might have to explain the procedure and send the confirmation fax themselves, eg: from a post office, which costs about €4.50. All in all, it's a lot of hassle, unless you are stuck on Príncipe.

When buying from street vendors or from the market, **change** (*troco*) is a constant issue, so it is a good idea to have 5,000$ and 10,000$ notes handy, plus plenty of coins. Especially on the market, prices are often given in multiples of *contos*, ie: 1,000. So a piece of jackfruit might be *três contos*, a clutch of ripe bananas *cinco contos*. A colloquial word for money is *verba*, or, more refined, *meios*.

BUDGETING These daily budgets are per person (on the basis of a couple sharing; rates approx). Bear in mind that the prices for many goods and services go up about 20% each year.

Luxury Staying at a top hotel/resort, hiring a car with guide, eating at resort/top-end restaurants: £100/US$200/€150

Mid-range Staying at a small hotel/city guesthouse, one organised activity with picnic, one meal at upmarket restaurant: £50/US$100/€75

Cheap and cheerful Staying at a basic guesthouse, getting around by shared taxi or bike, hiring a local guide, eating street food and one meal at a popular restaurant: £30/US$60/€45

GETTING AROUND

BY CAR The country has about 380km of roads, three quarters of them tarmacked and most of them on São Tomé island, supplemented by countless dirt roads and tracks. Whilst there are a fair number of pot-holes on the capital's road, the **roads** inland and north from the capital are pretty good overall and, in particular the north coast road, navigable by ordinary saloon car. The interior road goes past the suburb of Madre de Deus to Trindade and leads up 1,000m to the botanical gardens at Bom Sucesso and the Monte Café plantation. You can do these by saloon car, though it will get badly rattled. The northern road links Guadalupe, hugs the coast from Lagoa Azul to Neves until eventually fizzling out into a grass track past Santa Catarina on the northwest coast. It is the road south towards Angolares and Porto Alegre that is the problem – diabolical pot-holes easily qualifying it as a national shame, *vergogna*. The Santomeans have been promised a better road for a while; for the time being, you only see patches being repaired. Meanwhile, the number of cars and motorbikes is increasing, as are accidents; as a pedestrian in towns, watch out when crossing the road. The few road signs I have seen were in the capital, pointing out the main roads south to Angolares or north to Neves. People are happy to give directions; sometimes they might ask for a lift, *boleia*. Santomean drivers sound their horns a lot, Italian-style, to alert other road users. While traffic drives on the right, outside the city, cars coming from different directions are often competing for the same bit of road with the fewest pot-holes. **Car rental** is expensive; for details of car hire on São Tomé island, see page 98, for Príncipe, see page 173; alternatives are **motorbikes** and **bikes**. Most Santomeans travel by shared **yellow taxis**; these can also be hired individually (called a 'frete'), paying for all the seats.

AROUND THE ISLAND BY BOAT A great way to see the island. Flogátours (see page 101) can take on a *volta a ilha*, with two nights beach camping and excellent birdwatching opportunities. A new venture offers a **day trip round the island**, with lunch on the Ilhéu das Rolas, on the 14x2m two-motor *S. Cristovão*. In principle, departures are every Saturday at 06.00 from the Cais das Alfândegas port, leaving Rolas at 16.00. The cost, 600,000$, includes drinks and snacks and has to be paid by the Thursday before. The same boat makes a trip to the **Ilhéu das Cabras** ('Goats' Island') on Sundays at 08.00, with an opportunity for snorkelling, and returns at 16.00 (cost: 100,000$, payable by Saturday). These trips can also be organised on other days, for the same price, with sailings to Príncipe planned for the future. Ring Júlio Silva for details (☏ *908148*).

ACCOMMODATION

Accommodation on the islands ranges from a beach shelter made out of palm fronds by your guide and basic dives for €10 through city hotels and restored plantation houses to a five-star resort. Although São Tomé and Príncipe does not have a developed backpacker infrastructure, there is now a lot of choice, with new places springing up all over the place: from guesthouses in the city, ecocamps, B&B stays with expats, to international standard hotels and resorts with four or five stars. The high season is August and the Christmas/New Year period. You shouldn't need to bring a mosquito net, as it is provided free of charge in nearly all hotel/hostel rooms I've seen. However, the nets might have been hanging there for years, losing their impregnation, so bring a permethrin spray to treat them. When you get to your room, it's a good idea to check everything is working: that the taps are running and the loo flushing, and that there is toilet paper. You can **camp** anywhere on public land in the islands (ask for permission for the Obô National Park) but have to bring practically all your own equipment; also, in practice, unless you know exactly what you are doing with a compass, etc, it is always better to have a guide. The Navetur agency can arrange tents and sleeping bags for hire. I've found that in the dry season a hammock with mosquito netting and strong poncho-style rain flaps is enough, so you can get away without carrying a tent. If you find yourself stuck, build a shelter from palm fronds. Some travellers staying for a longer period of time choose to rent a cheap room to use as a base where they can leave their stuff while off on camping trips.

EATING AND DRINKING

The staple item of the Santomean diet is **fish** – *grelhado* – grilled, baked (*asado*), or to a lesser degree cooked (*cozido*). The most popular are flying fish (*peixe voador*), that you will see cut open and laid out to dry on the beach or drying sheds in large quantities; it has a delicate taste, but you won't find it much in restaurants as it is full of little bones. One of the most popular fish you will be

HOTEL PRICE CODES

Double room per night:

Luxury	$$$$	£60–100	US$130–200	€80–130
Mid-range	$$$	£30–60	US$60–120	€40–80
Budget	$$	£15–30	US$30–60	€20–40
Shoestring	$	< £15	<US$30	<€20

served in restaurants is the red grouper (*cherne*). Another is the sea bass (*corvina*), with firm flesh and great flavour, associated in *forro* culture with prestige, luck and knowledge. A good option for a **beach lunch** is to buy a fish directly off the fishermen, around midday. Expect to pay around 20,000$ for a big fish, and ask whether you can grill it over the fisherman's fire (*pode-se grelhar o peixe?*); if you bring a lime and some salt from town, you can yourself a real feast. In *forro* culture, to be well-fed is a sign of wealth and status; here are two words that are commonly used to describe people outside the norm: *massabruta* is a portly person, *socanina* a very thin person. For breakfast, or *matabicho* (literally, 'kill the little beast', ie: hunger, inside), most Santomeans reheat the remains of the previous evening meal (*jantar*), and only eat a snack for lunch (*almoço*), while a standard tourist breakfast is rolls, jam/cheese, fresh papaya. Currently, 90% of food is imported; small agricultural ventures, often funded by NGOs, are trying to promote more self-reliance.

Small eating establishments – *petisqueiras*, *churrasquerias*, *quitandas* and *quiosques* – might not all be immediately visible to you. For those with a sweet tooth, *pastelarias* are a welcome Portuguese heritage. At lunchtime, in every village, there should be at least one person who will serve simple cooked food; you just have to ask: *Onde há comida quente?* The food, mostly fish or chicken with manioc, fried banana or jackfruit, is often very tasty.

Roadside food – grilled corn-on-the-cob, *safú* fruit, stews from big pots – can be an excellent and cheap choice. Expats will usually warn you off street food and eating dangerous food items such as salads, but everybody's stomach reacts differently; try and acclimatise it gradually to the unfamiliar bacteria (see *Health*, page 61). One minor ripoff to look out for at some of the plantations on both São Tomé and Príncipe island already used to visitors; I've heard about travellers being charged a hefty 300,000$ for a simple dish. Be sure to discuss prices beforehand.

TRADITIONAL SANTOMEAN DISHES The grilled fish 'belly', *barriga de peixe*, for example, comes with rice (*arroz*), bread fruit or manioc. Beans (*feijão*) are a staple food. Another staple is *banana cozida* (cooked banana), the blandness of the banana offset by wonderful spicy sauces, like the red *malagueta* piri-piri sauce found in every restaurant, or a green parsley *salsa* sauce at more upmarket places. The **Santomean signature dish** is *calulú* (see box on page 76 for a recipe): dried smoked fish in a delicious sauce made from *ocá* leaves, palm oil, lady's fingers, *malagueta* chilli, and watercress, plus a variety of fresh herbs, resulting in a multilayered flavour. *Calulú* takes about five hours to prepare. Other typical dishes are *blablá* and *djogo*, and *cachupa* is a popular Capeverdian dish cooked with corn, green and broad beans. It is not that easy to find these time-intensive traditional specialities; the upmarket restaurants tend more towards Portuguese cuisine and fish dishes; in most places, you have to request them a day in advance. I only know of one place where you can just turn up and have a *calulú* – in the market building

RESTAURANT PRICE CODES

Average price of a main course:

Above average	$$$$	£10–15	US$20–30	€13–20
Mid-range	$$$	£5–10	US$10–20	€7–13
Cheap & cheerful	$$	£2.50–5	US$4–14	€3.50–7
Rock bottom	$	£1.50–2.50	US$3–5	€2–3.50

With kind permission from the author and publishers of Na Roça com os Tachos and Façam o Favor de Ser Felices (see Appendix 2).

The following recipe for the Santomean signature dish *calulú* is taken from João Carlos Silva's cookbook accompanying his 2006 RTP Africa TV programme *Na Roça com os Tachos*, 'On the Plantation with Moustaches'. You can get all the ingredients at the market; the vendors will love the idea of a *branca*, or better even, a *branco*, trying their hand at cooking this dish! Palm oil is essential to Santomean cuisine; in the West, it is usually available from ethnic stores, or buy some on the islands to take home.

INGREDIENTS *Galinha fumada* (smoked chicken), *óleo de palma* (palm oil), *maquêquê* (green tomato-like fruit), *tomate* (tomato), *cebola* (onion), *quiabos* (lady's fingers), *pau pimenta* ('pepper wood'), *óssame* (red bulbous fruit), *mosquito* herb, *couve* (kale cabbage), *gimboa/jimboa* herb, *malagueta* (chilli), *folha de louro* (laurel), *pimento* (pepper), *cominhos* (cumin), *beringela* (aubergine), *mússua* (hibiscus), *fruta-pão* (breadfruit) or *farinha de trigo* (wheat flour), bananas.

PREPARATION Chop all the vegetables, including the pieces of breadfruit, and cook them in a saucepan with palm oil until all the ingredients turn into a big 'soup'. Add the smoked chicken, cut into pieces. Pull out the breadfruit after cooking and mash it in a small mortar, to thicken the sauce. If you don't have breadfruit available, you can get a similar result using wheat flour. Leave everything to fall in love, until you smell the aroma of a kiss... A few moments before serving, pull out the *mosquito* twig. Serve accompanied by an *angú* of bananas (see below), or rice and manioc flour. Be creative: replace the *gimboa* with spinach or the *mosquito* with basil or any other aromatic herbs. Instead of the chicken, you can use fish or other smoked meats.

For the *angú* accompaniment, peel green bananas and leave them to cook until slightly soft. Then beat them in a mortar until you have a paste, which, using a spoon, you can form into the number of patties you like.

in the capital. If you've made friends locally, you could ask them whether you could try specific dishes at their house. I've usually bought a few beers from the local *loja* if I found myself invited for some food in a village. Beach picnics on agency excursions are an opportunity to try cocoyam, matabala, papaya, banana snacks, etc. At popular celebrations (*festas*), such as saints' days, you will get the opportunity to try delicacies like *estufa de morcego*: bat stew. The poorest sections of society, lacking the money to buy fish, often eat forest/sea snails (*búzio*) as a source of protein. You'll see the yellow-red flowering wild **manioc** by the wayside sometimes; its roots are a popular food, ground into flour and made into a pudding. Sold occasionally by kids on plantations, the fluffy starchy white heaps don't honestly taste of much.

BEING A VEGETARIAN IN SÃO TOMÉ AND PRÍNCIPE The good news: you won't get any hassle for being a vegetarian, and you will eat fairly well, if a bit on the boring side. If you eat fish, you're in heaven of course. Western-style restaurants are used to vegetarians, but in a popular eating place, to say that you are a *vegetariano/vegetariana* does not mean much to people, and the person serving you might panic and say they have *nada*, nothing, for you! Just explain that you don't eat meat or fish, *nem carne nem peixe*, and know what to ask for: *feijão* (beans), *arroz* (rice), *tomates* (tomatoes), *banana frita* (fried banana). As long as you trust the storage facilities for eggs, an omelette (*omelettes*) is a good fallback – just make sure to ask for an *omelettes simples*, or *omelette de queijo*, cheese omelette, otherwise you might find bits of *chouriço* sausage in it as a well-meant treat. Occasionally you can get an omelette with fresh herbs (*ervas frescas*). Try asking for an *omelette de micôcô*; this famous thyme-like herb is a Santomean favourite. And there's always chips/French fries: *batatas fritas*. Some other **vegetables** you can ask for are *cenoura* (carrots), *pimpinella* (a white tree vegetable), and *couve* (cabbage). They'll usually come boiled, *cozidos* (use hot *malagueta* sauce or green *salsa* to spice them up); if you would prefer them grilled ask for them *grelhados*. Less commonly available in restaurants are peppers (*pimentos*), aubergine (*berengela*), and *maquêquê* (a green tomato-like fruit). If you're staying longer and know an informal eatery, you could try bringing in your own vegetables for them to prepare. For **vegans**, the choice is similar, as dairy products don't really form part of the Santomean diet anyway.

FRUIT Everybody's favourite is the **jackfruit** – *jaca* – a big, ballooning, pock-marked yellowish-green fruit, sold along the roadside, the pieces covered with banana leaves to keep the flies away. In Europe, a whole *jaca* can cost up to €40! Here, it might only set you back 40,000$. The only problem is the fruit's incredibly sticky sap, so bring a plastic bag if you want to take a piece (*pedaço*) back to the hostel/apartment. Jackfruit sellers always keep a cloth and oil for cleaning the sap off their hands; at the worst, use moisturiser or sun cream. Be prepared that people think it's incredibly funny to see a Westerner eating a piece of jackfruit on the go. Mangos (*manga*) grow in most plantations, but it's difficult to find homemade mango juice. *Cajamangas* have a lovely fresh acidic taste. **Safú** is a small oblong fruit of a beautiful purply blue with a taste reminiscent of olives and artichokes. The basic way to prepare *safú* is to top and tail them, scratch off a few strips of the skin (*casca*) and boil them in salted water for a couple of minutes. *Safú* are sometimes eaten in the morning with butter, or to accompany bread or breadfruit; they are often sold grilled along the roadside. Kids break open **cocoa** pods with stones to eat the citrussy-tasting flesh, and suck on **sugar cane** (*cana*), which is sold cheaply at the roadside and at the market. In the 16th century, sugar cane, brought to Europe by the Crusades, became the island's first cash crop, turning São Tomé and Príncipe into the first African producer of sugar cane. Probably the most important fruit on the islands is the **breadfruit**, the spiny *fruta pão*, with starchy spongy whitish flesh; the trees often grow next to erythrinas on cocoa plantations. Originally from Malaysia, the breadfruit was brought to São Tomé and Príncipe in the mid-19th century by the first baron of Água Izé. It is eaten with fish dishes and to mop up palm oil, or as a dessert; Santomeans travelling to Lisbon often carry a few in their luggage. The prize for the weirdest-looking fruit could go to its cousin, the **African breadfruit**, *izaquente*. Originally from equatorial Africa and looking like a huge spiky, slightly squashed, green football, an *izaquente* can weigh up to 10kg. You sometimes see the seeds being washed at the beach, waiting to be made into a paste and a sweet pudding, or into a savoury dish with palm oil. Kids eat the fresh seeds of the oblong fruit of the *carozeiro*, one of the most common trees in urban areas. The taste is not unpleasant, similar to coconut. The fruit of the *coleira* tree, coca nuts, are also eaten; they contain caffeine and contain hunger. A tropical fruit much in evidence on the islands is of course the **banana**, introduced to Africa 2,000 years ago, and a good source of potassium. Generally, *banana madura* ('ripe') is the yellow one you eat as it comes. Various varieties grow in São Tomé and Príncipe. The green plantain banana you will eat cooked (*cozido*) and fried (*frito*) are *banana prata*, the 'silver banana', and *banana pão*, 'bread banana', larger, with dark yellow flesh, which is also the one used most for frying. For snacking and dessert, the popular small *banana maçã*, 'apple banana', indeed has a lovely appley taste. Much coveted too are the less-common *banana d'ouro*, 'golden banana', whose skin has a red colour, and the *Gran Michel*. Even though banana plants are found in every *quintal* in the country, their cultivation is a lot of work. Banana plants grow fast, their large elliptic leaves unfurling from the stem at the rate of one a week, but they need regular watering and removal of excess shoots to channel all the plant's energy into fruit production. Also, they are easily blown over by the weight of rainwater – when you're out hiking, you'll occasionally hear one of them come crashing down. Each stalk produces one huge flower cluster on a violet trunk that bears the fruit, tightly packed clusters of small, square-looking bananas, and then dies, new stalks growing from the underground rhizome (bulb). Bananas are made into all kinds of snacks: *banana seca*, shrink-dried whole bananas, with a smoky flavour, a small sausage-shaped banana snack called *fios*, made with corn flour, and the Príncipe speciality *bobofrito*, a delicious high-energy snack made with ripe bananas fried in coconut oil. Other popular **snack foods** are *gigumba* (peanut brittle), sometimes sold in bars and restaurants – usually by the bottle only – and *palla-palla*, sweet or savoury crisps made of banana or cocoyam (*matabala*).

A common **street food**, corn-on-the-cob (*milho*) costs around 3,000$. *Arroz doce* is sweet rice prepared with coconut and sweetcorn traditionally eaten for breakfast. Street kids sell it for 2,000$ in sawn-off soft-drink cans. My favourite sweet snack is *açucarinhas*: patties made from coconut and sugar fried in palm oil. Sold outside bakeries for 500$–1,000$ they work especially well put inside a corn roll (*broa*). Some prefer the coconut a bit burnt (*queimada*). Another desert is *aranha* ('spider'), filigrane sugar strings stuffed with food colouring, prepared with eight coconuts to one kilo of sugar. For **dessert** (*sobremesa*, 'on the table'), chocolate mousse is a favourite (as in Portugal), but as this involves raw eggs be careful, as the generator might have broken down or the eggs spent too long sitting in the shop in the heat. **Self-catering** is a great idea. Buying fresh produce from the market gives you a real experience of Santomean culture; complemented by forays to Western-style supermarkets, you can eat well and cheaply. The only problem is power cuts, disabling the fridge and electric hobs; also, if you don't want ants crawling around your cereals, make sure you put all opened food packaging in the fridge.

DRINKS The ubiquitous refreshing Sagres lager (you will notice blown-up bottles as decorations in restaurants) and the slightly sweeter Super Bock are imported from Portugal. The national Rosema beer, Nacional, brewed in the north of São Tomé, comes in big bottles with no label; easier to drink is their Pilsner-style Criollo. Wines sold in the cheap restaurants/shops are usually Portuguese table wines such as Faisal or the light Casal Garcia *vinho verde* 'green wine'. Upmarket restaurants and supermarkets have a large selection of Portuguese wines (including a pleasant red Capote Velho), plus French/South African vintages and even champagne; at the other end of the scale, on Príncipe, I came across white wine mixed with Sprite lemonade. Wine is usually sold by the bottle (*garafa*); it's difficult to get wine by the glass (*copo*) – that and the hot humid climate turned me into a dedicated Sagres drinker. *Aguardente* (from *agua ardente*, 'burning water') is made of sugar cane, as is Gravana rum; if you come across an artisanal distillery, you can see it being produced and buy some cheaply. Locals often drink the hard-hitting cheap *cacharamba* gin-style firewater. Less commonly available is *ponche*, a basic cocktail made from *aguardente* and honey; other versions are made with white rum, quinine leaves and lemon. Mé-Zóchi is a sweet liqueur (43%) that comes in various flavours: orange (*laranja*), *cajamanga* and pineapple (*ananas*). Miniatures make a nice souvenir, but few shops sell them.

The national drink, however, is **palm wine**. *Vinho de palma*, or *vim pema* in creole, comes in three qualities; the purest, most undiluted variety is made at high altitude, decreasing in quality the closer to town you get. Buy a small bottle (sealed with a bit of twisted palm leaf or newspaper) from a street stall (around 400$) or, even better, buy some straight off a palm wine worker in the forest. Bring your own container/thermos cap, as the sawn-off mineral water bottles or beer cans used can be pretty filthy. The wine ferments during the day. In the morning, it is like milk (*doce*, sweet); the longer the liquid ferments, the more acidic it becomes. Come night a cork will come flying out of the bottle, champagne-style, and the increased alcohol content makes it a lot more explosive too. Unfortunately, alcoholism is a growing problem on the islands, in the wake of a degradation of living conditions and loss of trust in the future over the past decade. One curiosity you might notice: don't be surprised if your waiter/waitress asks whether you want them to open your drink (*posso abrir?*). The reason for this cautious approach is to reassure the customer that the bottle hasn't been tampered with. In the past there have been cases of poisoning on the island when romantic scores or workplace grievances needed to be settled; tourists were never involved. **Soft drinks** all go by the same brand name here: 'Sumol' (passionfruit, orange or pineapple, lemonade, even Coca Cola sometimes). The main type of juice is mango juice (*sumo de manga*), imported from Lebanon. If you would like/rather not have ice in your drink, ask for *com/sem gelo*. Fresh **coconut water** is not often sold commercially, but it's usually easy to ask somebody on the beach to find a green coconut and open it for you. *Dawa* is meant to be incredibly healthy, but the slightly sour juice didn't agree so well with my stomach at least. As for **coffee**, in Western cafés on São Tomé you can find the range of Portuguese-style variations: *café, garroto, carioca*. A *galão* has more milk than coffee (my favourite is a *galão escuro*, with two shots of espresso, which is like a *latte, or latte macchiato*). On Príncipe (apart from the Bom Bom Island resort), coffee means a pot of the local earthy coffee. Unfortunately, few hotels and cafés actually serve Santomean coffee, but you can always try and ask for local coffee (*café de cá*). **Tea** (*chá*) is available in Western hotels/restaurants and in some local places too, often the Lipton brand, in varieties such as peach or green tea. You can ask for milk, *leite*, or a lemon, *limão* – though it is more likely to be a lime. Or you could try asking for a delicious alternative common in Portugal and used by the locals to treat colds: *carioca de limão*, hot water with lemon peel.

PUBLIC HOLIDAYS AND OPENING HOURS

PUBLIC HOLIDAYS Check the weekly *Correio da Semana* newspaper for details of events/celebrations, etc, also for the many saints' days.

1 Jan   **New Year's Day** Santomeans gather on the beaches to celebrate; there is a tradition of putting on a new set of clothes after a bathe in the sea to represent the new year.

3 Feb   **Heroes' Day** Commemorations of the 1953 'Massacre of Batepá' on Praia Fernão Dias on 2/3 February, with dancing, oral history, a march by secondary school pupils, wreath-laying, etc.

1 May   **Labour Day** International Workers' Day.

12 Jul   **Independence Day** Celebration of independence from Portugal in 1975; festivities centre around Independence Square in the capital and start on the eve of 12 July, but the big gathering for speeches, cultural performances, etc, is switched to a different town each year.

| 6 Sep | **Armed Forces' Day** Parades through the streets of the capital. |

| 30 Sep | **Agricultural Reform Day** Celebration of the 1975 nationalisation of the largest plantations. |

| 26 Nov | **Algiers Agreement Day** Celebration of the 1974 decolonisation treaty between Portugal and the MLSTP that paved the way for independence. |

| 21 Dec | **São Tomé Day** Discovery of São Tomé island in 1470. |

| 25 Dec | **Christmas Day** |

OPENING HOURS Most shops and services observe the regular opening hours of the 'English week', *semana inglesa*: 08.00–12.30 and 14.00–17.30 Monday–Friday, 08.00–13.00 Saturday, with variations. Restaurants usually stay open late until around 23.00, in Príncipe until about 22.00. In the capital, banks and a few other places relevant to tourists, such as the TAP agency, close early and institutions such as libraries are only open on weekdays, while the phone exchange stays open until 21.00 and the central petrol station until midnight. There are a few nominally '24-hour' kiosks/shops. All opening hours quoted have to be taken with a pinch of salt, not least to accommodate the frequent power cuts.

SHOPPING AND SERVICES

MARKETS sell fresh fruit and vegetables and many other items, such as shoes, clothes, stationery, cosmetics, etc. Small shack stores (*lojas*, sometimes called *cantinas*) exist in countless numbers – every plantation and fishing village has at least one – selling very much the same basic foodstuffs: biscuits, cheap wines, soft drinks, tomato paste and cooking oil.

SOUVENIRS One of the greatest pleasures on the islands is discovering the range of unique produce and quality crafts available – just watch your luggage allowance. Coffee and chocolate, as well as vanilla, are the most obvious souvenirs to take home; children will enjoy a wooden rattle or carved boat. Príncipe, while not great for souvenir shopping, is the home of *bobofrito*, and you can pick it up very cheaply (10,000$). *Bobofrito* keeps well and makes a welcome present for friends on the main island, and for hillwalking friends back home, as an exotic high-energy snack. To remember nights at the *discoteca* or to give to friends with an interest in music, have some CDs recorded at a recording studio (*estúdio de gravaçao*) found on both islands; at only around 60,000$, these make a great souvenir. A wide range of T-shirts, flags, caps, some with slogans of the 'Kiss me, I'm São Tomean' variety, are available on the internet (eg: *www.amazon.com*). In the capital, **necklaces and bracelets** made of brown, grey, black or red seeds are on sale in hotels (expensive) or touted by kids in the centre of the capital for around 10–20,000$. If you don't want to buy because you've already got some, you can say: *Obrigado/a, ja tenho*. Otherwise, just say *Obrigado/a, não quero* ('Thanks, I don't want') or *não preciso* ('I don't need').

Chocolate In Europe, the deservedly famous **Claudio Corallo** chocolate is sold through retailers Fortnum & Mason in London, Printemps in Paris and in some malls in Portugal, but at about three times the price (*www.claudiocorallo.com*). Some Portuguese supermarkets, such as Continente, stock a good bar made in Belgium, for about €2.30. While you're in the capital, you can try and pop into the chocolate factory on the coast road and buy some off the man himself; there are no formalised tours and Signore Corallo doesn't speak English, but he will probably be happy to show you around. In the UK, Marks & Spencer sell a very nice 100g chocolate bar (70%) with cocoa nibs, and a 218g selection box (72% cocoa, £8): sophisticated design, OK chocolates. The best bargain in Europe comes from Germany, where a nice 100g bar of Sarotti No 1 São Thomé 75% with cocoa nibs sells for under €1 (£0.70/US$1.35; unfortunately, not available to buy online). The Santomean consul in Marseille is importing cocoa for processing in France, buying from small planters; the website (*www.sao-tome.st*) has a long list of French stockists.

Chocolate lovers should try the following websites:

www.chocolove.com Beautifully wrapped 70% cocoa 'Chocolatour' bars (vintages 2004 and 2005, 3.2oz/90g)

www.lakechamplainchocolates.com 3oz/85g 'Sao Thome' 70% cocoa (fruity vanilla) vegan kosher bars (US$3.75)

www.chocolats-pralus.com The 80% Criollo/Trinitario bars (100g/160g) from this French chocolatier have been getting rave reviews & also feature in the beautiful 'Tropical Pyramid' collection.

www.cluizel.com/www.chocolatmichelcluizel-na.com (US) The 67% cocoa chocolate bars & miniatures made from the Trinitario cocoa variety (a mix between Criollo & Forastero) have 'subtle grassy & liquorice notes'. Paris-based chocolatier Michel Cluizel prides himself on not using child labour on his Vila Graçinda plantation near São João dos Angolares. Check the website for retailers; in the UK, the chocolates are available through Transmanche in Surrey (✆ 01483 793 926; e transmanche@tiscali.co.uk).

www.latasybotellas.com Chocolates and hot chocolate made with cocoa from Príncipe by Barcelona chocolatier Enric Rovira, the author (with Corallo) of a book homage to cocoa.

HAIR AND BEAUTY Visiting a Santomean salon is great fun and an inexpensive cultural experience, especially having your hair braided (women) or an interesting pattern shaved (men). The artificial hair (*postiço*) woven into braids (*tranças*) and the little transparent or multi-coloured beads (*missangas*) can usually be picked up cheaply in a shop or market. Braiding takes time, but is a morning or afternoon well spent, listening to the women's gossip and banter. Apart from being a great conversation item, this style is practical in the tropical heat. If you have Caucasian hair, especially if it's fine, a style that will hold for months on local ladies' heads will start unravelling after two weeks. In any case, for most people, enthusiasm for African hairstyles usually unravels just before boarding the plane home; keep in mind that unbraiding (*distrançar*) takes a good while too. Make sure you communicate what you want – I had an odd fringe cut in one place and some hair colour I'd brought in just slopped on to my head. You can usually get other beauty treatments, like waxing, at salons, too.

ACTIVITIES

Both islands are ideally suited to hiking, sports fishing, and diving. **Hikes** can range from gentle walks to waterfalls and a few hours' beach-hopping to rainforest treks lasting several days. Cycling and kayaking are only beginning to take off.

GUIDES In São Tomé, the Navetur and Mistral agencies employ excellent guides, who usually speak French (some of them English); some are available for private work, too. Of the few English-speaking guides on the island, musician **Oswaldo Santos** (✆ 914571; e oswaldosn@yahoo.co.br), working for Navetur, is an ideal cultural guide, very entertaining and knowledgeable; he also speaks French. At Mistral Voyages, **Agostino Espírito Santo** is a good bet for Francophone and Anglophone visitors. Taxi driver/guide **Joaquim Ribeiro** (☎ *906491*) is very experienced; he has some French and a bit of English. **José Spencer**, based at the Ponta Figo plantation (☎ *919305, evenings*), is a very knowledgeable hiking guide who runs trips to the Pico, around the northern waterfalls, and treks along the remote southwestern coast/island crossings; he only speaks Portuguese. The **best bird guide** is **Norberto Vidal** (see *Flogátours*, page 101), who has very good French. Other excellent forest guides are **Lucio Primo** (☎ *904468*), your best choice for orchid hikes, and his younger brother **Brice** (☎ *923984*); both are based at the Monte Café plantation and speak French. Some guides have no phone and have to be contacted via a neighbour, invariably in Portuguese. HABA's **Sesaltino** (☎ *905939/918200*) also speaks English. The **Monte Pico guide association** (e *montepico@yahoo.com.br; www.montepico.blogspot.com*) has 25 members and is involved in looking after the main island's botanical garden and the Obô National Park. Its president, **Luis Mario Almeida** (☎ *911670*; e *lumanovamoca@hotmail.com*) speaks good French. Monte Pico's General Secretary, botanist **Faustino Oliveira** (☎ *905279/225647*), might be able to offer tailor-made botanical tours at weekends and, if you don't have your own transport, take you on his motorbike; he speaks French and Italian. On **Príncipe**, there are fewer English-speaking guides still, but most activities can be organised through the Bom Bom Island resort. In general, a guide is worth having; most impromptu 'guides' on plantations for example can tell you very little about the history of the place (even in Portuguese), and rainforest hikes are practically impossible without a guide.

DIVING The bumpy underwater relief of the island's volcanic ocean floor mirrors the archipelago's mountainous surface. Enjoy the undisturbed natural beauty of a habitat where the equatorial currents at the meeting point of the eastern and western Atlantic create a wealth of species, with sharks, rays, turtles, fan corals and many fish you won't see anywhere else in the world. However, don't come with a tick-list of big fish, but with a spirit of discovery. The agreeable water temperature, averaging around 26°C (79°F), is unusually warm for the Atlantic. The only times when diving is hampered somewhat by choppy waters are the months of March and April. If your primary reason for visiting São Tomé and Príncipe is diving, **Príncipe** is the better choice for your main base, as there is even less human intervention and even fewer fishermen, trawlers and dragnets disturbing the marine fauna and flora of the shallow littoral. 'At night, with the coral flowering, it turns into a garden,' says Jean-Louis Testori, owner of Club Maxel, currently the only diving base on São Tomé island, who also comes over to the exclusive Bom Bom resort to run courses there. As there is a lot less infrastructure on Príncipe, you'll probably have to stay at Bom Bom. The second-best choice is the Ilhéu das Rolas just off the southern tip of São Tomé, but there are plenty of good sites dotted around the coast of São Tomé too. If you are spending any time in **Lisbon** before your onward flight, visit the magnificent **Oceanarium**, one of the biggest in the world (☎ *+351 21 8917002; www.oceanario.pt*), for a flavour of what you could see.

Diving instructors/centres

Club Maxel Praia Lagarto; ☎ 904424; e info@clubmaxel.st; www.clubmaxel.st. The owner of this diving centre, Frenchman Jean-Louis Testori, is a diving instructor who is very knowledgeable & passionate about the islands' underwater world. Operations are based in the capital; courses are run in French, Portuguese, & English. A 1-day Discover Scuba Diving course costs €65, a 3–4- day PADI Open Water Diver €350, an Advanced Open Water Diver or Rescue Diver course €300 & an Emergency First Response course €170 (Divemaster courses on request). At the time of writing, Jean-Louis was running the diving base on Rolas. Ask him to show you the fantastic photographs of São Tomé and Príncipe's underwater life on his laptop.

Nacho e nachosaotome@hotmail.com;. Nacho Gonzalez's diving school, *Gandú* — the creole word for shark — is currently closed, but the friendly Spanish-born instructor is happy to share information on his famous diving sites (Santana islet, the reefs between Cabras island & Lagoa Azul & around Morro Peixe) for see sea bass, manta rays, endemic invertebrates, barracuda, etc.

Pestana Equador (see page 159, Ilhéu das Rolas) Excellent diving around the equator mark on a tiny island off the southern tip of São Tomé. There is usually a resident diving instructor & sometimes a German diving instructor (see *Tour operators*); both can teach any guest of the resort. It is possible to learn how to dive here, but Rolas is not ideal for complete beginners as after the initial swimming pool tuition, all dives are made from a boat; you can't just gradually wade into the water. Also, there are only 2 sites for beginners, & because of the open Atlantic the swell is quite strong; you still feel it at 20m depth.

Dive sites São Tomé
Thanks to Jean-Louis Testori from Club Maxel

Santana Diving around the islet of Santana just off the resort on the east coast goes down to 35m & offers good visibility. The islet is traversed by a wide channel of 6 metres' depth; on the channel's seaward side, a small cave extends about 8m into the rock. Expect to see barracudas, red carp, red snapper, turtles, the rare cusk eel, the electric-blue deepwater cardinalfish & various corals. Diving through the tunnel at a depth of 12–19m deep is especially rewarding at night, as you see very large fan corals.

Uba-Budo A new discovery, there are two sites (8–25m), with lots of butterfly fish & angelfish, plus many different small fish.

Kia Two levels 2km off Ilhéu das Cabras: 12m & 22m, with red carp, a nursery of moray eels & red snappers, manta rays, rock fish, yellow, green & orange tubular coral, & sometimes a nurse shark. Even sand sharks of up to 6m in length have been seen here. Good night diving.

Morro Peixe 12–20m depth, small caves with big red snappers, nurse sharks & hawksbill turtles.

Lagoa Azul This popular snorkelling spot with good visibility also accommodates different levels of scuba diving. Complete beginners can do their first scuba dive down to 3m. The next levels go down to 8–20m & 20–45m. Expect to see intense marine life along the lagoon's reefs: various hard & soft corals, including fan corals (mind the rare 'black' coral — actually, it is white — it stings!), red snapper, butterfly fish, large red carp, pork fish, soldier fish, & sometimes turtles. This is also one of the most beautiful sites on the island for advanced divers, who can explore a 10m rock wall, looking for moray eels & barracudas. Excellent night diving.

Diogo Vaz Initial flat section down to 15m, with a garden of small fan coral at 10–12m in all the colours of the rainbow, then a drop down to 40m, & another to 65m — for experienced divers only. Scuba diving down to this depth is touching the absolute limit of what is recommended; bear in mind that there is no decompression chamber on the island. Large red, yellow, brown & black fan corals, red carp, jackfish, butterfly fish & rock fish around walls & big rocks on brown sand. Look out for a blue-grey worm with two heads — unless this is some diver's joke I didn't get...

São Miguel A star site featuring turtles, nurse sharks, barracudas, & various jackfish, which can be reached from both the capital and the Ilhéu das Rolas.

For Ponte Baleia & Sete Pedras, see Ilhéu das Rolas; for Príncipe, see page 189.

KAYAKING In theory, you can paddle all around the islands. In practice, there is a shortage of kayaks. At the time of writing, on São Tomé island only Club Santana is currently able to arrange commercial kayak hire and trips on a turn-up-and-go basis, but you can contact qualified local kayak trainer Gato (℅ *905328*; e *gedmaygato@hotmail.com*), who speaks English and French, for details of personalised trips: a *saída* from Praia Lagarto beach in São Tomé town to the Ilhéu das Cabras, for example, takes about 45 minutes, and there is some nice snorkelling around the islet. On Príncipe, the Bom Bom resort is now offering kayak hire and guided kayak trips. Once the problem of lack of kayaks is solved, trips on both islands may be organised, from a gentle half-hour paddle in a double kayak for complete beginners and crossings between Porto Alegre and the Ilhéu das Rolas in the south, to expeditions along the Príncipe coast.

OTHER WATERSPORTS

Swimming At the time of writing lessons are still held at the Hotel Miramar pool in the capital by Kenyan English-speaking instructor Job Kania (\ *925028;* e *kaniaj@hotmail.com*) and Nacho (see above). When you visit, the **Club Nautico** might be ready. Once refurbished, the historic watersports club on the capital's coast road, incorporating the saltwater pool where many Santomeans learned to swim, will offer various activities and facilities, from jetski to a disco.

Surfing Very few surfers have been to São Tomé and Príncipe, although a handful of French and US surfers have explored both islands, provoking the glee of fascinated local kids joining them on wooden floats; check forums such as *www.globalsurfers.com* for current information. One crew left a surfboard propped up against a house in Porto Alegre in the south of São Tomé and the local kids now use it to paddle around the bay. Due to the lack of serious waves, São Tomé and Príncipe will always be more of a novelty attraction than a fixture on the surf circuit. Summer, August in particular, has the best swell. You will have to bring all your gear. Apparently, Praia Pombo beach in front of the Voice of America transmitters outside the capital has good waves, but only part of this beach is open to the public. Others worth a try are the sweeping southern beaches of Micondó, Sete Ondas and Praia Grande, and the Ilhéu das Rolas.

CYCLING Cycling on the islands might be hot work occasionally, but is a great way to explore the landscape, due to the lack of serious traffic and roads for all abilities, from the flat coast road to strenuous inland hills, plus exciting off-road tracks used in the 2003 national championship races. You can **rent a bike** fairly cheaply, in the capital and from the Roça São João in the south (with advance notice). In general, if you ask around, somebody will probably know somebody who can hire out a bike to a tourist. Consider cycling to one of the plantation houses and stay overnight or just cycle around exploring; this mode of transport will ensure you get plenty of interaction with Santomeans more used to Westerners in 4x4s. The area around the capital is fairly flat, to the south in particular, but as soon as you go further, you will find gentle hills and some steep inclines too. On Príncipe, biking is harder work and the choice of good bikes is less good. One (German) tour operator already includes cycling in their São Tomé itinerary (see *Tour operators*). In São Tomé, the **Cycling Federation/Federaçao de Ciclismo** (*secretary Eneio Pereira,* \ *922587, otherwise Tiziano Pisoni,* \ *908737;* e *aliseistp@cstome.net/tizimari@hotmail.com*) is opening up a number of **circuits** for all abilities, exploring plantation houses or beaches, or a combination of the two; every circuit can be customised. Tiziano and Mari Pisoni speak basic English. **Sample itineraries** starting from the capital are: 1) Plantations and Beaches of the North (40km, 3–4hrs); 2) São Tomé's Popular Quarters & Fishing Village (25–30km, 2–3hrs); 3) Plantations and Beaches of the East (35km, 4–5hrs). Taking the bikes by car opens up 4) the West Coast (40–50km, 5–6hrs), and 5) Bombaim plantation/waterfalls, with two options for the return journey, depending on ability. Experienced cyclists can **cross the island** from the northwest (town of Neves) to the east (Água Izé plantation). Count €10 for a hybrid bike hire per day, plus €10 for the guide. If you want to set out on your own, you will be given a **roadbook** to navigate by. Bike trips lasting various days are possible too, for example:

- **Day 1:** São Tomé–Monteforte plantation house, via the northern beaches (35–40km)

- **Day 2**: Monteforte–Chamiço plantation house (usually very difficult to access) via Agôstinho Neto plantation (1,000m ascent, 35km)
- **Day 3**: Chamiço–Bombaim plantation house, via the historic Monte Café plantation (45km)
- **Day 4**: Bombaim–São Tomé through the rainforest (30km)

This itinerary can be extended: Day 5: São Tomé–São João dos Angolares (45km); Day 6: São João dos Angolares–Praia Jalé ecolodge (40km).

CLIMBING For pioneers only! The president of the guide association, Luis Mario Almeida (see *Guides*, page 82), is hoping to open up climbing trails, to use São Tomé's distinctive volcanic phonoliths for *alpinismo*. In 2001, an Italian group of climbers achieved what other alpinists had failed to do, scaling the 664m Cão Grande! Long-term, there are ambitious plans to establish a one-week climbing parcours, including Formosa Grande and Cão Pequeno. Waterfall climbing is also planned.

ARTS AND ENTERTAINMENT

In the near-absence of formalised cinema or theatre, much of Santomean art happens on the street: from murals and *bulaué* music to the islands' unique dramatic traditions of Dança Congo (page 27), *tchiloli* (page 28), and Auto de Floripes on Príncipe (page 171). Popular entertainment revolves around dancing, in a *discoteca* or a public dance area (*terraço*). There is no real bookshop on the island, but an excellent art gallery in the capital, as well as various libraries/cultural institutions.

PHOTOGRAPHY

In a way, the archipelago is a photographer's dream: the majestic trees of the rainforest, the picturesque colonial architecture, colourful cocoa pods and flowers of the plantations, cultural spectacles in bright colours, the catchy smiles of Santomean children, and, for the specialists, a rich bird and underwater world. However, as you will see when you look at São Tomé and Príncipe pictures on the web, the country is not actually the easiest for photographers. Often, a haze hangs over the islands, especially in January/February, but also during the main tourist season in June–September. Whilst the high-level cloud forest yields magical shots, beach shots can end up disappointing even if you manage to exclude that annoying corner of grey 'nothing' sky. In theory, the rainy season is better for taking pictures of dramatic skies and strong contrasts; in practice, trekking becomes difficult. Digital photography allows great interaction; children in particular are delighted to see their smiling faces (though you often end up taking photographs of large groups, as they all come running) or their *capoeira* martial arts' manoeuvres. Try and keep dirty hands off the screen (*Cuidado!* Careful! / *Não mexer!* Don't touch!). With adults, there is a marked difference. You should ask before you take anything that isn't a general scene, especially for a close-up (*posso tirar foto?*). At the market in particular, vendors are often reluctant to be photographed; it's better to first establish contact by buying something. Apparently, there is still a belief that a photo takes away the soul of the person; on the other hand, I've had a few fruit-sellers asking to have their photograph taken – and then ask for money. If you are particularly keen on people/portrait photography, make sure you visit Príncipe, as people there see far fewer tourists and are generally more open to having their picture taken. In general, if you have the chance to have a couple of pictures printed off (on São Tomé only in the capital and Trindade, on Príncipe only in Santo António) and give them to the person you took a picture of, this will be immensely appreciated. A photographer friend of mine even travelled with a portable printer! If you promise to send prints at a later date, try and actually do it. Take care with your equipment; digital cameras in particular are very vulnerable to humidity, so pack them into a separate plastic bag. I carried my compact Panasonic Lumix on a two-day hike where it rained most of the time and forgot, so water entered the camera body corroding the contacts. (Be careful with laptop computers as well, limiting their exposure to the humid air.) If you are shooting on print film, take more rolls of film than you think you will need; Sensia 100 is one of the best.

C MEDIA AND COMMUNICATIONS

MEDIA Communication is second nature to Santomeans, who love to talk and banter mercilessly with each other. In a society that runs on gossip and networking, most news still travels by mouth-to-mouth, *radio BB, boca-a-boca*. There is no daily newspaper, but a couple of good daily online news sites, such as www.jornal.st. Since 2005, the weekly *Correio da Semana* (out every Saturday) has been valiantly attempting to report objectively on the state of the nation, pointing out scandals from toxic landfill fumes to worsening corruption, even lambasting the national power company in the same issue that carries EMAE's regular ad with an appropriately blurred photograph of power lines. The *Correio* sells for 10,000$ at various outlets; look for signs saying *Correio da semana em venta aquí*. There are a number of low-budget weekly publications; *O Parvo* ('the Idiot', on sale at the Passante café in the capital) is considered one of the better ones. The glossy magazine *Pía* is good on current affairs. You can read most publications for free at educational institutions, such as the National Library/Historical Archive/Mediateca in the capital. French publications may be consulted at the Alliance Française, but it is impossible to get hold of English-language newspapers or magazines. The government controls most radio and television. While freedom of the press, and issues like corruption and domestic violence are more openly discussed in the media, in a small island society journalists sometimes practise self-censorship. The US radio station **Voice of America** (❟ *223400; www.voanews.com*), its twinkling red signal lights visible across São Tomé bay, relays programmes made in Washington to 25 million listeners across Africa. The VoA transmitters were moved to this strategic position in the early 1990s from Liberia, when civil war broke out. On the islands, the English programme is broadcast via MW 1530. To visit the site, contact the Director General, Ken Tripp. The national radio, **Radio Nacional**, with its headquarters on the Marginal, is an important community medium, broadcasting 24/7, news as well as information on ships due to sail, health campaigns, lost and found items, seasoned with a lot of music (FM 93.7, MW 114.7). The Portuguese state broadcaster RTP (*www.rtp.pt*; podcasts available) broadcasts by satellite a 24-hour mix of programmes produced in Lisbon with local content produced by the local delegation of RTP Africa (São Tomé: FM92.8; Príncipe: FM101.9). Santomean television company TVS broadcasts RTP content during the day, replaced in the evening by home-grown music videos and the local evening news. Radio France International, RFI 1 Afrique (*www.rfi.fr*) broadcasts 24 hours on FM102.8. In the evening, neighbours crowd around the few village TV sets to watch Brazilian soap operas. You will soon learn to recognise the signature tunes of the current favourites: *Cobras e Lagartos* ('Snakes and Lizards') and *Furia de Viver* ('Will to Live') when I was there. Although very few books are read, poets are held in high regard.

MOBILE PHONES Cellphone use is growing (about 10% of the population own one), but **network coverage** is haphazard. On São Tomé island, you can call your mother from the highest mountain on the island, but driving south you lose the network very quickly, and there is practically no coverage until you retrieve the signal again on the Ilhéu das Rolas. Mobile coverage on Príncipe is more or less limited to the capital area, Santo António. **Buying a mobile phone** (*telemóvel*) is expensive in São Tomé and Príncipe; expect to pay at least 1,500,000$ for a new handset with charger and SIM card. By asking around, you can probably get hold of a second-hand handset and sell it on or donate it before you leave. If you're not staying for longer than a couple of weeks' holiday, you won't really need a mobile. Any longer than that it does make sense to have one, especially if you are researching something and have to make arrangements with guides, etc. I've also found that Santomeans and expats alike are reluctant to make firm appointments; they will ask you to give them a ring nearer the time: 'Ring me tomorrow': *Liga para mím* (or *Dá-me um toque*) *amanhã*. **Hiring a mobile phone** is fairly expensive. The Miramar Hotel on São Tomé, for instance, used to hire out mobile phones with SIM cards for US$10 a day. If you've brought your own phone: a US phone will not be usable, due to the different bandwidth; it has to be *disbloqueado*, **unlocked**, with specialist equipment which does not work with all models. Some Portuguese mobiles don't even need to be unlocked. Ask at CST who can *disbloquear* your phone for you. CST staff can also often sell and hire out phones and give you general advice. A *Cartão Beijo* SIM card with 100,000$ credit costs 315,000$. All *telemóvel* numbers start with 9. Calls from mobile to mobile cost 2,400$ per minute. You buy a top-up card, *cartão de recarga* (100,000$ and 300,000$) from CST or several small shops or kiosks, usually with a sign up. To top up your phone credit, follow the instructions on the back: scratch to reveal your recharge code (*código*), call the *recarga* number (☎ 902021), type in the code, and press '1' to confirm. You can't leave messages on people's phones yet, and very few people use text messaging. Be prepared for haphazard service; I had extra work done on my UK handset to be able to send text messages across to Europe, but a couple of weeks later, all of a sudden, I couldn't receive any messages anymore, only send them. Keep your phone safe (see *Crime and Security*, page 69).

Contacting São Tomé and Príncipe from abroad
If you need to contact somebody urgently in São Tomé and Príncipe, don't email, – call them, even though it's expensive. Many email addresses with the national provider (cstome.net) have very limited quotas, and mails may take days to bounce. And although some 15% of Santomeans already use the internet, they don't necessarily reply; this can even happen with people working in tourism or a plantation with tourist accommodation. Calling São Tomé and Príncipe from the UK on a BT landline costs over £1 per minute. Few Santomeans use Skype yet, and at £0.75/€1.11/US$1.37 per minute offers calls to Santomean landlines for €0.30, and to mobiles for €0.40, plus a €0.05 connection fee. In practice, connections are extremely haphazard; most times, you will only hear a recorded message in incomprehensible languages and be billed for a minute's call anyway. From the UK, try www.telestunt.co.uk, where calls to STP landlines cost £0.35/min. From Portugal, PT's »Hello« cards work out best, at €0.23/min. to both landlines and mobiles, with good line quality and an option for instructions in English. They can be used from public phone boxes and PT landlines. Be careful: from some countries, for instance from Germany, calls to STP mobiles can only be connected through the operator, for an additional operator fee of over €5 – per call!

Calling within/from São Tomé and Príncipe
When you're in the country, the easiest way to call home is from the Companhia Sãotomense de

Telecommunicaçoes (CST), which is half-owned by Portugal Telecom, half by the state. There is a CST in the capital, in São João dos Angloares, and in Santo António on Príncipe. There are public phones in most larger places, and often private ones in shops; look for a sign: *Telefone aquí*. Calling the UK from São Tomé and Príncipe costs around 13,000$ per minute, the US 15,000$ per minute; there is no on/off peak period. Calling the UK from a hotel can cost €3 per minute. Public phone cards are sold to the value of 50,000$ and 150,000$, but they don't last long on calls abroad and you hear an annoying beep after each unit (*impulso*). Call the International Operator on 100, for Portugal direct 102 or 104, Directory Enquiries on 103 (*www.cstome.net*), and for a Portuguese-language weather forecast (*meteorología*) call 151.

INTERNET There are a dozen public places to access the internet, of which two are on Príncipe, and a few wireless areas. Whilst only 15% of Santomeans are internet users, some three quarters of the porn sites using Africa-based internet addresses are using the (unprotected) .st suffix. . If you're writing long emails, make sure you save/copy frequently, then you won't lose them if the power goes suddenly.

LANGUAGE COURSES

People are friendly and most will make the effort to understand what you are saying, even if you don't have a single word of Portuguese. French and Spanish will definitely help somewhat – many visitors get by in *Portunhol* – but I can't stress enough how much more fun you'll have on the islands if you make the effort to pick up some Portuguese before you go. I've found it very helpful to do some 1:1 conversation classes before I went. Contact your local university or ask at a Portuguese café/restaurant. There are Portuguese communities in most larger towns in the UK, the US (New Jersey, New England, California), Canada (Ontario, Quebec, BC) and about half a million in South Africa. The Portuguese cultural institute, Instituto Camões, has language centres all over the world, in the UK (Edinburgh, Newcastle, Oxford), the US (Newark), South Africa (Johannesburg), France (Lille, Lyon, Poitiers), Germany (Hamburg) and Hungary (Budapest); www.instituto-camoes.pt. Of the **self-taught language courses**, Manuela Cook's *Teach Yourself Portuguese* (paperback & CD, 2004) and Hugo's *Portuguese in Three Months* (2003) come recommended. Listen to the dialogues on the CDs over and over. Even if you already speak French and/or Spanish, the Portuguese nasal sounds and 'sh' sounds, together with a fast speech and joy of word play can make it difficult to understand. One tip: if you need receipts or even if you're just buying a phone card, you usually need to give your name, so it's handy if you know how to spell your name in Portuguese (*www.learningportuguese.co.uk*). As most travellers will pass through Lisbon on their way to São Tomé and Príncipe, consider combining **language classes** in the Portuguese capital with sightseeing and getting to know the country that colonised STP for 500 years – on the islands, you will recognise a lot! Whilst not the easiest to learn, Portuguese is the fifth-most spoken language in the world – by some 200 million people – so if you're planning to ever travel in Angola (gradually opening up to tourism), Brazil, Guinea-Bissau, Mozambique, the Cape Verde islands or indeed Portugal, learning the language is an excellent investment for your travels, and the cost of living in Portugal is lower than in the UK or the US. I've heard good reports from CIAL (*Av da República, 41–8° Esq, 1050-187 Lisbon;* ☏ +351 21 7940448; f +351 21 7960783; e *portuguese@cial.pt*). A good option is to take the three-hour course in the morning and a one-to-one lesson in the afternoon. CIAL also has an Algarve branch in Faro, 3hrs from Lisbon, if you want more sun with your language learning (*Rua Almeida Garrett, 44 r/c, 8000–206 Faro;* ↘ *289 807 611;* f *+351 289 803 154;* e *algarve@cial.pt; www.cial.pt*). If you are based in Lisbon, try contacting the São Tomé and Príncipe community association, Associaçao de Communidade de STP (ACOSP) (↘ *21 7648068/968274476*). Every Tuesday at 13.00, Santomeans, former colonial staff and others interested in the country meet for an informal dinner in the unpretentious **A Gamba Real** restaurant on central Lisbon's restaurant mile, Rua das Portas de Sant'Antão. To taste Santomean dishes, **A Caixinha** is a wonderful small restaurant owned by a Santomean (*Rua das Farinhas, No 7;* ↘ *21 8862990*). If you want to pick up some dance steps beforehand, visit a club featuring African music such as the Angolan club **Mussúlo** (*Rua Sousa Martins 5–D;* ↘ *21 3556872;* e *mussulo.discoteca@clix.pt*). You can probably find a club or workshop in most big cities outside Portugal by Googling for 'kizomba' or 'African music'.

If you want to combine learning Portuguese with your stay in São Tomé and Príncipe, so far this can only be done informally, although a few accommodation providers are planning to offer it in the future. In the capital, contact Sandra Beirão for **Portuguese classes** (↘ *914583*), put a note up at Café & Companhia or try and set up a **language exchange** with an English-speaking student or a member of the hotel staff; many now want to improve their English. Try contacting Fernando Nunes da Silva at the Centro de Língua Portuguesa at Instituto Camões (↘ *223876;* f *224244;* e *fnunesdasilva@instituto-camoes.pt/isp@cstome.net; www.instituto-camoes.pt*). If you want to **learn forro**, contact Claustrino through the Navetur agency in the capital. Have a few basic **greetings and small talk** ready and you'll have a lot more fun. Even if you have very few words, starting questions with *Faz favor,...* is a good idea, then you can always explain the rest with your hand and feet. *Oi!* does not have the impolite connotations that it does in English. As a sign of respect, often, the third person singular form of the verb is used. For example, if you are a woman, somebody might ask you *A Senhora é inglesa...?* (literally: 'The lady is English?'). Conversely, if you want to ask (a man) whether he knows where something is, you would ask *O Senhor sabe ónde é...?* Santomeans tend to be **polite** in their speech, and you will hear few people use swear words. Unlike in continental Portuguese, the informal form of address for young people and friends, *tu*, is less used; it suggests a degree of intimacy. Even children are often addressed as *você* (plural: *vocês* as in Brazilian Portuguese). Any woman above teenage age should be addressed as *Dona*, men as *o Senhor*.

In the street, Santomeans attract attention in different ways: the French *Monsieur/Madame* is commonly used for tourists, and *Amigo/a!* ('Friend!') to a younger person, tourist or local. Hissing is used to hail friends. If you hear this, it could be a bunch of schoolkids who want to get a wave and a smile off you, or, if you're female, a generic response to a white woman walking around on her own.

BUSINESS

Due to the *léve-léve* factor, a slow and politicised bureaucracy and problematic energy provision, you need a strong vision and unflagging stamina to do business in São Tomé and Príncipe. You need to be outgoing, too; a lot of deals are down to personal introductions. Personal contacts are very important; get hold of the 'Who's Who in São Tomé and Príncipe' book (see *Appendix 2*) and a phonebook (*lista telefónica*), learn Portuguese and be prepared to do a lot of networking. Local entrepreneurs face interest rates of nearly 30% and complain that the state does not support the private sector. Some of the sectors where the state is looking for investment are tourism, transport and alternative energies. However, due to the amount of red tape, statistically, setting up a business in São Tomé and Príncipe takes 192 days. Foreign investors face the added difficulties of government whims dictating the allocation of plots of land or the granting of permits. Dynamic Lisbon-based Swiss business consultant and plantation owner Reto Scherraus (✆ +351 917917917; www.saotome.eu/com) offers advice in English, French, German, Spanish and Portuguese (and in Russian, written only). A useful contact aiming to help clients, in particular with the **free trading zone** (zona franca) currently being established on the islands, is Licinio Santos, who speaks English, French and Spanish (✆ +351 964347052; e licinio.santos@gmail.com), or Miguel Teixeira, who runs a major tropical flower business on the island (see page 136) and speaks English (✆ 925390). Another useful platform is www.businessinstp.st. Last but not least, check www.juristep.com for the laws of the land (tax, constitutional, oil, labour, etc), most are translated into English.

BUYING PROPERTY

The few available apartments sell for around €90,000. Expect to pay €150,000 for a house near the sea within easy reach from the capital, less in zones further away, where there is more choice still. Plots of land within a radius of 5–10km from the capital sell for €20,000–40,000. Prices shoot up, of course, if it is known that a foreigner is buying. A useful contact is Reto Scherraus (see above).

Condomínio Vila Maria ✆ 223600; e vilamaria@pestana.com; www.pestana.com. Connected with the Pestana Hotel across the road, this luxury residential complex will have 51 villas with pool, for personal use, investment, or for buy-to-let. There is a games field, & residents have free access to the hotel facilities & casino. Most units should be ready now; you can see a white/orange model villa right along the Pantufo road. Ask for Manuel Fuzeta or Magdalena Gaio.

TOURISM

In 2007, some 9,000 tourists came to São Tomé and Príncipe, over half of whom were Portuguese, followed, far behind, by the French, who have a long tradition of development aid and cultural exchange with the country, and Angolans, probably most of them on family business. On my visits, I met German, Hungarian, Italian, Spanish, Dutch, British, US-American and Israeli travellers. Generalising wildly, the Portuguese were more after the beach and bar experience, the other Europeans, in particular the Germans and the few British, more after the active forest adventure. Given the ongoing vagaries of flight connections, the tourism authority's target of 25,000 visitors per year by 2010 seems wildly optimistic, but if the country can preserve its natural beauty, manage the potential oil wealth in a socially sustainable way, and bring down the prices of flights, tourism could become a more dynamic part of the economy. Things are definitely on the move: long-established hotels that were beginning to look a bit tired are getting spruced up in the face of sudden competition; new guesthouses, rural tourism ventures and restaurants are springing up all over the place, and also, gradually, in the towns outside the capital. As for Príncipe, the potential for *turismo rural* on their romantically crumbling plantations is only now being discovered. Over the next few years, quite a few beaches that today have only a couple of fishermen's shacks on them will be ringed with holiday developments, and the first cruise ships have started to include São Tomé on their tours of the west African coast. However, as long as flights and accommodation costs stay relatively expensive, São Tomé and Príncipe will never be a mass tourism or backpacker destination. At the moment, few people speak English. And never underestimate the *léve-léve* factor. Essentially, don't be discouraged if nobody, apart from established agencies and hotels, replies to your emails, and be aware that a lot of online information is out of date. If you are independent-minded and not in a mad rush, just book your first couple of nights' accommodation to get your bearings, and organise the rest once you get here. As a general rule, going to an office in person is always better than ringing, and ringing is nearly always better than emailing. The big resorts are never full, but book early for some popular favourites, such as the Avenida guesthouse in the capital, or places with very limited space, such as the Praia Jalé ecolodge in the south of São Tomé island.

CULTURAL SENSITIVITIES Santomeans in general are friendly and relaxed (and very helpful when you are driving around on the un-signposted roads or walking on plantation trails). There are no cultural no-nos in terms of clothing or topics of conversation, even though the recommended answer to the common question of what you think of the country is probably *muito lindo*, 'very nice'. While speaking some Portuguese greatly enhances your experience, travellers can have a fantastic time even just communicating with hands and feet. One thing the Santomeans really appreciate is if you are willing to try unfamiliar things: a local fruit, mix on the dance floor, show curiosity about the local language or traditional remedies. I've found the best response to children's persistent cat-calls of *Brancaaaa*! ('white woman') was to acknowledge them with a *Tudo bem?* and a smile and wave. Have a few simple phrases in Portuguese for children, such as asking their name (*como é que te chamas?*) and age (*que idade tens?*). Many will be pleased to try out their French on you, or you could teach them a couple of words in English. If you need information on anything, ask for the oldest, *o mais velho*. Brother is *irmão*, sister *irmã*, cousin *primo*. For adults, too, a few basic words of greeting go a long way, especially if you pick up a couple of local expressions; replying *léve-léve* (literally 'slowly-slowly', meaning 'I'm fine') to *Tudo bem?* always gets a positive reaction. Last but not least, if you are planning to stay longer, small island society gossip is an occupational hazard.

BEGGING There are few beggars, but considering São Tomé and Príncipe sees relatively few tourists still, children in the villages have quickly learned to shout for sweets (*Doce, doce!*), money (*Dá-me dobras/dinheiro!*) or, less often, for a lift (*Boleia!*) when you drive by. While it is less harmful to give biros (*esferográphicas*; kids will often specifically ask for them), notepads or balloons to kids than sweets, local NGOs and others will tell you that giving presents to individuals divides families and communities – tourists should not encourage begging. If nothing else, it makes life more difficult for the travellers that come after you. At Agostinho Neto plantation, for example, visitors are already routinely asked for gifts. It is true that with the tourists' money usually just going to the tour company, the people living on the plantations and serving as living attractions and photo opportunities are not getting anything out of it. It's also understandable that travellers want to give gifts and help, that presents help to establish contact, and, seen from the Santomean perspective, all white people seem to have money. If you are taking pictures of an amateur cultural performance (dance, *capoeira*), you might be asked for *patrocínio*, sponsorship – which seems fair enough. But giving indiscriminately encourages a mentality of expectation that is already, some would say, quite developed in São Tomé and Príncipe. As a responsible traveller, try to establish a relationship in a different way. Say *Não tenho* ('I don't have') or *Não temos* ('we don't have'). Some travellers like to ask what they will get back in return, *Que me vai dar?* If you want to make a donation, give it to the community leader or an NGO (see below).

GIVING SOMETHING BACK

Buy local goods and use local services wherever possible. Buying a piece of jackfruit or sugar cane, a sip of palm wine, or some wild strawberries helps the local economy and is a good way of getting into conversation. For travellers with a bit more time, voluntary work is an excellent way to engage with the country. Teaching English, for instance, would do enormous good in helping Santomeans earn some of the money that tourism is bringing in, enabling them, for example, to work as guides on the plantations and get better-paid jobs generally, a better education and a way to engage better with tourists. If you are resourceful, you might be able to set up a placement informally through a school or a plantation, funding yourself. Consider choosing Príncipe, which is way behind its larger sister island in development and should offer a very rewarding experience; contact Manuel Valentim Trovoada (☏ *919169/231013/251188;* e *matrovoada@hotmail.com*) of the regional president's office; he speaks some French. On both islands, the churches can distribute unwanted clothes to those who need them most. Over 80 NGOs are represented here, most of them Portuguese; check which humanitarian organisations in your country might have ties with São Tomé and Príncipe. In Portugal, contact details for humanitarian and friendship associations for both islands can be found on www.imigrantes.no.sapo.pt/page2comunidades1.html. The northern town of Aveiro has been twinned with Santo António, capital of Príncipe, since 1988. There are various ways to get involved; contact António Martinho (☏ *+351 969347983;* e *tozecassandra@mail.telepac.pt*) or Domingas Santos (e *do_mingas@hotmail.com*). Other towns twinned with Santo António are Odivelas and Oeiras. The French consulate in Marseille has a charitable association, and the Italian honorary consulate website (*www.saotomeprincipe-roma.it*) includes details on how to donate and appeals for concrete projects. You might in the future be able to volunteer/sponsor a marine turtle again through ECOFAC (*www.ecofac.org;* see page 101); for the moment, all activities are on hold due to lack of funding. Meanwhile, the local conservation NGO MARAPA (see page 37) can probably find you some informal volunteering work cleaning beaches or helping with turtle patrols or at the new ecomuseum.

LOCAL NGOS

ADRA Praia Emilia; ☏ 224324; e www.adra.st. Any US citizen, regardless of faith, can apply to volunteer with the Adventist Development and Relief Agency, in the areas of health, marketing, computers, English teaching, monitoring & evaluation. Apply to ADRA International (*www.adra.org*), who offer travel costs & other benefits. To apply locally, contact the dynamic head, Emanuel Costa, direct; ADRA STP can provide accommodation in its compound & an allowance. For **online volunteering** (translation, marketing, public health) see www.adra.st/en/index.php?men=4&main=2&lang=en. Donations are welcome for primary school meals, libraries, glasses, etc, & it is possible to sponsor a child as part of a successful long-term community project in the south of the island. Through ADRA Canada, you can sponsor a fruit tree (CAN$6).

Alisei/Nuova Frontera Rua Barão Água Izé; ☎ 223346/908737; e nuovaf@cstome.net/tizimari@hotmail.com. For volunteering with this Italian NGO involved in various projects in the areas of agriculture, education and sexual health, contact Tiziano & Mari Pisoni. Basic Portuguese required.

AMI Main road, São João dos Angolares; ☎ 261116; e ami@cstome.net; www.fundacao-ami.org. The Portuguese charity Asistência Medical Internacional sends international medical staff to São João dos Angolares village for humanitarian postings lasting from a few weeks to several years.

Caritas Bairro Quinta St António; ☎ 22 25 65; e caritas_stp@cstome.net. The Catholic relief organisation runs an orphanage & offers the opportunity to sponsor individual children or to volunteer. Contact Maximo Aguiar.

English Students Association of São Tomé and Príncipe With a lot of goodwill, but practically no money for teaching materials, young Santomeans give up their free time to teach English summer classes. If you want to support the project/get involved, contact Quintino Cabral (☎ 915353) or Benício, through the Liceu Nacional high school.

FONG STP Bairro Quinta St António; ☎ 226754/926589; e fong@cstome.net; www.fong-stp.org. This association of NGOs working on the islands should be able to direct you to a suitable charity/agency according to your abilities & requirements, but you will need some Portuguese. Contact Maria do Céu.

Fundação Stiftung Waldhaus Passadeira do Hospital; ☎ 221461/906469; e gianmeyer@samedan.biz. Tireless Swiss doctor Gian Meyer runs a charitable foundation (*www.saotome.ch*), which has built schools & medical facilities on the islands, as well as running a travelling clinic operating on cataracts. Volunteering is possible for trained medics with a willingness to engage in the difficult situations that working in a developing country presents, with ideally basic Portuguese.

Natcultura ☎ 222573/904492. Community/responsible tourism projects co-ordinated by Nora Rizzo at the Diogo Vaz field school (see page 127), where you can put your skills to work & live among the locals. In Europe, Natcultura is represented by the **Amis de São Tomé** in Marseille, affiliated with Mistral Voyages (see page 100). With a donation of €140/US$190, you can sponsor a section of the school for a year.

OSJ Bairro Quinta Santo António; ☎ 227511/904618; e jpvnbe@skynet.be; www.osj.fr. The Ecumenical Maltese Order can accommodate volunteers in various projects on both islands. Work with young girls at risk in Santana, older people or children in the capital or on the Diogo Vaz plantation in the north, or with a public health project on Príncipe. Divers can get involved in a new project training Santomean coastguards. Contact the project co-ordinator Christina Barbosa by phone or by email, or the head of the Embassy, Count Jean-Philippe van Nyen, by email. Both speak English, Jean-Philippe also speaks French and Spanish, plus a bit of Dutch & German.

Projecto Pagué/Missão Católica Rua de Santarém; ☎ 251067; e parsenio@iol.pt. Volunteers are welcome Jul–Sep to help with training, game, etc, activities for children, assist with development work on the plantations or social work with the disabled. Through the Sisters of the Holy Family you can also sponsor (become *padrinho/madrinha*, literally 'godparent' of) a child or old person to receive a daily meal & necessary medication. A community centre for educational & medical support is opening near Santo António airport in 2008. It's best to email in the first instance, as Padre Senio speaks good English.

Santa Casa de Misericordia Rua Juventude; ☎ 227311/2. The São Tomé branch of the oldest Portuguese charity is involved in social care & collects leftover medicines that travellers don't want to take back. You can support the charity's work by stopping for some ethical souvenir shopping at the **Ossobô** shop next door (page 111), just across from the National Museum, where you can also drop off your unwanted medicines.

StepUp Vila Dolores; ☎ 221285/915350; e ned_stepup@yahoo.com; www.stepup.st. The director of the STEP-UP NGO, US-American Ned Seligman, can find you volunteering work at his English school. You don't have to speak Portuguese to apply!

ZATONA-ADIL Av Independência; ☎ 221230/223363; f 223363; e zadil@stome.net. An umbrella organisation supporting local development initiatives. Some French spoken.

Part Two

SÃO TOMÉ

3

São Tomé: the Capital

HIGHLIGHTS

Explore the commercial and political heart of the country, see contemporary Santomean art and the collections of the National Museum, and taste your way through local specialities, from fried banana to the national dish *calulú*. Dive into the buzz of the market, sip coffee on a seafront terrace, learn how to dance *kizomba* and stock up on delicious chocolate and coffee. And, within a short drive of the city, discover atmospheric plantations, snorkelling/diving, and rainforest hikes.

BACKGROUND INFORMATION

Established around the wide sweep of Ana Chaves Bay in 1493, São Tomé became the capital of the island when the Portuguese left their first settlement Anambó, 30km further north. Some 50 years after São Tomé was granted city status in 1525 by the Portuguese king João III, the cathedral and the fort of St Sebastian were built. Today, many of the old colonial buildings, with their carved wooden wraparound balconies running around the houses, arched windows and balustrades, are falling down, while others have been restored, in pretty bright or pastel colours. With market traders pulling along a swordfish by its beak, street vendors selling cheap watches, hair bands and brushes, jackfruit sellers, music blaring from a car stereo or a shack shop, and a lot of chat and laughter, the city has a Caribbean feel to it. In the streets, yellow taxis are vying for space with buzzing motorbikes and mud-caked jeeps; the sidewalks are populated with teenagers in baseball caps, businessmen and functionaries in suits. Moneychangers chat on corners, school children in uniform mingle with older men and street vendors sporting torn and faded election T-shirts and mothers carry babies in a sling on their back. Stray dogs rummage in rubbish on dusty streets, black kites divebomb the harbour for fish, while the citizens negotiate the broken pavements on the broad avenues leading towards the odd imposing architectural relic of 1950s Salazarist aesthetics, garden villas and small white stone residences with red tiles. The sea spray crashes on to the wide boulevard of the Marginal running around the bay, past sandy inlets strewn with black rocks. A short walk out the other side of the city towards the popular Riboque neighbourhood reveals traditional wooden houses on stilts, humble shacks with zinc roofs propping each other up, but in between delicately carved wooden roofs reminiscent of Swiss chalets.

GETTING THERE AND AWAY

The airport is a quarter of an hour's drive out of town. There is no public transport link. If you have booked with an agency, somebody will meet you there; this is of course the easiest option if you're arriving on your own. On the other hand, there is no problem getting a shared taxi for about 20,000$ – or offer €3, as you probably won't have any dobras yet and your luggage will be taking a whole seat. A private run will cost about €10 as you will have to pay for all the seats. Even if your phone should work here, there is no taxi company that you can ring, but a few taxis will always be waiting outside the terminal building, waiting to fill up with passengers. None of the taxis is on a meter.

GETTING AROUND

One of the first things that strike you about the city is the abundance of **taxis** – all yellow, New-York-style, and mostly Toyota models of varying ages and sizes. You can get a ride to almost anywhere on the island from the central **market square** (*praça de taxis*). You can also easily flag them down from the road. Very few taxi drivers speak English, though some will have French. There are no taxi companies, but some of the taxis on the square have signs up on the roof with their destination often nearby suburbs. These will wait till they're full before they leave and cannot be hired for an individual ride. The locals use them to transport chickens, fish, petrol, car parts, electrical goods, pots and pans. I once saw a tied-up live goat being heaved into the boot of a cab, bleating. If you're not in a hurry and if you want to travel as the locals do, this is a very cheap way to get around. Sample fares are: ST–Neves 15,000$, ST–São João dos Angolares 15,000$, ST–Porto Alegre 25,000$. As a white person, especially a woman, you will usually be given the front seat. Try and have the correct change. At the end of a journey, you can always ask the driver to take you to a specific location and pay a bit more. If you choose to hire a taxi for yourself, ie: to go *em frete* (in French: *une course*), you will pay a lot more, effectively as much as the driver could have earned if all the seats were taken (and a lot of people can fit into these taxis) – plus the return journey, even if you're only going one way. A great new initiative is the **motorbike taxi** service, offering cheap and fast rides to anywhere on the island, even to the places that taxi drivers might not consider because of the state of the road. However, because of the dust on the roads and the discomfort of a long ride, they're best for short runs in the city. Bear in mind also that no helmets are available, and that there have been accidents; ask to go *devagar*, slow. A lift to the new Pestana Hotel will cost around 20,000$, to the airport 35,000$. Motorbike taxis can be found at the western side of the taxi square, at the bottom end of Rua 3 de Fevereiro. If you speak Portuguese, you can also try ringing Charles (↘ *917174*) or Lenim (↘ *926348*) and organise a pick-up. Another bunch of *mototaxistas* work from the Feira do Ponto market, right next to Residencial Baia.

CAR HIRE Car hire is expensive. Expect to pay at the very least €40 per day, though the average is more like €50–60. Fuel costs extra, and there is usually a 5% consumer tax to pay on top of the total. Normally, there is no insurance available, so make sure your travel insurance covers you for third-party damage. By and large, you get what you pay for. Make sure you have dobras to pay for the fuel, to avoid detours. **Navetur** and **Mistral** (see *Local Travel Agencies*, page 100) hire cars; Navetur can sometimes do you a deal. A group of young men rent out bikes (€5), motorbikes of different sizes (€20–25) and cars (€50) from the square next to the Boa Conceição church on Feira do Ponto market; contact Klaus (↘ *913234*). Two other hire car options to try are:

🚗 **Turiart** Av 12 Julho; ↘ 225339/912280/905153; f 223748; e turentacar@cstome.net or alexpsantos@hotmail.com. I've not tried them, but Turiart, next to Mistral Voyages, seem to be the only company offering insurance, with a range of cars from a Suzuki Jimny to a 10-seater Toyota Prado. A guide/driver costs an extra €10/day. Daily rates, decreasing for rentals of 5–10 days & over 10 days, start from €60. Turiart's manager, Alex dos Santos, is the head receptionist of the new Pestana Hotel &

SÃO TOMÉ

N

Bradt

Atlantic Ocean

Ana Chaves Bay

0 ——— 500m
0 ——— 500yds

Guadalupe ↗ | Hospital, Diving Club, Airport, Omali Lodge

Cemetery

São Pedro chapel
Blue container
Praia Brazil

Cocoa Residence
Discoteca Kizomba

Claudio Corallo chocolate
Turiart

Mistral Voyages

Boa Conceição
Mototaxis

Police station
Hotel Residencial Baía

Riboque

Boa Morte ↙

AVENIDA GIOVANY
Residencial Giovany

TAAG Angolan Airlines

New market

Open-air market

Recording booth
Bakery

Photo Ramos Costa

Pastelaria Cajú

Navetur Apartment

RUA 3 FEVEREIRO

Portuguese Quarter

↙ Madalena, Trindade
Madre de Deus

Port

Bom Despacho
MARAPA
Red Cross

Ossobô EcoSocial ethical souvenirs
ECOFAC
Immigration office
Alliance Française
Le Minigolf

Pié-Museu
Tété (fish)
UNEAS

Fort São Sebastião
National Museum

(Self-catering) apartments

Casa Amarela
Radio Nacional

Watersports Club Nautico (currently not open)

School

Portuguese
Café Passante
Hotel Miramar

Boutique Deli

PNUD/ United Nations

Stadium

Quinta Santo Antonio ↓

MJ's B&B, Parliament,
US diplomatic mission, Santana,
Pantufo, The South

Parque Popular
Kizumba
National Library

AVENIDA 12 JULHO
INDEPENDÊNCIA
National Archive

Historical Archive

Agôsto Neto
Mediateca
Hotel
AVENIDA DE
Copyshop
Residencial Avenida

Casa Cinema

AVENIDA KWAME NKRUMAH
Angolan
Discoteca/
Tropicana Cyberbar

Loja Kitoli souvenirs/ bamboo furniture

Praça da Independência
Old Pier
Tourist information
see page 103

TAP Air Portugal
Presidential Palace
Cathedral
CST phone exchange
Policlinic

UK Honorary Consulate
Navetur Tourism

Casa da Cultura,
Salão de chá Jasmin
Teia d'@rte
BISTP

AVENIDA ÁGUA GRANDE
Sum Secreto
Hair salon
Sombra do Caroceiro
Sombra da Coleira

Hotel Phénicia & Le Pagué
Pensão Carvalho & Café

Toka-Cara
O Farol
Ulisei/Qua Tela
Vila Saúde
Casa Vermelha

Evangelical

↓ Clubs Orbita, Dolores,
Santana, The South

↙ Madalena, Trindade,
Madre de Deus

↙ Madalena, Trindade

São Tomé: the Capital GETTING AROUND

3

speaks good English. Other English-speaking staff: Nuno (☎ 905155) and Godinha (☎ 907660).

🚗 **Elisio Costa** c/o Foto Ramos Costa; Rua 3 Fevereiro; ☎ 224233/903317; f 224233. The friendly owner of the photography store can arrange jeep hire (€45/day) with a free SIM card for your mobile phone thrown in. You can also ask him about accommodation; he is planning to set up a Residencial near the Pestana Hotel.

Filling up The most reliable and central **petrol station** in town is the one with the BP sign on Praça de Amizade e Solidaridade entre los Povos; it stays open till midnight and there are usually money changers around to convert your euros/dollars – as well as youngsters taking advantage of stationary motorists to push seed collars and bracelets.

BIKE HIRE The Navetur agency (see below) rents out bikes for €5 a day, as do the guys next to the Boa Conceição church and the Cycling Federation (see page 84) – double the price, but probably a better bike, plus lots of advice.

TOURIST INFORMATION

📋 **Tourist Information** Av 12 Julho, CP 40; ☎ 226162/3; f 221542; e turismo@turismo-stp.org; www.turismo-stp.org; ⏰: 08.00–17.00 Mon–Fri, 00.80–12.00 Sat. The *posto de turismo* on the Marginal sells maps, a handful of books & postcards, & a wide selection of crafts. At the moment they can only give general advice, not book hotel rooms. Also, the phone service is not always that helpful or friendly, & they don't really speak English. As the tourism authority is only gradually waking up to tourists' needs, travel agencies are a better bet.

LOCAL TRAVEL AGENCIES

Gold Tours & Services Rua da Palma Carlos, CP 501; ☎ 221136/903296; f 225178; e info@goldtours.st; www.goldtours.st. New agency with website in Portuguese and English. Can book TAAG and STP Airways flights, arrange excursions and car hire with insurance (from €65).

Mistral Voyages Av Yon Gato, CP 297; ☎ 221246/223344; hotline ☎ 904050; f 222142; e mvoyages@cstome.net/vilanova@cstome.net; www.mistralvoyages.com. Situated next to the Feira do Ponte market, Mistral is the best point of contact for French speakers. The smaller sister of the Libreville & Marseille operations can sell & confirm air tickets for Air Service, TAP, TAAG, SCD Aviation, etc, & arrange car hire (up to a 14-seater minibus with driver). Excursions include a half-day city tour, trips to Bombaim, to the south, including a crossing to Rolas, early-morning sport fishing of marlin, sailfish, tuna & barracuda, boat trips to the beaches of the north, including Ilhéu das Cabras & Lagoa Azul, & visits to Príncipe. 'A la carte' excursions can be organized too. It's best to send your enquiries to both email addresses, & phone if you haven't heard back. The office manager's name is Carlos Vilanova. A good guide for English-speakers is Argentino Espirito Santo; he also has excellent French.

Navetur-Equatour Rua Viriato da Cruz, CP 277; ☎ 222122/910395; logistics co-ordinator Guitola Dória, ☎ 910395; f 221748; e navequatur@cstome.net/navetur@cstome.net; www.navetur-equatour.st; ⏰: 09.00–12.30 & 15.00–17.30 Mon, 08.00–12.30 & 15.00–17.30 Tue–Thu, 08.00–12.30 & 15.00–17.00 Fri, 08.00–12.00 Sat. Located in a lovely yellow-blue colonial building & run by Santomean Luís Manuel Beirão & Bibi Braunstein, Navetur is the most dynamic travel agency in town, & their internet site is the most helpful for tourists on the web before travelling. For English speakers, the best person to talk to is Bibi, who speaks English, Portuguese, French & Danish & is passionate about the islands. Navetur's friendly staff can confirm air tickets for TAP, TAAG, Air Service, SCD Aviation & Aero Contractors to Lisbon, Libreville, Príncipe, Accra, Luanda, Port Gentil, Douala, & Lagos, & book tickets for SCD Aviation flights to Príncipe & Air Service flights to Gabon. You can book stays at the plantations of São João, Bombaim & Monteforte (and possibly Ponta Figo), as well as the Praia Jalé ecolodge, trekking, sailing trips, diving, sightseeing, & trips to Rolas Island. If you want to go to an out-of-the-way plantation or beach, they will try everything they can to make it possible. For a 2-week holiday for a couple in Jan, staying at a variety of hotels & plantations on both islands, with a three-day trek including the Pico de São Tomé & a 3-day car hire with guide, count around €2,150 excluding flights. The guides are always knowledgeable & the picnics thoughtfully put together, with lots of local produce to try. The agency is also a good contact for scientists planning a research trip, and offers research and translation facilities.

Equador Viajens & Turismo Rua Independência/Rua 3 Fevereiro, PO Box 421; ☎ 222045/905400; f 222375; equador@cstome.net/ americorolas@cstome.net. Affable English-speaking manager Americo Cabral offers car hire, shipping services (logistical assistance to cruisers & cargo boats), 4-night/7-night packages & can change your money for you at a good rate. Most interestingly, he is also currently setting up *turismo de habitação*, stays at the smaller plantations on both islands that aren't yet on the tourist circuit. At the time of writing, it was already possible to stay at Colonia Açoreana on the east coast of São Tomé island &

Sundy on Príncipe. Others, inc Roça Java in the interior of São Tomé island & Roça Abade on Príncipe to follow.

Flogátours Budo-Budo, 45A, CP 984; ☎ 224394/909199; e flogatours@cstome.net. Flogá means 'play' in creole, & the charismatic Norberto Vidal offers turtle-watching, sport fishing – from catching flying fish the traditional way, on grass mats spread out on the water, to deep-sea fishing using live bait for sailfish & marlin – to camping expeditions, snorkelling trips to the Ilhéu das Cabras & dolphin- & whale-watching trips. One of the best birders on the island, Norberto speaks fluent French. His birding trips in small groups of up to 6 people run primarily Jan–Mar, when conditions combine dry weather & conspicuous mating plumage, but can be arranged at any time of the year. Expect to see all the endemics on a 1-week expedition up the Xufe-Xufe river in the southwest; São Miguel has a particularly propicious micro-climate. Amazingly, Norberto claims a 100% success rate with the elusive São Tomé grosbeak (see page 33). Best phone Norberto on his mobile (or email) as he is often away.

LOCAL CONSERVATION AGENCIES

ECOFAC Rua Juventude; ☎ 223284; e bureau_ozono@cstome.net/gefamb@cstome.net/ ecofac@cstome.net; www.ecofac.org. ⊕: 07.30–12.00 & 14.00–17.00 Mon–Fri. Looking after the Obô National Park & the Botanical Garden at Bom Sucesso, ECOFAC is housed in the INAE building next to Ossobô EcoSocial, at the back of the car park; look for stickers. Contact: Salvador Sousa Pontes or Doutor Bonfim.
MARAPA Bom Despacho; ☎ 222792; www.marapa.org. Friendly NGO protecting artisanal fishing & turtles. Contact them for information on the ecomuseum at Morro Peixe turtle beach, & on turtle watching/patrols. There are usually some French

volunteers, but the only English-speaking member of staff I know is Étienne.
Montepico e montepico@yahoo.com.br; www.montepico.blogspot.com. The guides' association has 25 members and is a good point of contact. Its dynamic president, Luis Mario Almeida (☎ 911670; e lumanovamoca@hotmail.com), speaks good French. However, there is no office as such, and Luis Mario can be difficult to get hold of; try his workplace: the Gabinete de Desporte sports ministry halfway up Rua 3 Fevereiro on the right-hand side. It's best to send enquiries to both email addresses. Montepico's General Secretary is botanist Faustino Oliveira (☎ 905279/225647); he speaks French and Italian.

🏠 WHERE TO STAY

HOTELS In São Tomé town, accommodation ranges from US$15 hovel-like establishments to US$200-a-night international-standard hotels, with the few B&Bs probably the best value for money. Most of the cheap places have ancient mattresses that dip in the middle. If you are basing yourself in one of these places for a longer period of time, but still want a good night's sleep, it might be worth buying a mattress, *colchão* (around 600,000$) from the Feira do Ponto market, next to Boa Conceiçao church, and donating or selling it again before you leave. Rate-wise, single travellers get heavily penalised; often, there is only a very small difference in price. There is no formal set-up for **staying with local families** yet, but guides like Luis Mario Almeida (✆ *911670*, e *lumanovamoca@hotmail.com*) may be able to put you in touch with Santomean families and/or a plantation. Ask around and explain you want to experience how 'normal' Santomeans live, *conhecer a vida do dia em dia dos Santomenses*; as a guideline, a fair rate to offer for B&B could be €15.

Luxury (\$\$\$\$)

⌂ **Miramar (by Pestana)** (54 rooms, 5 suites, 6 junior suites) Av Marginal 12 de Julho, CP 69; ✆ 222778/222511/221346; f 221087; e hmiramar@cstome.net; www.miramar.st. For years, most business visitors, diplomatic representatives & development consultants fetched up in the oldest 4-star hotel on the island, built in 1986 & renovated in 1996. In June 2008, it was scheduled to close for renovations, as the new owner, the Pestana group, were opening a new five-star hotel nearby; the following refers to the 'old' Miramar. The hotel is equipped to an international standard, with all modern amenities, & very friendly staff with excellent English. About half of the rooms have a sea view. The airy **Café Passante** is one of the best features of a hotel that's still a bit rustic-dark in decor. The 'Barracuda Bar' (🕐 08.00–midnight) is good for a nightcap, but has a slightly fusty ambience; most people seem to prefer to sit in the comfortable lobby, a popular meeting place for the local elite & expats to check their emails in this wireless hotspot. **'The Baron'** restaurant, with view of the garden where the sumptuous breakfast is taken, offers international cuisine. Some visitors are just staying one night, before flying home; on those days, b/fast is served very early. The friendly receptionists can organise most things for you; head receptionist is Alex dos Santos (✆ *905153*). Guided tours, trips to Príncipe, etc, are arranged through the Mistral agency. Business facilities include a conference room. If you don't have your own transport, the hotel can call you an (expensive) taxi into town; walking only takes you 15–20 mins. The shops attached to the hotel sell spangly party dresses, linens for men & women & swimwear. Reception has sand postcards & CDs by local *kizomba* artists (€10) for sale. The 600m² pool with waterfall is set in a 10,000m² tropical garden, excellent for birdwatching. There is no swimming beach nearby.

⌂ **Omali Lodge Luxury Hotel** (formerly **Marlin Beach**) (30 rooms) Praia Lagarto, CP 463; ✆ 222350; f 221814; e reservations@africas-eden.com and omalilodge@africas-eden.com; www.africas-eden.com. On the airport road in front of Praia Lagarto, this resort-style complex, set in a tropical garden with pool, is a favourite with South African guests & has a friendly, service-oriented atmosphere where English is spoken as a matter of course. All suites are on the ground & 1st floor and have AC, en-suite bathrooms with bath &/or shower, phone, satellite TV, fridge – &, probably unique in STP, tea- & coffee-making facilities. Prices range from €100 to €350. There is a business centre and a conference centre. The hotel is being refurbished as a boutique hotel, with a more up-to-date 'modern Africa' look. Previously owned by German-born South African businessman Chris Hellinger, the hotel was bought in 2007 by Dutch engineer & conservationist Rombout Swanborn, who owns the ecotourism venture Africa's Eden in Gabon & is aiming to implement the Africa's Eden concept – tourism pays for conservation – at the hotel. Whilst fairly close to town & separated from the hotel by the busy airport road, the beach is pleasant enough & never gets crowded, apart from Sun, when the locals come out for a swim, fortified by fresh coconuts for sale on the beach. The hotel restaurant has a famous b/fast (6.30–10.00) & good international cuisine for lunch (12.00–15.00) & dinner (19.00–22.00), with attentive service. The 'Léve-léve' bar has a snack menu (burgers, pizzas, etc) & stays open till 01.00. Prices have now switched from US$ to €, although you can pay in US$ & dobras at the day exchange rate; credit card payments are accepted from €50 onwards. Omali Lodge has a pool table, plus the only tennis court on the island, free to use for guests & tennis club members (US$20/month, inc pool use); for lessons, contact Nacho (✆ *904455*). Flood-lit, it is open to non-residents too; borrow a racket & balls for a few euros. A **shop** connected with the Santa Casa charity sells Santomean produce. Birdwatchers can scan the garden for weavers, the São Tomé thrush, harlequin quails, white-winged widowbirds & common waxbills. Omali Lodge's sister operation is the Bom Bom Island resort on Príncipe (see page 187). A taxi into town & back should cost about 70,000$. Brand new in 2008: Avis car hire is now available from the hotel ✆ 226992/927482.

⌂ **Pestana São Tomé** (105 rooms) Vila Maria; ✆ 223600; e manuel.fuzeta@pestana.com;

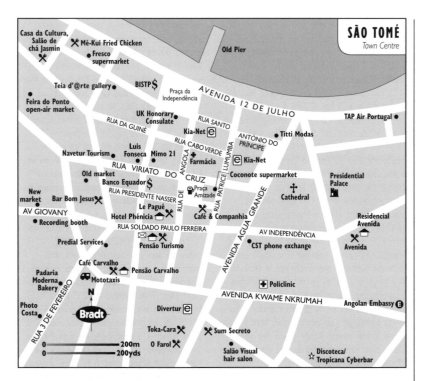

Casa da Cultura, Salão de chá Jasmin ✗
✗ Mé-Kui Fried Chicken
• Fresco supermarket

Old Pier

Teia d'@rte gallery •
BISTP $
Praça da Independência
AVENIDA 12 DE JULHO
TAP Air Portugal •

• Feira do Ponto open-air market
RUA DA GUINÉ
UK Honorary Consulate •
RUA SANTO
Kia-Net e
ANTÓNIO DO PRÍNCIPE
• Titti Modas

Navetur Tourism •
Luis Fonseca • Mimo 21 •
RUA CABO VERDE
Farmácia ✚
e Kia-Net

RUA VIRIATO DO
• Old market
RUA DE ANGOLA
CRUZ
Coconote supermarket
Presidential Palace ⌂

New market •
Bar Bom Jesus ✗
Banco Equador $
RUA PRESIDENTE NASSER
Praça ✝ Amizade
RUA PATRICE LUMUMBA
Cathedral ✝

AV GIOVANY
Le Pagué ✗
Hotel Phénicia ⌂ ✗
Café & Companhia ✗
RUA AGUA GRANDE
Residencial Avenida ⌂

• Recording booth
RUA SOLDADO PAULO FERREIRA
✗ Avenida

• Predial Services
✉ ⌂ ✗
Pensão Turismo
AV INDEPENDÊNCIA
✗ CST phone exchange

Café Carvalho
✗ ⌂ Pensão Carvalho

Padaria Moderna Bakery •
🏍 Mototaxis
N

Photo Costa •
RUA 3 DE FEVEREIRO
Bradt
Divertur e
AVENIDA KWAME NKRUMAH
✚ Policlinic
Angolan Embassy e

0 ——— 200m
0 ——— 200yds
Toka-Cara ✗
O Farol ✗
✗ Sum Secreto
Salão Visual hair salon
☆ Discoteca/ Tropicana Cyberbar

---

www.pestana.com. Due to open in 2008, this 5-star resort hotel on the spit of land across from the Parliament is built around the foundations of the historic São Jerónimo fort established by the Dutch during their occupation in the mid-15th century. A sign of confidence in São Tomé tourism, the latest in the Pestana group of hotels features a jetty for pleasure boats, an outdoor salt-water pool, a private beach, a diving centre, a disco & casino in an octagonal building overlooking the sea, as well as a health club. Business facilities will include a conference room for 200 people, with natural lighting & a panoramic sea view. Summer packages available with Euroatlantic Airways (www.terraafrica.pt).

Mid-range ($$$)

⌂ **Hotel Agôsto Neto** (16 rooms) off Av da Independência; ☎ 223584/226728; e netagosto@cstome.net. Opened in 2007, this small & friendly central hotel has rooms with AC, TV, radio/telephone, minibar, plus a tea kitchen. B/fast is included, with the option of local coffee. Wireless throughout, plus one terminal for guests. To discuss long-stay discounts, speak to the manager.

⌂ **Hotel Residencial Baía** (13 rooms) Av da Conceição; ☎ 242100/221155; f 222921, e hotelrbaia@cstome.net. This is a central base, if a bit noisy due to its position right on the busy Feira do Ponto market, & might struggle with all the competition opening up in the city. The comfortable rooms have AC & a fridge, but my phone line was pretty dodgy. The staff is very friendly. The upstairs restaurant, like the downstairs fast-food bar, never seems to be busy, but you can pre-order *calulú* & the Capeverdian speciality *cachupa* (min 4 people). There are various fish dishes, steaks, chicken, as well as tomato rice & vegetable soup for vegetarians; try the chilled tamarind juice. Due to slow staff, b/fast can take a good while; make sure your order is taken properly, otherwise you might have to ask individually for juice, sugar, etc. Currently under change of management.

⌂ **La Provence** (12 bungalows) Praia Nazaré, CP 3; ☎ 221038/909205; f 222335; e laprovence@cstome.net; www.a-deux.com/Laprovence.htm. Pleasant base 5km out of town on the airport road (ie: less suitable if you haven't got your own transport), with a swimming beach just across the road. 8

comfortable bungalows with a living room area, AC & satellite TV (€90 B&B for two, sharing, €120 HB, €150 FB), two apartment-studio sleeping 4 (€130) & 2 studio bungalows sleeping 2, with a kitchen & space for a couple of additional beds €25 each. B/fast is taken in the large & beautifully tended garden with lots of plant & bird life, & a lovely freshwater pool. Lunches & evening meals are served in the restaurant. There is a bar with a big TV screen, serving snacks. Other eating options nearby are Dona Hortência in Campo de Milho, or, in the other direction, the Omali Lodge Hotel or the Filomar (see *Where to eat*). For a quick daytime drink, you're close to the Club Maxel pier. Sat evening barbecue with live *musica nacional* (€12.50) & Sun morning brunch is served on the terrace. La Provence is one of the few places to accept credit cards; it belonged to a French couple for many years until they finally sold in 2007. There is a phone at reception (in the restaurant), where local chocolate & other souvenirs are for sale; you can access the internet in the office & send a fax. If you haven't got your own transport, keep a couple of taxi numbers handy or just stop one of the frequent yellow taxis working the airport road.

🏠 **Residencial Avenida** (17 rooms) Av Independência; ☎ 222368; f 221333; e ravenida@cstome.net. Owned by Santomeans, this small light-blue hotel right opposite the Presidential Palace was the first guesthouse on the island. With its nicely tended garden & good standard of

accommodation, the Avenida remains deservedly popular with a good mix of tourists, politicians & business travellers & makes you feel very welcome. Book as early as you can. All rooms are on the ground floor, with AC & private bathroom, hot water, TV & room service. Prices range from a sgl for €60 and dbl for €85 (B&B) to a trpl suite for up to €155 FB. The personal & friendly service extends to the bar. At reception you can buy postcards & maps, & use the internet terminal; it's free for residents, but bring a jumper, the AC is always on full. The bar & restaurant already have wireless access, & *sem fios* coverage should soon extend to the rooms. For last-minute crafts souvenirs, there is a stall up most days next to the bar.

🏠 **Hotel Phenicia** (14 rooms) Rua Angola, CP 836; ☎ 224203/4/5, fax 224206; e phenicia@ cstome.net; www.phenicia.st. Very central, with comfortable, spacious & light dbl rooms, of which 4 have twin beds, AC & satellite TV. The only criticism: the 2 rooms I tried smelled a bit of smoke (probably only a non-smoker would notice), & if the power fails, the generator can be quite noisy if you're staying in a room giving out onto the back. There is wireless internet access in the rooms & the restaurant/bar. B/fast, served in Le Pagué restaurant, costs €5 per person & is served between 06.30 & 10.30. HB is €15, FB €25. Staff are very friendly & helpful, less so in the restaurant/bar (see page 104), which is open 07.00–23.00. Reception should have a leaflet with a handy map of the city.

Budget (⑤⑤)

🏠 **Cocoa Residence** (9 rooms) 33b Rua Padre Martinho Pinto da Rocha; ☎ 915588. New guesthouse (due to open in 2008), good for sgl travellers, as there are 6 sgl rooms (€40), plus 2 dbls & 1 suite with internet terminal. Opposite the popular Kizomba club, so great to crash after a night out, but maybe not so great for light sleepers. Take advantage of the good car-hire rates.

🏠 **Pensão Turismo** (7 rooms) Rua Soldado Paulo Ferreira; ☎ 222340. Very central location; 5 rooms share 2 bathrooms. There are 2 additional rooms in a different building at the corner of Rua Santo António do Príncipe, opposite the Presidential Palace – which is where I stayed, very comfortably. The spacious comfortable room had nice little touches. The only problem was a smell of plumbing; if you're

staying for a few days, buy some air-freshener from the supermarket. B/fast, taken in the restaurant with its beautiful stained-glass windows, doesn't start before 08.15. Overall, pretty good value for money.

🏠 **Residencial Magni-Bi** (10 rooms, 3 suites) Bairro Quinta Santo António; ☎ 227562/920887; e cameix2000@yahoo.fr . New guesthouse, right next to the Caritas building. All rooms ensuite; prices (sgl $35/dbl $50, large suite $75) inc b/fast.

🏠 **Residencial Pereira & Helena** (8 rooms) Bairro Quinta Santo António; ☎ 914753. New guesthouse, en-suite rooms (US$35/400,000$). Airport transfer and car hire can be arranged. The same owner, French-speaking Emile Pereira, also has a place with 2 rooms in the Campo de Milho residential neighbourhood, closer to the airport and another in Trindade town (page 137).

Shoestring (⑤)

🏠 **Pensão Carvalho** (9 rooms) Rua Moçambique; ☎ 222955/911856; ⏰ 07.00–22.00 *daily*. One of

the best shoestring options in the city centre. Rooms Nos 1–3 are the bigger ones, No 4 has a good mattress, No 5 smelled a bit mouldy, Nos 6 & 7 are the quietest. The biggest corner room, No 3, costs a bit more, but I'm not sure it's worth it. There is a veranda at the back, but you might have to ask for a chair/table. 3 bathrooms, with 2 cold-water showers. There is no generator, but power cuts don't affect the water supply. Get your own b/fast in the pleasant shaded café downstairs, separated from the busy Av Nkwame Nkrumah by a bamboo wall, & also selling ice creams, beers, juices, etc.

🏠 **Residencial Costa Mar** (6 rooms) S. Gabriel; ✆ 221113. These light-blue beach cottages (plus 2 more rooms in another seafront building) next to the popular Pirata restaurant/club on the Pantufo

road seem a good proposition. The rooms have either AC or a ventilator, & a shower without curtain. Unfortunately, there is a musty smell in the dark dining room, & the place can't shake off rumours of prostitution. B/fast (must be pre-booked) is €5, lunch & dinner can be arranged, but you're probably better off next door at Pirata. *Bar* ⏰ *08.00–23.00.*

🏠 **Residencial Giovany** (18 rooms) Rua Giovany; ✆ 223929/931617. Central location up from the market, but not that clean, & my mattress was pretty ancient; if you can, have a look at the rooms before choosing. On the plus side: hot water, a nice balcony & friendly staff. B/fast can be arranged.

APARTMENTS Living in an apartment gives you great independence, and being able to cook means you don't have to rely on restaurants and can also try cooking some Santomean dishes yourself. The drawback of living like the locals is that if the power or water fails in your district, you will have the same problems. Apartment rentals start at around €250/month. Ask around or put a notice up at Café & Companhia; somebody might know somebody who is at the end of a contract and leaving their apartment.

🏠 **Navetur Apartment** (3 rooms) Rua 3 de Fevereiro; ✆ 222122; f 221748; e navequatur@cstome.net/ navetur@cstome.net. Bookable through the Navetur agency, a clean double room with AC, on the 1st floor of a house in a popular neighbourhood, a few mins' walk from the market square, costs €25 per night (€20 sgl occupancy), less on a weekly/monthly basis. Outside, ladies sell fruit & veg in the mornings (usually jackfruit too), & corn-on-the-cob & *safú* fruit by candlelight in the evenings. You can survey proceedings from the balcony, with a beer. The house is next to the popular local shop/bar Pedra-Pedra so it can get a bit noisy at night, whilst in the daytime the odd toddler likes to take a nap in

the doorway. A leaflet in the cupboard explains what to do to the taps if there is a power cut, which also disables the electric hob. The meticulous & radiant *empregada*, Nini, comes in every morning Mon–Sat to wash up your kitchen stuff, tidy & fetch water if necessary. She can wash & iron your clothes for 5,000$ per item.

🏠 **Dona Delfina** (2 apts) Rua Caixa; ✆ 904689. Clean apartments in a residential area, 10min walk to the centre: 1 with kitchen, but without natural light (€30), 1 without kitchen, but with natural light €25). The cost for dbl occupancy is only €5 more, so good value for couples. Next to Ralux restaurant (currently closed, ✆ 918151/910040).

B&B

🏠 **Casa Amarela** (2 rooms; 1 overflow sgl) Av 12 Julho; ✆ 222573/904492; e ciacnat@cstome.net; www.casaamarelacasavermelha.blogspot.com. The 'yellow house', a colonial villa next to the National Radio building, comes thoroughly recommended. €40 sgl/€50 dbl gets you a tastefully furnished room with ventilator & a beautifully presented b/fast, inc various breads, homemade papaya jam, fresh fruit, & freshly squeezed pineapple juice. There is an equipped kitchen for self-catering & a living room. Laundry is included. The whole house can be rented for €65, €80 in Aug & during the Xmas & Easter hols. The lovely garden with palm trees & orchids is overlooked by a porch with

deckchairs, where you can sit & listen to the waves. The beach across the road is not really a swimming beach, but sometimes people set up a volleyball net there, & it's on the expats' running/powerwalking circuit. Casa Amarela is a favourite with visitors who have an interest in culture & sustainable tourism; the Argentinian owner, architect Nora Rizzo, knows the island intimately & runs excellent **community tourism** projects. You can stay for half the price at either of the 2 houses (see Casa Vermelha, below) if you have a skill you can share with the young people attending Nora's field school in the north of the island, about an hour's drive away. $$

🏠 **Casa Vermelha** (2 rooms) Barão d'Água Izé; 📞 222573 904492; e ciacnat@cstome.net; www.ciac/casavermelha. Stylish & comfortable colonial house in the centre of town, with a veranda & kitchen. At €60 B&B for 4, the 'red house' is excellent value for a family or small group. You can also just rent 1 room: €30 sgl. $$

🏠 **MJ's** (2 rooms) Av 12 Julho; 📞 905450/226622; e mjpombo@hotmail.com. The dynamic owner of Café & Companhia offers relaxing accommodation at her house a few doors down from the National Assembly; excellent value. I room in the main house, I in the annexe apt. Great b/fasts, served by the friendly *empregada*: coffee, muesli/granola with fresh fruit, fresh bread, etc. Handy for the National Museum & Pirata restaurant/club; the city centre is a 20min walk away. Guests have free access to the internet laptop at Café & Companhia. A month's stay will cost around €250. $$

✗ WHERE TO EAT

RESTAURANTS

✗ **Al-Gharb** Praia Nazaré; 📞 907830; ⏰ 11.30–15.00 & 18.30–23.00 daily. The 'Algarve' used to be the most expensive restaurant in town, but with its move to the La Provence hotel, prices seem to have come down a bit. This is a good place to splash out on good ol' Portuguese favourites such as *bacalau com grão*, codfish with chickpeas, tasty meat & local fish (barracuda, Atlantic sailfish) & seafood. Salads & interesting side dishes make this a good choice for vegetarians too. Every Sat barbecue with live music (€12.50), & Sun morning brunch (same price). Take-away available (eg: *menu económico*: bread, soap, dish of the day, fruit from€10), count €4 for delivery within the city. $$$$

✗ **Avenida** Av Independência; 📞 222368; ⏰ 08.00–22.00 daily. Unlike the popular bar, I've never seen this restaurant exactly buzzing; with its fairly standard fare for the money, it's more of a default option for hotel guests. The fish dishes are good though, & the place is airy, with linen table cloths, murals – & a TV. $$$$

✗ **O Bigodes** Praia Francesa; 📞 223944. This expensive restaurant with a spectacular setting on a platform sticking right out into the ocean, on the road towards the airport, is currently closed, but might be open again when you visit, to cater for the clients of the pousada (hotel) next door, currently being built by Senhor Lima (📞 904937). 40 rooms are planned, 20 sgl, 20 dbl. $$$$

✗ **O Farol** Rua Patrice Lumumba; ⏰ 09.00–23.00 daily. The 'lighthouse' is a popular meeting place on the square across from the Instituto Camões, with an extensive Portuguese/international menu (good *calulú*) & attentive service, some in English. The open-air screen in the outside seating area shows various programmes & football matches. If it's closed when you visit, don't be surprised; there have been frequent changes of management over the years. The toilet is outside, around the corner; you have to ask for the key (*a chave para a casa de banho*). $$$$

✗ **O Pirata** Estrada de Pantufo; 📞 227821; ⏰ 09.00–24.00 daily. Great location on an airy wooden porch full of artworks & right on a palm-fringed beach just past the Parliament, with a picturesque shipwreck rusting away in the middle distance. The new management has brought in a new menu, with a good selection for vegetarians & some nice touches using local ingredients (*sap-sap* fruit mousse), & service is attentive; some of the waiters speak English. There is art everywhere, inc changing exhibitions by local artists. On days when there is a party on, *festa*, there might be an entrance charge. $$$$

✗ **Chez Eva** Bairro Quinta de Santo António; 📞 920887. New restaurant attached to the Magni-Bi guesthouse (see page 104) serving Cameroonian specialities, such as *ndole* (beef cooked with a special herb, smoked shrimps, crushed peanuts...). Vegetarians can ask for a veggie version. French and some English spoken. Highly recommended locally. $$$

✗ **Dona Hortência/ Os dois Pinheiros** Campo de Milho; 📞 221743/905825. Book in advance for excellent Portuguese and African home-cooking. For vegetarians, Dona Hortência can make a lovely vegetable tart (*torta de hortaliza*). As is often the case with these familial places, you might be the only one dining. Make sure you ask the way, either when you book or get your hotel to explain it to you. $$$

✗ **Filomar** Bairro Hospital; 📞 221908; open for lunch/dinner daily. Run by Capeverdian Filomena, this restaurant is a popular choice with ministers & expats, couples & tour groups on their last day. It serves various local fish, cod, chicken drumsticks, an omelette with vegetables for vegetarians, & fresh fruit for afters. There is an air-conditioned inside dining space & – a more preferable option in the evening – a nice terrace with view over the bay. (I must have been unlucky on the first evening I dined there: I got scores of mosquito bites on my legs, despite wearing long trousers, trainers & repellent.) The small top terrace is nice for romantic dinners. Service is OK, but mineral water only comes in huge bottles, & fruit juice only in one-litre packs. The sign for the restaurant is hard to spot; when you come down Hospital Hill from town, the turn is a dirt track on your right. **$$$**

✗ **Le Pagué** Rua de Angola. The main draw of this central restaurant, attached to the Phenicia hotel, is that it offers something different, namely so-so pizzas, salads & Lebanese specialities, such as *mezze*, which makes it also a good choice for vegetarians. Prices in €. The staff speak French, but seem bored. The menu is in Portuguese & French, but don't expect all the dishes shown to be available. Wi-Fi hotspot: 60,000$ for non-guests. **$$$**

✗ **Sum Secreta** Av Kwame Nkrumah; ☎ 224604; ⏰ 07.00–22.30 Mon–Sat. Great place for value-for-money food eaten around big round linen-covered tables with wooden chairs on a spacious covered terrace with a constant cool breeze. Santomean specialities such as *calulú* (80,000$) & *blablá* are only available if you ask for them in advance. Service is friendly if sometimes slow. 'Mr Secret' is popular with visiting groups & courting couples for a sorbet ice cream. This is one of the few places where you can get a homemade mango juice, *zumo de manga caseiro*, & for 40,000$ they can prepare you a vegetarian selection of vegetables with rice.

CAFÉS AND PASTELARIAS

✗ **Café & Companhia** Praça de Amizade e Solidariedade entre os Povos; ☎ 226622; e cafecompanhia@gmail.com; ⏰ 07.00–22.00 Mon–Sat. Serving excellent home-cooked food: great salads (with avocado, olives, carrots, tomatoes, peppers…), sandwiches, hamburgers, crêpes, filled pastries & home-baked cookies, Café & Companhia is *the* meeting place for travellers, expats, aid workers & Santomean professionals. Overseen by dynamic owner Maria-João, or 'MJ', as she is known to the English-speakers, the place is always cool (thanks to strong ventilators), & there is a strict emphasis on food hygiene. On balmy evenings, customers spill out onto the tables outside. Thu 18.00–20.00 is Happy Hour, with a selection of snack food to go with your *caipirinha* rum cocktail and often live music. The café is a **wireless hotspot**. A bottle of MJ's

The pastelaria section has a good selection of cakes, but nowhere near as nice a feel. **$$$**

✗ **Pensão Turismo** Rua Soldado Ferreira; ☎ 222340. Once you've found the entrance (opposite the pharmacy with the BAYER sign; go up the stairs), this family-run affair is a good choice for lunch or dinner, which you can see being prepared in the open kitchen. In the corner stands a bust of Lenin from the olden days, when STP was a one-party state, whilst 'Jacko', the grey parrot from Príncipe, likes to roam around picking at punters' backpacks. **$$**

✗ **Tété** Av 12 Julho; ☎ 904353; ⏰ 18.00–22.00 Mon–Fri, but larger groups should phone ahead. Unmarked, family-run fish restaurant on the Marginal, next to the UNEAS office, with *concón* flying gurnard a speciality. Calulú and other specialities can be ordered, again, phone the day before. **$$**

✗ **Tia Chinga** Bairro Verde; ☎ 905029; ⏰ by arrangement. 'Aunt Chinga' makes the President's *calulú*, São Tomé's signature dish, & serves pre-booked dinners on her porch in this popular neighbourhood. When I visited, the food was nice, but there was no mineral water to drink & no running water in the bathroom either. Tia Chinga's husband speaks French. To get here, turn off the main road towards Vila Maria at the roundabout just before the National Assembly & continue on through Vila Maria; take a right at the crossroads. If you haven't got your own transport, get a taxi to take you there & pick you up again, unless you fancy wandering along dark pot-holed roads at night. **$$/$**

famous aphrodisiac cocktail, made from local ingredients such as *pau três*, will set you back 250,000$. Read the *Correio da Semana* weekly newspaper here for free. A word of warning: if you start giving in to the entreaties of the street boys outside the café, in the words of one long-term expat, 'you're doomed; they will never leave you in peace for the duration of your stay'. **$$$**

✗ **Café Passante** Av 12 Julho; ⏰ 08.00–21.00 daily. The outdoor *esplanada* next to the (currently closed) Hotel Miramar has excellent coffee, plus cakes & pastries, hamburgers & pizzas. There are a couple of indoor tables, but it's much nicer to sit outside & watch the sea. Sat barbecues (€25 inc drinks). In this favourite meeting place for expats, the Great Café Passante Challenge was always to try to open a book & actually read more than a few lines before somebody turned up who you knew. With the closure of the café foreseen for the end of August 2008, this role will probably fall to the new Pestana Hotel terrace. **$$**

✗ **Jasmin** Rua Município; ☎ 227130; ⊕ 07.00–23.00 Mon–Sat. This new pleasant tea salon with an airy terrace, situated in the beautifully restored **Casa de Cultura**, has become immediately popular. Hamburgers, shwarma, pizzas, etc are served, and thanks to a generator, power cuts don't affect operations. Yoga classes are held in the same building (☎ 226291), which is now beginning to be used for more cultural activities, such as chess, theatre, rehearsals. **$$**

SNACK RESTAURANTS

✗ **Asas de Avião** Bairro Aeroporto; ☎ 226950; ⊕ 08.00–24.00 daily. This bar/restaurant under the wings of a stranded plane next to the airport is one of the most curious places for a snack meal, or some late-night fried bananas & a beer. There are a few tables right under the wing, with the TV & bar within view, while strings of little light bulbs lead you to more private tables, often, it seems, used by couples on a secret assignation. It gets busier around departure time. The story behind these two planes is fascinating: these Lockheed Constellations, 'Connies', were used during the Biafra war (1967–70) to transport vital food aid & to evacuate people. The Portuguese government supported the break-away Nigerian province, while the Soviets & the UK supported Nigeria. São Tomé became the centre of the relief operations & over 5,000 relief missions were flown from São Tomé to a dangerous makeshift airstrip in Biafra. The Barcelona-based CAUÉ Association is campaigning for the second plane to be turned into a museum to this humanitarian relief effort; in a separate development, a disco was scheduled to open here later in 2008. **$$**

✗ **Bar Bom Jesus** Old Yellow Market, off Rua Município; ☎ 907196; ⊕ 08.00–18.00 Mon–Sat. It took me a while to find this small inexpensive restaurant because the name on the wall outside is completely different, 'Ristorante Delice'. Right inside the yellow market building, it's a bit dark, but this is one of the few places on the islands where you can just walk in & ask for a *calulú*. Run by a nutritionist, the restaurant also serves a tasty vegetarian kebab. **$$**

✗ **Contentor Azul/Paraíso dos Grelhados** Av 12 Julho; ☎ 224469/913612; ⊕ 09.00–23.00 Mon–Sat. Operating out of a blue ship container right on the seafront, this informal, popular & friendly barbecue

✗ **Kilumba** Parque Popular. In the middle of the park, this *pastelaria* serves good coffees, sweet & savoury pastries, cakes & filled croissants, wines & beers, best enjoyed outside under the almond tree overlooking the pond, watching the world go by. **$$**

✗ **Pastelaria Cajú** Rua 3 Fevereiro; ☎ 221729; ⊕ 08.00–19.00 Mon–Fri, 08.00–16.00 Sat. Pleasant ventilated space on popular road near the market, with a nice selection of savoury pastries, cakes & soft drinks. Guaranteed no tourists; the only thing is: they don't serve any hot drinks! **$$**

place is good for watching the daily catch coming in from one of the outside tables. A popular starter is chunks of marinated marlin stomach, the speciality mains is the flying gurnard fish, *concón*, with grilled breadfruit & *malagueta* chilli sauce, washed down by local Rosema beer. No toilets. **$$**

✗ **Papa-Figo** Av Kwame Nkrumah; ☎ 227261; ⊕ 07.00–23.00 daily. Popular with both locals & staff from the United Nations HQ across the street, this friendly terrace snack bar gets nicely busy in the evenings. The shwarma for 50,000$ (also take-away) is very popular. **$**

✗ **Mê-Kui Rei do Frango** Feira do Ponte; ☎ 909353; ⊕ 08.–22.00 daily. The 'King of Chickens' is a popular *churrasqueria* for sit-down & take-away. **$$**

✗ **Le Minigolf** Parque Popular; ☎ 913561; e peetpj06@yahoo.fr; ⊕ 12.00–22.00 daily. Whilst I've never seen anybody actually play minigolf, this friendly spot run by a Belgian is where *tout* Francophone São Tomé (Congolese, Gabonese, Senegalese…) comes together for a beer & a chat. Jean-Pierre serves local dishes at midday, & European dishes in the evening. The toilets are across the road; you need to ask for the key, *chave*. **$$**

✗ **Plê-Museu** Rua Juventude; ☎ 912019; ⊕ 08.00–20.00 Mon–Sat. Handy stop for a quick snack between the museum & the Ossobô souvenir shop, though they seem surprised to see tourists. Proper meals, such as *calulú*, have to be ordered in advance. **$$**

✗ **Petisqueira Contentor** Av 12 Julho; ☎ 224018; ⊕ 08.00–23.00 daily. Off the beaten track, this unpretentious restaurant on the main road opposite the Bigodes turn also has a couple of tables outside. **$$**

✗ Sombra da Coleira ☎ 906992; ⊕ 08.00–22.00 daily. Good simple food, good atmosphere, with football or films on a big screen under the cola-nut tree. Special recommendation: filet steak, pork, *lombinho de porco*, 140,000$, veal, *de vaca*, 180,000$, pork cutlets, *costoletas de porco*, 130,000$. Good selection of teas: green with mint, chamomile, peach, lemon. The biscuits are a bit boring (like most of the dry Portuguese-style *biscoitos* you get here), but feel free to order an ice cream; the affable Portuguese owner assures me they never have a power cut, as they're on the same electricity feed as the police next door. Handy: phone recharge cards on sale. $$

✗ Sombra do Caroceiro ☎ 904231. ⊕ 08.00–late. Right next to Sombra da Coleira, this is a more recent operation – & shameless copy, some say – but it's perfectly OK for a plate of rice & beans & a beer. $$

✗ Toka-Cara Rua Patrice Lumumba. Small informal eating place for a quick snack of fish-&-rice, a doughnut or slice of madeira cake, across from the Instituto Camões. I've often had an early evening Sagres & a plate of fried bananas here, waiting for a free terminal at the internet café opposite, & usually ended up chatting to curious passers-by. Toilet facilities (in a barrack opposite) are pretty dire. $$

ENTERTAINMENT AND NIGHTLIFE

ENTERTAINMENT For young Santomeans, nightlife usually means a club, *discoteca*, and you should try and go at least once to see what the local dancing culture is all about. Local women will sometimes tell you that there is too much *confusão*, a commonly used word meaning 'trouble', in clubs, but for a tourist, even as a woman on your own, there is no problem. If you enjoy dancing, you will get a lot more out of the experience if somebody shows you a few steps in advance. Try a **dancing lesson** with Miguel Watson; he charges €30 for a two-hour lesson for a couple, (€25 for one person), including venue hire in the Chácara neighbourhood (*top of Rua 3 Fevereiro;* ☎ *914558;* e *batalhador_07@hotmail.com*) or, for a two-hour lesson in a club €20 for a couple (€15 for one person), excluding the entrance fee.

CLUBS

☆ **Dolores** Bairro Dolores; ☎ 914090; ⊕ 21.00–03.00/04.00 Wed–Sat, 18.00–24.00 Sun. Recently reopened club of the moment in the Fruta-Fruta neighbourhood (head for Bom Bom), with the obvious advantage over the currently closed Kudissanga: it's closer to the town centre. There is a chance of taxis outside waiting to take clubbers back into town. If you don't want to rely on that, arrange a pick-up with a driver beforehand, go with friends, or, at worst, ask for a lift (*boleia*) from a car with a mixed group of men & women. Entrance charges vary between 20,000$ and 50,000$, depending on the day and your gender. Smoking room. Women go free Wed.

☆ **Kudissanga** San Guembú; ☎ 911330; ⊕ 21.30–03.00 Fri/Sat, 18.30–22.00 Sun. Currently closed, the most popular *discoteca in 2006/7* is in a pink building at the end of a dirt track some 4km south of town on the Angolares road, past Bom-Bom. A taxi costs about 70,000$; the return might be a problem as there are no taxis waiting to take clubbers back to town. 500m before the Kudissanga is a new club called Orbita that you could try.

☆ **Kizomba** Rua Martíres Pinto Rocha; ☎ 905355; ⊕ 21.00–04.00 Fri–Sun. Taking its name from Santomeans' favourite style of dance, the Kizomba has a young clientele, especially on Sun, the day recommended by the locals. Within walking distance from the centre on the parallel road to the Marginal, the club gets unbearably hot on popular days such as Sat. 15,000$ (women), 20,000$ (men).

☆ **Tropicana Club** Av Água Grande; ☎ 225301; ⊕ 22.00–04.00 Thu–Sat, 18.00–02.00 Sun. The Tropicana has a reputation as a bit of a meat market, but this central club is where most expats fetch up at night. *Kizomba* rules here too, but sometimes more Western music is played. The entrance charge is around 50,000$, but there is a free cloakroom.

OTHER ENTERTAINMENT The lively **Parque Popular** is a common venue for concerts, competitions and shows. Every evening (if the equipment is working), Jean-Pierre shows **films** on an outdoor screen in his **Minigolf** bar at the far end of the park. As the Belgian will tell you, the Santomeans prefer actions films, the more dead bodies the better – and it's true that I did once meet a baby boy called Van Damme! In the bars, restaurants and small shops, Santomeans crowd around the TV screen to catch Brazilian soap operas, *telenovelas*, while the news shows the latest from the other former Portuguese colonies: Guinea-Bissau, Angola, Cape Verde, Mozambique, and, incongruously, the rush-hour traffic snaking around Lisbon. The bar at Residencial Avenida is a cosy place to watch the news at night and listen to the comments. Of the countless music videos on TV, most are blatant male fantasies of girls writhing around the singer; while the less professionally produced ones might feature impromptu bands of goats scuttling past between the cameraman and the recording artist. Men play a card game called *bisca* or checkers with beer bottle caps. *Oril* is a Capeverdian game played on a board with holes, made from *pau feijão* with chips made from black wood, *pau preto*. For more high-class entertainment, a **casino** opened its doors in Campo de Milho, towards the airport, in 2008.

BARS

♀ **Bar Avenida** Av Independência. This round bamboo-furnished bar/café, attached to the Residencial, is a meeting place for politicians, functionaries & journalists — São Tomé's 'second parliament', plus tourists & assorted regulars. In the daytime, there is a crafts stall outside; evenings, there is TV with news & football matches, alongside 'Radio BB', *boca-a-boca*, mouth-to-mouth news, & now also wireless internet access. Open late & always friendly. Excellent coffee, plus a selection of teas; snack food, eg: rolls with salad garnish. There are some plastic tables outside too. This is also a handy toilet &/or phone stop en route between the centre & the Hotel Miramar area; both are located next to the hotel reception.

♀ **Tropicana** off Av Água Grande; ☎ 225301. A popular meeting point for expats, as it stays open daily 19.00–02.00 & is handy for a late drink (also if the club opposite is too empty still), but it's not the most congenial place. Every time I went there, there was a Céline Dion video on the screen, & businessmen with bored-looking local girls drinking *caipirinhas* propping up the bar. This is the only establishment in town where drinks are added up on a *cartão*, a swipe card checked at your exit. There is an internet terminal too.

SHOPPING

Check the Navetur agency website for current details and photos of shops and initiatives selling local produce palm oil, bread, both in the capital and further afield.

CLOTHES If your luggage was not on the same plane as you, there are various places to shop for replacements. The open-air market sells a variety of clothes, fabrics and shoes; second-hand clothing is sold on Rua Giovany.

Kuma Elegância, Av Kwame Nkrumah; ☎ 224848 / 908001 ⊕ 09.00–12.30 & 15.00–18.30 Mon–Fri, Sat 09.00–12 & 15.00–17.00. Fancy jewellery & clothes, mainly imported from Portugal & Brazil, plus some São Tomé T-shirts.
Mimo 21 Rua Viriato da Cruz; ☎ 223993. Good selection of clothing & shoes; helpful staff.

Novidades Praça Amistade. I found a couple of linen & cotton trousers here that were a good fit & good value. Friendly owner.
Titti Modas Rua Santo António do Príncipe. Expensive young fashions; prices are displayed in €. There are always far more sales staff in here than customers, but if you're looking for something for the *discoteca*, this is the place.

FOOD AND DRINK

Padaria Moderna Rua 3 Fevereiro; ☎ 223217; ⊕ 03.00–21.00. The best bakery in town, possibly thanks to German involvement, selling fresh rolls (*pão*), bread (*pão de forma*, white & with cereals), French-style pastries (*pain-au-raisin* & *pain-au-chocolat*), dry cakes (*quêquê*), coconut-topped sweet

rolls (*pão de Deus*), etc. There are a couple of other bakeries nearby, eg: Miguel Bernardino on the market square.
Carla Charcuteria Av Kwame Nkrumah; ↘ 225192; ⏰ 09.00–12.30 & 15.00–18.30 Mon–Sat. Deli, with

a selection of beverages, dairy products, cereals, olives, nuts, fairly expensive local coffee/chocolate, etc. Aimed at clients from Hotel Miramar around the corner.

MISCELLANEOUS
Luis Fonseca Rua Moçambique; ↘/f 221039. Store selling hardware & useful items like torches (but for

batteries you have to go to Intermar), snorkelling gear, backpacks, shoes, etc.

MUSIC
Estudio de Gravação Av Giovany; ↘ 903759. Blue shack selling music by Santomean bands & singers. For 60,000$, Dédé, who also works as a DJ at the

Orbita club, will record you a good sampler of whatever you like.

PHOTOGRAPHIC EQUIPMENT
Foto Ramos Costa Rua 3 de Fevrereiro; ↘/f 224233. Senhor Costa offers digital services, sells memory cards (1GB 700,000$) – & can order Sensia 100 print films from Lisbon within 10 days. You can have

passport pictures taken, your images burnt on CD & paper prints made from any Nokia mobile phone. You'll spot the yellow Kodak sign of the shop from the market square.

POSTCARDS For the nicest postcards, *postáis* (5,000$), go to the central post office (see *Postal services*, pages 114–15); they have a good selection featuring plants and birds. Hotels such as the Miramar, Baia and Avenida sell postcards, too, but they're more expensive. Navetur sells nice cards with images of waterfalls and plantations that will convey some idea to friends and family of where you've been. For more arty cards, visit G&B Arte (see below).

SOUVENIRS People will sometimes just stop you in the street and offer crafts, and there are a few stalls dotted around, selling little carved boats (some more polished than others), coconuts carved into cups, spoons and bags, seed collars, etc. The tourism office (see page 100) on the Marginal has a good selection of *artisanato*. If you want something more enduring, stop at the art gallery (see *What to see*, page 118).

Atelier G&B Arte Hospital Hill; ↘ 911286. ⏰ 14.00–18.00 Mon–Fri (or by appointment; it's best to call ahead to make sure somebody is there to receive you); e brunospagnol@hotmail.com/ guilcar7@hotmail.com. Beautiful sand postcards/paintings and paintings by local artists (French-born) Bruno Spagnol and Guilherme Carvalho. Heading towards the airport from town and going up Hospital Hill, look for a yellow wooden house on the right hand side of the road, level with the *quartel* army complex on the left.
Pica-pau Casa Cinéma, Praça Cultura; ⏰ 08.00–20.00 daily. An association of two dozen artisans, friendly guys selling wooden boxes & carved tableaux of Santomean scenes, cocoa pod sculptures, jewellery made from a variety of local seeds, &, my favourite: beautiful trays (300,000$) with intricate designs made from different local woods, such as

cedrela. They also sell tortoiseshell products, so apart from not buying this (rightly widely banned) merchandise, it's up to you to support this place or not. With the development of the cinema building, their location might move again.
Ossobô EcoSocial Praça de Juventude; ↘ 227933; www.cstome.net/ossobo.html. This one-stop souvenir place with a social conscience – it's attached to the Santa Casa de Misericordia charity – sells chocolate (various flavours: coffee, ginger, orange), coffee (Claudio Corallo Jambo, 250g 90,000$), little bags of pepper, beautiful crafts: wooden inlaid trays, rings, bracelets & hair accessories using cow horns instead of turtleshell, for a similar effect. An unexpected find was a USB stick (pen drive) carved from beautiful woods. Of the selling price (€25), the artist receives €5; this is part of a crafts development project involving local artists & craftspeople.

Loja Kitoli Av Kwame Nkrumah; ✎ 222592/904212. Banana products (*bobofritto, banana seca,* banana chips), spices (ginger, saffron), rum & *aguardente* in

large & medium bottles (20,000$ for a half-litre bottle of rum), textiles & crafts. You can watch bamboo furniture being made right here.

STATIONERY

Livraria de São Tomé Biros, notepads, cards, candles — & maybe even a couple of books... Photocopies (1,500$).

SUPERMARKETS

Coconote Praça Amizade; ✎ 226031; ⏱ 08.30—12.30 & 15.30—19.00 Mon—Sat. Enticing selection of French specialities, cookies, wines. No AC. Belgian agronomist Odile can arrange jars of her delicious homemade banana jam from her base at Nova Moca, refined with orange & lime, for 60,000$. Don't take them home in your hand luggage though; my two jars stayed behind at Sal airport in Cape Verde, classified as 'liquids'.

Economax Rua Sold Paulo Ferreira; ✎ 224626; ⏱ 08.00—12.30 & 15.00—21.00 Mon—Fri, 08.00—20.30 Sat, 09.00—13.00 Sun. French wines, Belgian beers, a large selection of cosmetics & household goods, fresh cheese, stationery, etc. The owner is always friendly, & sometimes certain things you will find nowhere else, like 'Marie-Rose' cream for mosquito bites (*pomada para picadas*).

Fresco Rua Municipio; ⏱ 08.30—13.30 & 18.30—23.30 Mon—Sat, 15.30—18.30 Sun. Owned by French restaurateur Yves Peladeau. Wide selection of imported goods: drinks, chocolate, cereals, etc. The vanilla from Peladeau's Santo António plantation is sold at the same price as elsewhere (€7), but from €100 onwards he'll give you a discount... Talk to him or Navetur about organising a visit to the plantation.

Intermar Praça Amizade; ✎ 221250; f 222262; e intermar@cstome.net. The most popular local supermarket sells a wide range of foodstuffs, including Portuguese dairy products (butter, cheese), cosmetics & a good selection of local chocolates & coffees that you can pay for in US$/€ if necessary.

PRACTICALITIES

DRY-CLEANING

Aquasec Vila Maria; ✎ 225025/904770; ⏱ 07.30—12.00 Mon—Fri; contact management for

Sat opening details. A few doors down from the National Assembly. A pair of trousers costs 20,000$.

HAIR AND BEAUTY

Salão Glamour Rua Patrice Lumumba; ✎ 223294; ⏱ 08.30—18.00 Mon—Sat. Dona Nanda is hairdresser to the expats, but prices are low: a complete women's cut costs 70,000$ & a trim 30,000$, a men's cut 40,000$, a few front braids, *tranças,* 25,000$, & eyebrow waxing 20,000$. There is no sign outside; go up the stairs of the yellow building opposite Golf Trading. Also manicures, pedicures, waxing.

Salão Visual Av Kwame Nkrumah (entrance Rua P Lumumba); ⏱ 08.30—18.30 Mon—Sat. Nice

atmosphere. Teresa, the French-speaking manager from the Ivory Coast, speaks French, but Didi also cuts hair well.

Vila Saúde Rua Barão de Água Izé; ✎ 226520/904971; e vilasaude@cstome.net; ⏱ 08.00—18.00 Mon—Sat. Health centre offering a bit of everything: therapeutic massages (250,000$) & detox, natural beauty treatments (steam bath 150,000$), hairdressing & a snack bar. Brightly painted & nicely decorated & shaded outside seating; handy for a rest stop & an ice cream, juice or hot-dog.

MEDICAL FACILITIES

✚ **Hospital Dr Ayres Menezes** Bairro Hospital; ✎ 221222/223932; e bsangue@cstome.net/ham@cstome.net. In an emergency, 24hr provision is given by the hospital up on Hospital Hill. Up to very recently, I could not have recommended this

much: I have memories of visiting a friend's sick relative in the hospital, of two dozen people crammed into one smelly room. However, in 2007, a brand-new 24hr **Accident & Emergency** unit with X-ray, plastercast & surgery services was set up by

Gian Meyer, a genial Swiss doctor & philanthropist & founder of the Waldhaus foundation (see *Giving Something Back*, page 93). Treatment at this *banco d'urgência* is free. Don't phone for an ambulance, which can take a while; it's best to get the injured person straight here. In the extremely unlikely event of being bitten by the black cobra, this is where the anti-venom should be held (see *Health*, page 66). The hospital is named after Dr Ayres Menezes (1894–1965), son of the island's first black doctor & anti-colonial activist.

✚ **Policlínica Água-Grande** ➲ 227258/221991; **Taiwanese Medical Mission** ➲ 227766/224074/ 224075/227084; e missmedicardis@cstome.net. For non-urgent general medical services, from dentistry to gynaecology, this central policlinic is much preferable to the hospital. Appointments can be made by turning up at reception at 07.00–12.00 & 13.00–15.30. If you come at 14.00, your appointment could be as late as 21.00 though. A list of treatments with prices is displayed, & there is an on-site pharmacy, where medicines with a prescription are very cheap. The Policlínica is also a good bet for finding English-speaking medics & dentists, as the **Taiwanese medical mission,** *Missão Médica Taiwan,* is based here; when you come in, take a left.

✚ **Consultorio Esperança Carvalho** Campo de Milho; ➲ 225944/903212; e efcarvalho@cstome.net. Dr Carvalho, who speaks French and Spanish, too, was recommended to me by several expats. Her surgery is signposted on the road out to the north, past the Capeverdian Cultural Centre just over the brow of the hill. Make an appointment by mobile phone.

PHARMACIES The pharmacies take it in turn to open at night.

✚ **Farmácia Epifánia de Franca** Rua Angola; ➲ 221209. Well-stocked pharmacy in a beautiful white colonial building; pharmacist Senhor Damião is very friendly, & his assistant, Senhora Violetta, speaks some German.

✚ **Farmácia Cabral** Rua Moçambique; ➲ 221254. Old-fashioned pharmacy. Look for the black & white BAYER sign.
✚ **Farmácia Sum Tomachi** Rua Moçambique; ➲ 226125.

A CONSULTATION WITH A TRADITIONAL HEALER

If you would like to do as the locals do, go and see a herbalist practising *medicina tradicional.* Experienced herbalist and bone-setter Mestre Horatio works from his home, a herb garden with aloe vera and other medicinal plants at the back, and treats stomach infections and ulcers, hepatitis B, haemorrhoids, and many orthopaedic cases. When I visited, one patient was having heated drinking glasses applied over judicious cuts around the knee, to suck out the 'bad' blood from the haematoma suffered during a fall. The blood gradually congealed in the glass; afterwards, the cuts looked amazingly neat and didn't bleed. Meanwhile, another patient, a young woman, was having her knee reset, wailing and screaming; nothing for the faint-hearted. I came away with free advice for my sore throat: to buy a herb called *samagugu* and chew it with sugar (a market trader selling lots of different herbs organised some for me the next day). Mestre Horatio's speciality concoction however is an aphrodisiac that also fights intestinal infections. The Mestre's claims of successful cancer treatment might ring hollow to Western ears, but his patient agreed that bone-setting works much faster than hospital treatment. Many patients come to Mestre Horatio with conditions that have not improved with conventional medicine (as happens in the West); others with serious diseases have to wait too long to go to hospital. To get to Mestre Horatio's house, take the Água Porca road parallel to Rua 3 de Fevereiro, turn right at a shoemaker's shack in front of the *prédio* (a taller stone-built house), and follow the dirt track about 200m down. Look for a ramp on your left; anybody will be able to direct you. Mestre Horatio is a Christian, not a traditional healer but, if you're interested, it should not be too difficult to find a *stlijon* if you ask around. (**Mestre Horatio** Riboque; ➲ 227423; e jazict16@hotmail.com; ⏰ 13.00–17.00 Mon–Sat.)

MONEY A dozen banks cluster around Praça da Independência. The **Banco International de São Tomé and Príncipe** (BISTP) is the most reliable. With your VISA, Mastercard or Diners card (both debit and credit cards) you can arrange a money transfer (cash advance) in 10 minutes. Bring your passport. Travellers' cheques are cashed too, if with a bit of reluctance. Queues can get long. Do check your pile of dobras carefully; in the rush, currencies can get confused, and once I found a 5,000$ note in between a wad of 50,000$ notes. BISTP can check banknotes for you, too. In recent years, there was a problem with fake banknotes printed, it seems, on Príncipe, in particular US$100 and €5, handed out on occasion even at reputable places. I once heard about an American traveller who was given some fake notes at one bank and then had several notes refused at the airport when he needed to pay his departure tax. New security measures have now curbed the problem somewhat. Money changing is not illegal; there are many **money changers** in the city, *cambistas*, touting for business (US$/€) on the corners of central roads and elsewhere in the centre of São Tomé town. One who is very friendly and reliable is Walter. If you don't want their services, just say *'Ja está'* ('already done') or *'Não preciso, obrigado/a'*, 'I don't need it, thanks'. The rates are more advantageous than those at the bank; be aware however of the current rate of exchange and count the notes you are given. You will get a low rate if you change small US$ notes as the money changers have to pay a charge for banking them. If you have a cheque account with BISTP and run out of money at the weekend (not that this has happened to me, of course…), most money lenders can lend you money against a personal cheque, but they will ask for about 20% commission. If you are looking to change larger sums, ask around; people will come to your hotel. One person to contact is Americo Cabral, of the Equador Viajens agency (see page 101). If you don't have access to a Visa/Mastercard account and need to have money wired quickly, there are **Western Union** (*www.westernunion.com*) services at Banco Equador. This only costs the sender. Banco Equador cashes travellers cheques and, at the time of writing, was in the process of setting up a cash advance system similar to the one offered by BISTP. Handy lunchtime and Saturday opening.

$ **BISTP** Praça da Independência; ☎ 243100/243108; f 222427; e bistp@cstome.net; ⏱ 07.45–11.45 & 14.00–15.15 Mon–Fri

$ **Banco Equador** Rua de Moçambique 3B; ☎ 226150/241950; f 226149; e be@bancoequador.st; www.bancoequador.st. 08.00–15.00 Mon–Fri & 08.30–12.30 Sat

$ **Ecobank** Travessia do Pelourinho; ☎ 222141; f 222672; e ecobankstp@cstome.net; www.ecobank.com. ⏱ 07.30–15.30 Mon–Fri & 08.00–12.00 Sat. Santomean branch of Togo-based Pan-African bank with excellent connections for African transactions and agencies in over 20 countries on the continent. At the moment (2008), the cash mashine dispenses dobras only, unfortunately, and only to account holders. More services planned. Opposite INDUS. Contact José Cardoso.

POLICE (*Polícia; Av Conceiçao;* ☎ *221622;* ⏱ *24hrs daily*). To report a crime, the relevant station in São Tomé is the ***Polícia de Investigaçao Criminal*** (**PIC**), next to Residencial Baía. The police service is being reformed, but, for the time being, you will struggle to even get a crime report for your insurance company. Bring your passport and somebody who speaks Portuguese and stress that you will be leaving soon. Be prepared to answer all the questions (name of father & mother, number of children), but don't agree for the paperwork to be sent to your home address; it's not going to happen. In the case of my stolen phone, it was retrieved months afterwards by a friend, having been sold on six times. 24hr emergency ☎ 222 222 (Polícia Nacional); fire service: ☎ 112.

POSTAL SERVICES The central post office (⏱ *07.00–12.00, 14.00–17.00 Mon–Fri*) on the Marginal, next to the tourist information, offers the whole range of services and has a separate room with postcards for sale (also a map of STP). There is a postbox, *caixa de correio*, outside. The smaller post office (⏰ *08.00–15.15 Mon–Fri*), on Rua Soldato Paulo Ferreira, looks like it might fall down any minute, but it is more central, and the friendly lady working there also sells a few postcards and envelopes alongside stamps. There is no postbox outside. The airport also has a post office next to where you pay your departure tax, but it is open only on flight days, and the post box outside is not in service. Club Santana has a postbox, too, and the bigger hotels will take care of your mail. For urgent mailings or valuable documents, **courier** DHL has an office in the Mistral Voyages office (📞 *221246*; ⏰ *08.00–17.00 Mon–Fri*). Expect to pay around €40 for sending a document to Europe.

TELECOMMUNICATIONS There are **public phone boxes** (*cabinas*) outside the CST phone exchange. Otherwise, look for signs for '*Telefone aqui*', eg: around the market square.

CST Av Independência; 📞 222226/222982; 📠 222500/226020; ⏰ 07.00–21.00 daily. By day, CST is a hub of activity, with people chatting into the six posts. This is the procedure: go to one of the posts, lift the receiver & dial 555, then wait for the tone. You will be asked to type in, *marcar*, the number you want & press the hash key (*cardinal*). The line is often crackly, but this will clear once you're connected. You will already be charged while the connection is being made. Should you hear '*Este posto não está activo*', call back to the counter '*Número/Cabina..., faz favor!*', giving the relevant number (above the post) & staff will activate the phone for you. You pay afterwards at the counter; local calls cost 1,500$ per minute, but international calls are expensive. You can also ask to be called back (📞 221101). Make the first call from one of the inside cabins or use a phone card & take the call-back at the public phone on the wall outside CST (when you exit, to your left). The mural above the big counter was made by Angolar painter Nezó (see *São João dos Angolares*, page 151) & shows scenes from the *tchiloli* drama. If you need help, Asterio Seca is the local CST's Mr Fixit (📞 908748; e asterio.seca@gmail.com); he speaks some English & can find you a mobile phone for the duration of your stay, as well as arrange other tourist services. If he is not there, explain that you are looking to rent a mobile phone (*alugar um telemóvel*).

Internet Public **Wi-Fi spots** are the lobby of the Hotel Miramar, the Phénicia bar/restaurant, and Café & Companhia, a relaxed place to check your emails (day rate 50,000$/€3). Owner Maria-João can hire out a laptop. Within 10 minutes, CST can set up a free cstome.net **email account** for you, which is handy for communication with people here as everybody recognises it, and you get little spam. First go to the counter at the back of the building to pick up a form, fill it in and choose a simple user name (joebloggs@cstome.net), plus a password. To pick up your mails, go to www.cstome.net, click on the green 'mailsite' icon & enter your username and password. One word of warning: many months later, I unexplainedly lost my entire inbox.

Internet cafés There are about five internet cafés with the going rate of 15,000$ for 80 minutes. You will be given a slip of paper with a number to type onto the screen. If you want to communicate via MSN Messenger – probably the most popular service with Santomeans – you'll probably have to do it without live voice, as headsets are not often available.

🖥 **Divertur** Av Independência; ⏰ 10.00–22.00 daily. This central & easygoing internet place across the road from the Instituto Camões, with 6 terminals, is my favourite. There is a sign, but it is a bit tricky to find: cross over from the Instituto to the centre of the various wooden buildings & turn back on yourself; the entrance is opposite the Toka-Cara snack bar. Apart from hiring out videos, the place also sells mobile phones & accessories – & biscuits. The AC is always on full. There is a generator, but if the power fails late in the day, staff might go home early.

🖻 **Kia-Net** Kia-Net's two branches, one in the video shop in Rua Patrice Lumumba (🕘 08.00–22.00 daily), another around the corner in Rua Presidente Nasser (🕘 08.00–22.30 Mon–Fri) are popular with Santomeans. However, in my experience their computers are often desperately slow, & staff are not that helpful. Still, the one in Rua Patrice Lumumba

is the only internet place in town with a printer, & the other one the only one with a toilet.

🖻 **Tropicana** off Av Água Grande; ✆ 225301; 🕘 daily 09.00–21.00, closes Sun at 18.00. Fast connection (90 mins 25,000$) from 6 terminals behind the cloakroom of the Tropicana club. Users with a valid student card get a discount: 90 mins 15,000$.

TRANSLATIONS/INTERPRETING

Flatela 012B Bairro Dolores; ✆ 913126 (skype); e flatela@flatela.com; www.flatela.com. New agency offering all combinations of languages, translation rates start at €0.04 per word.

WHAT TO SEE

CATHEDRAL (*Lg Água Grande*; ✆ *222209*; 🕘 *07.30–12.00 & 15.00–19.00 Tue–Sun, 04.00–12.00 & 15.00–20.00 Mon; Mass Sun 06.00–07.45, 10.00–11.45 & 17.30–19.15*) Who would have thought that sub-Saharan Africa's oldest cathedral was the **Santa Sé** here in São Tomé? Across from the presidential palace, Nossa Senhora da Graça (Our Lady of Grace) took some 400 years to complete, from 1576 to 1958. The impressive cathedral occupies the dividing line between the business part of the city and the administrative part. The story of its construction is the story of São Tomé. In 1493, Álvaro de Caminha, the island's third feudal lord, had a stone and quick-lime chapel built on the site of the present cathedral. Dedicated to the Virgin Mary – maybe as a thank you for not succumbing to malaria as had the first settlers ten years before, it was finished in 1499, only to be destroyed in 1501 when Dutch pirates sacked the town. Rebuilt in 1505, the new Avé-Maria church was elevated to the status of Sé, 'cathedral', for the newly created Diocese of São Tomé and Príncipe in 1534, and renamed Nossa Senhora da Graça. A new Dutch/French incursion in 1562 destroyed the building, and construction of the current cathedral did not start until 1576, by orders of the pious Portuguese king Dom Sebastião (1557–78) when the whole building was moved closer to the river. When Portugal and its territories fell under Spanish rule in 1580, works carried on, but another Dutch invasion in 1599 left the cathedral badly damaged. This was the beginning of the legends that have attached themselves to the cathedral. One said that if the cathedral was ever finished, the island would sink below the waves. The first mixed-race marriages in sub-Saharan Africa were held here, as members of the different ethnic groups on the island – *forros*, mulattos and colonials – carried on mixing. In 1814, the frontispiece and the roof fell in. In 1937, the towers were raised by another 10m, and raised again in 1952. The cathedral was only completed in 1958. Today, the spacious interior has a beautiful frieze of simple **blue-white tiles** (1970); one of the 200-year-old originals is kept in the sacristy, together with the valuable ivory crucifixes and silver liturgical instruments. Ask for Padre Zé; if he is around, he will be happy to show you. More blue-and-white *azulejos* form a large **fresco of the Holy Trinity** above the main altar. It is said that under the altar lie the (transferred) bones of Ana de Chaves, a local noblewoman who died in 1566, giving her name to the bay. To the right, a **statue of St Thomas** is holding the saint's symbol, a palm frond. The stained-glass windows are recent, as are the Stations of the Cross in bas-relief from Madrid, and the paintings of the Annunciation and the Sacred Heart of Jesus, from Braga in Portugal (1950s). At the back of the cathedral, the marble baptismal font is kept behind an Art Nouveau-style grill. Since 2006/7, the diocese has had a new bishop, the Portuguese Rev Dom Manuel António Mendes dos Santos, who worked as a missionary on the islands in the 1990s. A ten o'clock Sunday mass I dropped into was full of young people; during another visit, in the evening, atmospheric shadows of the congregation coming and going played on the outside wall. The cathedral's feast day is 24 March or the following Sunday. Custodian Albertino de Lima speaks a bit of French.

MARKET The *Mercado Grande* is held in and around the large yellow **Mercado Municipal** building plastered with posters on the taxi square. Negotiating the narrow walkways between pyramids of limes, tomatoes and charcoal, spices, chillis and ginger, garlic and onions, and stacks of aromatic herbs, white tourists will often be urged (*Amiiiiga! Madame!*) to look at a particular vendor's produce. Agencies such as Mistral offer a tour of the market as part of their half-day exploration of São Tomé town, but the best thing to do is to come when you actually have some shopping to do, as you can shop very cheaply here, and the experience is a lot more fun. Try and get an idea of prices and carry small change. Buying small quantities can be difficult. It helps if you know roughly the prices of the produce (see *Daily Groceries*, page 72); then you can just offer the 1,000- or 2,000-dobra coins, *moeda*, rather than handing over a large note and then fighting for your change or being handed a large clutch of bananas or such like that you didn't want. If you see a vendor pulling her ear it means 'it's good!' Also on sale are very nice sugary doughnuts, buttered corn bread, *milho*, cakes… The **Feira do Ponto** market, selling mainly fish, meat and vegetables is located towards the shore, next to the Boa Conceição church; also on display are biros, toothpaste, flipflops, clothes and fabrics from plain to exuberant west African designs (expect to pay around 100,000$ to have a skirt made). The litter and unhygienic conditions of Feira do Ponto, with flies buzzing around the fish, was for a long time an embarassment to many locals and Santomeans returning from abroad. The **Mercado Novo**, located in a brand-new yellow market hall on Avenida Giovany, built with Taiwanese money and inaugurated in 2007, should help. Fish is landed on **Praia Brazil**, right opposite Feira do Ponto. Wandering amongst the women offering fish, tomatoes, charcoal, rice, etc, and pulling sailfish by their long bills along the (pretty dirty) foreshore is interesting, but not exactly one of the highlights of São Tomé. From early on, palm wine is drunk from plastic cups, and in the afternoon inebriated market traders line the Marginal celebrating the end of the sales.

NATIONAL MUSEUM (*Av 12 de Julho;* ✆ *221874/227167;* e *musna@cstome.net; admission 2,500$ locals, 3,000$/€3 foreigners/tourists*) A must if you have any time in the city. Since 1975, the **Museu Nacional** has been housed in the striking cream-coloured former fort of St Sebastian, built by the Portuguese in 1576 on this strategic point to guard against the frequent attacks on the island by the French, the Dutch and the Spanish. Looking at the tall statues of the Portuguese seafarers who discovered the archipelago from the museum entrance, Pedro Escobar is the one to the right, with the Prince Ironheart haircut – alongside the island's first administrator (1485–90), nobleman João de Paiva, and João de Santarém. The statues were temporarily dismantled after independence. As you enter the museum, look up; through this opening hot oil used to be released onto enemies' heads. Today, a declaration by the country's first president Manuel Pinto da Costa reminds visitors of the tragic history of human enslavement. Items from five centuries of Portuguese colonialism and 30 years of independence, furniture, agriculture and nature are spread over two storeys, with the few explanations, unfortunately, in Portuguese only. You have to visit with a guide, who might speak French, less so English. If you can arrange an outside translator/guide (such as Oswaldo Santos, through Navetur for instance), your experience will be greatly enhanced, as a lot of the objects will mean very little otherwise. Opposite the entrance, the cobble-stoned courtyard features a chapel dedicated to the Roman martyr and favourite Portuguese saint Sebastian, in honour of the pious Portuguese king Dom Sebastião (1557–78) who had this fort built. The **first room**, showing sacred art and liturgical garments, illustrates the continued presence of the church during the two centuries of decline between the sugar cane cycle in the 16th century and the beginning of the coffee/cocoa cycles in the 19th century. The niche between the two rooms has a sandstone sculpture of the Virgin and Jesus with Sant'Ana, the island's female patron saint. There is impressive dark-wood furniture in the Indo-Portuguese style from the pharmacy at Bombaim plantation. The **agriculture room**, dedicated to coffee and cocoa cultivation, has portraits of João Baptista da Silva, who introduced coffee to Príncipe in 1800: your guide will lift the lid of a wooden casket to reveal the bones of Brazilian-born João Maria de Sousa e Almeida, who first brought cocoa to the islands in 1822. A black-and-white photograph shows Santomeans' joy at the nationalisation of the plantations in the autumn of 1975. The **turtle room** has a lot of information and displays on São Tomé and Príncipe's marine turtles, with ping pong balls not doing such a bad job representing turtle eggs – and a life-size reproduction of an *ambulância* leatherback turtle. There are **great views** out to sea from the parapet running around the top out to sea and down to **Praia Museu**, or simply 'PM', where local youngsters go for a swim, but no one else. One day I visited, an evangelical mass baptism with a lot of singing was taking place, whilst on the other side of the museum, a *capoeira* group were rehearsing their moves; they are usually there Saturday 08.00 and Sunday 10.00. The museum office to the left, when you come in, sells a handful of postcards. No photography is allowed inside the museum. The director's name is Manuel Barros.

PRESIDENTIAL PALACE (*Av Independência;* ✆ *221143;* f *221226*) The guards of the impressive 'Pink Palace' wear impassive faces, and if they feel you are coming too close to the office of the President of the Republic they will make it clear you should keep your distance. Alternatively, they have been known, in the unprofessional way of many Santomean officials, to whistle at women walking past on their own. Despite its official name, *Palacio do Povo*, 'the People's Palace', the guards will also try everything to stop you from taking photographs of the building – probably a security hangover from the military coups of the past.

TEIA D'@RTE ART GALLERY/CIAC (*Rua Mártires da Liberdade 4;* ✆ *225135/906900;* f *221333;* e *ceiarte@cstome.net, www.bienal-stp.org;* ⊕ *08.00–19.00 Mon–Fri, 08.00–14.00 Sat, 08.00–12.00 Sun*) The best place to pick up Santomean artworks – from unsigned pieces of painted tree bark to paintings by award-winning artists, and see excellent exhibitions. The next Bienal, involving artists from the former Portuguese colonies and accompanied by an excellent cultural programme of films, talks, music and drama, will be in summer 2008 (mid-June to mid-July), and then again in 2010.

CULTURAL/RESEARCH INSTITUTIONS

Alliance Française Rua Gago Coutinho; ✆ 242300; alliancefr@cstome.net; ⊕ 08.00–12.00, & 14.30–17.00 Mon–Fri. The French Cultural Institute. The **Aliança Francesa** library has maybe the best range of STP titles in town, alongside French books to buy & borrow. If you're staying for a while, it's worth getting out a reader's card for 100,000$, but

even without a *cartão* you can surf the net on one of the 5 terminals. There's a photocopier too. This is the place to meet young ambitious Santomeans taking French classes.
Centro Cultural Português/Instituto Camões Rua Soldado Paulo Ferreira; ✆ 221455; f223713; e ccp@cstome.net; www.instituto-camoes.pt;

⏲ 08.00–12.30 & 14.30–17.00 Mon–Fri. A nicely cool space to sit down with a wide range of books & magazines, in Portuguese only. Sometimes, there are books by local authors for sale & exhibitions of local artists. Free ½-hour internet access at 8 terminals.

Centro da Língua Portuguesa Bairro Quinta Santo António; ☎ 224244. This cultural centre functioning in the ISP polytechnic building near the French Embassy has occasional cultural activities.

Historical Archive Praça Cultura; ☎ 222306; e ahstp@cstome.net; ⏲ 07.30–12.00 & 13.30–15.30 Mon–Fri. The **Arquivo Histórico** is a good place to buy books on STP & to browse magazines. The Historical Archive holds the *Câmara Municipal* records of the city. If you would like to do some research, access is refreshingly informal.

Casa Cinéma/Teatro Marcelo de Veiga Praça Cultura. Despite the name, this impressive building, built with forced labour in the 1950s and restored with Taiwanese money, has not shown any theatre productions or films for a while, but was a venue for fashion shows, political rallies & music events. This should change with the recent takeover by a couple of brothers who want to show films again in the capital. The balcony is normally locked up but can be opened up on request, giving a magnificent view of Ana Chaves bay.

Mediateca Praça Cultura, ☎ 243106; e medbistp@cstome.net. Serene, climatised study space, with shelves of reference books on economics, politics, sociology, copies of African magazines, such as *Africa Today* (*Africa Hoje*), the STP glossy magazine *Piá* (meaning 'to see'), and newspapers, to be read in comfy chairs. You can access the video & CD library, & various databases. Olga at reception is very helpful. There are 10 computers that you can use free of charge; unsurprisingly, the service is very popular. You are entitled to 30 mins if you're surfing the net (*navegar*), 60 mins if you're researching. You have to sign up & leave your bag with reception.

National Library Praça Cultura; ☎ 226013; ⏲ 08.00–12.00 & 14.00–17.00 Mon–Fri. The giant plastic breadfruit outside the entrance of the **Biblioteca Nacional** was used as the central prop in the film Frutinha do Equador (see page 217). To get a foreigners' reader's card (*cartão de leitor*) you need to bring a passport picture & 35,000$. Don't expect a vast selection of STP-related books though. Their photocopiers often break down, but if you need to photocopy anything **Lexonics** office services are only a couple of minutes' walk away, on Av Independência (☎ 222644).

UNEAS Av 12 Julho; ☎ 222483/226889; e uneas@cstome.net; ⏲ 08.00–17.30 Mon–Fri. Housed in a pretty colonial house on the seafront, the Writers' & Artists' Union has a library with many books on STP, inc a range of UNEAS publications. If you're in luck, you might see the president, poet Alda Graça Espírito Santo, the *grande dame* of Santomean politics & culture.

ONE-DAY WALKING TOUR

Start your day with a coffee and a pastry on the terrace of the brand-new Pestana Hotel. Walk along the seafront towards the centre, between almond trees, past the secondary school and the National Radio to the **National Museum** at the fortress of São Sebastião, and spend a couple of hours discovering the history of the country through the collections of paintings, photographs and sculptures. From the battlements, there are fine views out to sea. Carry on along the seafront, pick up some colourful stamps at the post office (postcards are sold next door), and take the small road to the left of the post office up to **Praça de Cultura** ('Culture Square'), the hub of Santomean cultural activity, with the cinema, the Historical Archive and the National Library. Look out for the giant breadfruit outside the biblioteca, and the fictitious likeness of Rei Amador, the 'slave king' who in the late 16th century led the most successful revolt against the exploitative plantation economy, outside the Arquívo. Once you've done the round of the square, turn into the **Parque Popular**, where a rusty plane overlooks a collection of brightly painted snack sheds. Stop here for an inexpensive lunch (for instance, with Dona Fernanda at the *barraca* with the number 20), or a cake at Pastelaria Kilumba, next to the artificial lake.

Coming back out of the Parque Popular entrance, take the second road to the right, broad Avenida da Independência. After a few hundred metres, to your left, a marquee signals the light-blue Residential Avenida, with its shady bamboo bar that is also a good place for a post-lunch coffee stop. Coming out of the bar, turn left to carry on along the Avenida da Independência again, and head for the nearby **Santa Sé Cathedral**; admire the frieze of blue/white Portuguese tiles and the statue of St Thomas to the right of the altar, holding a palm frond. Coming out, try your luck taking a snap of the pink **Presidential Palace** before the guards warn you off. The fairly filthy canal is where the Água Grande, 'big water' (Santomeans often call rivers just *água*), runs into the sea; Água Grande gave its name to the capital district. The source of the river is near the Nova Moca plantation up in the hills.

Carry on along the seafront, to reach, very soon, **Independence Square**, where in 1973 independence was proclaimed. Every 11/12 July, the square is the focus of Independence Day celebrations: on the 11th, after musical and Dança Congo performances, the president enters at midnight, accompanied by a torch parade, and makes a rousing speech. Out in the bay, it's difficult to tell which of the ships are picturesque wrecks left to die, and which are tug boats out on harbour business. Amongst the banks clustered around the square, the splendid white colonial building across from the BISTP (the important one for travellers, see *Money*, page 114) is the country's central bank BCSTP, which in the 1990s was implicated in fraud, embezzlement and other assorted scandals marring the country's reputation. Take this road, Rua Angola, towards the brightly painted colonial houses surrounding **Praça Amizade**. Have a drink and a chat with fellow travellers at **Café & Companhia**. As you leave the café, turn left, left again and then right; Rua Soldado Paulo Ferreira, one of the main thoroughfares, will lead you to the '**Taxi Square'/Praça dos Taxis**, where hundreds of yellow taxis vie for business. Put your camera away to spend some time wandering around the fruit and veg, spices, herbs and other wares displayed inside the yellow central market and, if you're hungry, grab a buttered *broa* corn roll, a *banana madura* or an *açucarinha* sweet to go (have small change ready). Rejoin the Marginal coast road passing Bôa Conceiçao and, turning left, carry on along Praia Brazil, where the fish is landed around midday. A bit further along, the chapel of **São Pedro** was built in the early sixties, its sail design a homage to St Peter's, the patron saint of fishermen. Inside, you can see two statues: one of St Thomas, the second, smaller, of St Laurent, patron saint of Príncipe (with Santo António). Senhor Dedi, who looks after the chapel, might well ask you for a contribution for a candle. Further along, to your left, look out for the **Sporting Club**, set slightly back from the Marginal. This pretty green colonial building was a focus for the *Santomense* drive for independence. Under cover of a football club, founded in 1940 (Sporting is the name of one of the most famous clubs in Lisbon, with green kit), nationalists met and schemed resistance against the colonial government. Reward yourself with a beer and the catch of the day at the famous 'blue container' snack shack.

top left   Boy selling raspberries in porcelain rose leaves, Monte Café plantation (CW) page 141

top right   Young São Tomensé husking a coconut, Rolas Island (CW) page 158

above left   Woman selling jaca fruit at São Tomé city market (CW) page 110

above right   Selling fish, Praia dos Burros, Príncipe (CW) page 184

top   **Traditional fishing boats** (KB)

above   **Bom Bom Island resort** (CW) page 187

left   **Praia Piscina beach** (KB) page 158

top left   **Drying kippers** (KB)
top right   **Looking out to sea, Praia dos Burros, Príncipe** (CW) page 184
above left   **Squid, breadfruit and banana, Café & Companhia** (KB) page 107
above right   **São Tomensé woman selling fish, Santo António market, Príncipe** (CW) page 178

top   **Capoeira practice, Praia Sete Ondas**
(KB) page 151

above   **Auto da Floripes performance, Santo António**
(KB) page 171

left   **Religious procession, Santana**
(KB) page 147

above left **Cocoa beans at the processing plant in Água Izé** (CW) page 144
above right **Coffee bush flower,** *Coffea arabica* (CW) page 30
below left **Sorting cocoa beans, Diogo Vaz plantation** (KB) page 127
below right **Plantation building, Água Izé** (CW) page 144

top **Blue marlin,**
Makaira nigricans
(WF) page 193

above **Flying gurnard,**
Dactylopterus volitans
(WF) page 194

left **Male greenthroat
parrotfish,**
Scarus prasiognathos
(WF) page 34

above left **Blue-breasted cordon-bleu,** *Uraeginthus angolensis* (RJ)

above right **São Tomé fiscal shrike,** *Lanius newtoni* (RJ) page 191

below left **Western-reef egret,** *Egretta gularis* (NB) page 192

below right **African grey parrot,** *Psittacus erithacus* (CW) page 192

4

The North and Northwest

HIGHLIGHTS

Go shell-hunting at Praia das Conchas, snorkelling at Lagoa Azul and swimming at Praia dos Tamarindos. Drive the winding coast road through the baobab and tamarind savannah, stopping for a crab lunch in Neves, until you hit the end of the road – and maybe explore even further. Admire the archipelago's most impressive plantation, Agostinho Neto, and hit the roof of the archipelago on a two-day climb up the Pico de São Tomé.

BACKGROUND INFORMATION

On the northern coastal strip, some of the best beaches on the island lie within half-an-hour's drive from the capital, and the relatively flat coast road makes this good terrain for biking. Past the town of Guadalupe begins the real savannah landscape, with its dry open plains, dotted with small baobab trees, their branches reaching for the sky, their distinctive stems dangling downwards. This area is home to a plentiful birdlife: many introduced by settlers, such as the conspicuous black-winged red bishop, but also the endemics Newton's yellow-breasted sunbird and the São Tomé prinia. Past Neves, the landscape changes again, as the road lined by waterfalls in the wet season leads past black basalt beaches.

GETTING AROUND

The northern road to Neves is well served by yellow taxis; a shared one-way ride costs 15,000$ and takes about an hour. You can ask to be dropped off anywhere en route.

NORTHERN BEACHES

Due to a large fishing village here, the vast **Praia Micoló** turtle beach is not that clean, unfortunately, but, as it's served by yellow taxis from the capital, makes a good starting point for **beach-hopping** along the coast, swimming or looking for sea and shore birds, starting with the palm swifts building their nests in the coconut palms. You can pick up a picnic lunch at the village market. The next beach along, **Fernão Dias**, holds special significance for the Santomean collective memory and the independence movement. During the repression of the 1953 insurrection (see page 5), there was a labour camp here, and the bodies of killed *forros* were dumped into the sea from the pier. Other prisoners were shackled together and forced to fetch sand for construction, or, in a pointless humiliating exercise called 'emptying the sea', had to fetch water in a pail on their heads and empty it onto the beach. Each year, on the night of

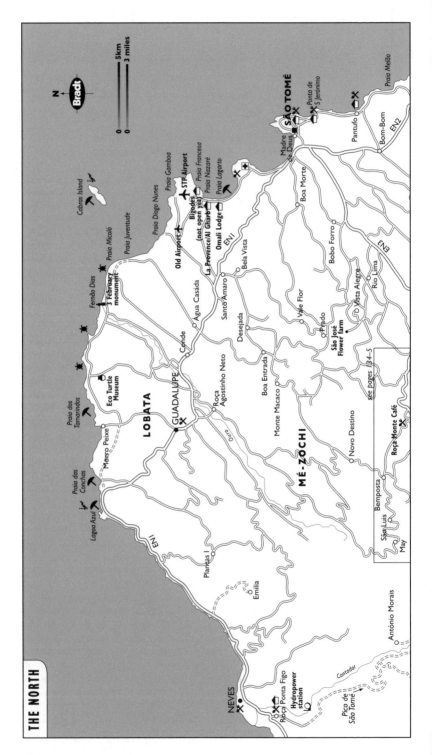

2–3 February, traditional music is played and the *puitá* danced, and the events of those days re-told by storytellers in commemoration, *soiá*. The next day, a procession of high-school pupils marches from the capital, wreaths are laid and speeches made. If you want to attend, check the *Correio da Semana* weekly newspaper for details or phone the municipal department of culture, Direcção de Cultura (↘ *224201*). Fernão Dias is the only potential site for the deep-water port that would be a central feature of the Free Trading Zone currently being set up in this area.

Visible out to sea from the coast, the **Ilhéu das Cabras** is geologically the oldest part of the archipelago. Boat/snorkelling and diving trips, and possibly kayak excursions, go out to 'Goat Island' (see page 83).

Through the sand-dredging operation alongside, the small **Praia dos Governador** has lost a lot of the appeal that made Portuguese author Miguel Tavares use it for some central scenes in his bestselling *Equador* novel (see page 27). The next proper beach along, **Praia dos Tamarindos**, is one of the best on the island, fringed by tamarinds, an indigenous African tree with edible if acidic fruit and high-quality wood used in cabinet-making/joinery; the leaves are cooked to expulse intestinal parasites. Unless you're unlucky and a cluster of jeeps from the capital descend on it, this is a quiet and clean stretch of white sand. Herons and egrets like to sit in the tree tops. It is only the area around the stagnant water to one side that is fairly littered; I once spent a lot of time stalking a green-backed heron with my camera, but couldn't get a frame without a beer bottle floating in front of it. **Praia Morro Peixe** is OK for swimming, though a bit close to the village (don't leave your mobile phone on the beach). To get to Morro Peixe from the main coast road, turn right at the big monument near the Guadalupe exit. This is a turtle beach, and an **ecomuseum** dedicated to the marine turtles nesting on this strip of coast was inaugurated in 2007 right at the beachfront. For information on visiting or taking part in turtle patrols (see page 37), ask for Hipólito (↘ *913792*), or contact the MARAPA conservation NGO in the capital (see page 37); Elísio (↘ *914510*) is one of the senior 'turtle officers', and Etienne (↘ *933622*) speaks English MARAPA can organise transport, lunch, night patrols, etc. There is no entry charge at the museum and the trips are free; visitors are encouraged to give a donation. Simple meals are served too; phone Hipólito on the above number.

Another nice swimming beach is the next one along, **Praia das Conchas**, reached from the main road by taking a right turn at a large baobab tree. Just ten minutes rummaging between the cracks in the rocks at the end of the beach shows you why this beach is called 'shell beach', yielding broken shells in various colours: pink, yellow and red. The beautiful (whole) shells sold by local kids could be a nice souvenir. At the weekend, it can get a bit crowded. Prominent politician Patrice Trovoada has a house here, bought off the current president, Fradique de Menezes.

About half an hour's drive from the capital, **Lagoa Azul** ('blue lagoon'), surrounded by baobab trees and fossilised corals, is a favourite spot with visitors; you can see its turquoise waters peeking out from the road as you approach on the coast road. The clear water and shallow gradient make Lagoa Azul a great snorkelling spot, especially over on the right-hand side of the lagoon. Local kids will love trying out your snorkelling mask if you let them, and take you up to the little outcrop to the left to play in the branches of the baobab. A South African company is currently building a resort complex with golf course, which is likely to privatise access to Lagoa Azul and Praia das Conchas. Their vision is outlined on a big panel at São Tomé harbour; luckily on São Tomé and Príncipe these projects can take a long time to materialise…

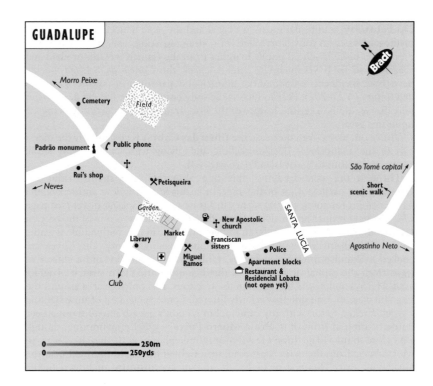

GUADALUPE TOWN

The capital of the Lobata district, with some 6,000 inhabitants, is said to be the most Catholic town in the country. The pretty church, **Nossa Senhora da Guadalupe**, completely rebuilt in 1939 and containing statues of St Joseph and St Benedict flanking one of Our Lady, is worth a visit. The key is held by the Franciscan sisters (✆ *231124*), based at a large house at the entrance of town on the left, opposite the New Apostolic church. Home to the dance company Leoninos, Guadalupe is a stronghold of the MLSTP party. Half way to Guadalupe, consider turning off towards Madalena to have a look around the **Boa Entrada** plantation with its Art Nouveau veranda.

 WHERE TO STAY

🏠 **Restaurante & Residencial Lobata** (10 rooms) Main road; ✆ 913417. Opened in 2008, the restaurant will have specialities from the Portuguese region of Alentejo & Santomean dishes. Private dancing area. $$

✗ **WHERE TO EAT AND DRINK** Pick up something from the **market** on the main road in the centre of town or the little **shop** run by Senhor Vera Cruz's wife, on the left-hand side of the road just after the monument marking the turn off to Morro Peixe. The famous Paladar restaurant is shut, unfortunately, but a couple of new restaurants have recently opened.

✗ **Petisqueira** Main road. Watch the Neves traffic go by, with some grilled fish or a plate of rice & beans. *Mains* $

✗ **Miguel Ramos** Rua de Chalé; ✆ 231117. This informal restaurant serving Santomean dishes opened in 2008. *Mains* $

PRACTICALITIES

Police/Polícia Main road; ↘ 231168   **First aid/Área de saúde** ↘ 231155

WHAT TO SEE AND DO

Roça Agostinho Neto The biggest (3,380ha) and most impressive plantation on São Tomé might seem familiar: it features on the back of the 5,000-dobra note. Built in typical Portuguese colonial style, this plantation was once one of the biggest producers of cocoa, alongside bananas, wood, coffee and copra. Originally called Rio do Ouro ('golden river'), the plantation was renamed Agostinho Neto in 1979 after the first Angolan president and poet (1922–79) to celebrate the political, military and financial help his government gave to the young republic; his bust still greets visitors on arrival. Most of the people living here are descendants of Angolan contract labourers. Various tracks lead to the plantation off the main road: either take a left at an unmarked crossroads before you reach Guadalupe, or wait for the left-hand turn just after entering the town; look for a big panel with educational health drawings next to a pink shack. On arrival you might be surrounded by a flurry of children and/or asked for money/a present by adults too as you ascend the sweeping avenue up to the imposing **hospital**. Following the old railway tracks up, the drive is lined with offices and workshops once used by the colonial administration. The government is planning to restore the hospital, unused for the past dozen years, and maybe turn it into a campus for São Tomé's new private university. From the upstairs window you get a sweeping view of the plantation. Behind the hospital are the former kitchen quarters and the mortuary. The key to the pretty **chapel** beside the hospital, over 200 years old, is held by Dona Nanda, who lives in a yellow house to the left when you come in, or a visit can be organised by Du, who lives two-thirds up the big avenue in a light-blue house with the number 031; you can also contact him via his neighbour Nedi. He can also show you around the impressive botanical garden or take you to the **waterfall** (*cascata*) about a half-hour walk away, which not many visitors take the time to explore. The **botanical garden** is great for relaxing in in the shade; you might have to ask for it to be opened (*pode-se abrir o jardim?*). A few of the trees have labels, but it's better to bring/find a guide who knows about their medical properties and other uses.

Hiking Coming from the capital, some 500m before you reach Guadalupe, a dirt track turns off to the right for a gentle 1–1½-hour hike up a hill, *morro*, to the telecommunications mast, with great views of Guadalupe and Agostinho Neto. Early on, passing a field of sugar cane on your right, look out for an artisanal *aguardente* **production** operated by a friendly bunch of workers. Watch the sugar cane stems being squeezed through the metal rollers, the liquid distilled in a large cast-iron container and through a cooling tube, and buy this clear sugarcane firewater for a few hundred dobras. Bring a clean container. As you continue walking up, every now and then you'll see small edible orange fruit on the ground: *guégué*, the African grape. Try them; the local deputy of the MLSTP party, Rui Vera Cruz Pereira, who showed me this walk, is starting to use those juicy fruits in *aguardente* to be sold locally. Ring Rui (↘ 907556) if you need more information on Guadalupe or would like to arrange a **car/guide**. He speaks French and a little English.

FROM GUADALUPE TO NEVES

The northern road winds along the coast, overlooking rocky beaches; out to sea, wooden pirogues plough through the waves, while closer to the shore the occasional lone snorkel is sticking out of the water. Taking a right at a turn off the main coast road, marked by a big almond tree, brings you to **Anambó**, where the first

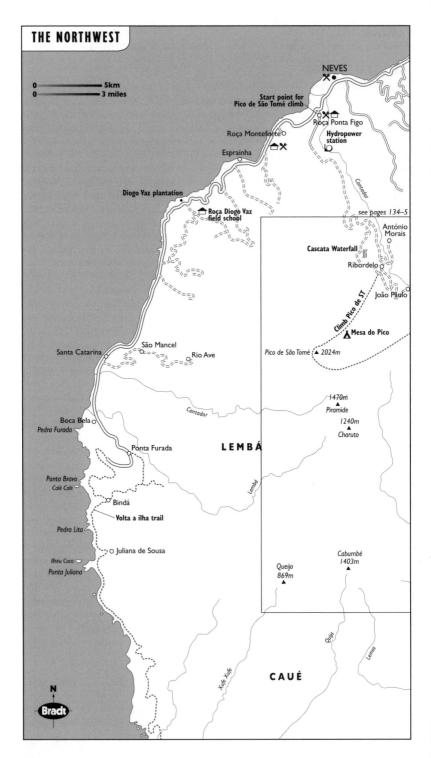

0 ————— 5km
0 ————— 3 miles

NEVES

Start point for
Pico de São Tomé climb

Roça Ponta Figo

Roça Monteforte

Hydropower
station

Esprainha

Cantador

Diogo Vaz plantation

Roça Diogo Vaz
field school

see pages 134–5

António
Morais

Cascata Waterfall

Ribordelo

João Paulo

Climb Pico de ST

Mesa do Pico

São Mancel

Santa Catarina

Rio Ave

Pico de São Tomé ▲ 2024m

Cantador

Boca Bela

Pedra Furada

1470m
▲
Piramide

1240m
▲
Charuto

Ponta Furada

LEMBÁ

Lembá

Ponta Bravo

Calé Calé

Bindá

Volta a ilha trail

Pedra Lita

Juliana de Sousa

Ilhéu Coco

Ponta Juliana

Cabumbé
1403m

Queijo
869m
▲

Xufe Xufe

Quija

Lemos

CAUÉ

N

Bradt

Portuguese explorers landed in the late 15th century. The white stone pillar decorated with the Portuguese coat-of-arms and topped by a cross is a 1939 copy of the monument, *padrão*, that marked every Portuguese landfall since 1483. The monument stands on a square framed by almond trees, near the mouth of the river that the first settlers called *agua bom*, 'good water', ie: safe for drinking. In colonial times, Anambó was a popular place for society events: afternoon tea on Friday afternoons, swimming, picnics and dancing. Today, there is only a seasonal snack bar. Mountain bikers can brave an old colonial road now much in disrepair, leading past the Água Sampaio waterfall to Neves; contact the Cycling Federation (see page 84).

WHERE TO STAY

🏠 **Roça Monteforte** (7 rooms) ☎ 911362. Small quiet plantation house under an hour's drive from the capital. Nice-looking rooms; ask the manager, Senhor Jerónimo, for the *quarto da ponta* at the corner: the best room, with a sea view. Sea views can also be had from the balcony; enjoy them from the comfy armchairs, keeping an eye on wandering pigs & birds flying over the trees. Monteforte is a good base both for exploring a working plantation, for **birding expeditions** & for trips around the north of the island. A guide can be arranged locally, even English-speaking, though I'd recommend some advance planning. **Lunches/dinners** ($10, pay in dobras, US$ or €) on the upstairs terrace are relaxing, but service can be on the slow side. Monteforte **beach** has fine black sand. §

WHAT TO SEE AND DO

Roça Diogo Vaz The next major plantation along is a working plantation. As you enter, to the right-hand side are the cocoa driers, with the pigeon tower in the background. Back on the main road, if you turn left up the paved road and take another left up the dirt track at the chapel, you reach the **field school**, *escola de campo*, run by Nora Rizzo (☎ 222573/904492). The president of the 'Natcultura' association and owner of two guesthouses in town, Nora has rehabilitated the pink former hospital building for her **solidarity tourism** project: guests stay for free in simple rooms at the former hospital (which now has electricity), exploring the rainforest and taking part in cultural activities with the youngsters (12–18) from the plantation. In exchange, depending on their background and experience, they help with activities that can range from agriculture, apiculture, breadmaking and hairdressing to painting walls. Visitors with specific skills, such as fine arts, photography and crafts, can share them, as did, for example, the Portuguese photographer who spent time here, teaching the youngsters how to set up and use a pinhole camera (*http://lrocha.mef.googlepages.com/projectos_fotograficos*). Alternatively, you can choose to stay in Nora's guesthouses in the capital, paying half-price and coming up here to teach. Solidarity tourists come from Portugal, Italy, France or Spanish-speaking countries, including Nora's home country Argentina. Nora is aiming to empower the young people to take responsibility for the place – the ultimate goal is for the field school to be self-sufficient. When I visited, young boys were at work in the back garden, carving coconut crafts and collecting natural sponges growing on climbing plants for sale. The aim of the Marseille-based 'Natcultura' association is sustainable tourism through development of the local community (see *Giving Something Back*, page 93); with a donation of €140, supporters can sponsor a sector of the school (eg: vegetable garden, hairdressing) for a whole year.

Roça Ponta Figo (☎ 233142). This plantation used to be a nursery, providing plants to other *roças*, and has a beautiful church. One of the best treks you can do on the island leads through São Tomé's deepest valley to an impressive but fairly unknown **waterfall**, the Cascata Angolar (or Contador). Eight **tunnels** are dotted around the area; let the bats (*morçegos*) escape first before you go in, and keep your

When the driver rings the doorbell at 04.30 to pick us up, it is still dark in São Tomé town. Luckily, the bakery down the road is already open, so Helmut and Karin from Germany and myself pick up some warm *pains-au-chocolat* and fresh rolls for the drive north. Shuttling through the spreading daylight, there is little conversation as we drive up past the Ponta Figo plantation, picking up the guides, José and Brice, to our starting point at about 500m altitude. While we load up with bottles of water, Nilo the driver is rustling in the forest nearby, trying to drag a *pimpinela* vegetable within his reach; whenever I see him, he is always collecting herbs and plants for food or to make up some potion for a member of the family, in true *forro* style.

On the long slog up, through big ancient trees, light-green ferns and dangling lichens, Brice keeps us entertained: he carves off some bark from a tree and holds a match to it, lighting it with a steady flame that carries on burning on its own. This is the oil tree, *pau d'óleo* – handy to know if you should ever find yourself stuck in a rainforest with no dry wood. Not that I would recognise the tree the next time I saw it; you could spend a lifetime learning tree recognition on these islands. Growing under our feet is *capim colchão*, mattress grass – and after a few hours' hiking, it does look inviting! As we climb, José taking the lead, once in a while we hear a crash from below: a banana plant falling over, weighed down by rain water. Suddenly, a shout! There is only one thing that could make a guide cry out like this: the black cobra. And indeed, a *cobra preta*, seeing its escape route blocked, had hurled itself through the air to get out of our way, right past the guide, who, understandably, thought it was going for him. Meanwhile, the forest is changing around us, the trees are getting more stunted and the canopy more open. We are entering the mist forest, its subtly reduced colour range of nebulous greys and greens creating a magical atmosphere. At some 1,850m, we reach the campsite at **Mesa do Pico de São Tomé**, surrounded by lots of white-blossoming *kata d'obô* trees covered

head down. Local guide José Spencer will lead you (⚲ *919305, evenings; if you don't speak Portuguese, you can get a message to him through Oswaldo, see page 81, or Navetur*). José can also organise informal cheap accommodation on the plantation, with running water and electricity. On the 2½-hour walk taking in the waterfall and six tunnels, and crossing a bridge with huge trees fallen across it, you will see plenty of interesting plants and birds; I got tantalisingly close to spotting the elusive *ossobó* bird. There is the option early on to do a short detour to see the ruins of **Communidades**, a satellite of Ponta Figo. If you haven't got your own transport, the easiest way is to get a taxi (around €25 for the return trip) to drive you to Ponta Figo, pick up the pre-arranged guide and drop you both off further up. If you want to save money, start early in the day, take a shared taxi and start walking from the plantation, leaving enough time to catch a return taxi towards the capital. Bring a picnic to share towards the end of the walk, at the working hydraulic plant. Here you have a great view down to Neves, across the hills and out to sea before going downhill back to the pre-arranged taxi pick-up point. Even if you just turn up, you should easily be able to find a guide, and there is a **shop/canteen** for a meal or quick snack. Ponta Figo is the most popular **starting point for the Pico de São Tomé**, and is also the start/end point for a three-day northwest–east **crossing of the island** via Bombaim and the Pico towards Água Izé (rarely undertaken, as far as I know; contact José Spencer for details). A possible **bike** excursion could run to the **Manuel Morais** plantation; contact the Cycling Federation (see page 84).

Climbing the Pico de São Tomé (2,024m)
Climbing the island's highest point (also, on old maps, called 'Pico Gago Coutinho' after the colonial admiral who first

in tree ferns, a quinine tree, and a passionfruit tree. We collapse onto the grass in the sun, saving our energy for the last bit up to the top. At some 1,300m, this is already one of the longest ascents I've ever completed in a day, and I can't believe my luck: we've not had a spot of rain! One more hour on an overgrown path gets us to the summit of the Pico. As there is not much of a view, we take pictures of ourselves. Back at camp, shamefully, we don't do anything, while the guides prepare dinner: spaghetti with fish and vegetables. I am dropping hints about 'celebrating in style', fishing for a swig of Karin's Bell's whisky. Unfortunately, this apparently very effective family remedy to ward off stomach bugs is strictly rationed. An electric storm is rumbling over the hills somewhere as we crawl into our tents. The next day, after a breakfast of coffee and rolls, it's time to switch the camera to macro mode for a bit of orchid photography. Right under the wooden sign pointing the way to the Pico sits a *bobofilho* ('yellow son', a local name with no claims to botanical correctness), and a one-minute walk up through the grass yields a beautiful epiphyte *polystachia* orchid clinging to the trees. Unfortunately, we soon find out that today we are not going to be so lucky with the weather. The rain starts as we start trudging along towards Calvário, and continues for three hours, soaking us through and through. All of a sudden, like a flash, José's machete comes down on something: a small *samagungú* tarantula: hairy, brownish and dead. Apparently, if you are bitten, it's not a major problem, but don't drink any water. On the way down from Calvário the view occasionally opens up to reveal the top of Ana Chaves and other peaks in the mist. Possibly we should walk a little faster, I'm thinking, as behind me, Brice is managing to carve a spoon out of a piece of wood picked up on the way as he is walking. Continuing down past rows of bright-red monkey flowers, through bamboo forests, and crossing a couple of rickety bridges, we are only too glad to see Nilo waiting to take us to the Bombaim plantation, where a cold beer on the balcony beckons.

measured what, in 1918, was the highest mountain in the Portuguese empire), is one of the most physical and rewarding things to do on the island. You will hike through different types of forest, with views of misty peaks in the distance, and see amazing plants, trees and orchids close-up. Even experienced hill-walkers have found the climb demanding, unrelenting even, but the determining factor here is the weather. If you hit a lot of rain, the Pico is a tough walk indeed, slip-sliding your way up and/or down, carrying a backpack laden with water and overnight gear. Otherwise, the Pico is a perfectly possible proposition for anybody in good physical condition who doesn't mind using roots and lianas to get ahead. There are **two ways** to climb the Pico. The **first route** leaves from above the **Ponta Figo** plantation (see box above), for a fast and steep climb to camp at Pico Mesa (1,875m), from where it is only an hour or so to the summit. The following day, you descend via **Calvário** (1,595m), with the only slightly exposed part of the walk involving a bit of scrambling. At the Calvário rest area, ask the guide to point out a mature *cubango* tree; its bark is burnt to chase bad spirits away. On the way down, listen out for the metallic cries of the São Tomé oriole and look around for the São Tomé giant sunbird and the maroon pigeon. You finish (or overnight) at the **Bombaim** plantation house (see page 140). The **second route** leaves from the botanical gardens at **Bom Sucesso** (see page 142), reaching Calvário after about 3 hours, with camping at Estação Sousa/Mesa: look for tall fig trees and the endemic *pinheiro-de-São-Tomé* pine, bearing round green fruit, amongst the (introduced) quinine trees. The next day you climb the Pico via Calvário and descend towards **Ponta Figo**. It is possible to do a night climb from Ponta Figo, to see the sun rise from the Pico, but only privately as far as I know, not through the agencies. It is

Santomean coffee is expensive; not because it is the best – in fact, the robust taste of some of the basic Santomean brews isn't everybody's cup of coffee – but because it is so rare. The coffee plant originates in Ethiopia. In São Tomé, arabica coffee can only be grown in a narrow horseshoe belt, at an altitude of between 800 and 1,400m around the Pico de São Tomé. Robusta coffee bushes, with a higher number of coffee cherries and bigger leaves, can be grown at a much lower altitude; this coffee has about double the caffeine. Robusta is used to give bulk; what provides the quality is arabica. The small coffee trees bear white coffee flowers, with a scent not unlike jasmine. Coffee berries take eight to nine months to ripen; they are hand-picked when they are ripe and red. The main season for this is the *gravanita* (mid-January to mid-February). The cherries are pulped, then fermented, revealing the two seeds inside, the coffee 'beans'. These are washed and dried in the sun, raked every few hours, but only lose their green colour with roasting. Most Santomeans pick, roast and grind their own coffee, without blending.

also possible, if you are more interested in the physical challenge than the natural world, to climb the Pico in one day, in an 18-hour round trip, again from Ponta Figo. Whichever way, bring a couple of changes of clothing; they don't weigh much, and it is sheer bliss to change into a dry T-shirt and trousers half way through a day's rainy hike. The most important item to bring, however, is walking boots with a good grip.

✕ WHERE TO EAT AND DRINK

✕ **Choupana** ↘ 223586/917609. Carrying on from Ponta Figo on the winding coast road towards Neves, past a bend to the left just before you get to kilometre mark 30, look down to your right: there is a restaurant half-way down the slope. Sometimes flagged up by a huge inflatable Sagres bottle, this place really only functions at advance notice, mainly for Sun lunch. Cooked bananas with kebab, *churrasco*, baked chicken/meat, grilled fish, with breadfruit. There is a nice shaded terrace overlooking the sea; a 5min walk leads down to a rocky beach. Owner Armindo Carvalho is setting up accommodation on the hillside on the other side of the road. *Mains* $$

NEVES

Populated mainly by Angolares, this town has some 5,000 inhabitants and shelters the harbour where all diesel and petrol supplies come in by ship from Angola. One of the few factories in the country, the Rosema brewery (↘ *233158*) employs some 200 people in the production of *Criolla* and *Nacional* beers. Up until the late 1950s, Neves was a whale-fishing port, with a Norwegian company processing 1,000 tons of oil out of 100 animals caught in the record year of 1946. In 2007, São Tomé and Príncipe drew the wrath of Greenpeace by expressing interest in a Japanese whale-hunting proposition. The town's most famous daughter is Maria dos Ramos (1916–?), who was taken prisoner and deported to Príncipe with her Portuguese husband for protesting against arbitrary injustices of the colonial government in the run-up to 1953. Her daughter Angela still lives locally. Neves is also the home of the island's oldest and most famous **Danço Congo** (see page 27) ensembles, Aliança Nova. The name comes from a tiny yellow ant with a painful bite, suggesting the frenetic quality of the dance. The group's oldest member, playing the devil, is over 90 years old. Aliança Nova president Senhor Urbano (↘ *916673*) can probably tell you where to catch a performance. The hills above Neves are excellent **trekking country**, in particular because they are in a semi-arid zone.

Roça Ponta Figo (see page 127) is a good starting point. Just before you get to the Ponta Figo turn (coming from the capital), crossing the Contador river, look out for a good early morning view of the Pico de São Tomé.

WHERE TO STAY I'm not aware of any commercial place to stay in town; but you should be able to arrange informal accommodation at the nearby Ponta Figo plantation.

WHERE TO EAT Visit the **market** at the entrance of town, or pick up something from one of the countless roadside stalls: bread rolls, coconut/sugar sweets, corn-on-the-cob...

✗ **Santola** Rua Água Tóma; ✆ 916736/905562; 🕐 10.00–22.00 daily. Famous restaurant serving huge red crabs (100,000$/kg) & other local dishes, such as *búzios do mar* sea snails. Downstairs is a little dingy; go upstairs to get a bit of a breeze.

The kids outside are only too happy to pose for pictures, but can also be quite cheeky. Coming from the capital, take a sharp right at the fountain (there is a sign), just before you reach the river Provaz. *Mains* $$

PRACTICALITIES
District Hospital/Área de saúde ✆ 233173   Police/Polícia ✆ 233167

WHAT TO SEE Neves had the first church on the islands, **Nossa Senhora das Neves**, 'Our Lady of the Snows' (feast day 5 August or the following Sunday), next to the Água Ambó River. After extensive restoration in 1939, not much remains of the original structure, and it is not in use any more. Coming from the capital, you reach the old church by taking a right into Rua Bengá at the blue headquarters of

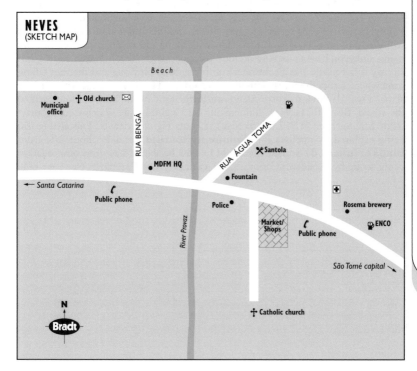

NEVES
(SKETCH MAP)

Beach

Municipal office
✝ Old church ✉
RUA BENGÁ
● MDFM HQ
RUA AGUA TOMA
✗ Santola
● Fountain

← Santa Catarina
☎ Public phone

Police ●
Market/Shops
☎ Public phone
Rosema brewery ●
☎ ENCO

River Provaz

São Tomé capital ↘

N
Bradt

✝ Catholic church

the MDFM party. Senhor Ramos, who lives in the house next to the church, has the key. When the Franciscan Sisters, Irmãs Franciscanas Hospitaleiras da Imaculada Conceiçao (✆ *233115*) arrived on the island, they built a new, much bigger church. To get to it, take the first left past the Rosema brewery, Rua Madre Santa Clara. The church, featuring a wooden cross and some stained-glass windows, is only open at mass times, but the Sisters can give you the key.

FROM NEVES TO THE END OF THE ROAD

From Neves, the road winds on around the coast, past various waterfalls (for example at kilometre markers 40/41), which are at their best, of course, in the rainy season, and through the short tunnel of **Santa Catarina**. Not many visitors seem to make it to the last village on the west coast; it will always stay in my mind as the only place in the whole country where, I guess, my unfamiliar skin colour made young children shriek and run away! A worn sign at the entrance points to an arts cooperative, but that does not seem to have got off the ground yet. If you're planning an end-of-the-road picnic, pick up bread rolls, *chouriço* sausage and jackfruit here.

Reached by the next (fairly hidden) right turn a bit further along, the **Roça Boca Bela** plantation is locked and not open to the public; only a couple of goats balance along the top of the walls. The Capeverdian guard told us the sad story of robbers killing the last pigs with stones and rowing them away in canoes. A path leads to the grey-sand **beach**, with the Ponte Furada rock hole visible to the left. From here, you get a good view of Cabumbé mountain (1,403m). Back on the road, turn right after a few hundred metres for **Roça Ponte Furada**, a cluster of houses around a square. Most inhabitants live by extracting palm wine; people see few tourists. There is a tiny shop selling *chouriço* sausage alongside the usual biscuits, etc, and you can ask who has bananas to sell. Not long past the turn-off to Ponte Furada, the road turns into grassy track and then, after another kilometre or so, runs out completely at Bindá. But in fact, the old colonial road carries on, rising, only you have to explore on foot. I stopped after a few hundred metres, but already it felt magical, with thunder rumbling, loud birdsong and the rain falling somewhere across the forest sounding like a river. This is where the **Volta a ilha** starts, a two-day trek to Porto Alegre, through some of the most remote parts of the island. Beautiful beaches and exciting bird sightings are guaranteed. Contact guide José Spencer (✆ *919305, evenings*) at Ponta Figo for details. This area is also being explored by **cyclists** for **community tourism**, eg: a 1½ hour ride from **Bindá** to **Juliana de Sousa**; you might by now be able to stay in accommodation being set up by Teodórico Campos; contact the Cycling Federation (see page 84).

5

The Interior

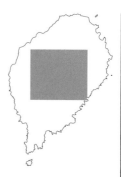

HIGHLIGHTS

Tick off some endemic birds at Bom Sucesso botanic gardens and enjoy an easy walk in the Obô National Park up to the dry crater lake of Lagoa Amélia. Relax at the historic plantation house of Bombaim, learn to tell your arabica from your robusta coffee at Nova Moca, delve into the colonial past at Monte Café plantation, and taste the fragrant and delicious mountain raspberries sold by the roadside.

BACKGROUND INFORMATION

Leaving the capital on the road following the Água Grande river leads through the historic town of Trindade into the heart of the island, through coffee and cocoa plantations, unique species of trees supporting a host of endemic forest birds and orchids, and on to the islands' highest summit: the Pico de São Tomé (see *Chapter 4*).

GETTING AROUND

Taxis go to Trindade, and some on to Monte Café, but very few go to Nova Moca, and none to Bom Sucesso. To visit these places, it usually makes sense to go on an organised tour. Otherwise, check with the Ecofac office in town (see page 101); it might be possible to get a lift to Bom Sucesso. No shared taxis seem to go to Bombaim, and the extortionate rate demanded for an individual taxi (1,000,000$ round trip) make it better value to either hire a car or visit that plantation as part of an organised driving/hiking tour.

MADRE DE DEUS

This is a friendly neighbourhood, just within walking distance of the capital on the way to Trindade, where you can visit one of the oldest churches on the islands and an easily accessible waterfall, or just pick up a few bits and bobs from the little shops and catch up with the soap operas in a bar. Coming from the capital, just before you get to the church, on your left, Aquiles Amaral's *Os Fidos* ('the reliable ones'; \ *914346/924107;* e *aquilesamaral@hotmail.com*) **craft shop** sells beautiful objects made out of coconut: coffee pots and cups, jewellery boxes, cooking spoons... It's worth buying direct: the fun coconut purse on a cord I'd seen on sale at Hotel Miramar in town for US$12 cost 100,000$ here. The only problem is that coffee spoils in the untreated coconut cups; unless you want just to look at them or use them as storage containers for spare change and suchlike, try and find a food-neutral varnish when you get home. Continuing on past Madre de Deus, at the **Bobo Forro** fork in the road – where the hopeful inscription on the façade of the primary school reads *Deus quer, o homem sonha, a obra nasce*: 'God wants, man dreams, the work is born' – you can drive two ways, right towards Madalena and

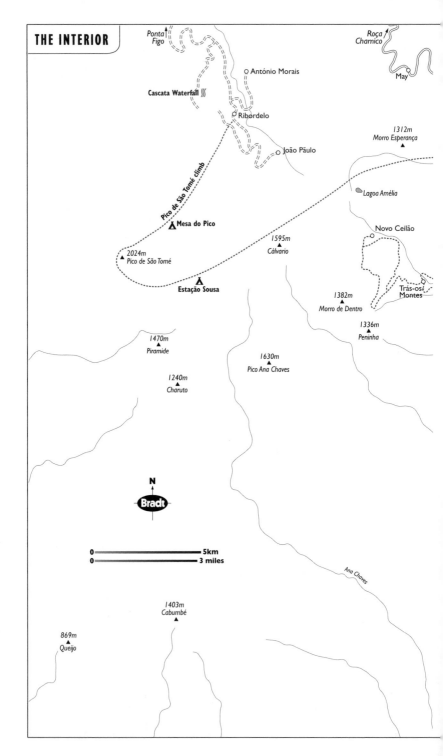

THE INTERIOR

Ponta Figo

Roça Charnica

May

António Morais

Cascata Waterfall

Ribordelo

João Paulo

1312m
Morro Esperança

Pico de São Tomé climb

Lagoa Amélia

Novo Ceilão

Mesa do Pico

1595m
Cálvario

2024m
Pico de São Tomé

Trás-os-Montes

Estação Sousa

1382m
Morro de Dentro

1336m
Peninha

1470m
Piramide

1630m
Pico Ana Chaves

1240m
Charuto

N

Bradt

0 ————— 5km
0 ————— 3 miles

Ana Chaves

1403m
Cabumbé

869m
Queijo

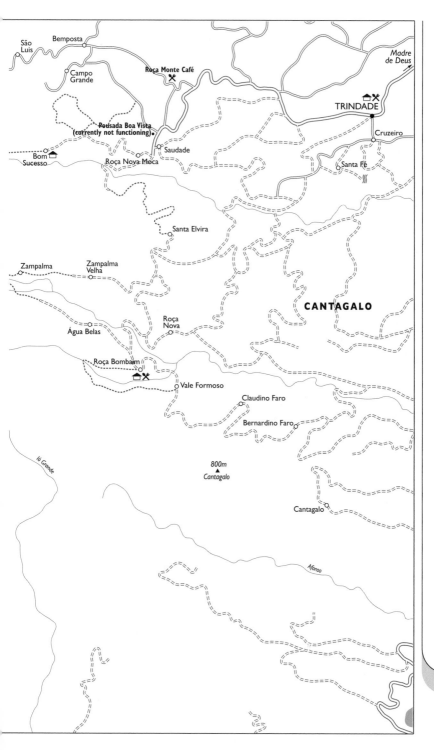

some little-visited plantations, as well as the tropical flower plantation of São José (see below), or continue on straight towards Trindade (see page 137).

WHAT TO SEE The yellow-stone **Nossa Senhora de Madre de Deus** church (⏱ *04.00–10.00 Sun; Mass Sun 08.00, Mon/Tue 07.00, & Sat 06.00*), set slightly back from the main road, on the left-hand side, dates from 1562; this is where the former (until early 2008) prime minister, Tomé Vera Cruz, worships; it is also where traditionally, young mothers bring their seven-week-old babies to put them under the protection of Our Lady. The **key** to the church is held by an elderly brother and sister, Senhor Silva and Dona Rosaria; they live down the road (going back towards the capital), on the opposite side of the church, in the house with a small wooden bench in front, next to a house with a large fan palm tree in the garden. Go through the yard, past the first house – you want the house at the back. You cannot visit on your own; Senhor Silva, who has looked after the church for some 40 years, has to come with you. If you can, bring a small present: a candle (*vela*) for the church, some sweets or, if you really want to make Dona Rosaria happy, a perfume miniature. The church's feast day is the second Sunday in September.

Blú Blú waterfall Only a 20-minute walk from here, this is a lovely little *cascata* that is very easy to get to. Take a left off the main road where a dirt track crosses the main roads, just before the football pitch (the track right next to the pitch joins that path after two minutes, too). From there, it is only a five-minute walk to a concrete bridge crossing the river. Just before the bridge, cut through to the left and follow the river for 10–15 minutes down to the waterfall. This is easier if you get one of the kids you will meet on the path to show you the way. It was also quite helpful when I visited, as some unpleasant *folha ganha* was growing right next to the path (see *Hazards*, page 69).

WHAT TO SEE FURTHER AFIELD
Roça São José/Flora Speciosa (☎ *222143/908847;* e *informacoes@floraspeciosa.com; www.floraspeciosa.com*). Spend half a day at the second-biggest tropical flower plantation in sub-Saharan Africa, wandering around 35ha of majestic tropical plants: waxy pink porcelain roses (the signature flower of São Tomé, if not endemic), the amazing bright-red endemic giant ginger, *bastão de macaco*, which has a new yellow flower appearing every day, various varieties of 'parrot beak' heliconias (one of them called 'Lady Di') and tropical foliage – glossy leaves with spots, or red or yellow stripes. The *roça* is open to the public every day, but the best day to visit, especially if you want to take pictures, is Friday, when the flowers are cut. If you visit just before your return, you can buy some flowers here; they come with a customs certificate. A stem costs €1–2, rare varieties €4–5; pay in euros, dobras or US dollars. At two tons per week, tropical flowers are now apparently the country's number two export after cocoa. Situated at an altitude of 400m, the plantation, with its large ancient trees and idyllic river, is also great for birdwatching, and you are free to wander around. A small bar serves water, coffee and beer. The friendly Portuguese owner, Miguel Teixeira, speaks English, but is not always on site; his business partner Agostinho Dória, speaks French and Spanish, and a little English. In 2006, the Roça de São José was the venue for the first 'hash harrier' run: two groups of participants (running or walking) follow a ribbon-marked trail – a great piece of English eccentricity in the tropics.

On the drive up to São José from the capital, passing through the famous popular **Bobo Forro** neighbourhood, watch out for the **wooden benches** with slogans – they make nice photographs. After 3km, before you reach Madalena, you will see the first sign to the plantation. **Yellow taxis** can drop you at Roça Vista Alegre (30,000$), from where you can walk; for the return, you might be able to catch a lift. At worst – or just for fun – there is a nice walk from nearby **Prado** to **Praia Lagarto** just north of the capital, which should take about 1½ hours, downhill all the way.

Where to stay Agostinho Dória from the São José plantation is setting up a **campsite** in the shade of huge *cidrela* trees, starting with two army tents holding up to six people, to be followed by lodge-style -bed safari tents, plus spaces for your own tent. A **walking map** will be available, showing what you can visit around here. The nearby plantation of **Vista Alegre**, with sweeping views over the two bays of the capital, is now owned by the brother of the former president, Pinto da Costa; ask the guards whether you can have a look around the beautifully kept *casa grande*. One of the oldest and richest plantations on the island, with a beautiful example of colonial-style architecture is **Santa Margarida**. Within hiking distance, the campsite also plans to have mountain bikes for hire.

Roça Chamiço As the crow flies, the atmospheric plantation of Roça Chamiço is only a few kilometres from São José, but situated on a squiggly, difficult broken-up road, becoming near-inaccessible in the rainy season, so very few tourists come here. Taxi drivers are also reluctant to go up; Joaquim Ribeiro (⤵ *906491; e joaquimribeiro@hotmail.com*) will go, but at a price. For more information, also on **hiking trips** up here, contact Nora Rizzo (see page 105). To stay here (€35 dbl, €25 sgl), contact Adolzinda (⤵ *905453*), the daughter of the female plantation manager (one of the few) and who has been here for many years; she can cook you a monkey or rabbit curry for dinner. Adolzinda works at the Ministery of Foreign Affairs next to the Portuguese Embassy. For a **bike expedition** out here, contact the Cycling Federation (see page 105).

TRINDADE

If you carry on straight at the Bobo Forro fork, towards Trindade, Monte Café and Nova Moca, you will pass a cemetery on your right, and the house of the president, Fradique de Menezes, heavily guarded Quinta da Favorita, on your left.

Lying at just above 400m, surrounded by good agricultural land, Trindade, the second-largest town on the island and capital of the Mé-Zochi district, has historically been both a place of refuge from attacks on the capital and a centre of anti-colonial resistance. When pirates came to plunder and burn in the 16th century, priests, nuns and friars would come up the hill to seek refuge in the church; Trindade church was also where 'King' Amador started his bloody slave revolt in 1595. In the 20th century, the town became a focus for the struggle for independence. One of the most famous Santomean families, the Graça Espirito Santos, hail from here, eg: primary school teacher Maria de Jesus Neves (mother of politician/poet Alda Graça), whose portrait hangs in the National Museum in São Tomé, and anti-colonial activist Salustino; they all came to prominence in the 1953 rebellion, whilst Julieta da Graça Espírito Santo was the first female medic in the country. Artist and essayist Almada Negreiros (see page 141) and poet Caetano Costa Alegre, as well as classical composer Viana da Motta, were also born in Trindade.

WHERE TO STAY

🏠 **Pensão Cantinho** (8 rooms) Rua Viana da Motta; ⤵ 906307. Cheap & cheerful rooms with ventilator at the corner with the main road. No b/fast. $

🏠 **Residencial Pereira** Main road; ⤵ 914753. New in 2008, above the supermarket. Rates inc b/fast. Airport transfer and car hire can be arranged $$

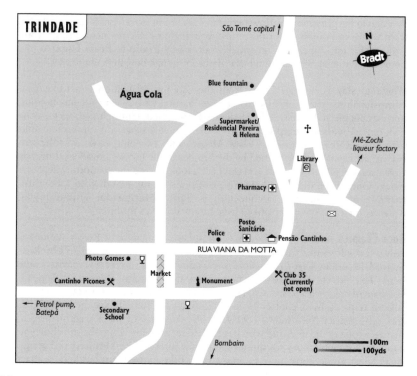

✕ WHERE TO EAT AND DRINK

✕ **Cantinho Picones** Main road; ⏰ 08.00–21.00 daily. Flying fish or *concón*, chicken *churrasco* with chips or fried bananas. A couple of outside tables. **$**

✕ **Clube 35** Main road. Currently being refurbished & looking for a new taker, this basement club with upstairs snack restaurant used to attract people all the way from the capital. **$$**

SHOPPING For **clothes**, especially jeans, there are a couple of places in the Rua Viana da Motta/market area. The nearest **petrol station** is above the town, on the right-hand side on the road leading to Monte Café.

Pereira & Helena Main road; ☎ 271567. Well-stocked supermarket (from groceries to TV sets), with a French-speaking owner, Emile Pereira. Curiously, the place is closed Sat, but open Sun 08.00–12.00.
Farmácia Irmão Viena; Main road ☎ 271026; ⏰ 08.00–20.00 Mon–Sat, 08.00–13.00 Sun. Well-stocked pharmacy in the centre of town.

Mé-Zochi ☎ 271280, 903645; ⏰ 07.00–14.00 Mon–Sat. You can buy some bottles of liqueur from the factory, a 5min walk from the centre & see the production.
Foto Gomes Rua Viana da Motta; ☎ 906418; ⏰ 07.00–20.00 Mon–Sat. Photographic supplies.

PRACTICALITIES
Post office/CTT Main road
First-aid/Posto de Saúde Rua Viana da Motta; ☎ 271332

Police Rua Viana da Motta; ☎ 271333. The *polícia* occupies a discreet dusty salmon-pink building.

Internet
🅴 **Library** ⏰ 08.30–12.00 & 13.00–17.00 Mon–Fri, 08.30–12.00 Sat, 13.00–17.00 Sun. 4 terminals in the *biblioteca*, next to the yellow

Claretian Missionaries' house. 10,000$/hr, printing 2,000$ per page. No USB sticks or CDs allowed.

WHAT TO SEE Dedicated to the Holy Trinity, the current stone **Igreja de Santíssima Trindade**, surrounded by a wide flights of steps, dates from the early 18th century. To get to it, take a sharp left a couple of hundred metres after entering the town, nearly doubling back on yourself, just before the sign pointing the way to the Mé-Zochi sweet liqueur factory. This building replaced a wooden church that had suffered various attacks and had had to be rebuilt twice. Slave 'king' Rei Amador and his Angolar soldiers stormed the church during mass in 1595. In 1641, giving shelter to clergy fleeing from the Dutch in the capital, it was given the status of temporary cathedral for a year. The church's popular name is 'Lord God Father', *Senhor Deus Pai*; a festival of the same name, the biggest in Trindade, is celebrated in May, on the Sunday following Whitsun. In the late 19th century, the church was given a sculpture of the Eternal Father, carved into a terrifying face. It looked so fearsome that the locals would pray to him to destroy their enemies, so it had to be replaced. Inside, there are the usual three altars. The chapel to the left of the choir displays a statue of its patron saint, in memory of the well-known Portuguese legend of the miracle of Our Lady of Nazaré. A horseman, following a deer at full gallop, is unaware of how close he is to a precipice, when the horse suddenly freezes in mid-leap, alerted to the danger by the Senhora de Nazaré. The saint's feast day is celebrated here on the Sunday following 8 September. The last renovation dates from 1962, when the tower was added. The church is open daily from around 06.00–08.30, novena mass is said at 18.00 and Sunday mass at 09.00; at other times, get the key from friendly Padre Domingos next door in the yellow house; the priest has been here a good dozen years (\ *271369/908273*).

FROM TRINDADE TO BOMBAIM

To get to Bombaim, take a left in the centre of Trindade, 200m past the (currently closed) Clube 35 (see page 138).

WATERFALLS The way to **Cascata Fundo do Morcego** is an easy 1½-hour downhill walk through the abandoned cocoa plantation of **Santa Fé**, past beautiful old trees. (Luckily, I only found out later from an expedition report that the area around Santa Fé is a prime spot for finding tarantulas…) Park the car near the entrance to the plantation. Bring a picnic to have at the river, watching the bats flitting in and out of the basalt rockface. To see the waterfall, you unfortunately have to wade (and swim) across into the opening and climb up onto the rocks. Be careful in the rainy season though: if the water turns brown, get out quick. Back on the Bombaim road, the next right turn leads to the Milagrosa plantation. **Cascata Milagrosa** is a beautiful double waterfall; symbolising man and woman. Contact Tiziano Pisoni (see *Activities*, page 84) to arrange a good waterfall walk guide.

HIKES FROM BOMBAIM A good stop-off point coming down from the Pico de São Tomé, Bombaim is also a great base for various hikes. A guide can take you on a 2-hour morning walk (€10) to the showpiece waterfall: **Cascata Formosa**, a series of three waterfalls over 100m high. Your guide can also tell you which of the waterfall pools are safe to swim in, depending on the season. According to a friend who did this walk, there are actually three paths you can take to this waterfall: a (slightly unsafe) shortcut, a medium-distance path and a much longer one. A half-day hike around the nearby hills costs €20, a day's hike around the peak of **Formosa Grande** €30. One hiking trail leads to São João dos Angolares. It might also be possible to hike the beautiful 6-hour 'Bom Sucesso to Bombaim' (see page 142) trail in reverse; see if the manager can call ahead to make the booking for the overnight accommodation and transport the following day. A very pleasant 5–6-

5

hour walk to the **Roça Bernardo Faro** plantation leads through various cultivated areas – a great opportunity to learn about different plants and trees: avocado, acacia, guava and the tall *capitão* tree. (Less welcome, on my hike, were the horrible big flies buzzing around the river area early on.) You can have lunch under a big *cajamanga* tree, munching some watercress (*agrião*) picked at the wayside. One thing I remember from arriving at the Bernardo Faro plantation, because it's such a rare sight, was a young man sitting in the shade, reading a book. Passing the primary school at the end of the village at break time, you might have to shake the hand of every single child. When we went through, a delegation followed us for quite a while, asking us to pick some *comida de cobra* (cobra food): small orange berries, hanging too high up for them.

Where to stay

Hotel Bombaim (11 rooms: dbl/sgl) Distrito de Mé-Zochi, CP 177; ☎ 227788/226439/907097; f 227788; e hotelbombaim@cstome.net/ edupires85@hotmail.com/ emersonsousa9@hotmail.com. The best person to ring is probably Emerson Sousa (☎ 907097), as he speaks English. This historic colonial plantation house has plenty of atmosphere, with beautiful stained-glass windows & romantic wraparound balcony with views over the peaks (Formosa Grande, Formosa Pequeno, Carvalho), great for relaxing after a day's hiking. The 5 downstairs rooms have their own bathroom; the other 5 share a couple of bathrooms on the landing – the price is the same! Shower is by bucketfuls of heated-up water. Upstairs is a living room with TV, the dining room & kitchen; downstairs is a bar. The power is usually turned off at around 22.00, but candles are provided (maybe bring your own matches) & if you pay a little surcharge, you can have the light on for longer. I have heard more than one report of rats in the rooms, so be careful not to keep any food there; just hand it to the kitchen staff to put in the fridge. The service can be a bit haphazard when there are few guests. Ask whether they have *sap-sap* juice for b/fast; this big green spiky fruit grows in the garden. **Food** ranges from grilled fish with vegetables to spaghetti with chouriço sausage. There is plenty to discover here. Explore the various plants in the garden, starting with the vanilla orchid growing on a nearby wall. Next along, the pillars that used to support the roofs of the cocoa driers now stick out forlornly into the sky. Foreman André will be happy to tell you about the plantation, where today two dozen families rear livestock. Don't leave without tasting the **mangosteen** (*mangostão*). The subtly citrussy-tasting fruit originated in Asia; in São Tomé, Bombaim is the only place where it thrives.

Take a walk along the abandoned *roça* buildings opposite the hotel, with the railway tracks all but disappeared under the grass. The railway once went from Bombaim to Água Izé on the east coast. The big white house alongside the workshop (*oficina*) belonged to the foremen, *capatazes* or *brancos de mato*, literally 'whites of the forest' (referring to their lives adapted to the rough conditions of the island), the storage rooms, the bookkeepers' office, the workers' quarters & the hospital. There are several **waterfalls** nearby; confusingly, all seem to be called *cascata de Bombaim*. A 20min walk out of the entrance & up the road leads you to two, one after the other, on the left-hand side of the road. There are more, with caves, down to your right, but they are difficult to get to. $$

TOWARDS BOM SUCESSO/MONTE CAFÉ/NOVA MOCA

To catch a yellow taxi to **Batepá** and further inland from Trindade, try alongside the market, but don't expect them to be that frequent; most traffic goes in the direction of the capital. The events of 1953 were triggered by a killing here, but there is not much to see – the monument to the 'War of Batepá' being at the beach of Fernão Dias (see page 121). Today, the Santomeans come to Batepá for the best, purest **palm wine**.

WHAT TO SEE AND DO Past Batepá, a short grass track off to the right leads to the **Pousada Boa Vista**. There is indeed a beautiful view out to Santana and the coast from the terraced grounds in front of the hotel. The Pousada is currently closed and, despite rumours that it was to be developed and reopened by an Angolan businessman, nothing has happened so far. Nearby is the Roça Saudade plantation where the writer and artist **Almada Negreiros** used to live in the early 1900s before moving, at three years of age, to Lisbon – where he went on to become one of the major exponents of avant-garde art and literature in Portugal. His Cubist-inspired portrait of writer Fernando Pessoa at the Gulbenkian Museum in Lisbon is amongst his most well-known works. His father José wrote one of the first ethnographic studies of the island.

Roça Monte Café (❧ *223234/910089*). At an altitude of 500m, two white stones on the right mark the entrance to the plantation that used to produce most of the island's coffee before independence. Founded by pioneer planter Manuel da Costa Pedreira, Monte Café had ten dependencies and employed thousands of workers. The bell that marked the labourers' work day is still here, along with other photogenic industrial ruins. The inscriptions '1914' and 'Technologia' indicate this plantation's heyday. The wagons on rails and driers are still used for the *roça*'s small-scale coffee production, whereas a big brand-new hospital building is standing empty, only receiving a weekly visit from the Taiwanese medical mission. Charismatic foreman Osvaldo can show you around – and maybe point you to a house where you might be able to taste the local *ponche* drink, difficult to find in town. A **coffee museum** with **café** is being set up in the former administration building and should be a fascinating experience as well as a good example of plantation tourism benefitting the locals. You will see displays and a documentary on the coffee harvest, featuring interviews with plantation workers (with English/French/Portuguese/Spanish subtitles). For the time being, you can usually buy some local coffee at the shop (*loja*) on the right-hand side. Also sold cheaply (40,000$) in transparent bags in the capital's supermarkets, it has an earthy flavour.

Roça Nova Moca Continuing up the windy road brings you to the Nova Moca plantation, where, at an altitude of between 800 and 1,000m, in the shade of flame trees, most of the country's coffee for export is produced. Some 70 people live here, and there is electricity and water. Nova Moca is becoming the powerhouse for new agricultural initiatives in São Tomé and Príncipe. Park the car next to the football pitch; or, if you park a bit lower down and walk up, you can see robusta coffee bushes and, over to your right, little stone walls put in place to retain the humidity of the terraced soil. Foreman Camilo (❧ *906739*) can probably find somebody to show you around; or just ask anybody working there. The owner of Nova Moca, who single-handedly revived coffee culture in São Tomé, is **Claudio Corallo**. Born in 1951 in Florence, the tropical agronomist is passionate about cocoa and coffee and first gained his expertise cultivating coffee in Zaire (now DRC) in the 1980s. In 1983, Corallo's wife brought back some coffee plants and cocoa pods from a visit to São Tomé and Príncipe. Studying the properties of these ancient varieties, Claudio Corallo found an arabica with the most body he'd ever tasted. The family moved to São Tomé in 1995 and, undeterred in their gourmet quest and despite his wife Bettina nearly dying from malaria, also acquired a cocoa plantation on Príncipe: Terreiro Velho (see page 183). The Corallos now cultivate four varieties of coffee here – three arabica and one robusta – to produce the single-estate blends 'Jambo' and (the more expensive) 'Selecção'. The yield of these varieties is as low as 200kg per hectare – modern hybrids can yield up to 4,000kg. To see what these ancient varieties look like, take a right before the tumble-down former administrator's house, walk up a few metres and look to your right; you will see trees marked with different tags – CAT, BB and NM. If you want to experience the difference in taste, Corallo produces a presentation box with coffee

5

beans from the three varieties enrobed in chocolate made with cocoa from his Príncipe plantation. They offer different taste sensations, with coffee and cocoa hitting the palate in a different sequence, explained in a leaflet that's also available in English. Unfortunately, none of the produce is on sale here as yet, but you can buy a presentation box (150,000$ well spent) at Intermar supermarket in the capital (see *Shopping*; with the leaflet in Portuguese). If you're really organised, buy a box before coming up here and have your own tasting session by picking coffee cherries off the relevant bushes (ask first) – great fun! Coming down again, on your right, a few steps lead up to a porch where tastings are held for larger groups. The porch overlooks the solar driers for the coffee beans, covered with plastic sheeting when rain threatens.

Waterfall São Nicolãu At some 30m, this easily accessible *cascata* is possibly the most visited waterfall in the country. The way to the waterfall is not signposted, but the dirt track leading to it turns off to the left about 200m from the Pousada Boa Vista, just before the sharp right-hand bend up to Bom Sucesso. Leave the car there and walk; there is a wealth of trees and plants to be seen along the short walk to the waterfall above a hazardous-looking broken bridge. It is only a short walk up to the São Nicolãu plantation, where people don't see many tourists and are very welcoming. There are a couple of forest paths you can take around the plantation that give you a new perspective on the waterfall, without worrying about getting lost.

Botanic Gardens Bom Sucesso (*www.jardimbotanico.st. Contact ECOFAC Rua Juventude; ℡ 223284/909132; e bureau_ozono@cstome.net/gefamb@cstome.net/ ecofac@cstome.net; www.ecofac.org – though best visit in person or phone*). At an altitude of 1,115m, the **Jardim Botânico** of Bom Sucesso, managed by the EU-supported (but always cash-strapped) conservation organisation ECOFAC, has over 400 typical plants and 140 orchids. The trees and some of the plants carry a label with basic botanical information, but you really need a guide to explain the native trees' various medicinal qualities, from stomach-calming *canela* to the 'rainforest Viagra', *pau três*, ie: 'third leg'. The main building, used for botany classes, contains some educational material (dried specimens of ferns and other plants, bird posters) and a basic toilet. If you want to stay overnight, the bungalow has three rooms with en-suite bathroom (cold shower) and two (none too comfortable) beds for US$10 per person, payable in advance. There is no electricity. Usually, but not always, a guard can let you in and show you around. If not, try asking a plantation worker on the road how to get hold of somebody. The guard can't take your money though; you can arrange to pay the day after at the ECOFAC office in town; however, it's best to book in advance, as I've heard of people finding the place shut. The communal kitchen with crockery and cutlery has a gas stove, but not gas, as far as I'm aware, so bring your own supplies (inc toilet paper, candles and matches, plus maybe a bottle of wine and a corkscrew…) and a camping stove if you have one. Put on a warm jumper, open the wine, and sit on the porch overlooking the garden and listen to the owls. The next morning, get up early and enjoy some easy birdwatching at dawn in the botanical garden.

Hikes from Bom Sucesso Bom Sucesso is a relaxing if basic base where you can really feel close to nature, as well as an excellent starting point for walks in the Obô National Park: the most popular is an easy walk up to the dried-up crater lake of Lagoa Amélia (see opposite). A recommended 6-hour hike to **Bombaim** (see page 140) leads past rows of porcelain roses, bamboo, the incredibly atmospheric and photogenic ruins of **Trás-os-Montes**, a *dependência* of Bombaim, past the abandoned *roças* of Nova Ceilão and Zampalma, then following the River Abade. (You can make a detour to Lagoa Amélia.) Another option is a two-day walk up to the **Pico de São Tomé** (see page 128). With ECOFAC struggling for funding, it is rumoured that Bom Sucesso could be sold – in which case it would likely become a lot more upmarket and comfortable, but a lot more expensive too. For information and reservations, phone ECOFAC. If you don't have your own transport, they can probably arrange for you to get a lift with the workers early in the morning, even if you're not going to stay.

Lagoa Amélia A very popular walk of an hour or so leads west through fertile agricultural land, growing beans, carrots and cabbage, to the ancient crater lake of Lagoa Amélia (1,483m) amongst primary rainforest. In theory, you could do this walk on your own if you make sure you take the right-hand path at the fork in the road up from Bom Sucesso and just head up southwest following the track. However, taking a guide not only enhances the experience – learning about the trees, plants and birds you encounter on the way – but also supports the local economy. Last but not least, it is safer, as guides know to look out for the black cobra, just in case. (On one occasion, we saw a juvenile *cobra preta* right at the entrance to the forest, blending in very well with the leafy soil, and, untypically for the black cobra, not looking very interested in slinking away.) Early on, to the left of the path, look for a magnificent tree trunk, where the famous strangling fig, *figo estrangulador*, has killed off its host tree completely, leaving a magnificent hollow space amongst the roots to step inside. After about half an hour's walking you enter the **Obô National Park**, marked by a wooden sign. One of the aims in creating the park was to stop agricultural land from encroaching further on the important forest habitats around the crater lake. Continuing up, the path is strewn with beautifully coloured leaves and discarded monkey nuts; ask the guide to point out the most distinctive trees. Take your time exploring, as the beauty of this walk lies less in the Lagoa itself as in the rich bird and plantlife encountered on the way; it might be a good idea to make clear early on that you will be stopping frequently. Apart from the common endemics, look out for the maroon pigeon, the São Tomé scops owl, the giant sunbird, the São Tomé oriole and the São Tomé white-eye. Be prepared: 'Lake Amelia', at 1,483m altitude, is not a lake anymore, but a filled-in crater surrounded by trees and giant begonias. There is a sign asking you not to step on the spongy grass, which most visitors ignore of course. You may see some São Tomé spinetails flitting across, hunting flying insects. There is the possibility of **camping** at the weather station just before you walk down to the crater; there is not much shelter, but it would be a wonderful opportunity for early-morning birdwatching in the middle of the primary rainforest.

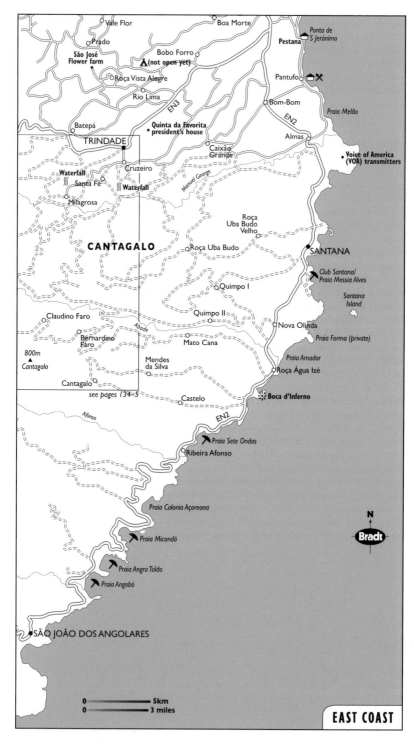

6

The East and South

HIGHLIGHTS

Relax at the Club Santana resort, taste imaginative Santomean food at the atmospheric São João plantation, swim at Praia Piscina and watch turtles at Praia Jalé. Stand on the equator line on Rolas Island, or join the hard-core birders on an expedition up the Xufe-Xufe river.

BACKGROUND INFORMATION

The coastal road south from the capital leads past São João dos Angolares, a town at the centre of Angolar culture and the heart of the contemporary arts scene outside the capital, and on to a stretch of fishing villages, alternating with beaches of different-coloured sand. Many visitors agree: the southern beaches are the most beautiful on the island. There are plenty of undiscovered ones, clean and with rich wildlife, kept that way by the advanced state of disrepair of the only access road and lack of development and communications. The further south you go, the poorer generally the people. At the tip of the island, the first ecotourism projects have begun to break the south's isolation and poverty, whilst across the narrow stretch of water a resort next to the equator mark beckons – a temptation hard to resist. The southwest of the island is still only visited by pioneering travellers.

GETTING AROUND

Yellow taxis ply the coast road from the capital via Santana and São João dos Angolares down to Porto Alegre. A shared taxi to Santana, for instance, costs 10,000$, to São João dos Angolares 15,000$ and to Porto Alegre 25,000$. After 15.00 it will probably be tricky to find a taxi to go south; the same goes for the return journey. A private taxi to São João dos Angolares would cost around $150,000, which makes car hire a better proposition. Transport to Rolas Island is usually organised through the resort (see page 158). The friendly Pestana driver picking up passengers coming off the island on the 14.30 boat may be able give you a lift back north. An individual taxi from the capital to Porto Alegre will cost you about €60 – the road is a real car-wrecker, and even in a 4x4 will take you at least 2½ hours.

FROM SÃO TOMÉ TO SÃO JOÃO DOS ANGOLARES

Heading south from the capital on the Marginal, the coast road leads past the parliament on a stretch of straight road to the pleasant fishing village of Pantufo.

PANTUFO If you are self-catering and based in town, Pantufo is a good place to pick up fresh fish for dinner, maybe on your way back from a day at Club Santana. The yellow church dedicated to St Peter's, patron saint of fishermen, is recent (1939). On the left-hand side of the coast road, opposite the church, you can't miss the O Império 'boat', which should be set up as a full-time bar when you visit and belongs to the guesthouse and restaurant opposite (see below).

Where to stay and eat

Estalagem Pantufo (6 rooms) Estrada de Pantufo; 224119/903588/910500; e conceicaovalerio@ gmail.com. Run by Portuguese journalist & chef Dona Conceiçao, this lovely guesthouse is a great place to stay if you want to experience life in a fishing village. The rooms are simple & tastefully furnished; No 1 is the nicest. An additional bed costs €10. By the time you visit, b/fast – with a fresh coconut if you want – might already be served on the palm-bedecked boat bar, looking out to sea. HB is an additional €10, FB €15. There is free internet access in a small office at the front & a meeting room. Day trips, around the plantations for example, cost €50, including car hire with driver & the services of guide Domingos. Bike hire can be arranged – the run into town would be a pleasant ride; going the other way, you could cycle towards Santana & recover at the beach club – & possibly Portuguese tuition; most things you want to do can probably be organised with some advance notice. If there are at least 10 of you, a traditional *bulaué* band can be brought in to perform, for around

€10 per head. French is spoken, Domingos also speaks some English. The Estalagem is less suited to a beach holiday, as the local beaches are too rocky & not suitable for swimming. $$

The **restaurant** (open for lunch & dinner, except Tue) is a good place for fresh fish, well prepared & nicely presented on the outdoor terrace; *cherne* is a favourite. Vegetarians are well catered for too; I had a very imaginative salad there one evening, sitting in romantic darkness, with candles, as the generator had blown – life in São Tomé... Phone a day in advance for Dona Conceiçao's famous *calulú* (100,000$ per head, min 4 people). For her book of recipes, see *Appendix 2*.

✗ **O Esconderijo da Ganda**; 222058. Pleasant fish restaurant famous for its grilled octopus (*polvo*) – & for the private bamboo huts where you can have dinner with somebody you shouldn't officially be seen with (*esconderijo* means 'hideaway'). Take a right (signposted) just past the viewpoint on the left-hand side. As it's a bit off the beaten track, better call ahead to make sure they're open. $$

Entertainment

☆ **Oasis** The greatest advantage of this *discoteca* is that it's open-air. The locals might still know the club under its former name, 'Argentimoa'. Take a right in front of the church &, some 200m on, take a left; the club is on your left-hand side. Don't get

there too early & have a get-away plan, as it's not a place to sit & chat, nothing else will be open in the area at that time & few taxis will be available. Also, as the club was closed again for a while in 2007/8, check locally that it's open before you go.

WHAT TO SEE ALONG THE COAST

Voice of America At weekends, there is a bar service on Praia Pomba. To visit the transmitter station, contact Ken Tripp (see page 86).

Roça Uba Budo (265117). This small plantation has a beautiful administrator's house and, as the site of a recent electrification project, can give you an insight into successful development work on the islands. One kilometre before Santana, a road turns off to the right towards Uba Budo (if you miss that, you can join that road from the centre of Santana; ask for directions as it's easy to get lost). I don't know of any shared taxis going to Uba Budo (check at the taxi square in São Tomé); if you can get on one bound for Santana and ask to be dropped off at the turn, you will still have a long walk. Electricity has only recently come to the plantation, through a pilot project managed by **Columbia University's Earth Institute** (see page 219). In the past, only expensive kerosene lamps and candlelight were available; today, a low-cost diesel generator managed by the community provides affordable electricity and, with it, a basis for better education, health and economic growth. There is now a power-saving 7-watt fluorescent bulb in every residence, and a television for watching cartoons and soap operas of course. If you want to hear more about it (Portuguese only), ask for the president of Uba Budo's community association, Pedro Semedo Tavares. Contact José Spencer (✆ *919305, evenings*) to organise a **bike trip** from São Tomé to Uba Budo.

SANTANA The attractions of the Cantagalo district capital, with some 8,000 inhabitants, are strung out along several kilometres. *Cantagalo* translates as 'the rooster sings', and you will notice that on the islands the roosters indeed start singing very early – at around three in the morning! In the home town of the famous *socopé* (traditional dance) group 'Linda Estrela', you will see many malaria and health education panels; the town was recently chosen by the Red Cross and the National Malaria Control Program for the distribution of thousands of impregnated mosquito bed nets.

Where to stay

⌂ **Club Santana** (31 bungalows) Praia Messia Alves, CP 144; ✆ 222023/242400; f 221664; e clubsantana@cstome.net/ clubsantanareservas@cstome.net; www.agencewta.com. The beautiful location of this French-owned lodge-style resort on a rocky cliff makes Club Santana very popular with day visitors too. Individual bungalows (21 dbl, 10 suites) with AC, mini-bar, TV, phone (UK €2.80/min, US €3.20/min). Rates range from €95 B&B/€120 HB/€145 FB for a standard bungalow with sgl occupancy, to €205/€255/€305 for a bungalow with suite with dbl occupancy. Half-boarders may choose between lunch & dinner on a daily basis, depending on your planned activities. As in all Western-style hotels, laundry is expensive (count €7.50 for a skirt, €4.50 for a shirt). There is a post box, but reception does not sell stamps. Residents may use an internet terminal in the reception area. The entrance is at the top end of the main Santana road. Look for a wooden sign pointing to the left; often, palm basketware is sold here. From the turn, it's still a 20min walk down to the resort. Excellent b/fast, served in the air-conditioned restaurant up top or, if you prefer, at tables outside overlooking the sea, next to a cage with local birds, inc lovebirds. With its calm waters, the **beach** is great for snorkelling & cleaned regularly, so you don't have to worry about stepping onto anything. On one memorable summer visit, dozens of dead squid (*lulas*) washed up on the beach just as I wanted to go into the water, to the great delight of the locals. A few times a year, the *lulas* come ashore to die – a ready-made meal; for hours afterwards you could see people along the coast road swinging their catch. There is a small turtle project. Trips out to the tiny **Santana islet** cost €5 for non-residents. The boat will take you right

into the islet (the lighthouse on top dates from 1997). Climbing begonias colonise the higher reaches of the basalt rocks, oysters & yellow/orange corals cling to the waterline. This is a great spot for snorkelling or diving (contact Club Maxel; see *Dive sites*, page 83); the seaward side of the islet has an 8m cave. A Hobbycat katamaran is for hire; kayaks & windsurfing boards can be arranged. At the moment, this is the only place on the island where you can hire a kayak (€3/hr for non-residents) on the spot. Food & drink at the beach snack bar is expensive, but the resort does not charge a day fee, & hire charges for deck-chairs (€3) & towels (€2) for non-residents are reasonable. There is a manned barrier at the entrance; just greet the guard & say *para o clube Santana*. Picnics are not allowed, & minimum consumption per table is €10, but I doubt the friendly staff is going to keep tabs.

As for **food**, French-speaking Santomean head chef Lurdes Silva creates amazing French dishes with a local twist & Santomean specialities, using herbs & produce from the garden at the back. The resort keeps livestock, & fish is bought fresh off the local fishermen or personally by Lurdes at the market in town. The coffee & chocolate served is Santomean. Every Saturday evening, a fantastic if pricy outdoor buffet (€30) on the beach, with live music (there is a small dance floor), draws the expats. There are very few mosquitoes here, due to the resort's elevated position & scrupulous cleaning, & I didn't see any. The one annoying insect occurring here in high numbers & various sizes is ants. If you are in the mood for more exercise, a new **fitness trail** starts behind the kitchen, with various natural-wood training features blending in with the forest. Book a personal fitness session with Luis Mario Almeida & get a botany lesson thrown in: an oil extracted from the deep roots of the *cólema* tree chases away bad

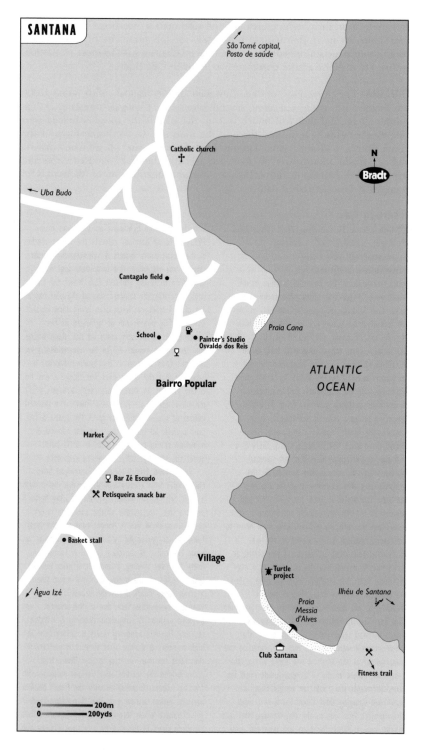

SANTANA

São Tomé capital,
Posto de saúde

Catholic church

← Uba Budo

Cantagalo field ●

Praia Cana

School ●   ● Painter's Studio
            Osvaldo dos Reis

ATLANTIC
OCEAN

Bairro Popular

Market

♀ Bar Zé Escudo
✕ Petisqueira snack bar

● Basket stall

Village

★ Turtle
   project

Ilhéu de Santana

↙ Água Izé

Praia
Messia
d'Alves

Club Santana

✕
Fitness trail

0 ━━━━━ 200m
0 ━━━━━ 200yds

spirits, & the carpet of pink flowers at a scenic viewpoint are 'turtle bean' (*feijão de tartaruga*). Bike hire & a swimming pool are planned. For a glimpse of life beyond the resort, walk up (15 mins) through the **fishing village**. The resort can arrange a taxi (€40) to take you on a tour of the plantations; good value if there's at least two of you. If you're on a budget, walk or hitch a lift up the access path with staff or a guest & flag down a yellow taxi. $$$$

Practicalities
Red Cross /Área de Saúde (entrance of town, left-hand side); ↘ 265113.

What to see The pretty yellow **church** overlooking the rocky bay is a good place to start a walk up the hill through the town, picking up a snack of fruit from roadside vendors to keep you going. Over the next few years, one of the companies owned by the president is apparently planning to build a resort here. The church (only open Sundays; ask who has the key, *a chave*) is dedicated to Santa Ana, the (apocryphal) mother of the Virgin Mary, patron saint of São Tomé and of women in labour. Santa Ana's feast day is 26 July, but the grand procession in her honour takes place in early September. The 1939/40 restoration of the early 16th-century building kept only a few parts of the walls. Inside, under a wooden ceiling, painted blue and decorated with stars, look for a statue of St John the Baptist and a marble statue of Santa Ana, in the traditional representation with the Virgin Mary in her lap. Carrying on up the hill, past the Cantagalo field, you will come across the studio of one of the island's most popular painters, Osvaldo dos Reis, above the large brand-new petrol station to the left. Reis has been painting his exuberantly colourful scenes of Santomean daily life, work, leisure, food and traditions for over a decade (↘ 920159/265100; e *reis56@hotmail.com*). Some of the little kiosks sell bread rolls and grilled *safú*. There is a bar next to Reis's house (Petisqueira Girassol) selling phone top-up cards, too, and a couple more along the road, such as **Zé Escudo**, with a porch. The entrance to Santana's popular quarter (*bairro popular*) is opposite the market, taking the left of the two dirt tracks; judging by the reaction I got, not many of Club Santana's guests make it here. The houses in the *bairro popular* were built in the early 1950s by a campaign of forced labour, with local men conscripted into this public works effort, building a house every few days and often starting at two in the morning and working for 20 hours at a stretch. This brutal treatment, repeated elsewhere, was one of the contributing factors to the uprising of 1953 (see *History*, page 5). To rejoin the resort, double back on yourself and make an immediate left, walking back down through the fishing village. On the other side of Club Santana, there is currently no access to private Praia Forma (*www.praiaforma.com*), a beautiful beach of dark-grey sand, *areia mulatta*, but an agritourism project with 21 chalets is planned.

ROÇA ÁGUA IZÉ Back on the coast road, Água Izé, a half-hour drive from the capital, is one of the biggest (2,600ha) and most-visited plantations. This is where commercial cocoa production first started in the mid-19th century. When the man responsible for introducing cocoa to the islands, João Maria de Sousa e Almeida, was made First Baron of Água Izé in 1868, he was the first *mulatto* nobleman in the Portuguese colonies. In 1884, Água Izé had 50km of internal railway lines running through its 80km² territory and 50 European employees overseeing 2,500 Angolan contract workers. Today, the brown hues of the cocoa beans and hemp sacks in the dusky workshop in the bright yellow repainted buildings make for excellent photo opportunities (our cover photo was taken here). If somebody is there, you should be able to taste the cocoa beans. Palm oil is produced here, too, as well as furniture, as part of a Portuguese co-operation project. Walk up through the plantation where

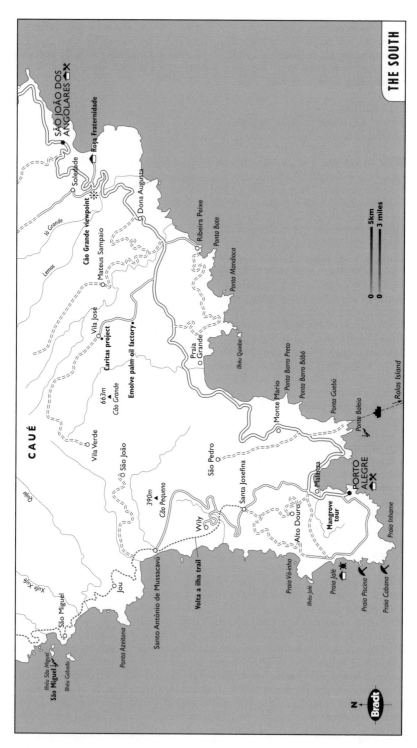

kids are selling fluffy manioc, past the soup kitchen run by a Portuguese charity, keeping to the left. From the top of the hill, you have one of the most photographed views on the island: the beautiful staircase of the crumbling **hospital**, dating from 1928. To the left, inside the building, sits the rusty hulk of a car. From up here, you have a good view all the way down to the church, the stumps of the pier in colonial times used to ferry the beans to the capital, and the beach where a new restaurant/hotel development is being built. From here, it is possible to hike to Bombaim via the plantations of Bernardo and Claudino Faro. 13 May is the local feast day, dedicated to Santa Filomena.

BOCA D'INFERNO Probably the oldest tourist attraction on the island, much-photographed 'Hell's Mouth' is reached by turning off left past Água Izé onto the promontory. Here, the water shoots through rocky basalt channels and gushes high up into the air. Don't be tempted to go too close.

PRAIA SETE ONDAS Next along is the beautiful sweeping beach of the 'seven waves'; it makes a great picnic spot. You might be joined by youngsters coming down to play with their homemade wooden toys and to practise the Brazilian martial art *capoeira*, quite popular in São Tomé and Príncipe. As with other beaches on this stretch of the coast, a resort is planned, but again, as with others, nothing has really happened yet.

Just before Santa Cecilia, a path to the right leads in a few minutes to the plantation of **Colónia Açoreana**, passing first by the houses of the workers, painted in light pastel colours. Behind is the main house, still a ruin, but there are plans to renovate the building for tourism. At the time of writing, the smaller house was setting up a room for guests; for details, contact Equador Viajens (page 101). On the left-hand side of the main road, the large abandoned drying facility might be revived again, with a projected plant for the transformation of coconuts, using the whole potential of tree, bark and fruit to produce oil, soap, grated flakes, ropes, cork substitute and isolating material.

Past the fishing village of **Ribeira Afonso** (its famous São Isidro saint's day festivities at the end of January draw many Santomeans), the second beach, **Praia de Micondó**, is a good swimming beach and also one of the best beaches for wildlife watching. When you see a breach in the metal fence to your left, park the car and walk down. To the right of the access path to the beach live massive land crabs with blue-grey bodies and fiery red legs. They make great photos, but you have to be quick as they are fairly shy, scurrying back into their holes among the coconut palms fringing the beach if they feel threatened. A trickle of water crossing the path is a favourite haunt for kingfishers, and flocks of smaller birds take off from the bushes as you approach. An Angolan investor is planning a resort here, but after problems with the government the project seems to be apparently on hold. This is the kind of story that you will hear frequently.

SÃO JOÃO DOS ANGOLARES

The main attraction of this fishing village and centre of the Angolares community (see box, page 154), in the shade of the Pico María Fernandes, is the Roça de São João working plantation, a cultural and gastronomic gem and handy stop-off point on your way south (and/or on the return journey). The blue house opposite Nezó's studio and restaurant (see below) belongs to one of the island's most interesting personalities, Fernando Mendes (✆ *261159*). Now nearing 80, the charismatic owner of the large Fraternidade plantation has been living on São Tomé for over 50 years and has many stories to tell. When the prominent

SÃO JOÃO DOS ANGOLARES
(SKETCH MAP)

São Tomé capital/swimming beaches

Roça São João,
Vale do Carmo abandoned plantation

AMI

Bar Pépé

N

Bradt

Shop selling petrol

Mionga

Police

Bar Pépé

Prédio
apartments

Market

Shops

CST

MAIN SQUARE

Post office/CTT

Bakery

Chez Nezó

Beach

Catholic church

Senhor
Fernandes
House

Irmãs
Teresianas

Cão Grande viewpoint,
Roça Fraternidade, Porto Alegre

Portuguese Socialist politician and anti-colonial activist Mário Soares was deported to São Tomé in 1968, all letters to him used to be sent via his friend Senhor Fernando to escape the prying eyes of Salazar's secret police. One of the very few Portuguese who stayed on the island after independence (though initially with several bodyguards), he is clearly a well-loved patriarchal figure today. In his house, there is a constant coming and going, people bringing in coconuts and fish, or workers presenting an injury to be patched up. Should you ever get really stuck, Senhor Fernando will probably make sure you have a roof over your head, even if it's a bed in the spare room.

WHERE TO STAY

Roça São João (7 rooms) 261140; f 221333; e turimar@cstome.net/ceiarte@cstome.net; www.ecocultura.st/index.htm. Signposted to the right as you come into town, this is a successful rural eco-tourism venture in the lovely old administrator's house. Overlooking the bay of Santa Cruz & managed by artist Olavo Amado (907405) & Inácia Monteiro, the place has a very inviting feel, with paintings & sculptures by local artists everywhere. The rooms share 3 bathrooms; extra beds can be arranged (€9–15). HB is an extra €15, FB €20. There is no need for AC as the *roça* lies above the village's humid microclimate. A balcony runs all around the house, with seats to put your feet up & look out over the misty forest or

past the huge fig tree to the bay; read, or listen to the birds — sometimes white-tailed tropicbirds come in — & a few muffled sounds from the *roça*, maybe workers picking herbs for dinner. There is only cold water, but if you ask nicely, as we did after arriving after a day-long forest trek, they can heat a bucket of water for you.

The *roça* serves some of the best **food** in São Tomé and Príncipe, cooked with fresh local ingredients, using lots of herbs & spices (if a bit heavy on the cinnamon maybe) & lovingly presented. Head chef is the local 'Mr Culture' João Carlos Silva, presenter of a successful TV programme on RTP Africa, *Na Roça Com Os Tachos* — literally 'On the Plantation with Moustaches' (see *Eating and Drinking*, page 76, for his *calulú* recipe), & voted 'Santomense Personality of 2006' by a local newspaper. B/fasts include homemade jams & fresh fruit; for lunch/dinner, guests have a choice of fish or meat. For vegetarians, São João is possibly the best place on the island. Portions are not huge; if you like one dish, make sure you ask for more before the next course arrives. Some travellers have found it overpriced & complained of a lack in hygiene, but many expats travel here from the capital just for the food. The cool airy veranda where meals are taken is great for relaxing, with hammocks, comfy bamboo furniture, art books, & local produce for sale: coffee from the *roça*, Corallo chocolate, fantastic mango jam & palm oil, pickles & wooden spoons. You are also welcome just to drop in for a coffee.

A bit set back, past the calabash trees, is the former hospital, which has spaces for art/music classes & workshops, where local girls produce woodwork, plus an overflow room for guests. There are various guided **nature trails** on foot, by bike or canoe; reserve at least a day before (there are no bikes on site); picnics cost €7. A *bulaué* band can be organised (€45). Now there is a new generator, lights are no longer turned off at midnight; still, if you're planning to come back late at night, make sure you tell the guard, otherwise you might find yourself locked out. Birdwatchers can track down the rare endemic **dwarf olive ibis** with friendly guide Zeca, spotting fabulous other (endemic) birds on the way: the speirops, *olho grosso*; Newton's yellow-breasted sunbird, *tsélélé*; the Gulf of Guinea thrush, *toldo*; & the oriole, *papafigo*. You may also get tantalisingly close to the elusive emerald cuckoo, *ossobó*. For most of the time, you are walking on the **old Bombaim road** (a 12hr walk in total, requiring camping; if you fancy it, one of the guides could probably take you, with advance planning), passing the palm-wine seller's place, marked by cut-off plastic bottles upended on sticks, & the abandoned plantation of **Vale de Carmo**. Zeca can

also take you on a giant sunbird mission to Dona Augusta & around the peaks of Maria Fernandes or Cão Grande. The services of the guides cost €20 for half-a-day, €40 for a whole day. There is a waterfall 30 mins walk away, but I'm told it's only worth a visit in the rainy season. $$

⌂ **Irmàs Teresianas** (1 room) ☏ 261124. One simple room with twin beds right next to the church. One of the friendly Sisters can show you around. The feast day of Santa Cruz de Angolares is 13 September. $

⌂ **Prédio** (1 room) ☏ 261163. One cheap apartment in the building on the market square. The rooms look OK, with a kitchen (you cook with coal or kerosene) & a large dining table, but apparently there are often problems with water pressure. Ask for Dona Aurea at the bakery, next to the church. $

⌂ **Roça Fraternidade** (14 rooms) ☏ 261159 (Fernando Mendes, in São João, see above). A hardy traveller who stayed here described the experience of staying at this plantation 6km out of São João as 'the loneliest night of my life'. You might want to bring some company then, but the views over the mountains of Trás-os-Montes, Bombaim & Maria Fernandes are spectacular. To get there, head south on the road lined by the white-flowering wild ginger, & turn left up a dirt track when Cão Grande comes into view on your right (the track to the right leads to Roça Soledade). Some 50 families live here; the grounds of the plantation cover 900ha, & span 7km. The rooms, in a yellow house built on stilts, have various degrees of comfort, but you should be able to take your pick. Ask for *o cuarto do doutor* in the corner at the back; 'the doctor's room' is nicely furnished. There is drinking water from the spring, but no electricity, so come prepared. Simple meals can be arranged through the friendly young foreman, João. At sunset, wander down the path towards the main road again for a good view of Cão Grande. $

✗ WHERE TO EAT AND DRINK

✗ **Roça São João** (see above). $$$

✗ **Chez Nezó** Main road; ☏ 261149. Good food at good value, cooked by Kady, the wife of acclaimed Angolar artist Nezó, served on the narrow porch; nice atmosphere. Upstairs is Nezó's atelier; if you visit during the daytime, he will be happy to show you his work. Currently a large extension, with an elevated restaurant, atelier & budget accommodation (4 rooms), is being built (due to open in late 2008), overlooking the bay. $$

✗ **Mionga** Main road; ☏ 261141. Simple restaurant, named after the Angolares word for 'ocean' or 'sea' & run by Nelito and Kela, recommended by a Dutch traveller. A sample menu could be *mokeka de frango*, chicken prepared in palm oil with coconut and vegetables, with ripe banana for afters. Like Nezó's, they are open to suggestions and prefer diners to book in advance. Upstairs is a porch with a disco that really only operates at the weekend; when I went there for a mid-week nightcap, the

SÃO TOMÉ'S MAROON COMMUNITY: THE ANGOLARES

Thanks to Gerhard Seibert and Paulo Alves Pereira

The *angolares*, a fishing people populating the coastal stretches of the island, from Santa Catarina in the west down to the Ilhéu das Rolas in the south, have fascinated the local imagination and Western researchers for a long time. A distinct socio-cultural group of several thousand people, the *angolares* speak their own language, *n'gola*, not intelligible to other Santomeans (see box, *Languages in São Tomé and Príncipe*, page 20). For centuries, mystery surrounded the question of how the Angolares people came to be on the island. The traditional story is that the Angolares are the descendants of a slave ship shipwrecked on the Sete Pedras rocks to the southwest of the island. Some 200 slaves are said to have swum ashore and founded a community. This romantic notion, handed down by oral transmission and promoted by a colonial government embarrassed by the draining of their workforce, has been disproved by recent historical, genetic and linguistic research. The Angolares are, in fact, a 'maroon' society established by runaway slaves, who, in the early 16th century in particular, were fleeing the harsh conditions on the plantations to form communities of fugitives (*fugões*). From the impenetrable *obó* forest they would mount raids on plantations, destroy sugar mills and take slave women and provisions back to their *quilombos*. The most successful slave uprising was led in 1595 by 'Rei' Amador. Whilst the portrait of Amador on dobra banknotes is pure fiction, and the claim that he was 'king' of the Angolares and the date of his feast day commemorating his execution by the colonial government (4 January), are now disputed, he remains very important to the culture of the Angolares and Santomean national identity. In any case, it was only in 1693 that the Angolares were defeated by the Portuguese. Apart from the prisoners, who were enslaved, the rest of the community remained fairly autonomous until, in the mid-19th century, Angolares and Portuguese met again during re-colonisation. With new cocoa plantations encroaching on their lands, the Angolares were obliged by arrangement to provide fish to the plantations in exchange for not being conscripted to work there.

only entertainment was geckos falling from the rafters. **$$**

✗ **Bar Pépé** Main road/market. Pépé seems to have a bit of a monopoly in town, running a restaurant with disco next to the market, a bar at the corner of the main square & setting up a guesthouse on the main road, behind the bar (200m past the entrance to the Roça São João). **$$**

PRACTICALITIES

Hospital Santa Cruz Main square; ☎ 261127. The hospital doesn't look so grim, but has only limited facilities.

AMI Main road; ☎ 261116. The pink house slightly set back from the main road just past the entrance to the Roça São João is the base of the Portuguese medical charity. The volunteers are usually happy to help with any advice.

CST Phone exchange Main road. There is practically no mobile signal in the village.

Police Main road; ☎ 261125

WHAT TO SEE AND DO The town **beach** is OK to walk along, but too close to the town and too popular with pigs and horseflies to swim. If you do want to swim here, make sure you go over to the far end. The track leading down to the beach with some house ruins and a pier (take a left past Nezó's house) is covered in litter. You can usually buy a coconut from one of the locals working down at the beach (local price 500$, tourist price 5,000$). The better swimming beaches, **Praia Micondó, Praia Angobó** and the dark-sand **Praia Angra Toldo** (currently being developed; *www.angratoldo.com*), are about 4km away to the north. If you don't have a car, hitch a ride with one of the many yellow taxis

Today, the Angolares make up the vast majority of fishermen on the island, following the fish along the coast. Politically, the Angolares are affiliated with the MLSTP/PSD party. Socially, as they have always refused work on the plantations, they remained outside mainstream *forro* and *contratados* contract worker communities. They continue to live in their typical fishermen's huts, called *vamplegá*, made of wooden planks and covered with interlacing palm fronds, and use the *dongo* dug-out canoe and harpoons for their artisanal fishing. The culture of the Angolares, *angolaridade* – art, music, a strong sense of tradition and of freedom – was celebrated by the late Portuguese author Fernando de Macedo (1923–2006), who claimed to be the descendant of the last Angolar king Simão Andreza. Poems such as 'Capitango, capitango' and 'Rema, Pescador, Resiste' ('Row, Fisherman, Resist') evoke the imagery of traditional Angolar society and the exaltations and dangers of the sea. The centre of *angolar* culture is around the town of São João dos Angolares in the southeastern Caué district. The most important site for meditation and the communication between the living and the dead is the Budo Bachana mountain, whilst the border between the Angolar kingdom, *Anguéné*, and the outside world is still taken to run at Praia do Rei. In the Angolar animist worldview, mountains, rivers and animals such as the owl and the shrew are holy. The *ocá* tree is particularly revered, and, as in the American Indian tradition, before any tree is felled, its spirit is asked for permission.

Linguistic studies reveal the *n'gola* lexicon to consist of 65% Portuguese, 14% Bantu languages, 1% from Kwa, with the remaining 20% still unidentified, disproving the cherished hypothesis that the *angolares* were the descendants of Angolan slaves or pre-discovery explorers. Whilst there is no written tradition, Angolar culture remains alive in language and rituals, in *bulaué* music and the work of resident painter and musician Nezó. If you are passing through São João dos Angolares in the second week of September, don't miss their biggest religious celebration in honour of the Santa Cruz. On any day of the year, impress the locals you'll meet along the main *monja* (street) with a few words of their language: *Ma vira-ó?*: 'Everything OK?' *N' sabóa!*: 'Everything OK!'

leaving São João. Explore the forest around the Pico Maria Fernandes with a guide from the *roça* (see above). If you want to save money, try dropping in to see Senhor Fernando; he might have a worker available who can take you on a walk to his Fraternidade plantation (see *Where to stay*), a 15km round trip with spectacular views. You can take a lunch-time trip over to **Rolas Island** to see the equator mark if you catch the 10.30 boat (phone ahead to make sure it is going) before getting back to the mainland on the 14.30 boat. There is another weekend disco to the right-hand side of the lane leading to the market.

FROM SÃO JOÃO DOS ANGOLARES TO PORTO ALEGRE

WHAT TO SEE AND DO On your way down south, a short detour to the **Emolve Palm Oil Factory** can be interesting, and not just if you have time to kill before the Rolas boat. You can see the heaps of red *dendém* and be shown around; nice for some photographs. Elsewhere, palm oil, much used in Santomean cuisine and medicine, has been getting bad press recently. As in other African countries, the rainforest is being threatened through the extensive planting of palm trees. Further along, the bridge at **Ribeira Peixe** fell in a few years ago; the detour is a couple of metres to the right. A quarter of an hour's walk up from the bridge is the Ribeira Peixe **waterfall**. Get a guide locally to show you the way, not least as the area is a favourite haunt of the *cobra preta*. This is also an excellent birding area; a Birdquest group I met camped two nights here and saw practically everything they needed.

For information on the 4km cycling circuit around this area, taking in Vila José, the orange plantation of Mateus Sampaio, and the Emolve waterfall, contact the Cycling Federation (see page 84).

Malanza Mangrove Tour A very relaxing and rewarding experience is to be steered through the quiet waters of São Tomé's largest mangrove in a traditional dugout canoe, organised through the NGO MARAPA, with all profits going directly to community development projects. The two-hour tour costs €10 per person, bookable/payable either at the MARAPA office in town (see page 37), at the Praia Jalé reception (see below) or directly with Senhor Vitalo in Malanza. Starting from the bridge just outside Malanza going south, your guide will paddle you across the calm waters bordered by red and white mangrove trees. The bark of the red mangrove was traditionally used on the plantations to dye the sacks for cocoa and copra; today the fishermen use it to tint the white fishing nets, to make them less shiny and likely to scare the fish away. However, taking the bark leaves the tree vulnerable to salt and water damage and the trees can die, destabilising the ecosystem. The white mangrove tree helps stop erosion through its roots sticking out of the water; it is also an important food source for the mudskipper (*cucumba*). The mangrove trees' underwater roots can also temporarily immobilise your canoe. Although many fish come here to reproduce, mangroves support only a few specific species of tree and animal. The most common bird species found here are the moorhen (*galinha-d'agua*), the malachite kingfisher (*conóbia*) and the reed cormorant (*pato-de-água*). As part of the tour, the guide moors the boat at a wooden walkway usually frequented by the only primate on the islands, the mona monkey (*macaco*). The Malanza brochure, in Portuguese and French, is sold in the Ossobô shop in São Tomé (€5; see page 111). Another **cycling circuit** is currently being opened around the Malanza Mangrove between Porto Alegre, Praia Jalé and Malanza; contact the Cycling Federation (see page 84).

PORTO ALEGRE

To be honest, there's nothing much in this large and very poor fishing village to detain you; consequently, most people just drive through on the way to the ecolodge at Praia Jalé. If that's where you're headed, to get to the **Praia Jalé reception** drive through the village, hugging the left, carry on straight at the 'Dancing' hut, drive up to the central square – surrounded by crumbling colonial buildings, such as the old army barracks, with painted figures and 'Jesus Saves' messages – and head for the path to the right at the back of the square; ask for Vado. The reception (✆ 261104), run by Vado's wife Milú, is usually crowded with kids. A local fisherman/diver should be able to offer **snorkelling trips**. A **guide can be arranged**, but if you just wander around, usually somebody will materialise to show you the place, and I've found people very friendly and appreciative of the interest. Goats hop among the ruins and abandoned farm machinery, while the tall brick chimneys are still in use for palm oil production. The most impressive building around here is the big white New Apostolic church up on the hill – most people assume this is the **old governor's house**, which is, in fact, a ruin on a bluff the other side of the bay. To visit it, leave Porto Alegre on the coast path leading towards Praia Jalé; five minutes after passing the Praia Jalé reception a gentle path leads up to your left. A pleasant half-hour walk up to the old governor's house gives you a good view over the town and the bay. Continuing along the coast track towards good swimming beaches (see below), you're likely to meet a fisherman with his colourful daily catch dangling from his harpoon, or a palm wine tapper working high up in the tree.

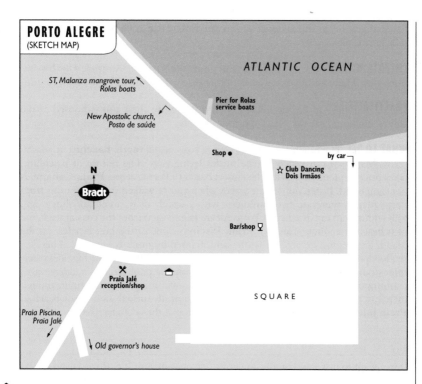

ST, Malanza mangrove tour,
Rolas boats

New Apostolic church,
Posto de saúde

ATLANTIC OCEAN

Pier for Rolas
service boats

Shop ●

by car

☆ Club Dancing
Dois Irmãos

Bar/shop ♀

N

Bradt

Praia Jalé
reception/shop

Praia Piscina,
Praia Jalé

Old governor's house

SQUARE

WHERE TO STAY
In Porto Alegre proper, a self-catering place with kitchen is now available (€20 for one or two people, with breakfast taken at the ecolodge reception). Check with Vado or his wife at Praia Jalé reception.

Praia Jalé Ecolodge (3 chalets, tent spaces) ☎ 261104 (reception), ☎ 222792 (reservations São Tomé; e marapa@cstome.net; as the ecolodge is very popular, it's better to phone). Sleep next to the crashing waves in a bamboo bed in chalets made from palm tree wood, or in a tent (bring your own). There is a toilet & a cold shower plus a cosy wooden house to share the meals prepared in Porto Alegre (can be vegetarian), with a hammock outside overlooking the sea, as well as an outside eating area. There have been organisational hiccups, with reservations not getting through, but for the moment this is one of the few locally managed operations & everybody who has

been has loved the experience; I met a couple who stayed for 10 days & didn't get bored. In season, you can see all the island's species of turtle laying eggs, or the release of hatchlings to the sea. Outside the season, at night, you'll have hundreds of crabs for company; bring flip-flops & don't worry if you step on them, they are very resilient. Praia Jalé is not really a swimming beach, nor is **Praia Va inhá**, a 20min walk away to the end of the track, but gorgeous beaches such as Praia Piscina are only a short walk away, back towards Porto Alegre. An extra bed costs €5, lunch/dinner €5 per person; meals taken at the reception at Porto Alegre, 3km away, cost €4. ⑤

WHERE TO EAT
Praia Jalé reception sells biscuits, spaghetti and rice, bottled soft drinks, beer and water, but there's only a wooden bench inside to sit down. Walking up towards the central square from the pier, taking a right before the 'Dancing' hut, there is a *loja* shop on the right-hand side selling biscuits and wines, with a shaded seating area with one table and one or two chairs. Toilet facilities are a hole at the back apparently. If you want a proper meal, ask for **Dona Fausta**, who lives a bit further down; she should be able to prepare you a slap-up slice of grilled

The East and South PORTO ALEGRE

6

fish, but give her as much notice as you can. Failing that, a shop down near the pier sells bread rolls.

ENTERTAINMENT Near the pier, you can't miss the 'Dancing Amizade Dos Irmãos' disco hut. There is supposed to be another disco; it shouldn't be too hard to find.

PRACTICALITIES Up on the hill; the **posto de saúde** (first aid) is housed in the yellow building near the New Apostolic church.

WHAT TO SEE The beaches on this stretch of coast are all **turtle beaches**. In season (Nov–Mar) you can watch female turtles laying eggs. The release of hatchlings takes place September–April. The closest beach to Porto Alegre, **Praia Cabana**, is not signposted. Listen out for the waves when you've walked maybe 15 mins from Porto Alegre; there are two entrances, with a widely disregarded anti-litter sign. Still within walking distance of Porto Alegre (signposted from the coastal track, the next beach after Praia Cabana), **Praia Piscina** is one of the best beaches on the island, a sweeping expanse of white sand, framed by black basalt rock. There's a shallow pool to the left (the small sea urchins are fine, but mind the big ones: their spines can bring on a fever), and beware: the middle pool receives sudden waves crashing over the rocks at the back. The best swimming is to the right, though there can be some strong currents too. The beautifully tucked-away turtle beach of **Praia Jalé** is mainly visited on an overnight stop at the ecolodge (see above).

ILHÉU DAS ROLAS/ROLAS ISLAND

If you want to just stand on the equator mark once in your life, Rolas Island can be visited on an organised lunch trip, but for relaxation and to really enjoy the island, a 4/5-night stay is ideal, longer if you are planning to do a lot of diving.

GETTING THERE There is a boat service (the crossing takes around 20 minutes) connecting the **Ponte Baleia** embarking point with the Ilhéu das Rolas. Ponte Baleia is a good 2 ½-hour drive on the bumpy road south from the capital, with wonderful views of the Cão Grande. As with 99% of places on the islands, the turn-off to Ponte Baleia is not signposted; look out for a cut to your left once you have passed Monte Mario (where, sometimes, monkeys play in the trees) and are going down the hill again towards Malanza. For €10 each way, you can get Pestana transport, leaving the Pestana office in São Tomé in the morning at 07.30 and making the return journey at around 15.00, picking up clients from the 14.30 boat from the island. In theory, the boat runs several times a day. However, the times given by the office are not to be taken literally and are liable to change according to management requirements; be sure to confirm in advance which boat you want to take. There is a very intermittent mobile phone signal on the way down here and, as the radio at Ponte Baleia is solar-powered, ie: doesn't work at night, staff can't alert reception if you are late. You are not encouraged to do this, but if you arrive too late, try and zoom over to Porto Alegre, a few minutes' drive further south, where a *carioco* wooden service boat with outboard motor leaves for Rolas between 17.00 and 18.00. If you are too late for that, then you'll have to find (and pay) a sympathetic canoe owner to get you across. The return journey is usually at 14.30, but if you want to leave earlier and explore Porto Alegre or one of the nearby beaches, talk to the head receptionist; he might be able to put you on an earlier boat taking staff across. All you need to do then is to make sure you are back at Ponte Baleia at 14.45 to catch the minibus back to town; the driver often starts the return trip in Porto Alegre, but don't rely on that.

WHERE TO STAY AND EAT

Pestana Equador (70 bungalows) CP 851;
261196; **f** 261195; **e** pestana.equador@
pestana.com; www.pestana.com. São Tomé office: Av
12 Julho; 223600; **f** 222703; **e** rct@cstome.net.
This 4-star resort is the only commercial
accommodation on the island. All the bungalows are
pleasant, with TV, fridge, AC & ceiling fan, & a
veranda with comfy chairs, set in well-tended
landscaped gardens, with hibiscus & pineapple
borders. The semi-detached bungalows have fairly
thin walls; as the resort is hardly ever fully booked,
ask for a bungalow without neighbours. They also
could do with a refurbishment sometime; mine at
least was a bit dark too. No **401/402 Standard** is
the best choice, as you get a sea view without
paying more for it, but it gets booked up quickly.
Only the front bungalows with the 300 numbers
have a sea view; the 600 numbers at the back are
more spacious, with cattle egrets grazing outside.
Another easy bird to spot around the compound is
the pin-tailed whydah (the male has a conspicuously
long tail); these were introduced as pet birds &
always live close to humans. Lizards flit across the
wooden walkways connecting the different parts of
the resort. From the island, you have gorgeous views
of both Cão Grande & Cão Pequeno, framing golden
beaches. A 2,300m² landscaped saltwater pool, the
largest on the west African coast, snakes its way
around a bar, with an infinity pool feature. There is
also a small Jacuzzi with a massage/acupuncture
table between the quay & the pool; book sessions at
the Bazar Sete Ondas. A 30min massage costs €20,
1hr €40; a 30min acupuncture (Tue/Fri/Sat) costs
€25. The climate on Rolas is even more hot &
humid than on the main island, & early in the
afternoon mosquitoes will start coming out; don't
invite them into your bungalow by leaving the doors
open. Always have a bottle of fresh water in your
bungalow, as you cannot buy anything after the bars
close. And don't forget, you might pay for your
splendid isolation with a few hiccups: power cuts,
though not frequent, do happen, despite the resort
generator consuming 600 litres of diesel every day.
There has also been the occasional problem with the
fresh water supply; in my case when I was literally
standing under the shower. With 90% of visitors
Portuguese, I've heard complaints that reception staff
don't have enough English. I've heard other
complaints about an inflexible approach to guests'
requests – for instance, a group of three wanting to
move because the 'family suite' turned out to only
have AC in the main room, or a tourist arriving

without luggage not getting much help with buying
supplies. If there's any problem, ask for the day
manager (their names are posted on the counter), or
head receptionist Jai; they can usually sort things
out for you. Bring cash for your drinks expenses,
just in case there's a problem with the credit card
reading device at check-out. (Also, the link-up with
Portugal for the processing adds €3 to the bill.) If
you fancy **getting married** on the equator, a 3-day
extravaganza including gala dinner with live music &
barbecue lunch around the swimming pool will cost
you €570 per person, plus transfers. The resort can
help you organise a civil &/or religious ceremony.
The honeymoon package (€1,000) consists of 6
nights' FB for the price of 5 & an upgrade to a
quarto suite or Superior, a welcome cocktail & bottle
of bubbly, a guided visit to the equator with
certificate & a trip to the Roça São João (on São
Tomé). For business visitors, there are also 2
conference rooms.

Resort guests take meals – breakfast, lunch (if
you're on FB, joined by daytrippers) & dinner – in
the **Sete Pedras restaurant**, situated on an elevation
on the eastern side of the island overlooking two
bays & the open sea with the Sete Pedras rocks in
the distance. The restaurant is a 5min walk from
the bungalows, past egrets feeding on the lawn. The
food is an excellent mix of international & local,
with always plenty of choice. The restaurant, with a
tasteful terracotta floor & wood carvings, is open on
3 sides, but gets surprisingly hot still; you can
escape to the simple wooden tables on the narrow
wraparound balcony. The b/fast buffet (07.30–10.00)
serves freshly squeezed fruit juices, rolls, brioches,
cereals, fresh fruit, Santomean coffee & a variety of
teas. Lunch (12.30–14.00) could be pumpkin soup, a
matabala stew or beef stroganoff, shrimp curry,
Santomean omelette with herbs, salads & homemade
juices. The dinner buffet (07.30–22.00) offers 3–4
main courses, fish & meat, prepared in international
& African style. Get there early; any buffet food will
suffer from being on hot plates for long, & the fish
in particular can get dry. There is an excellent
choice for vegetarians. At around €12, the Rotas
d'Africa house wines are good value. There are three
bars: the **Tartaruga Bar** next to the reception & pier
area serves excellent pizzas & salads, desserts &
coffees (11.00–19.00). The **swimming pool bar** is
open for drinks 09.30–18.00. **Bar Golfinho**, a
pleasant airy open space with comfy chairs & tables
on the way up towards the restaurant, is open
16.00–24.00. The Golfinho only serves the local

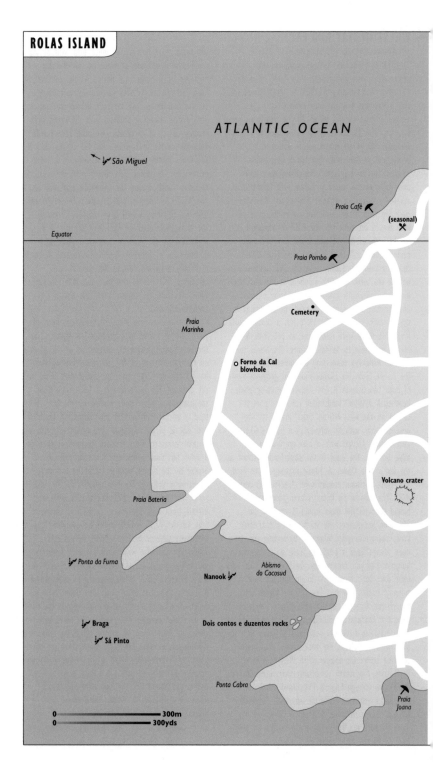

ROLAS ISLAND

ATLANTIC OCEAN

São Miguel

Praia Café

(seasonal)

Equator

Praia Pombo

Cemetery

Praia Marinho

Forno da Cal blowhole

Volcano crater

Praia Bateria

Ponta da Furna

Nanook

Abismo do Cocosud

Braga

Dois contos e duzentos rocks

Sá Pinto

Ponta Cabra

Praia Joana

0   300m
0   300yds

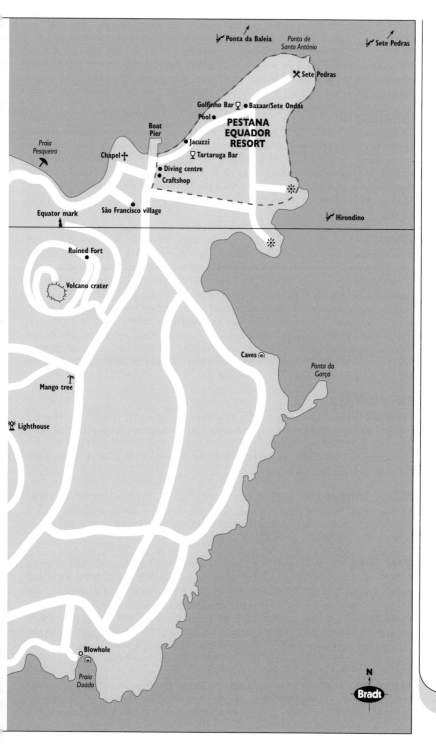

Ponta da Baleia

Ponta de
Santo António

Sete Pedras

Sete Pedras

Golfinho Bar ⚲ ● Bazaar/Sete Ondas

Pool ●

**PESTANA
EQUADOR
RESORT**

Boat
Pier

Praia
Pesqueira

Chapel ✝

● Jacuzzi

⚲ Tartaruga Bar

● Diving centre
● Craftshop

Equator mark

São Francisco village

Hirondino

Ruined Fort ●

Volcano crater

Caves

Ponta da
Garça

Mango tree

Lighthouse

Blowhole

Praia
Doado

N

Bradt

Criollo beer &, apart from port, no wines by the glass (consider buying a bottle & taking it through to dinner). You have to sign a chit for every beverage you consume (a beer costs 2€), & pay your collection of chits when you check out. Pestana understandably discourages eating food in the village; however, standards of hygiene are unlikely to be better or worse than on the mainland, so it's up to you. Also, if you are on a tight budget & have a sleeping bag/tent, there is nothing to stop you from asking about informal accommodation in the village. Chalets $$$, suites $$$, superior suites $$$$.

ENTERTAINMENT There is entertainment every night, in the resort's **Bar Golfinho**, from about 21.30 – even if there are only a dozen guests. The animation ranges from good-fun *bulaué* and *socopé* dance and *batuque* drum performances to excruciating party games (think passing an apple around without using your hands). There is usually a disco afterwards. Cooling off with a midnight swim in the infinity pool under the stars is a truly fitting finish to a night on the equator. During the day, you can use the pool table, and play a round of ping-pong; there is a beach-volleyball net too.

SHOPPING Above the Golfinho Bar, on the right-hand side, the (pricy) **Bazaar Sete Ondas** sells clothes (bikinis, shorts, flip-flops), toiletries, inc suncream and mosquito repellent, sunglasses, batteries, CDs and a range of souvenirs (sand cards, Corallo coffee, coconut cups). This is also where you book your massages and acupuncture sessions. The shop is open 08.00–12.00 and 14.00–18.00, but if you need anything, one of the staff can probably get the shop assistant to open up for you. There is also a crammed little local **crafts shop** – selling carvings, bowls and drums made from *cidrela* and *amoreira* wood – around the corner from the diving centre, at the beginning of the path towards the equator mark. Official opening hours are 06.00–16.30; if it's closed, somebody should be able to fetch artisan Edimilson Maral Santiago (✆ *919359*) for you.

PRACTICALITIES

Communications There is a mobile phone signal, and parts of the resort are a wireless zone – reception, the Golfinho Bar and the first two rows of bungalows – but be prepared for hiccups. For guests without laptops, internet access is free for 30 minutes, 07.30–22.00, at a terminal in the little room behind reception; the connection is fairly slow, though.

Medical facilities The only danger on the island, pointed out by a much-photographed wooden sign, is falling coconuts. A doctor comes over on Friday, a nurse three times a week, and two members of staff are trained in first aid. There is also a first-aid post at the entrance of the village.

WHAT TO DO The resort offers a range of excursions which allow you to make Rolas your base and still see a lot of what the main island has to offer: a half-day (€30) and day trip (€50) by boat around São Tomé island, visiting beaches and taking in dolphin-spotting; a day trip to the sights of the capital, including lunch at Dona Hortência's restaurant (€60); to Roça Bombaim (€65); to the south, including the plantations of Porto Alegre, São João and Praia Esqueira (€50); or the central and northern regions of São Tomé, including a visit to the National Museum and the plantations of Monte Café and Agostinho Neto (€80).

Beaches The best beach on the island is **Praia Café**, a 10-minute walk from reception across the staff area and past the Praia Pesqueira fishing beach with the beached rusty wreck, where you can make friends with the local kids, especially if you're willing to share your snorkelling mask. The Praia Café bar is only open in high season, but there is lovely sand and good shade. Here, snorkelling yields various colourful fish (*asma preto, bolião, caqui, garoupa* – see *Glossary*, page 193), with the occasional turtle or moray eel on the little reef to the right. According to the locals, the next beach along, down from the abandoned cemetery, **Praia Pombo**, is also good for snorkelling. The beaches at the northern tip, around the restaurant, are great for hiding away with a book or for following the daily dramas in the lives of the hermit crabs played out in the sand, only interrupted by the occasional thud of a falling coconut.

WALKS There are several walks you can do. The island is criss-crossed by a number of little trails cutting through the dense forest of coconut palms, but it is quite impossible to get lost. If in doubt, just plough on straight until you hear the sound of waves. You will hit the path going around the island; following that in either direction will get you back to the resort. **Guided walks** are offered free of charge (see below). When the resort was built in 2000, the Angolares villagers of **São Francisco** had to move, receiving some compensation. At the time of writing, the Pestana group were trying to entice the villagers to leave the island entirely, but there was some resistance and criticism of the low level of compensation offered. Still, the resort jobs are very sought-after locally, despite a waiter here earning only the minimum wage, about €30 a month. Look out for the little chapel dedicated to St Francis, to the right of the pier, when you arrive.

To the equator mark Some 300m past the village, the road forks: take a right (signposted). A 20-minute gentle uphill stroll leads to the equator mark, marking the imaginary line at equal distance from the North and South Poles, dividing the earth. Walking around a colourful mosaic of the world, you can have one foot in the northern hemisphere, the other in the southern. From here, there are good views over the resort and across to the southern tip of São Tomé. The length of the equator is estimated at around 40,000km. One traveller pointed out to me that according to his 2007 GPS reading, the equator now runs right through the village: something for you to verify!

To the lighthouse If you want a shorter walk, carry on straight at the sign pointing to the equator mark, turn right at the mango tree with the pile of coconuts beneath, and take the first left at another mango tree: you will wind your way up to the lighthouse. It's nice as a focus for a walk, but the top is fairly overgrown, and there is no view. The lighthouse keeper spends most of his time in the village, so won't usually be available to let you in.

Around the island This 2½–3-hour walk around the island is best done in the early morning; take advantage of the free guided walks. My guide was very knowledgeable, showing me all kinds of medicinal plants, ferns and trees along the coast trail, leading past blowholes and steep rocky cliffs. If you go on your own, you can either start behind the Golfinho bar, along Praia Santo António and along the coastline; after two thirds you will come across the blowholes, with the sea swirling beneath and coming up in great whooshing sounds, and return to the resort via Praia Café and the fishing village. Alternatively, take the track towards the equator mark, but carry on straight towards **Praia Joana**, a good swimming beach. If you start around 05.30–06.00, you'll still be back in time for breakfast (take an energy bar or other snack – maybe some fruit from the previous day's breakfast? – to tide you over). Wear trousers and good shoes and take some water. Most importantly, use a good mosquito repellent; I got my worst bites here; they itched like crazy and some of them turned into unsightly blisters. (Luckily, according to management, the last reported case of malaria on Rolas was eight years ago.) Quite a few of the beautiful beaches you see on your walk unfortunately have no access – there are plans to build some steps down the steep cliffs – while the stunning **Praia Bateria** is being set up as a secluded beach for honeymooners.

ACTIVITIES

Diving Diving off the island reveals an undisturbed underwater world: snappers, sweetfish, stingrays, octopus, sea horses, turtles, fan coral, moray eels, sea slugs, etc, with plenty of surprises for those who haven't got a fixation with the big fish. Sharks are visible, but are not guaranteed at every dive. Whales have passed by occasionally. There are fewer colours than in the Caribbean; visibility is also not quite perfect, and the open Atlantic brings a strong swell. While some of the German diving guests are used to more organisation and less *léve-léve*, a certain spirit of improvisation might be needed; in the past outboard motors were known to break down in the past, with spare parts weeks away, but this situation seems to be under control now. In 2007, only about 20 divers visited Rolas.

Dive sites

Hirondino is the first site you will be taken to if you are an inexperienced diver, as it is close by and protected, but you can go down to the rounded top at 14–17m, with the chance of seeing octopus, resident sea horses, soldierfish, sweetlips & parrotfish, as well as blackbar hogfish cleaning the bigger fish between six rock formations on an even sandy ground. This is a great site for night dives; check whether the night diving boat is back in service.
Nanook & Sá Pinto With luck, you can see sand sharks here between the tall rocks. Fish life is similar to Braga, but at a lesser depth (15–16m).
Ponta da Furna Recommended, but access is dependent on swell conditions.

Braga has a lot of hard coral & is an excellent place to see red snappers, rays of over 1m diameter & moray eels. All the action is at 22m.
Ponta da Baleia Good chance of seeing turtles, such as the massive leatherback, among the impressive blocks of rock on a gradient sloping down to 26–27m near the Rolas boat pier on São Tomé island. Red snapper, rock lobster, a few fan corals, & a cave, 1.5–1.8m wide, may hide some big fish surprises.
Sete Pedras Beautiful site, 8–30m, with sting rays, small angelfish, corals, etc, on sandy ground. There are more than 'seven rocks', by the way!

Diving courses At the time of writing, the situation was somewhat in flux, Jean-Louis Testori from Club Maxel is currently running diving operations there. There is no Pestana instructor on site but at times a German instructor looking after Ivory Tours (see page 46) clients. If you are organising your diving through the resort, the price comes down if you do ten dives or more. Diving with hired equipment costs about 20% more. A diving baptism costs €80 and a scuba review €70. If you are planning to rent equipment, check well in advance that your size is available. Filling your bottle costs €7. OWD, Advanced, Rescue and Divemaster courses are on offer here. Novices can book a 1:1 introduction to diving, *baptismo de mergulho*, in the pool. If you are familiar with snorkelling, ie: used to putting your head under water, then within the hour you can be gently trundling along the bottom of the pool, controlling your buoyancy by pressing a valve. You will practise taking the mask off under water and putting it back on – not easy, but a vital skill you need to master should your mask become dislocated at 30m depth. Your second session could already be out at sea! Make sure you don't arrive with a cold, as your ears can't cope with the difference in pressure. In this case, consider postponing your stay at Rolas if you're at all flexible; management can usually accommodate this. Make sure you drink lots of water and get sufficient sleep. Dives are made from high-sea fishing boats and occasionally a dug-out canoe. At the time of research, there was no boat available for night dives, but that might change. In any case, bring your own lamp for lighting up caves and rock holes. The diving centre is open 07.30–12.30 and 14.00–17.00. If you read German, check the diving forum www.tauchernet.de for up-to-date information.

Fishing Depending on how many of you there are, submarine fishing (*pesca submarina*) costs anything from €30 per passenger (if there are eight of you) to €110 (for one). There are three boats available for high-sea sport fishing (*pesca de alto mar*). In the resort restaurant I saw a group of Portuguese visitors happily tucking into the sea bass (*corvina*) they'd harpooned earlier in the day. Prices range from €300 for half a day for a two-person boat including skippers and picnic food to €850 for a six-person boat for the day.

Snorkelling Hiring a mask, fins and snorkel costs €15 a day. Head straight for **Praia Café**; don't waste your time scraping your belly across the rocks on Praia Santo António, buffeted by the swell, like I did.

THE SOUTHWEST

The remotest area on the island is currently really only visited by dedicated wildlife enthusiasts, mostly birdwatchers looking to tick off as many of the São Tomé endemics as possible. The area is good for the threatened giant sunbird, the São Tomé sunbird and the São Tomé paradise flycatcher. The base of the **Xufe-Xufe** river is a 4-hour drive by 4x4 vehicle or a 3-hour boat trip from São Tomé. Contact Luis Mario Almeida or Norberto from Flogátours (see page 101); the latter only leads groups there in the short dry season in January/February. Alternatively, you can hire a guide and porters at Santo António when you arrive; make sure the arrangements are understood, in particular, if you need them to stay the night with you and continue portering luggage up the river. You have to bring everything. Watch out for the horseflies. The recommended campsite for birdwatchers is 3km (2–3 hours' walk) upriver, next to the large eastern tributary, home of the giant sunbird. Hikers will enjoy a 2-day **volta a ilha** trek from Santa Catarina to Porto Alegre (contact José Spencer, see page 82), in territory explored by very few tourists, while a **boat trip** (see page 74) reveals beautiful coastal scenery.

Part Three

PRÍNCIPE

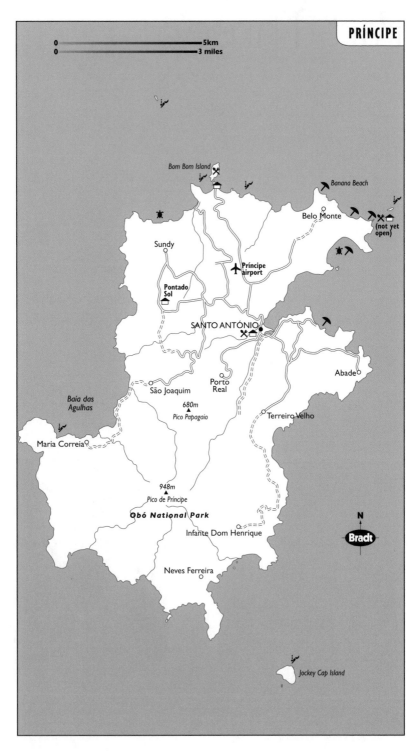

PRÍNCIPE

0 ▬▬▬▬▬▬▬ 5km
0 ▬▬▬▬▬▬▬ 3 miles

Bom Bom Island

Banana Beach

Belo Monte

(not yet open)

Sundy

Príncipe airport

Pontado Sol

SANTO ANTÓNIO

Porto Real

Abade

Baía das Agulhas

São Joaquim

680m
Pico Papagaio

Terreiro Velho

Maria Correia

948m
Pico de Príncipe

Obó National Park

N

Bradt

Infante Dom Henrique

Neves Ferreira

Jockey Cap Island

7

Príncipe

HIGHLIGHTS

Swim at Banana Beach, or relax at the Bom Bom resort – for a week, a beach day, a snorkelling session or just one magical dinner, depending on your budget. Tick Príncipe's endemic birds off your list, explore the magnificent plantation of Sundy, hike through the rainforest, climb Pico Papagaio, and learn to dance the *kizomba* in Santo António.

BACKGROUND INFORMATION

If you think São Tomé is beautiful if a bit isolated, wait till you get to Príncipe…

For the tourist, visiting the Green Island, *a Ilha Verde*, has advantages: an even more authentic travelling experience and sense of discovery, cleaner beaches, a pristine underwater world and great scope for photography. The risk of malaria is very low – a thorough 2006 Taiwanese study found few cases. The remoteness and laid-back atmosphere of this island, with a surface area of only 143km², has real charm; I met travellers who had spent two months on Príncipe without getting bored, and you don't need to stay here that long to be greeted like a long-lost friend. *Léve-léve*? Here, it's called *móli-móli* – it's the same thing, only slower. The flip side of this unspoilt beauty is a very rudimentary tourist infrastructure; if you're on a budget, organising excursions can be hard work. On Príncipe, tourists broadly fall into two basic camps: the well-heeled Bom Bom resort relaxers and the budget rainforest explorers.

For the people living here, the problems of São Tomé – isolation, poverty, lack of infrastructure and investment – are exacerbated. Levels of education are lower; schooling stops at ninth grade and 20% stay away from school altogether. Unemployment is higher, and alcoholism and mental health problems more visible in this community of some 6,000 people. The power is regularly cut between around midnight and 07.00 (bring a good torch). All consumer goods, vegetables and construction materials are more expensive. Between the people of São Tomé and those of Príncipe, inhabitants of one island nation separated by some 160km of sea, prejudices abound. The Santomeans believe their cousins on the smaller island – whom they like to call *moncós* – to be a bit simple, while the inhabitants of Príncipe, mainly *tongas* of Capeverdian descent, reckon the Santomeans want everything for themselves.

Discovered by the Portuguese on 17 January 1471, the island was first called Santo Antão in honour of the saint of that day, granted to the feudal lord António Carneiro in 1502, and made a crown colony in the name of Príncipe, to pay homage to Prince (later King) Dom João. Similar to São Tomé, the north and the south of the island have distinct climatic zones, determining the shape of the colonial economy. The north is well suited to the cultivation of the cocoa and coffee crops (that were introduced to Príncipe years before they were established in São Tomé), coconuts, bananas, breadfruit and pineapples, while the south is

Thanks to Wilfried Günther and Gilberto Gil Umbelina

In 1970, *lung'íye* (see box, page 20) was prophesied to suffer language death within the next 30 years (especially in the absence of a written tradition), yet it is still clinging on, with a couple of hundred speakers; some even claim a resurgence. Visitors will see manifestations of the language in the names scribbled on the wooden signs of snack bars and shops. Knowing a few common words will astonish and impress the locals. Rejecting the traditional epithet of *moncós*, the inhabitants of Príncipe prefer to call themselves *mínu íye*, 'children of the island', and a long-established dweller of the capital Santo António is *ibó*. For the first greeting of the day when you meet somebody, 'good morning, good day', *bon-dyá-ó* is used, later, *bwá-tádi-é*, good day, and *bwá-nóci-ó*, good evening. Today, a common greeting is *modiê?* ('all OK?'), with the response *malimentê, sá via via* ('all OK'). When you are walking past somebody or taking your leave, you say *pásó*, and the road is called *ulátu*. I am thirsty is *n sa ki sekúra*. How much does it cost? *kwātu kushtá â?* Many thanks is *désu pagá cí* (literally 'may God pay you'). Money is *dyó*, water *áwa*, firewater *deti*; banana *baná*, high/tall, nice, beautiful *gávi* or *átu*; to sleep *dimí*, and to wash laundry on a stone *dumú upánu*. A white person is *rupéu/a* ('European'). And finally, the local equivalent to the Santomean motto *léve-léve* is *móli-móli*. Informal classes are available; contact Manuel Trovoada (see page 92).

more mountainous, wilder, and subject to a lot more precipitation. The island was temporarily occupied by the Dutch in 1598, and attacked by the French in 1702. In the mid-18th century, the capital of the archipelago was temporarily transferred to Santo António by the colonial government, struggling to maintain order on the main island; the transfer of the capital back to São Tomé a hundred years later initiated the archipelago's second colonisation by Portugal. Later on, the island was used by the colonial government as a punitive place of exile for troublemakers. In recent memory, in 1981, hunger riots, when no boat with provisions had reached the island for months, were violently put down by the Santomean government, which in turn fuelled secessionist demands. The victims of months of arbitrary imprisonment are still seeking compensation. The island has had autonomy status since 1995, covering the Pagué district. The archipelago's second **Free Trade Zone** (ZFBA) and deep-water port being set up in the Baia das Agulhas in the southwest, the people of Príncipe were hoping to at least get a share of the wealth generated by this tax-free commercial hub; electricity and jobs for the surrounding fishing communities might be a start. However, at the time of writing, the prospect was on hold in favour of tourism. Currently, the whole economy on Príncipe runs on diesel (*gasóleo*). The oil deposits being found north of Príncipe (see box, page 16) have been accompanied by rumblings of nationalism, whilst the recent setting up of a dedicated website (*www.principe.st*) is an encouraging sign of the regional government's determination to increase tourism. At the moment, many paths leading to abandoned plantations are now disused; so few visitors come that they have to be cleared of vegetation again and again by machete. Spectacular basalt phonoliths and lower elevations (called *oques* here) dot the lush rainforest.

For volunteering opportunities, see page 92.

CULTURE

Due to the island's isolation and poverty, there is little artistic production, but Príncipe has its own distinctive traditions. Like other cultural manifestations on the island, the slow *dexa* dance shows a cultural link with the Minho province of northern Portugal, from where many immigrants came to São Tomé and Príncipe; look out for the **Vijyá Kôtê** group. There is the militant poetry of **Marcelo da Veiga** (1892–1976) and the lyrical expression of **Manuela Margarido** (1925–2007; 'A Ilha te fala'); the murals of **Protásio Dias Xavier Pina** (1960–99); the *musica nacional* of the (now dissolved) **Ilha Verde** band. The late **Camilo Domingos** sang very popular *kizomba* in Cape Verde creole and is remembered in town by a plaque on the square with the Padrão monument. The *puita* dance is being kept alive by a group from the Sundy plantation, the São Joaquim plantation has a *bulaué* percussion group, whilst the contemporary songs of popular singer **Gilberto Gil**

AUTO DE FLORIPES

With thanks to Paulo Alves Pereira

São Tomé has the *tchiloli*, Príncipe has the Auto de Floripes or *São Lourenço*, after the saint in honour of whom this dramatic piece of street theatre is performed, turning the whole of Santo António into a stage for the biggest party of the year. Based on an episode in the life of the Emperor Charlemagne, introduced to the island in the 18th/19th century (and much akin to a play performed in a village in northern Portugal), at the core of the Auto de Floripes lies a battle between the Moors and the Christians. Floripes is a young Moorish princess who converts to Christianity for the love of a young soldier in Charlemagne's army, Guy of Burgundy (*Gui de Borgonha*). The show lasts all day, with the main action taking place from around midday. Early in the morning, at 07.00, the inhabitants of Santo António hear the sounds of the first horns, as the two ambassadors, each accompanied by a tambourine player, start gathering their factions. They go on to pay their respects to the ancestors at the town's cemetery and beach. Around midday, the two rival armies meet: the Moors in red, the Christians in elaborate green, blue and white battledress, carrying shields showing their allegiance. Gathering on the main square over the course of the afternoon, they joust, clashing their swords, whilst their leaders hold forth, attempting to convince the adversary to change allegiance. In the same way as in the *tchiloli*, anachronisms such as telephones or plastic pistols feature alongside crucifixes and mirrors sown into gowns. The battle is commandeered from tall wooden structures, decked out in palm fronds: the 'castle' of white-bearded Charlemagne and the Pairs of France in front of the church, defended by Oliveiros, and the Moorish 'castle' of Admiral Balão, next to the pink regional government palace. With the Moors occupying most of the battlefield, Guy de Burgundy wounds the Moor Ferrabras, son of Admiral Balão, and is taken prisoner. While all this is going on, the fools (*bobos*), cracking whips and wearing frightful masks, hold the public in check and clear the lines of combat, scattering delighted kids. With Guy of Burgundy facing execution, the young Turkish princess Floripes, sister of Ferrabras and daughter of Admiral Balão, converts to Christianity, turning against her father, and marries Guy in a Christian ceremony, thus saving the life not only of Guy but also the other knights. The drama ends at night, around 20.00, with the Admiral, taken prisoner, refusing to convert to Christianity. The Auto de Floripes is performed by an all-male cast, with hereditary roles, except Floripes, who is played by a young girl who must be a virgin. To catch this colourful spectacle, you have to be on the island on 15 August (the Auto de Floripes is no longer performed on St Laurent's Day, 10 August), or on the following Sunday, when it is performed again in its entirety. For more information, contact culture officer Manuel Salomé at the Casa da Cultura or through his next-door neighbour (\ 251169), or ask for Marcelo Lopes de Andrade, president of the festivities commission.

Umbelina give the island's *lung'íye* language new life. Ask locally whether there are any saint's days (*dias santos*) or popular feasts (*festas populares*) being celebrated: Santo António do Príncipe 17 January, António de Pádua 29/30 May, Nossa Senhora da Graça mid/end August, when the *dexa* is performed, and Nossa Senhora da Conceiçao on 8 December. If you are on the island over New Year, try to catch the **Vindes Menino** procession on the night of 31 December, which satirises all the little scandals that have happened in the past year. The biggest celebration, however, is Saint Laurent's in mid-August (see box on page 171).

GETTING THERE

BY AIR This is the recommended option: a short hop in a comfortable two-propeller machine with great views of the Tinhosa Islands and the spectacular coastline of Príncipe. Currently, STP Airways flies four times a week (but was out of action for a while in spring 2008), and SCD Aviation has a twice-weekly flight serving Africa's Eden's (see page 46) clients going to the Bom Bom Island resort (the company is set to invest €45,000 into infrastructure and tourism facilities starting with the airport). Check with Navetur for updates, as the situation can change from week to week. The planes touch down on one of the world's shortest runways, with hens pecking around a stranded plane that has been rusting away for years, against the backdrop of rocky fingers rising out of lush tropical forest.

STP Airways

São Tomé – Príncipe	Príncipe – São Tomé
Dep: Mon 08.00 – arr: 08.35	Dep: Mon 09.00 – arr: 09.35
Dep: Wed 08.00 – arr: 08.35	Dep: Wed 09.00 – arr: 09.35
Dep: Fri 08.00 – arr: 08.35	Dep: Fri 09.00 – arr: 09.35
Dep: Sat 08.00 – arr: 08.35	Dep: Sat 09.00 – arr: 09.35

SCD Aviation

São Tomé – Príncipe	Príncipe – São Tomé
Dep: Thu: 10.30 – arr: 11.05	Dep Thu 15.20 – arr: 15.50
Dep: Sun: 10.30 – arr: 11.05	Dep Sun 15.20 – arr: 15.50

The flights leave São Tomé from the **old airport**, a couple of hundred metres along from the current international airport on the Praia Gamboa road. The journey takes about 40 minutes; however, often there is a delay. Sometimes, the plane can't land because of the mist hanging over the island and a plane chartered by STP Airways is sometimes needed to fight oil spills in the Gulf of Guinea. So, if you need to be back on São Tomé for your flight home, don't cut it too fine; make sure you're back with a couple of days to spare. Tickets (around €140 round trip) can be booked through Navetur or Mistral, but seats get booked up quickly, especially for festivities such as São Lourenço in mid-August. If the plane is not full, you can also just turn up and buy your ticket at the airport, but don't rely on this.

The **Portuguese air force plane**, *Aviocar*, used for evacuation services and for transporting functionaries and cargo, was suspended in December 2007, but an alternative should be in place by the summer of 2008. Officially, tourists are not meant to travel on this plane; unofficially, it might be possible, with luggage strictly limited to 10kg. Your best bet is to ask when the plane is due and plead with staff.

Within the airport, there is a small café serving meals and hot and cold drinks – handy for delays. There should be working lavatories when you visit, as the airport is being upgraded. Nearby is a good bakery, in an inconspicuous house marked 035 (ask to be shown), and the *Loja do Aeroporto* (🕐 *08.00–20/21.00 Mon–Sat*) behind a small embankment is a useful small shop.

BY SEA Few locals can afford the air fare; most go by cargo boat, on an overnight passage taking about 10 hours (fast charter boats can do the trip in 3½ hours). The most reliable vessel, equipped with toilets and rescue boats, is the *Tornado* (📞 *227511/920082 Captain Onildo;* e *jpvnbe@skynet.be*). The journey on the 26m, 70-ton capacity boat costs 300,000$ one-way. Owned by the local Ambassador of the Maltese Order, Jean-Philippe Nyen, the *Tornado* also operates once a month on various routes, including Douala–Libreville–Luanda and is available for charter. Departures are announced on National Radio. Other boats ('Thérèse', 'Africa no. 1') connect the two islands, at irregular times (usually sailing around 17.00/18.00) and with questionable standards of safety and comfort. Be aware that boats have gone down on this crossing, with loss of life, others lost their way and had to be rescued. Travellers who have taken the boat reported waking up to dolphins alongside the boat nearing Príncipe, but a rough return journey due to choppy winds. Budget travellers could consider taking the 'Tornado' from São Tomé to Príncipe and flying back. To find out which boats are due in/out, visit the harbour office in São Tomé (*Av 12 Julho;* 📞 *221520/222207*) or in Santo António: the Capitánia is the bright-blue building above the pier in front of the hospital (📞 *251246/909352, Senhor Armando;* 🕐 *07.00–12.00 & 13.00–15.30 Mon–Fri*). A regular, reliable and fast boat connection would be one of the best things that could happen to Príncipe and STP tourism in general, but as long as tourist numbers are low, and air fares to the country high, investors are understandably reluctant.

GETTING AROUND

There are only a few kilometres of paved road: between the airport and Santo António, westwards to Porto Real and to the south to Santo Cristo. Transport is the biggest issue for budget tourists on the island; part of the difficulties in organising trips lies in the local perception that all white visitors are either staying at Bom Bom or, even if not, can still afford the high prices. For backpackers or travellers/students/researchers on longer stays this can be frustrating. The daily going rates for a motorbike are 500,000$, and 1,000,000$ for a car with driver – a month's wages. Most visitors will eventually crack, as nobody wants to spend their holiday hunting around for transport. If you're on a budget, your best bet is to bring the price down by sharing with other people. If you hitch a lift, contributing to the cost of *combustível* is good form.

PUBLIC TRANSPORT There are two **yellow taxis**; a shared ride from the airport to Santo António costs 10,000$. You might be able to organise a run towards a beach and carry on by foot, and even arrange a return pick-up. There are new small state-operated buses now, operating from the airport and serving the northern and southern parts of the island from Santo António: Porto Real, Sundy, Abade, Nova Estrela, Santo Cristo, São Joaquim, airport, Picão and Paciência. Enquire locally for details; the 'timetable' follows the needs of the moment. The maximum cost for one leg is 8,000$.

CAR HIRE Hired jeeps come with drivers included and cost a whopping 1,000,000$ per day. The Bom Bom Island resort offers driving excursions with English-speaking guides and refreshments, while the owner of Pensão Palhota, Alex Metzer, and the Residencial Delmata guesthouse hire out jeeps, but prices will be steep. Your only chance to get a better deal is to ask around locally; try Carlos

7

Pinheiro (✆ 916024; e pinhero_2000@hotmail.com), who runs his own tourism and shipping agency Príncipe Tours in the centre of town and also handles all Africa's Eden local ticketing and plane bookings.

MOTORBIKE HIRE Ask around, at Residencial Delmata or Pensão Palhota; a motorbike will probably set you back around €25 per day.

Filling up There is a small petrol shop, *bomba de combustível*, just past the Deus E Amor church on the road west out of town towards Porto Real (✆ *910883;* ⊕ *07.00–18.00, Sun 08.00–17.00*). Check with Claudio for contacts for hire cars and motorbikes.

CYCLE HIRE The regular price quoted will be around 100,000$. To get a better deal, drop into the **Radio Regional** (✆ *251115*) building; the friendly journalists seem sympathetic to budget travellers and will probably be able to arrange to hire out a motorbike or a bike at better rates. I hired a regular bike for 50,000$/day from one journalist, José dos Santos Fred Bel. Alternatively, try José Roxa (✆ *251062*). Be prepared: cycling around Príncipe is no easy job; the road leading north out of town towards the airport and Belo Monte is particularly steep and sweaty, and the one running south is not much better. But if you don't mind that, it is possible to do a day trip cycling to visit Banana Beach, Roça Sundy (uphill all the way unfortunately) or the beaches along the southeastern rim of the island. The Belo Monte run is beautiful, passing cocoa trees bearing, in the *gravana*, pods in the whole range of colours, but if it's been raining you risk coming off your bike on the rutted track. In my case, coming back at night was good in a way, as the potholes weren't visible, but as the brakes couldn't cope with the steep descent, I found myself pushing the bike part of the way back down to Santo António.

BOAT HIRE Ask a guide or contact the head (*responsável*) of a fishing village direct. If you just turn up, expect to pay around 50,000$ for an hour's cruising along the shore in a dug-out where you might have to scoop water out of the bottom with a plastic bottle. Joaquim 'Gi' Varela, the head of the **Praia dos Burros** fishing community, is a good person to ask as he is keen to encourage tourism rather than make a quick buck. Senhor Varela lives opposite the first-aid post, *posto de socorro*; he has no mobile phone, but you can get hold of him through his friend Isaios (✆ *907996*). Much closer to town, Ministro, based at **Ponte Mina** beach, can probably help (see page 184). You usually have to pay for the diesel in advance (around 22,000$ per litre; 25 litres is a standard filling). Consider bringing a secret supply of extra diesel in a safe container; I heard more than one report of boat motors nearly packing up at sea for lack of fuel – not a great prospect.

SANTO ANTÓNIO: THE CAPITAL

The capital of Príncipe – the smallest city in the world, according to the Guinness Book of Records – is little more than a collection of dilapidated houses and shops in pretty pastel colours along the sluggish Papagaio river, with yawning gaps between them, slowly eroded by the salt air and choked by trees.

 WHERE TO STAY
Mid-range ($$$)

🏠 **Hotel/Residencial Delmata** (9 rooms, 1 suite) Rua Santo António; ✆ 251296/906098; e ddclube@cstome.net. Scheduled to open in summer 2008. With accommodation on the 1st floor (private bathroom, TV, b/fast), a restaurant (various types of food, inc Brazilian) & bar, disco (Clube

D&D), internet café & shops (*mini mercado*, clothes, video hire), this should be the closest thing to a mall Príncipe will ever have! The two brothers are full of enthusiasm to offer a 24-hr client-oriented experience. Make a good impression & the price might come down a bit. Preferential hire prices for Suzuki motorbikes (€20) & Galope jeep (€70) with or without driver) for guests. Airport transfers.

🏠 **Pensão Residencial Palhota** (10 rooms) Av Martires da Liberdade; ☎ 251060/906032/938153; f 251079; e pensaopalhota@cstome.net. Bom Bom resort apart, most agencies will book you into the Palhota. The rooms are spacious, but at €50 for a sgl & €80 for a dbl, even with b/fast & airport

transfer inc, a bit overpriced. It's probably best to ask to be put up in the brand-new Residencial building next door (2 rooms, 2 suites), with a restaurant/bar/club downstairs. There is a communal living room, with a big TV, & a downstairs porch. A swimming pool & a beauty salon should be ready by summer 2008. You can use the internet in the office of the friendly owner, Alex Metzer (€3/hr), who can also arrange transport & pick-ups to Banana Beach, Bom Bom, Sundy, etc. There is a security guard at night. B/fast is served in the Fakiri restaurant in the garden. You might have to ask for items individually (I seemed to get less every morning); cheese is extra.

Budget (⑨⑨)

🏠 **Casa de Daniele** (5 rooms) Rua Martíres da Liberdade; ☎ 906454; f 251320; e gsalvador@cstome.net/danyneves73@hotmail.com. This brand-new spacious bright-white colonial-style building, owned by Daniele Neves from the BISTP bank, was due to open for business in 2008, with 3 bathrooms, kitchen, 2 living rooms, patio & big garden, & internet room. Definitely worth a try.

🏠 **Pensão Arca de Noé** (6 rooms) Rua UCCLA; ☎ 251054/910813. The rooms in this budget hostel in the middle of town are not bad — brightly painted, with ventilators, mirrors & lamps — & there is a nice communal area & pleasant terrace out the back. There is hot water, a kitchen & a computer terminal for guests. Before the new owner took over, there was a general air of neglect, but the biggest problem was that travellers' belongings got stolen; double-lock the doors, & don't invite kids up to your room.

Shoestring (⑨)

🏠 **Pensão Residencial Osório** (3 rooms) Rua Trabalhadores; ☎ 251034/904056. Just across the river, this hostel (the pink building on the right-hand side of the pot-holed road) is popular with budget travellers (€ sgl occupancy, €15 dbl occupancy) . The cosy living room has a phone (☎ 251034), to receive calls or leave messages for other residents with the maid or owner. The shower is cold & you might have to chase for things like toilet rolls (just buy your own), but for the price, you can afford to stake your rainforest-trek base camp there; the owner, Osório Umbelina, is open to flexible arrangements. You are likely to quickly make friends with the children living across the road.

🏠 **Pensão Romar** (5 rooms) Rua Guiné-Bissau; ☎ 251124/251019. Best value-for-money option.

Although one of the two bathrooms had the tattiest shower curtain ever & there was the occasional loo roll crisis, they were cleaned every day. There is a living room with a grizzly TV, & a nice balcony from which to survey what goes on in the street; all meals are taken here. B/fast costs extra (coffee, rolls, & juice: 25,000$) & depends on availability of rolls from the bakery across the road. Lunch & dinner have to be booked in advance (Zozó's food gets good reports, but she can be moody). The Romar is run by Rodrigo Cassandra, the father of the current president of the regional government; if you can't find anybody in, ask for Senhor Rodrigo at the hardware store a few houses further down, on the left.

✗ **WHERE TO EAT AND DRINK** Snacks from the kiosks and street food is a good low-cost option; children will sometimes sell delicious ice cream, *sorbete*, for 1,000$. For more food options, see www.principe.st.

✗ **Bar Fakiri** Av Martires da Liberdade; ☎ 251060; ⏰ 07.00–21.00 daily. The Pensão Palhota restaurant in a round bamboo hut in the garden

offers good food & wines, with a lot of variety, if a bit pricy. If you have booked HB at the Pensão, you will be asked in the morning whether you prefer

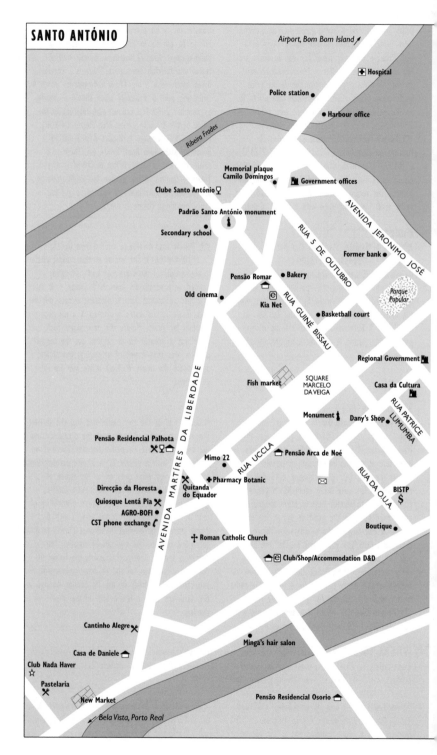

SANTO ANTÓNIO

Airport, Bom Bom Island ↗

Hospital

Police station ●

● Harbour office

Ribeira Frades

Memorial plaque
Camilo Domingos ● 🏛 Government offices

Clube Santo António 🍷

Padrão Santo António monument

Secondary school ●

Former bank ●

RUA 5 DE OUTUBRO

AVENIDA JERONIMO JOSÉ

Parque Popular

Pensão Romar ● Bakery

Old cinema ● 🖳 Kia Net

RUA GUINÉ BISSAU

● Basketball court

Regional Government 🏛

Fish market

SQUARE
MARCELO
DA VEIGA

Casa da Cultura 🏛

RUA PATRICE LUMUMBA

Monument 🗿 Dany's Shop

AVENIDA MARTIRES DA LIBERDADE

Pensão Residencial Palhota

Mimo 22

RUA UCCLA

🏠 Pensão Arca de Noé

Direcção da Floresta
Quiosque Lentá Pia ✕
AGRO-BOFI ●
CST phone exchange ☎

Quitanda
do Equador
✚ Pharmacy Botanic

✉

RUA DA O.U.A.

BISTP
$

Boutique ●

✟ Roman Catholic Church

🏠🖳 Club/Shop/Accommodation D&D

Cantinho Alegre ✕

Minga's hair salon

Casa de Daniele 🏠

Club Nada Haver
☆

Pastelaria
✕

New Market

Pensão Residencial Osorio 🏠

← Bela Vista, Porto Real

176

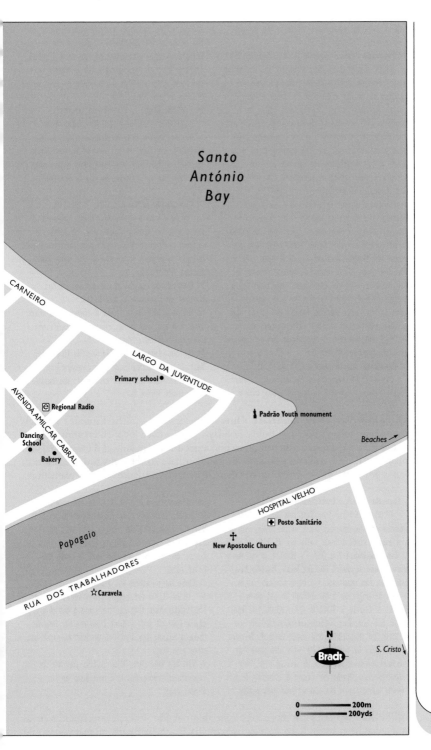

Santo
António
Bay

CARNEIRO

LARGO DA JUVENTUDE

Primary school ●

AVENIDA AMILCAR CABRAL

Ⓒ Regional Radio

Dancing
School ●
● Bakery

🏛 Padrão Youth monument

Beaches ➚

HOSPITAL VELHO

Papagaio

✚ Posto Sanitário

✝
New Apostolic Church

RUA DOS TRABALHADORES

☆ Caravela

N

Bradt

S. Cristo ↘

0 ▭▭▭▭ 200m
0 ▭▭▭▭ 200yds

fish or meat for your main course in the evening. Service varies. *Mains* $$$

✗ **Pastelaria** António Segundo II; ✆ 251150/919539; ⏰ 07.00–02.00 daily. Most travellers end up eating in the evening at this friendly wood-panelled place, reached by turning right past the Amor e Deus church. Excellent b/fasts: earthy local coffee, an omelette with or without cheese, mango juice, bread. The Pastelaria is reopening in early summer 2008 after a refurbishment; take the opening times with a pinch of salt. Afternoons are nice for pastries, savoury & sweet (such as a madeira cake drizzled with honey). The lovely Minga can cater for vegetarians & in the evenings will make a nice pasta or rice dish with tomato sauce & vegetables. You can bring in your own veggies from the market, to be cooked in your dinner. Sometimes, there are pizzas too. Minga's husband Ramos is head chef at the Bom Bom Island resort; on special request, he can make a wonderful black-bean vegetarian *feijão pintado*. The Pastelaria is also the best place in town to have your **washing** done; a big plastic bag of very well-cleaned laundry will only cost around 70,000$, but turnaround depends on drying time, ie: available sunshine. *Mains* $$

✗ **Bar Romar** Rua Guiné-Bissau; ✆ 251124; ⏰ 09.00–23.00, except Sun. Bar attached to the Pensão Romar, decorated in blue & green, with a ventilator. The barkeeper can tell you where to find the owner of the guesthouse. A glass of the cheapest Portuguese table wine, white or red, costs 13,000$. You can have an inexpensive lunch or dinner here, but must order early in the morning, or even better the day before. *Mains* $$

✗ **Cantinho Alegre** Av Martíres da Liberdade; ✆ 251108; ⏰ 07.00–21.30 daily; lunch from 12.00. Inexpensive tasty local dishes (such as squid/fish with rice) in a turquoise-coloured house set back slightly from the main road. If you want something specific, reserve the day before. *Mains* $$

✗ **Quiosque Beira Mar** Rua OUA; ✆ 916310; ⏰ 06.00–21.00 daily. Popular place for lunch. If you ask for something specific the day before, for instance a Príncipe *feijão* bean dish, Judithina should be able to prepare it for you. In the same road: **Analisa**. *Mains* $$

✗ **Quitanda do Equador** at the junction of Rua Martíres de Liberdade & Rua UCCLA; ⏰ 07.00–21.00 daily. Cheap & cheerful fish, fried banana & rice with beans, chicken kebab, *concón* flying gurnard fish.. *Mains* $

✗ **Quiosque Lentá Pia** Rua Martíres da Liberdade. Next to the Bobofrito outlet, with varying specialities, from chargrilled *concón* to the humble *búzio* snails. *Mains* $

ENTERTAINMENT AND NIGHTLIFE Outside the festivities of St Laurent's in mid-August and other saint's days/public holidays, there is not a lot of entertainment here, but at Príncipe *discotecas* you can often find a good party, mainly at the weekend and mainly playing *kizomba/zouk/kadance* music. You have to rely on word of mouth to know where the *festa* is. On Saturdays there is sometimes a dance on at the plantations.

♀ **Caravela** Rua dos Trabalhadores; ✆ 921479; ⏰ 19.00–02.00 Fri–Sun. Best club on the island, situated on the opposite bank of the river, with a nice view. Excellent food. Entry fee 15,000–20,000$

☆ **Escola de Danza** Rua OUA; ✆ 908024. If you fancy learning how to dance like the locals, Marcelo Boa Esperança can teach you the basic *kizomba* steps, though he might be a bit difficult to pin down.

☆ **L&L** S. Cristo; ✆ 904218; ⏰ –03.00 Fri, from 19.00 Sat–Sun. This bar/club/restaurant 3km out of town, on the uphill road south towards Terreiro Velho, is run by friendly Lélé, who also works at the harbour. Nice set-up, with several little blue palm-bedecked shacks for sitting & chatting, & a friendly atmosphere; the dance floor gets pretty hot. There is snack food, & there are rumoured to be toilets somewhere. Fri nights seem to be best, but ask around before making your way up there. I've walked there & back; it's feasible, if a bit creepy on your own on the dark & fairly pot-holed road.

☆ **Clube Santo António** Rua Martíres da Liberdade; ⏰ 18.00–02.00 (or longer) Sat & Sun, sometimes Fri. Popular disco that can turn into a bit of a sauna. Cool off with a drink from the bar outside; there is seating too. Handy & unusual: bar staff can store your bag.

☆ **Vivi Boa Vida** Praia Inhame. 'Live your life' in Capeverdian creole, this is a new disco on the airport road.

SHOPPING Groceries are more expensive than on São Tomé; every single tomato and green bean seems to come over by boat. Try to establish early on that you would like to pay the normal prices, not the double *preços de turista*. While the main biscuits for sale, 'Príncipe' (10,000$, with strawberry/vanilla/chocolate/banana filling) have nothing to do with the island, they make useful energy snacks for hikes. *Folha de chanela* is a stimulating lemongrass tea, also called *Chá Príncipe*. It is made at Roça Paciencia (a plantation you pass on the way to Belo Monte), and sometimes sold in the Ossobô shop back in São Tomé. The locals use the fresh or dry leaves for a stimulating diuretic tea. If you ask somebody, they will be happy to pick some for you; either use it fresh or dry it properly in the sun, otherwise it'll go mouldy.

Mercado Novo Av Martíres da Liberdade; ⏰ 06.00–16.00 Mon–Sat; 06.00–12.00 Sun. The handful of vendors in the covered market sell fruit & vegetables, yellow sachets of Evita margarine, clothes, etc. Go in the morning, for fresher produce. One of the vendors, Romana, seems to double up as a traditional healer.

Mercado de Peixe Independence Sq. Small enclosed fish market selling the night's catch.

Mimo 22 Rua UCCLA; ⏰ 08.00–12.00 & 15.00–17.00 Mon–Sat. Bags & shoes, pots & pans, TV/DVD players, perfume, clothes, nappies, rucksacks, etc.

Clube Santo António Av Martíres da Liberdade. This popular disco (see above) doubles up as a video club & recording studio, *estudio de gravação* (⏰ 07.00–21.00 daily), where you can have assorted CDs recorded for 50,000$ – but try & listen back to them there & then; the set-up isn't as professional as on São Tomé & mine jumped tracks when I got home. Next door, I've sometimes bought fresh vegetables from Antonia, when there weren't any to be found anywhere else. Expect to pay around 40,000$ for a clutch of tomatoes, beans, carrots & onions.

AGROBOFI Av Martíres da Liberdade. The Príncipe speciality of *bobofrito* – a long brown 'sausage' of *banana prata* fried in coconut oil – makes an excellent trekking food & souvenir, &, at 10,000$, it's half the price than in São Tomé. If *bobofrito* is available here, buy it; it won't spoil. If not, you'll always find it at the airport on flight days.

Padaria Mangaro Rua Guiné-Bissau; ⏰ 05.00–20.00 daily. Follow the aroma of freshly baked bread: rolls (*pão*), loaves (*pão de forma*) & wonderful *broas*

(corn rolls; also called *fuba*). Bring a plastic bag to take them away in. Margarine is sold, as are *açucarinhas* sweets sometimes. The bakers don't usually mind you coming in & having a look while they're working.

Padaria Rua OUA; ⏰ 05.00–21.00 daily. The elderly baker, Mario Jaco, might have rolls when the other bakery doesn't. The entrance is set back from the street, down a grassy track.

Foto Gomes Av Martíres da Liberdade; ☎ 906418; ⏰ 07.00–22.00 Mon–Sat. To reach this photo shop-cum-studio turn right just before the new market building & take the second entrance between the stalls. For 5,000$ each, you can have print-outs (*postáis*) made from digitals, a wonderful present for local families/kids whose picture you've taken. One word of warning: of the five print films I bought there (55,000$ each, all well within the best-before period), four turned out to have washed-out colours plus a web of blue veins running across all the pictures. The heat probably got to them. If you are shooting on film, bring more rolls than you think you will need.

Almazém de Dany Marcelo da Veiga Sq; ☎ 905135; ⏰ 08.00–13.00 & 14.00–18.00 Mon–Sat. Grocery selling cosmetics, cheese, soft drinks, biros, etc, wholesale & to individuals. The friendly manager Vadi sometimes opens 08.00–13.00 Sun; basically, if you see a light, try knocking on the door.

Comercio Geral Rua da UCCLA; ⏰ 08.00–12.00 & 15.00–17.30 Mon–Fri, 08.00–13.00 Sat. Stocks lots of useful things: toilet rolls, bottled water, UHT milk, olive oil, juices, Lipton tea, tinned food, yoghurts & mayonnaise, fabrics & the odd shoe.

PRACTICALITIES

Communications With the isolation of the island, communications aren't helped by constant unscheduled power cuts (on top of the regular one every night). Phone coverage does not extend much beyond a few kilometres outside the capital; even on the big plantations like Sundy and Belo Monte, coverage is intermittent. In any case, most people never seem to have any credit (*saldo*) on their mobile phones. To send a fax, ask at Pensão Palhota. In the summer of 2006, the transmitter mast was vandalised. If successful, the attempt would have left the island completely cut off from all telephone and internet communication. Unless the machine is broken, you can make **photocopies** for 1,500$ each in the Casa dos Padres, the yellow house next to the Casa de Cultura.

Telephone There is a phone booth for local calls at the corner opposite the shop with the big Sagres sign, open every day 07.00–20.00 (candle-lit when the power goes).

CST Av Martíres da Liberdade; ✆ 251100/251018; ℱ 251179; ⌚ 07.00–12.00 & 14.00–17.30 Mon–Fri. The phone centre across from the church has two telephones; both can put through international calls. You will hear a beep marking the units; pay after your call at the reception desk. People can ring you back, using +239 251100 or 251, but double-check beforehand. Recharge cards for 100,000$ & 300,000$ can be bought in the back office, where you can also buy top-up credit for your mobile, buy a phone &/or SIM card, but not have your phone unblocked. When CST closes for the weekend, that's when life can suddenly feel a bit lonely on this tiny island adrift in the Atlantic…

Postal services

✉ **CTT** off Marcelo da Veiga Sq; ✆ 251053; ⌚ 07.00–12.00 & 14.00–17.00 Mon–Fri. The small friendly post office offers all postal services & sells a few postcards with drab images from the sister island, not Príncipe unfortunately. Bring stamps from São Tomé if you can, as there are often none available. With the EMS service, you can send an item weighing up to ½kg within 72hrs (in theory) for about 200,000$.

Internet Internet communication on Príncipe is less concerned with education and more with breaking island isolation. You'll see youngsters in baseball caps working the MSN Messenger, chatting with family members in Angola – or Brazilian cyber-girls with few clothes on. One hour usually costs 20,000$. The central Marcelo da Veiga Square is technically a Wi-Fi area.

🖳 **Radio Regional** Av Amilcar Cabral; ⌚ 09.00–22.00 Mon–Fri. The 4 terminals used to be in the pink Casa de Cultura former church building, currently used for governmental purposes.

🖳 **Kia Net** Rua Guiné-Bissau; ⌚ 09.00–22.00 Mon–Fri. 4–5 terminals below Pensão Romar.

Hair and beauty

Salão Minga Horta Cana. Run by affable Minga Domingos Ribeiro, this salon is located below a pink house with a wooden balcony, next to the 'Bom Sitio' snack-bar. You might find yourself with a dedicated team of five females from three generations plus a neighbour braiding away. The barber's selling the *missangas* beads is just a couple of doors along; natural-looking hair extensions are sold at Foto Gomes (see *Shopping*, above).
Salão de Beleza Rua dos Trabalhadores/Rua Feliz; ✆ 903853. Hairdressing, eyebrow-shaping, etc. Ask for Senhora Didi's house.

Medical facilities Santo António has a hospital and a health centre. Possibly the biggest health hazard on the island are the unlit pot-holed streets of Santo António at night. If you sprain something, you might want to try the local *massagista* or *pusha-pé* Jéjé, who lives near the cemetery. A nursing student I met trusted him enough to (successfully) fix her ankle.

✚ **Central Hospital** Chimaló; ✆ 251005. The hospital, overlooking the bay, is open 24hrs; 3 doctors work here. Ask for Doutor José Dos Prazeres (✆ 903720); he speaks French & a bit of English. Emergency treatments are free.
✚ **Health Centre** Rua dos Trabalhadores; ✆ 251122; ⌚ 07.30–12.00 & 14.00–17.00 Mon–Fri; emergencies only on Sat/Sun. Sponsored by the New Apostolic Church, this **posto sanitário** on the southern side of Santo António bay has some diagnostic facilities (malaria test 1,000$) & an on-site pharmacy. However, their 'mosquito bite' cream turned out to be just a general-purpose ointment.

✚ Farmácia Botanic Rua UCCLA; ⏱ 07.00–19.00 Mon–Fri, 07.00–13.00 Sat; sometimes 08.00–12.00 Sun. Painkillers, various antibiotics, throat spray, Tampax, multi-vitamins, etc, usually available. If you find the pharmacy closed, it could be that the helpful pharmacist, Senhor Ramos, is up at the hospital.

Money

Bring your own! There is no ATM on the island, and no Western Union agent. Travellers who had spent two months on the island reported speaking to 'many' people printing money; unfortunately, I didn't meet any of them when mine ran out…

$ BISTP Rua OUA; ☎ 251140; f 251320; ⏱ 07.45–11.45 & 14.00–15.15 Mon–Fri. The Príncipe branch of the Banco Internacional de São Tomé and Príncipe, & the only bank on the island, is managed by genial Daniele Neves, who has various business interests on the island & speaks some English. You can change money (there are no money-changers in the streets of Santo António), but not arrange cash advances on credit/debit cards or cash travellers' cheques. BISTP does not have an IBAN number, so you cannot transfer money from your bank account in the UK or anywhere else. If you get stuck, there are three options: 1) borrow money off a fellow traveller; 2) open an account, using a copy of your passport (showing the original is not enough) & go down the route described on page 72 (see *Money*); or if there is no-one who can pay in money for you in Portugal, 3) open an account anyway & contact your ambassador/consul on the main island to ask whether they can help. If they agree, this is how it works: somebody in your country pays money into the ambassador's account in that country first; once the funds have cleared, the ambassador can reimburse the money into your BISTP account at the branch in São Tomé. This is not a formalised procedure, so don't rely on it, but I know of at least one UK traveller who was helped in this way by the consul.

Police

Police station Airport Rd; ☎ 251056. The sky-blue **Polícia** building next to the harbour as you leave Santo António on the northern road is the base of 24hr operations for the island's half a dozen police officers. Nobody speaks English here; the *chefe de serviço*, Commandante Jerónimo Luis has Spanish and a little French. While I was there, despite claims of extensive undercover operations, an MP3 player stolen from an American student was only recovered through the efforts of a local, recognising the conspicuous gadget in the hands of a young boy. Meanwhile, the police crime report took 3 weeks to be written & had to be picked up by a friend of the long-departed student. If you need something urgently for your insurance, bring somebody who speaks Portuguese & be prepared to insist; it might be a good idea to have a short statement in Portuguese/English already written up to try & get a stamp/signature on that.

WHAT TO SEE In the town centre, only the church, the government building and a handful of other pretty 19th-century colonial buildings found around the central square have been restored. One of the most poignant symbols – and one of the best picture opportunities, too – is the former bank building on the waterfront: the strangulator figs and other roots have completely taken over the ruins: a staircase leads up into thin air. One couple I met decided to visit Príncipe after seeing a photo of this building. In the centre of town you find the **Nossa Senhora da Conceição** church (☎ 251139; *06.00 Tue–Sat, 18.30 Mon & 09.00 Sun*). The church, restored in 1940, has a light-blue wooden ceiling and yellow-painted walls (⏱ *08.00–12.00 Tue–Fri, but often seems to only be open for mass*). Look for the baptistery font to your left when you come in and the beautiful stone-carved St Anthony to the left of the altar. On the square outside the church is a little stone pillar with a tile showing Santo António. St Anthony (feast day 13 June) is the patron saint of the poor and helps against shipwrecks, starvation, and to find mislaid items. Close by, at the cemetery, tamarind shrubs with bright red and orange flowers grow amongst the graves.

7

🏠 **WHERE TO STAY** Accommodation on plantations and in fishing villages is developing only gradually, but it is always worth asking the community leader (*responsável*), whether you can stay/camp somewhere. A small hotel next to the airport might be open when you visit; contact Ramos at the Pastelaria (see *Where to eat*, page 178).

🏠 **Residencial Ponta do Sol** ☎ 251223/925114; e brankinho_stp@hotmail.com. New rural tourism venture at small plantation in the northwest of the island; at €25 inc airport transfers & b/fast, this should be worth trying. Lunch €5. $$

PLANTATION HOUSES

Roça Sundy With a surface of 1,657ha, Sundy is the biggest plantation on the island and gives you a real idea of how self-sufficient some *roças* once were. This was the only coffee-producing plantation on Príncipe. Some 10km out of town, it would take a good while to walk all the way uphill; you could try and arrange a lift with the foreman, Senhor Firmíno (☎ 905502) or hitch a lift with one of the trucks going up there. Start early in the day, so you can take in the beaches as well as look round the plantation. The former hospital is to your left as you come in the entrance, majestically flanked by two towers. Kids will be happy to show you the only thing that is left from the time when this was the most important hospital on the island: an old dentist's chair. (They might also request your empty plastic water bottle.) Next to the hospital, a **marble plaque** in the middle of a field commemorates the experiments conducted here by British astronomer Arthur Eddington in 1919, proving Albert Einstein's relativity theory for the first time. During a total solar eclipse, Sir Arthur demonstrated that gravity would bend the path of light when a massive star passes it and published the results as 'A Determination of the Deflection of Light by the Sun's Gravitational Field'. The plantation belongs to the state, and the former owner's house is kept, waiting for state visits. There are gorgeous views out to sea from the balcony and the colour-coordinated bedrooms upstairs. The green one, closest to the bathroom and furthest from possible intruders, was the president's; his bodyguards slept in the red and blue rooms.

The whole place, with a large rectangular tree-lined square at its centre, is surrounded by a crenellated wall; over on the other side of the square, the former stables have beautiful horseshoe-shaped windows. Railway tracks can still be seen in the soil, with a rusting locomotive. Today, around 400 people live here – of whom about 10 have a job in town. The simple chapel, dedicated to Our Lady of Lourdes, contains a beautiful crucifix. The church is not open; ask for the key (*chave*). The way down to Sundy **beach** (and the other nearby beaches) starts next to the chapel; get an older kid to show you the way. In the workers' quarters you can also stock up on picnic food for the beach or provisions for the way back in one of the *lojas*. You might see some pet monkeys for sale. The plantation is not electrified, but there are a few generators. The concession is currently being held by a Luso-Finnish consortium; to see whether tourists can stay here, try Senhor Firmíno or the Equador Viajens agency in São Tomé, see page 101.

Roça Belo Monte You enter this plantation through a picturesque fairy-tale if slightly askew crenellated entrance gate, with an old rusty cannon outside. The *casa grande* is a double-storey mansion with arched windows and doors and bare wooden floors, with a large slave bell in one corner. Ask who can show you around. You might be able to stay overnight on the plantation, in a cosy house just to the left when you come in (contact Vitor Egídio, Projecto Belo Monte; ☎ 251167). A sweeping balustrade terrace is the best viewpoint for **Banana Beach** (see below). A track leads down to the beach (maybe a 15-minute walk), and from there you can carry on walking along the coast. I've found people here to be very friendly and chatty, and it shouldn't be difficult to arrange a guide. The beach down the other side is the black-sand **Praia Preta**, and the local name for the conical mountain behind is Pico Mae ('mother'). To reach Belo Monte from Santo António, head out towards the airport, but take a right at the tarmacked turn-off, going through a village. The tarmac soon turns into a red dirt road, only negotiable by 4x4. At the first fork in the road, take a right (the left-hand track leads to Roça Paciencia).

Roça Terreiro Velho Reached by taking the southern road out of Santo António, then the steep tarmaced road up past Santo Christo, this is where the Italian **Claudio Corallo** grows the Forastero cocoa for his famous chocolate. You might be able to see the women workers taking out the minuscule bitter stem out of each cocoa bean by hand; a job done by machine with industrially produced chocolate. You are welcome to wander around and might be invited to try some roasted cocoa beans. Although Corallo's chocolate is now beginning to become well known abroad, there is not enough work for all the people living here, and the one demand heard again and again here, is *emprego* – employment, work. One of the young men living here, such as Filesio de Rosario Silva (*neighbour's* ❯ *912120*), can take you to some **waterfalls** half-an-hour's walk away – and maybe show you inside the humble house in the *senzalas* workers' quarters where he lives with his wife and young son. Like so many of the people living on the plantations, Filesio works in the field, growing basic food crops like matabala and manioc to feed his family.

Roça Porto Real This abandoned but well-preserved plantation lies on the way west towards São Joaquim. The hospital of this second-biggest *roça* on the island was once more important than the one at Santo António, and vestiges of the railway lines may still be seen. There are plans to develop it into a luxury hotel.

Roça São Joaquim This plantation is the starting point for hikes down the southwest coast. Bands of half-naked kids push goats and kick makeshift footballs around the central square, overlooked by a friendly shop selling biscuits, soft drinks and *cacharamba* firewater. There are great views of the João Dias Pai and Filho ('father and son') phonolithic peaks and across to the Baia das Agulhas. A steepish track to the right of the stark grey façade leads down to the coast. Small **Praia Caixão** is the first beach you come to. Carry on west to **Praia Lapa**, home to a small fishing community of some 60 people served by a couple of shops. On a trek to Praia São Tomé, our small group of hikers gratefully huddled on the small porch of the first, out of the driving rain, cooking our spaghetti over their fire in exchange for a round of soft drinks.

BEACHES

Banana Beach The easiest way to visit the island's most famous beach – perfect for swimming, with white sand curving in a banana shape around turquoise waters – is on a 25-minute boat trip from Bom Bom or an abseiling expedition (see above) from the **Belo Monte** plantation, where you might be able to stay the night. You can also just walk down from Belo Monte in about 15 minutes. A famous ad for Bacardi rum was filmed here.

Other beaches In the north of the island, just before entering **Belo Monte** plantation (see page 182), a path leads down to two good swimming beaches: **Praia Macaco** (with new resort) and **Praia Boi**. Nearby **Praia Grande** is a good swimming beach and home to a turtle project. **Praia dos Burros** is reached by walking west along the coast from Banana Beach. This large fishing village, where you will see plenty of flying fish spread across solar driers, will give you a friendly welcome. Senhor Gi (Joaquim) Varela, the head of the village, is setting up simple tourist accommodation in a typical house on stilts and can also organise somebody to take you fishing (see *Boat hire*, page 174). Further along (take a guide), enjoy **Baia das Agulhas**, a wonderful spot for snorkelling, remaining unspoilt while the free trading zone is not yet set up. You can camp at the abandoned plantation of **Maria Correia** at the southwestern tip of the island, which is reached either by the (frequently overgrown) coast path or by skirting Pico Mesa.

If you take supplies and water, there are several good beach walks that you can do from Santo António without spending a fortune on transport. One possibility is to explore the **beaches to the southeast**, on foot or by bike. Head up the pot-holed road south out of town (coming from the centre of Santo António, cross the bridge and turn left). After a steepish incline, access to **São João** fishermen's beach just beyond town is on foot, by turning off the road past a kiosk and walking down through the houses; you might see kids washing the seeds of the *izaquente* African breadfruit by the river. Back on the main road, take the next left-hand turn for a pleasant downhill stroll; a beautiful swallowtail butterfly was alighting on a pineapple plant just before the entrance to the beach when I was there. This is **Praia Ponta Mina**, already better for swimming. Only one family lives here now, headed by the friendly 'Ministro', who speaks French and Spanish, and can organise fishing trips (*saidas de pesca*), with nets (*de rede*), rods (*com canna*), and snorkelling (*submarine, com masca*). This isolation might not last; if you look up on the hill along the coast, a tourist development is planned in the ruins of the old Portuguese fort. Back on the main road, turn left at the religious monument for **Praia d'Evora**, good for a swim and a romantic picture opportunity, sitting on the long trunk of a palm tree slumped across the sand.

Alternatively, if you take the right-hand turn (just outside Santo António) up the steep tarmacked road south (which continues on as dirt road towards Claudio Corallo's famous cocoa plantation, Terreiro Velho), there are beautiful **views** of the southern mountains, such as the Pico dos Dois Dedos ('peak of the two fingers'), as well as the distinctive Jockey's Cap out to sea. This is the way to the beaches of **Praia Portinho**, **Praia Salgada** and **Praia Abade**; as everywhere on the islands, the swimming beaches are the ones without a big community, as those beaches are often, unfortunately for the beach tourist, used as toilets. If you haven't got your own transport, try to find a bus going that way and either walk back down or catch a lift down at least part of the way. You get a nice view of Santo António from the **Pincate** plantation (formerly Roça São José) and there are beautiful **waterfalls** on the way to **Monte Alegre**, to the west of Santo António, along the river Frades; you will need a guide.

Where to stay

Pagué Beach Resort Macaco Beach. Check with the agencies in São Tomé whether this resort on the northeastern coast is up & running. The chalets already built looked nice enough; other great beaches, such as Praia Grande & Praia Boi, are nearby &, while the setting is not as spectacular, it will be good to have an alternative to the luxury Bom Bom resort. Contact the owner of Pensão Palhota (see page 175) for details. $$$

ACTIVITIES

Generally, booking island tours, boat trips, etc, with the Bom Bom resort guarantees you a professional set-up, reflected in prices not geared towards budget travellers. If you're on your own, or travelling as a couple, try getting hold of other travellers to get a group together; sharing can bring the price down to very reasonable rates. Also, it is always worth ringing up to see whether you can join an activity. For diving, Bom Bom is really the only possible base, unless you come on an organised diving trip from São Tomé island.

BOAT TRIPS

Islas Tinhosas These islands, about 22km southwest of Príncipe, are highly recommended for birdwatchers. They look like two islands, but are in fact three. The birds nesting there – sooty terns, often encountered in groups, black and brown noddies and brown boobies – are unused to humans, so you can get very close, although you are not advised to land on the islets as it will disturb them. In any case, only the larger island has conditions for landing. The Tinhosas have the greatest concentration of brown noddies in the Gulf of Guinea, and they often hover above the boats. Look for sandwich and bridled terns, and Wilson's storm petrels skimming the top of the waves searching for food. The most reliable, though expensive option is to hire a boat from Bom Bom. It takes around 4½ hours to get there, and 4 hours back; the return journey is faster thanks to the Benguela current.

Jockey's Cap The **Boné de Jocquei** (also called Ilhéu de Caroco), a large, rounded volcanic rock indeed in the shape of a jockey's cap and topped by oil palms, is prized by birdwatchers for the frequent appearance of white-tailed tropicbirds, and Príncipe seedeaters, rare in the north of the island. You can reach it by chartered boat from Bom Bom in about 90 minutes.

Praia Seca According to a traveller who has visited this beach, home to one of the most isolated communities on the island (2½ hours), the sea can be pretty rough and, in her case at least, the 'dry beach' also seemed a bit of a misnomer.

HIKING You could spend weeks exploring the peaks of the island. Be aware that even if you visit in the dry season, you are likely to catch a fair bit of rain; and that nothing dries easily on Príncipe, washing or walking boots, no matter how much newspaper you stuff into them. Take plenty of food. Daniel Ramos, from the forest ministry Direcçao de Floresta (✆ 251073/903048) can advise on hikes and has a motorbike; if he is free, you might be able to book an excursion with him, or else his colleague and guide Baltazar. As a deputy for the political party (ADI), Daniel is very interesting to talk to about life on the island. The forestry ministry took over ECOFAC's functions, when the conservation NGO had to close its Príncipe office, but a centre for parrot conservation is planned. One confusing thing is that the locals, even guides, have different names for the same peak, and are puzzled by visitor's obsession with knowing their 'proper' name.

Pico Papagaio Getting up to the top of the mountain overlooking Santo António is a 6-hour, moderately easy (if you don't mind pulling yourself up by roots on steep ground) and very rewarding forest hike, though the peak is often in cloud. There are different trails. Some guides start from the São Joaquim plantation; others from the path starting at António II, going up past the Pastelaria. There are several good birding opportunities. Personally, I'll always remember this walk: an hour into it, we were offered cola nuts to try by some young boys high up in a cola nut tree; two minutes later, one of them lost his footing and dropped out of the tree – a fall of 10m or so – so we all went back to Santo António, carrying the injured boy down the hill – and started again. Follow the red-earth road up past the

Quintal do Pico, where you can overnight (see below). There is a fence; you have to attract the guard's attention by ringing a bell and pay a nominal fee (20,000$) to pass. This should be a great base for forest walks, but it's probably best to organise a guide beforehand. Make sure your guide doesn't race you up to the top; a couple of travellers I spoke to ended up doing the Pico Papagaio in a record three hours or so. Tell him: *móli-móli*; as long as you're at the summit by around 14.00, it's no problem to get back before dark.

Where to stay

🏠 **Casa de Pasagem Quintal do Pico** (2 rooms) ☎ 251150 (Pastelaria)/906424. Halfway up the Pico do Papagaio mountain, this small plantation belongs to Ramos, the owner of the Pastelaria: 2 rooms in a simple wooden house on stilts, one twin, 1 sgl. Food can be arranged with the Pastelaria. $

Pico de Príncipe At 924m, the Pico de Príncipe, in the south of the island, is Príncipe's highest point and, although less than half the height of its sister peak on São Tomé, it is trickier to climb. Not many people attempt it; however, the claim that the Pico has only ever been climbed twice, in 1953 and 1999, is not true. Scientists from the California Academy climbed the Pico in the rainy season of 2001, and an Israeli traveller climbing it with the guide Bikigila in the 2006 *gravana* found it to be entirely feasible. It is definitely on my to-do list for my next visit! You can find a great reportage of a Pico climb in an internet diary written in 1999 by a British zoologist (*www.ggcg.st/jon_principe.htm*), sustained by lots of grilled forest snails. If you read French, there is another detailed report on http://www.ecofac.org/Canopee/N16/N1602_PicoPrincipe/PicoPrincipe.htm, which describes the route in some detail, and also posits the question whether in fact it is the Pico de Mencorne, further to the east, that might be the real highest point on the island. The hike up to the Pico starts at the **Roça São Joaquim**, and there is at least one night's camping involved. Mind when you are on top; there is not a lot of space to stand on – and a long drop down.

Towards Morro Leste An interesting 1½-hour walk up towards the peak of Morro Leste takes you through different habitats, very rich in birds. Head due south out of town along the river, passing through cultivated land and the *roça* Bela Vista, then follow the river, mostly on the right-hand bank, until you come to the remains of a hydro-electric plant. When it was inaugurated in 1992, it produced electricity for 30 minutes before breaking down. The lack of maintenance tools and know-how meant that it was never fixed. A new mini hydro-electric plant was being constructed on the Rio Papagaio in 2008, by the Portuguese Soares da Costa group. If you carry on up the stream, there is some climbing over rocks involved, passing, after a couple of hours, a tiny dam, with crayfish-filled rockpools. Camping upstream from the barrage, you will hear monkeys and parrots in the forest. You can carry on, but you need an experienced guide for this, otherwise you might end up at the top of an unknown waterfall with great views, but with food running out, feeling argumentative and relying on your compass to get you back down to camp. The lesson from that one was: on Príncipe, you can never have enough biscuits!

WATCHING WILDLIFE

Birdwatching The island is heaven for birdwatchers. A walk along any road or track will reveal most of the six to nine endemics: the Príncipe drongo, Príncipe speirops, Príncipe weaver, Príncipe sunbird, Príncipe glossy starling and Dohrn's thrush-babbler. Príncipe's emblematic grey parrots tend to flit around between the high trees outside the town, but their numbers have been depleted by parrot-trappers.

(The red-headed lovebird is already believed to be extinct on the island.) In town, at dusk, you are much more likely to see big brown bats (*morcegos*). Even around the airport there is plenty to discover. Ask somebody to show you the bat colony 200m from the airport in two small culverts. An area called Chada, also near the airport, with still water and thick forest, also comes recommended for scientific observation.

Turtle-watching Príncipe has two **turtle beaches**: Praia Grande, to the northeast, and Praia Sundy, some 10km out of town, where in season (Nov–Mar) you can watch turtles laying eggs (see *Chapter 2, Marine turtles*) and hatchlings being returned to the sea. Book an excursion with Bom Bom or contact Damião Matos, the local representative of the MARAPA conservation charity (↘ *251261*), for visiting information. A donation is expected. You could probably arrange informal accommodation at the Sundy plantation (see page 182). For the Praia Grande turtle project, you can also try Yodi (get hold of him at the Pastelaria, ↘ *251150*), who has a motorbike, and, diesel situation permitting, can take you on a half-day trip.

Whale-watching In season (Aug–Dec), humpback whales can be seen along the north coast of the island, especially at low tide, at around 17.00, 18.00 and in the early mornings. If you look out from Belo Monte plantation at 07.00, for instance, you should be able to see them passing. Bom Bom can take you out on a motorised pirogue

GUIDES One of the best guides on Príncipe is **Bikigila** (contact via neighbour; ↘ *909263*); very experienced, he is good company too. Bikigila can take you on a two-day trek to the Praia de São Tomé in the south of the island, and even up the Pico de Príncipe, which few people attempt. In Santo António, **Brankinho** (↘ *251223/925114*; e *brankinho_stp@hotmail.com*) can arrange transport and various town activities, including meals and transport. A recommended guide is **Balthazar**; contact him through the Direcçao das Florestas on Avenida da Liberdade (next to AGROBOFI). Some guides still charge in dobras (80,000$ per person for a day's guiding), which is good news for you. For a visit to the beaches, it is easy to find an informal guide – one day, struggling on my hire bike up the hill out of town, I fell into conversation with a 19-year-old carpenter and ended up getting a tour of the northern beaches and having dinner with his family. Be prepared for things to move slowly; guides may arrive late, the boat may turn out to be a wreck or there might be no diesel, or the trip might be postponed by a day. Try to avoid paying for diesel in advance before you have seen the boat. I did once pay the 425,000$ for the 25-litre standard tank filling for a trip. Five litres were siphoned off while the diesel was overnighting at the hostel; when the boat turned out not to be seaworthy, the remaining fuel was re-sold to the petrol station, but I never got my money back. If you are setting up your own guided walk, take enough **food and water** to share with the guides; unless it's an overnight camping expedition, they will invariably not bring anything with them. Energy bars brought from home are an invaluable top-up food, as is *bobofrito*.

BOM BOM ISLAND RESORT

WHERE TO STAY

🏠 **Bom Bom Island resort** (21 bungalows); CP 25; ↘ 251141/251114; e reservations@ africas-eden.com or bombomisland@africas-eden.com; www.africas-eden.com. Bom Bom means 'Good Good' in Portuguese, & this 4-star resort in the north of the island, run by Africa's Eden (see page 46, the owners of the Omali Lodge hotel in São Tome), is truly a slice of paradise. A very photogenic wooden walkway connects Bom Bom Island (holding the restaurant, bar & marina) with the bungalows/pool area on mainland

Príncipe. Accommodation is in spacious individual chalets (currently being refurbished) directly on the beach or built into the rock, with a couple of family bungalows next to the swimming pool. Be prepared: you might be the only person/couple there & have everything to yourself, including the resort's two lovely & very clean **beaches**. The firmer sand of the western beach, **Praia de Côco**, is great for an early-morning run/stroll before breakfast, while the one to the east, the more protected **Praia Rita**, is best for swimming & snorkelling. The pleasant, medium-sized pool has an artificial waterfall & a pool bar. Around Bom Bom Island there are beautiful rock pools with different ecosystems hosting coral and an array of small tropical fish. Around the pier, yellowtail sardinella can be frequently seen. At night-time, watch you don't step on the large land crabs, with a span of up to 20cm.

The price for this slice of paradise is €350 per day per person, FB, including all standard activities. As for **food & drink**, sumptuous b/fasts inc cereals, eggs, juices, brioches, croissants, fresh fruit, etc. From the restaurant, a great western reef-backed heron can often be seen fishing. For lunch, there is usually a choice of 3 dishes: this could be Indian brinjal soup starter (Indian chef Saju cooks wonderful food), a Santomean *calulú*, with a forgettable vegetarian pasta dish (I once had a little blip in the gorgeous & beautifully presented food). Make sure you work up an appetite for the lavish (often themed) dinners. You can also have your meal served on the marina pier. For visitors, dinner costs €35, & you need to make a reservation. The **shop** sells clothes & comfortable Crocs rubber sandals, postcards, as well as local chocolate & coffee. There is free wireless broadband **internet access** for guests (& a terminal

in reception) & a babysitting facility. When I visited, lights went out at midnight (you are given a torch at check-in) & there were occasional hiccups with the water provision, but management assures me that from 2008, power cuts will be a thing of the past. If you are coming straight into the resort on a charter flight without passing through São Tomé, **visas** can be picked up from Príncipe airport on arrival, but require 72hrs advance notice (US$50; members of a group of more than 10 people only pay US$20). The departure fee is US$12. Visa/Mastercards are accepted. Tips go into a staff kitty.

If you're staying at budget accommodation in Santo António, you can still treat yourself to a day or just dinner here. Entry to the resort, including use of the beach & pool, costs €20; the **day rate** for entrance, including transfers, lunch & access to a bungalow for the day, is €85. Budget travellers wanting to get to the resort for some early-morning birdwatching or to spend the day there can catch the staff truck at 06.00, leaving from the new market in Santo António. It is a fun experience & completely free; you will probably be forced onto the best seat in front. The truck makes the return journey from Bom Bom to Santo António at 16.30 (wait at the manned barrier). Maybe understandably, some tourists never make it out of Bom Bom but, considering how far out you've come, it would be a shame not to at least spend a leisurely half-day looking around Santo António or the plantations, organised through the resort or by yourselves. The resort is currently setting up an eco **tent camp** in the south of the island, which should open up excellent hiking possibilities. $$$$

ACTIVITIES

Adventure sports You can abseil to the famous Banana Beach from Belo Monte plantation (30 or 60m), with the option of returning by pirogue, try quad-biking, kayaking to a fishing village, gorge swimming, a (seasonal) turtle trip, and rainforest and coastal walks, or join an excursion to the island's major plantations, such as Ribeira Izé (with the ruins of a 400-year old church), or a working roça tucked-away amongst huge oka trees.

There is even an organised pub crawl! Check the resort website for details of excursions, which should be booked 12 hours in advance.

Birdwatching The resort is a great birdwatching base. You will quickly meet the resort's tame grey parrot, Chaplin, and both the blue-breasted and white-bellied kingfisher can often be seen flitting around the compound. An early morning walk before breakfast is the easiest way to encounter all six (possibly nine) island endemics. Joining a 2½-hour walk with a group from the UK, I got to see golden weavers, Príncipe starlings, bronze mannikins, swallowtails, Príncipe drongos, Dohrn's thrush-babblers (some of the most vocal birds on the island) and beautiful dragonflies. Don't forget to look down, too, for instance for the fascinating Príncipe blue-speckled mudskipper ('walking fish') that might be stretching motionless across a twig in a puddle just alongside the access road.

Boat trips The resort has boats available to visit a beach (the most popular being Banana Beach, 25 minutes away) or for whale/dolphin watching. Depending on the weather, the experience can be very different: during one grey, rainy birdwatching expedition I got soaked to the core peering out over the waves at indistinct moving shapes; the next day, on a 3-hour excursion, we saw different pods of humpback whales around Jockey Cap island, as well as plenty of dolphins and birds. Morning boat trips usually leave the jetty around 09.00, afternoon boat trips at 14.30. Be punctual; departures don't run on 'African time'. Flying fish will be your constant companions, propelling themselves out of the boat's path to whir across the waves for up to 300m! Ruffled brown boobies sit on the **Pedra de Galé** offshore rocks, and you might see storm petrels on the way to the **Misterioso** islets – one has a lighthouse, the other is just a small group of rocks popular with nesting noddies and tropicbirds. For a fun photo, strap yourself into the marlin-hunting seat. If you're not staying at the resort but would like to take a trip, it might be worth asking around to find other travellers to bring the price down.

Scuba diving An average water temperature of 26°C, average visibility of 20–30m and excellent dive sites only a 20-minute boat ride away make the resort a great diving base. Whilst beginners can take advantage of calm waters, experienced divers can go down to a depth of 30m. There is a resident PADI diving instructor and Dive Master at the resort. A diving 'baptism' (3hrs) costs €70. Courses for groups and individuals can also be arranged with Club Maxel from São Tomé (see page 82); book well in advance. Accompanied by an Open Water-qualified guide, dives cost from €35 to €80 depending on where you go and how many dives you book. Full diving kit hire is available. The water is clearest December to March.

Dive sites

The Arch A great dive for beginners, as you don't have to take a boat; you just walk into the water off Bom Bom island. Swim through the massive archway at 8m depth to see eels, puffer fish, octopus, snapper & maybe a beginner's luck barracuda.

Mosteiros The interlacing rocks of 'the monastery' is a beautiful & varied site ranging from 0–40m, but with plenty of surprises already between 8–20m: turtles, sand sharks, barracudas hiding in caverns, skates, goatfish, surgeon fish, parrot fish, snapper. All levels.

Pedra de Adálio Various fish, eel & octopus on the reef formed by two rocks at a depth of 15m. All levels.

Pedra Galé One of the best sites on Príncipe, with corals, big red carp, various big moray eels, king fish, wahoo & a good chance to see barracuda, nurse sharks & turtles. Depth: 12–40m.

Recommended for advanced divers only, as from the 33m rock plateau there is a drop of a few hundred metres.

Focinho de Cão ('dog's nose') Big rocks on white sandy ground, revealing sand sharks, big manta rays, red snappers, sea bass, barracuda, & fan corals in a depth of 15–30m. All levels.

Boné de Jocquei The giant rocks & big vertical walls of Jockey's Cap islet show similar fish life to the Tinhosas islands (hammer sharks, sand sharks, red carp, king fish), with the advantage of being much closer. Also surgeon fish, trigger fish, snapper, barracuda – & many sea fans. Depth range of 15–40m, suitable for all levels.

Ilhas Tinhosas Known for their seabird colonies, the islands are a long way off the southwestern tip of the island, but the 8hr round trip is rewarded by sand sharks, king fish alongside red carp, beautiful sea slugs, & rock lobsters at a depth of 25–30m. If you're lucky, you might see a hammer shark. Great site for night dives. Pedra de Werner is an amazing rectangular rock with a depth ranging between 18 & 50m. All levels.

Baia das Aguinas 20–25m. Listen out for the singing of passing whales.

Snorkelling Hiring a mask, snorkel and fins is free for guests and included in the day visitor's rate for non-residents. On the Praia Santa Rita beach, check out the reef to the left, where you can see west African butterfly fish and parrotfish. On a leisurely two-hour snorkelling trip around Bom Bom islet you have a good chance of seeing barracuda sharks, turtles and wahoo, golden African snapper, and the largest of the snapper family, the cubera snapper, as well as the yellow jack, all year round. You will find shoals of small yellowtail sardinella swarming around the pier.

Sport fishing The resort holds seven IGFA world records from the early 1990s, amongst them a 114lb Atlantic sailfish, locally called *peixe andala*, in the Line Class, and a 60lb barracuda in the Saltwater Fly Rod class. When I visited, four men were struggling to heave a massive marlin caught by a South African guest onto the weighing hook of the official IGFA weighing station (now removed). True to the motto of the Billfish Foundation – 'No Marlin on the Menu' (*www.billfish.org*) – marlins are always released after being caught. The Fisherman's Bar, *Bar Pescador*, is a nice, airy open space. Apart from marlins weighing 150–400kg, you can catch yellow-fin tuna weighing 20–45kg, wahoo, barracuda, rainbow runner and jacks. The 32ft *Black Fin* yacht and two 28ft *True World* marine boats are equipped with 25lbs and 50lbs Shimano tackle and 80lbs Penn International. The dry season, with southern breezes of 10–25 knots, is the best time to come. Chief skipper Argentino has been with Bom Bom for 17 years.

Other activities Check the resort website for details of excursions to plantation houses, rainforest walks, etc.

Appendix I

WILDLIFE GLOSSARY

This is a – by no means exhaustive – list of the birds, mammals, plants, fruit, vegetables and trees that you might encounter. The English name comes first, followed by the Latin, then (where known), the Creole/Portuguese and French names.

BIRDS with thanks to Patrice Christy, D E Sargeant, Phil Atkinson
Birds endemic to São Tomé

Dwarf olive ibis	Bostrychia bocagei	Galinhola Ibis de bocage	Ibis-de-São-Tomé
São Tomé green pigeon	Treron sanctithomai	Cessa Pombo-verde-de-São Tomé	Colombar de São Tomé
São Tomé bronze-naped pigeon	Columba malherbii	Rola Pombo-de-nuca-bronzeada	Pigeon de Malherbe
Maroon/São Tomé pigeon	Columba thomensis	Pombo (do mato)	Pombo marreta Pigeon de São Tomé
São Tomé scops-owl	Otus hartlaubi	Kitoli Mocho-de-São Tomé	Petit-duc de São Tomé
São Tomé spinetail	Zoonavena/Chaetura thomensis	Ferreiro-espinhoso	Martinet de São Tomé
São Tomé fiscal shrike	Lanius newtoni	–	Pie-grièche de São Tomé
São Tomé oriole	Oriolus crassirostris	Papa-figo Papa-figos de São Tomé	Loriot de São Tomé
São Tomé thrush	Turdus olivaceofuscus	Tordo	Merle de São Tomé
São Tomé prinia	Prinia molleri	Truqui	Prinia de São Tomé
São Tomé short-tail	Amaurocichla bocagei	P Nasique de bocage	
São Tomé paradise-flycatcher	Terpiphone atrochalybeia	Tomé-gaga	Tchitrec de São Tomé
Newton's yellow-breasted sunbird	Nectarinia newtonii	Selêlê Beija-flor-de-peito-amarelo	Souimanga de Newton
São Tomé giant sunbird	Dreptes thomensis	Selêlê-mangotchi Beija-for-gigante	Souimanga Géant

São Tomé oriole

São Tomé giant sunbird

São Tomé green pigeon

São Tomé white-eye	*Zosterops ficedulinus*	Tchili-tchili Olho-branco-de-São-Tomé	Zostérops Becfigue
São Tomé speirops	*Speirops lugubris*	Olho-grosso Olho-branco-sombrio	Speirops de São Tomé
São Tomé grosbeak	*Neospiza concolor*	Néospize de São Tomé	
Giant weaver	*Ploceus grandis*	Camussela Tecelão-grande	Tisserin Géant
São Tomé weaver	*Thomasophantes sanctithomae*	Tchim-tchim-cholo Tecelão-de-São Tomé	Tisserin de São Tomé

Birds endemic to Príncipe

Dohrn's thrush-babbler	*Horizorhinus dohrni*	Tchibi-fixa Rouxinol-do-Príncipe	Cratérope de Príncipe
Príncipe drongo	*Dicrurus modestus*	Rabotizoura Drongo	Drongo de Príncipe
Príncipe glossy starling	*Lamprothornis ornatus*	Estorninho Estorninho-do-Príncipe	Choucador de Príncipe
Príncipe sunbird	*Nectarinia hartlaubi*	Beija-flor-do Príncipe	Souimanga de Hartlaub
Príncipe speirops	*Speirops leucophaeus*	Sorli	Speirops de Príncipe
Príncipe seedeater	*Serinus rufobrunneus*	Padé Chamariço-do-Príncipe	Serin roux
Príncipe golden weaver	*Ploceus princeps*	Merlo Tecelão-do-Príncipe	Tisserin de Príncipe

Other commonly found birds

Black/white-capped noddy	—	Garajau-de-cabeça branca	Noddi noir
Black-winged red bishop	*Euplectus hordeaceus*	Padé-campo Cardeal-coroa-de-fogo	Euplecte monseigneur
Blue waxbill	*Uraeginthus angolensis*	Suín-suín	Cordon-bleu de l'Angola
Bronze mannikin	*Lonchura cucullata*	Queblan-cana-preto Freirinha	Capuchin nonnette
Brown/common noddy	*Anous stolidus*	Padé-do-mal Garajau-pardo	Noddi brun
Brown booby	*Sula leucogaster*	Matchia-vagé (ST), Pato-marinho (P)	Alcatraz Fou brun
Bridled tern	*Sterna anathetus*		Sterne bridée
Black kite	*Milvus migrans*	Falcão Milhafre-preto, Rabo-de-bacalhau	Milan noir
Blue-breasted kingfisher	*Halcyon malimbica dryas*	Chau-chau pica-peixe-de-peito azul	Martin-Chasseur à poitrine bleue
Cattle egret	*Bubulcus ibis*	Garça Garça-boeirra	Héron Garde-Boeufs
Common sandpiper	*Actitis hypoleucos*	Maçarico-das-rochas	Chevalier guignette

Black-winged red bishop

Pin-tailed whydah

African grey parrot

Príncipe seedeater

Common waxbill	Estrilda astrild	Quebra-cana Bico-de-lacre	Astrild ondulé
Emerald cuckoo	Chrysococcyx cupreus insularum	Ossobó/pássaro-de-chuva Cuco-esmeraldinho	Coucou foliotocol
Green-backed heron	Butoridis striatus	Chuchu/Tchongo Garça-de-cabeça-negra	Héron Strié
Greenshank	Tringa nebularia	Perna-verde	Chevalier aboyeur
Grey parrot	Psittacus erithacus		Perroquet jaco
Moorhen	Gallinula chloropus	Galinha-de-água Galinha-de-água-africana	Gallinule poule d'eau
Malachite kingfisher	Alcedo cristata thomensis	Martin-Pêcheur Huppé	
Palm swift	Cypsiurus parvus andorinha	Guincho-das-palmeiras	Martinet des palmes
Pin-tailed widow	Vidua macroura	Viuvinha Viuvinha-cauda-de-fio	Veuve Dominicaine
Reed cormorant	Phalacrocorax africanus	Pato marinho/Pata-de-água Corvo-marinho-africano	Cormorant Africain
Reef heron/ Western reef-egret	Egretta gularis	Garça	Aigrette à Gorge Blanche
Sooty tern	Sterna fuscata	Gaivina fosca	Sterne fuligineuse
Whimbrel	Numenius phaeopus	Meio-maçarico	Courlis corlieu
White-tailed tropic bird	Phaeton lepturus	Coconzuco Rabo-de-junco	Phaeton à bec jaune

MARINE LIFE

Fish NB: brackets denote the lack of common name; often the local name, '*moreia*' or '*cobra*' covers several different species.

African hind	Cephalopholis taeniops	Bobo quema Garoupa-de-pintas	Mérou à points bleus
Atlantic agujon needlefish	Tylosurus acus rafale	Agulha quio/Zanve Agulheta-imperial-da-Guiné	Aiguille voyeuse
Atlantic blue marlin	Makaira nigricans	Espadim-azul-do-Atlântico Marlim-azul do Atlântico	Makaire bleu
Atlantic flying fish	Cheilopogon melanurus	Voador panhã Peixe-voador	Poisson-volant
Atlantic mudskipper	Periophthalmus papilio	Cucumba Saltão-da-vasa	Sauteur de vase atlantique
Atlantic sailfish	Istiophorus albicans	Peixe andála Bicuda/ Espadarte-veleiro/ Peixe de vela/Peco	Voilier de l'Atlantique
Balao halfbeak	Hemiramphus balao	Maxipombo Agulha	Demi-bec balaou
Ballyhoo	Hemiramphus brasiliensis	Agulhinha	Demi-bec du Brésil
Barracuda	Sphyraena barracuda	Barracuda	Brochet de mer
Bennett's flyingfish	Cheilopogon pinnatibarbatus pinnatibarbatus	Voador rede/ anzol Tainhota-voadeira	Exocet de Bennett
Biafra doctorfish	Prionurus biafrensis	Peixe-cirurgião	Chirurgien biafra
Biglip grunt	Plectorhinchus macrolepis	António-boca Roncador-batata	Diagramme à grosses lèvres
Blackbar hogfish	Bodianus speciosus	Bulhão	Pourceau dos noir
Blackbar soldierfish	Myripristis jacobus	Mãe de caqui	Marignan mombim
Blue runner	Caranx crysos	Bonito Solteira	Carangue coubali
Bluespotted cornetfish	Fistularia tabacaria	Agulha buzina	Cornette à taches bleues
Brown chromis	Chromis multilineata	Donzela marron	Castagnole grise
Creole fish	Paranthias furcifer mulato	Bala bala Pargo-mirim	Badèche créole
Crevalle jack	Caranx hippos	Corcovado Xexém	Carangue crevalle
Cubera snapper	Lutjanus cyanopterus	Caranho	Vivaneau cubéra
Flaming reef lobster	Enoplometopus antillensis	Lagostim das grutas	Homard de récif

Flat needlefish	*Ablennes hians*	Agulha espada	Aiguille voyeuse
Flying fish	*Exocoetus volitans*	Peixe-voador	Poisson-volant
Flying gurnard	*Dactylopterus volitans*	Concon Cabrinha-de-leque/ Peixe-pássaro	Poule de mer, Poisson volant, Grondin Volant
French butterfly fish	*Prognathodes marcellae*	Tchintchin Peixe-borboleta	Labre
Golden African snapper	*Lutjanus fulgens*	Vermelho Luciano-dourado	Vivaneau doré
Greater amberjack	*Seriola dumerili*	Charuteiro-catarino	Sériole couronnée
Greater soapfish	*Rypticus saponaceus*	peixe sabão Badejo-sabão	Savonnette
Honeycomb moray	*Muraena melanotis*		Cobra Murène
Horse-eye jack	*Caranx latus*	Macaco	Cric
Horse mackerel	*Decapterus macarellus*	Carapau cavala Carapau	Carangue maquereau
Large-eye dentex	*Dentex macrophthalmus*	vermelho fundo	Breca Denté à gros yeux
Leopard eel	*Myrichthys pardalis*	cobra do mar Cobra-leopardo	Serpenton léopard
Lesser African threadfin	*Galeoides decadactylus*	barbudo Barbudo-de-dez-barbas	Faux-capitaine
Milk shark	*Rhizoprionodon acutus*	Tubarão-bicud Marracho branco	Requin à nez pointu
Nurse shark	*Ginglymostoma cirratum*	Tubarão-pagem	Requin dormeur
Offshore rockfish	*Pontinus kuhlii*	cangá	Rescasse du large
Parrotfish/Peacock wrasse	*Thalassoma newtonii*	Peixe verde	Girelle-paon
Pistol shrimp	*Alpheus glaber*	Camarão pistola	Crevette-pistolet
Rainbow runner	*Elagatis bipinnulata*	alada Camisa de meia	Comète saumon
Red grouper	*Epinephelus morio*		Garoupa de São Tomé Nègre
Redfin parrotfish	*Sparisoma rubripinne*	Bulhão congo Boião	Perroquet basto
Red Snapper	*Lutjanus campechanus*	vermelho-de-fundo	Vivaneau rouge
Rockhind	*Epinephelus adscensionis*	Glopim/Garoupa	Mérou oualioula
Round scad	*Decapterus punctatus*	Carapau cavala Carapau	Comète quiaquia
Sand tiger shark	*Carcharias taurus*	Mangona	Requin-taureau
Scalloped hammerhead	*Sphyrna lewini*	Tubarão martelo Peixe-martelo	Requin marteau
Sea bass	*Acanthistius brasilianus*	Corvina Badejo	Serran argentin
Shortfin mako	*Isurus oxyrinchus*	Mako Mako	
Snakefish/ Bluntnose lizardfish	*Trachinocephalus myops*	Rainha Traíra do alto	Poisson-lézard
Spot-fin porcupinefish	*Diodon hystrix*	Graviola	Porc-épic boubou
Squirrelfish	*Holocentrus ascensionis*	Caqui	Marignan coq
Stout moray	*Muraena robusta*	Moreia congra	Moreia Murène robuste
Swordfish	*Xiphias gladius*	Peixe ferro Peixe-espada/ espadarte	Espadon
Three-banded butterflyfish	*Chaetodon robustus*	Tchintchin Peixe-borboleta	Poisson-papillon
Wahoo	*Acanthocybium solandri*	Peixe fumo Cavala-wahoo	Thazard-bâtard
West African angel fish	*Holocanthus africanus*	Tchinchin de fundo	Poisson-ange africain
West African goatfish	*Pseudupeneus prayensis*	salmonete Chalino	Rouget du Sénégal
West African hawkfish	*Cirrhitus atlanticus*	Peixe-falcao	Poisson faucon
West African seahorse	*Hippocampus algiricus*	Cavalo-marinho	Poissons-trompettes
West African Spanish mackerel	*Scomberomorus tritor*	Serra Peixe-serra	Maquereau-bonite
Whale shark	*Rhincodon typus*	Má pinta tubarão-baleia	Requin-baleine
Yellow jack	*Carangoides bartholomaei*	xerelete-amarelo	Carangue grasse
Yellow sea chub	*Kyphosus incisor sopa*	Pirajica	Calicagère jaune
Yellowfin tuna	*Thunnus albacares*	Atum oledê Alvacora	Thon à nageoires jaunes
Yellowtail sardinella	*Sardinella rouxi*	Sardinela-rabo-amarelo	Sardinelle à queue jaune

Crabs and spiders

Cameroon red tarantula	*Hysterocrates gigas*	Samangungú	Tarantula Mygale
Hermit crab	*Pagurus*	Caranguejo ermita	Crabe hermite/pagure
Trap door spider	*Moggridgea occidua*	Simon Aranha alcapão	Araignée de trappe
Whip scorpion	*Amblypigida*	Escorpião sem rabo	Scorpion sans queue de fouet
Whip spider	*Damon tibialis*	Aranha do chicote	Araignée de fouet

Corals and anemones

Fan coral	*Gorgoniacea*	Gorgônia	Gorgone
Collared sand anemone	*Actinostella flosculifera*	anêmona de areia	anémone de sable
Cylinder anemone	*Cerianthus membranaceus*	Anêmona-de-tubo	Anémone de tube
Great star coral	*Montastrea cavernosa*	Cérebro Verde	Grand corail étoilé
Golden cup coral	*Tubastraea aurea*	Coral sol	Aiptasie jaune
Hydro/lace coral	*Stylaster blattea*	Coral-laço	Corail dentelle

MAMMALS

Mona monkey	*Cercopithecus mona*	macaco	Singe Mona
Civet cat	*Civectittis civetta*	lagaia	Civette
Black/ship rat	*Rattus rattus*	Rato preto	Rat noir
Pantropical spotted dolphin/bridled dolphin	*Stenella attenuata*	golfinho dauphin	tacheté pantropical
Brown rat	*Rattus norvegicus*	Ratazans castanha	Rat brun
House mouse	*Mus musculus*	fingi	Rato Souris
Humpback whale	*Megaptera novaeangliae*	Baleia-de-bossas	Mégaptère/Baleine à bosse
Common weasel	*Mustela nivalis*	Doninha	Belette
Bent-winged bat	*Miniopterus newtoni*	Morcego de asa grande	Rhinolophe
São Tomé day-flying bat	*Hipposideros ruber*	Morcego de nariz chato	Rhinolophe
Straw-coloured fruit-bat	*Eidolon helvum*	Guembú Morcego frugívoro cor-de-palha	Roussette paillée africaine
São Tomé free-tailed bat	*Chaerephon tomensis*	Morcego	Molosse de São Tomé
São Tomé giant olive-brown baboon	*Hysterocrates scepticus*	Tarantula Samangungú	Mygale
São Tomé little collared fruit bat	*Myonycteris brachycephala*	Pequeno morcego de fruta	Petite roussette
Common dolphin/porpoise	*Delphinus delphis*	Golfinho	Dauphin commun
Wild pig	*Sug scrofa*	porco do mato	Cochon forestier/sauvage

REPTILES AND AMPHIBIANS

Black cobra	*Naja melanoleuca*	melanoleuca cobra preta	Serpent Noir
Beaked snake	*Rhinotyphlops newtoni*	–	Serpent aveugle
Burrowing snake	*Rhinotyphlops feae*	–	Serpent aveugle
Day gecko	*Lygodactylus thomensis osga*	–	Gecko diurne
Gecko	*Hemidactylus greefi osga*	Gecko	
Green bush snake	*Philothamnus thomensis*	Soá-soá	Serpent Noir de São Tomé
Green turtle	*Chelonia mydas*	Mão	Grande Tortue verte
Hawksbill turtle	*Eretmochelys imbricata*	Sada	Tortue imbriquee
Leatherback turtle	*Dermochelys coriacea*	Ambulância	Tortue luth
Lizard	*Lacerta lagarto*		Lézard
Loggerhead turtle	*Caretta caretta*	Ambo	Tortue carouanne
Many-scaled feylinia	*Feylinia polylepis*	cobra cega	Serpent aveugle

Millipede	*Diplopoda*	Centopeia	Centipède
Moller's gulf frog	*Hyperolius molleri*	Raineta	Grenouille arboricole
Olive ridley turtle	*Lepidochelys olivacea*	Tatô	Tortue olivâtre
Palm forest frog	*Leptopelis palmatus*	Raineta	Grenouille arboricole des forêts de palmiers
Peter's river/ranid frog	*Ptychadena newtoni*	Rã Phrynobatrachus dispar	Grenouille riverine
São Tomé house snake	*Lamprophis lineatus bedriagae*	Cobra de casa	Serpent de maison de São Tomé
São Tomé tree frog	*Hyperolius thominsis*	Raineta de São Tomé	Grenouille arboricole
São Tomé white-toothed shrew	*Crocidura thomensis*	Musaranho	Musaraigne
Skink	*Panapsis africana*	Mabuya Lagarto	Eumèce
Rat snake	*Boedon lineatus bedriagae*	Gita Cobra-rateira	Serpent rat
West African mud turtle	*Pelusios castaneus*	Benco	Péluse de Schweigger
Yellow-banded blind snake	*Typhlops elegans*	Cobra cego	Serpent aveugle
Yellow caecilian	*Schistometopum thomensis*	cobra bôbô	Cécilie multicolore

GASTROPODS

Forest snail	*Archachatina bicarinata*	Búzio d'Obô/do mato	Escargot terrestre
Sea snail	*Aphlysia*	Búzio do mar	Escargot marin/Aplysie
São Tomé door snail	*Thyrophorella thomensis*	Búzio d'Obô/do mato	Escargot
Millipede	*Lobo centopeia*	—	Millipède
Anemone horseshow worm	*Phoronis autralis*	—	Grand phoronidien

FLOWERS, FRUIT, HERBS AND SPICES, PLANTS AND TREES

Acacia	*Albizzia moluccana*	acácia	Acacie
African breadfruit	*Treculia africana*	Izaquente	Arbre à pain d'Afrique
African corkwood/ Umbrella tree	*Musanga cecropioides*	Gófe	Parasolier
African grape	*Pseudospondias microcarpa/ Spondias lutea*	Guêguê	'Raisin d'Afrique'
African oak	*Chlorophora tenuifolia/ Milicia excelsa*	Amoreira	Chêne africain
African oil palm	*Elaecis guineensis andim/ déndém*	Palmeira	Palmier à huile
African plum/pear	*Dacryodes edulis*	Safú	Safous
Amaranth	*Amaranthus caudatus*	Jimboa/Gimboa	Amarante queue de renard
Avocado	*Persea americana*	Abacate	Avocat
Bamboo	*Bambusa arundinacea*	Bambú	Bambou
Banana	*Musa paradisiaca*	Banana Quitchibá	Banane
Baobab	*Adansonia digitata*	Micondó Imbondeiro	Baobab africain
Black pepper	*Piper nigrum*	Pimenta do reino	Poivre noir
(Blood tree)	*Harungana madagascariensis*	Pau-sangue	Arbre de sang
Breadfruit	*Artocarpus altilis/communis*	Fruta-pão	Fruit de pain
Cameroon cardamom	*Afranomum Daniellii*	ossame/ossami	Cardamome cameroonaise
'Cameroonian' tree	*Scytopelatum camerunianum*	Vilo Viro branco	Arbre du Cameroun
Cayenne pepper	*Capsicum annuum*	Pimenta malagueta	Poivre de cayenne
Chilli/Guinea pepper	*Capsicum frutescens*	Piripiri	Poivron
Cinnamon	*Cinnamomum ceylanicum*	Canela	Cannelle
Climbing begonia	*Begonia baccata*	Folha bôba vermelha Begônia	Bégonia grimpante

Cocoa	*Theobroma cacao*	cacaozeiro	Cacaoyer
Coconut palm	*Cocus nucifera*	Côcônja Coqueiro	Palmier de coco
Cocoyam	*Xanthosoma sagittifolium*	Matabala	Inhame Taro
Coffee	*Coffea Arabica*	Cafeeiro	Caféier
Common ginger	*Zingiber officinale*	gengibre fresco	Gingembre
Croton	*Croton stellulifer*	Cubango	Croton
(Endangered endemic tree, Flacourtiaceae family)	*Homalium heriquesii*	Quebra machado	Flacourtiacée endémique danger d'extinction
(Endangered endemic Pandanaceae tree)	*Pandanus thomensis*	Pau esteira	Pandanacée endémique vulnérable
False African currant ('third leg')	*Allophylus africanus*	Pó Tleche Pau-três	Fausse groseille Africaine ('troisième jambe')
Fan palm	*Borassus aethiopium*	Ulua palmeira lêque	Rônier
Fern	*Pterophyta*	Feto	Fougère
Flame tree	*Erythrina poeppigiana/ variegata*	Eritrina	Érythrine
Foxtail	*Setaria megaphylla/ chevalieri*	Uagá-Uagá Capim-de-burro/ Pé de Galinha	Queue de renard
Giant begonia	*Begonia crateris*	Fiá bôba d'obô Begônia	Bégonia géant de São Tomé
Giant lobelia	*Lobelia barnsii*	Lobélia gigante	Lobelia géant
Guava	*Psidium guajava*	Goiaba	Goyave
Kola nut tree	*Cola acuminata*	Cola/Coleira	Noix de kola
Lemongrass	*Cymbopogon citratus*	Chá do Príncipe Chanela/ Capim do Gabão	Citronelle
Jackfruit	*Artocarpus heterophyllus/ interger*	Jaca	Jacquier
Mango	*Mangifera indica*	Manga	Mangue
Mangosteen	*Garcinia mangostona*	Mangostão	Mangoustan
Manioc	*Manihot esculenta*	Mandioca Maioba	Manioc
Millet	*Poaceae*	Milho de sequeiro	Millet/Graminée
Monkey flower	*Costus Gigantus*	Flor de macaco/ cana-doce-dos-macacos	'Fleur de singe'
Oil tree	*Santiria trimeira*	Pó Oleo/Bálsamo de São Tomé	Pau óleo Arbre huilier
(Orange-flowering endemic heather)	*Erica thomensis*	Urze de São Tomé florescente cor de laranja	Bruyère endémique aux fleurs oranges
(Orange-flowering endemic Leeaceae)	*Leea tinctoria Cele-alé*	Árvore florescente cor de laranja	Arbre de fleurs rouge-oranges endémique
Oregano basil/Fever bush	*Ocimum viride/ Ocimum gratissimum*	Micocó	Basilic africain
Papaya	*Carica papaya*	Mamão/Mamoeiro (tree)	Papaye
Parrot beak	*Heliconia rostrata*	Hêliconia	Heliconia rostré/ Pince de homard
Passionfruit	*Passiflora*	Maracujá	Fruit de la passion
Pepper	*Piper spp.*	Pimenta	Poivre
Pineapple	*Ananas*	Bacatchi Ananás	Ananas
Porcelain rose	*Phoemeria magnifica*	Rosa porcelana	Rose porcelaine
Red mangrove	*Rhizophoraca apiculata/ racemosa Rhizophora*	mangle mangue vermelho	Palétuvier rouge
Saffron	*Curcuma longa*	Saffrom açafrão da India	Safrane
Salad burnet	*Sanguisorba minor/ Sechium*	edule pimpinela	Pimprinelle

Silk cotton tree	Ceiba pentandra	Oká	Fromager
Starfruit	Averrhoa carambola	Cálambola Carambola	Carambole
Strangler fig	Ficus aurea	Figo estranguladora	Figue étrangleur
(São Tomé chestnut)	Acanthus montanum	Cundú de muala vé Castanheiro de São Tomé	(Châtaignier de São Tomé)
São Tomé peach tree	Chytranthus mannii	Pessegeiro de São Tomé	Pêcher de São Tomé
São Tomé pine	Afrocarpus/ podocarpus mannii	Ofó Pinheiro de São Tomé	Pin de São Tomé
Sap-Sap	Annona muricata	Sap-sap Graviola	Corossol
Spanish cedar	Cedrela odorata	Cedrela	Acajou amer
Sugar cane	Saccharum officinarum	Cana de açucar	Canne de sucre
Sweet potato	Ipomaea batatas	Batata doce	Batate
Tamarind	Tamarindus indica	tamarino	Tamarin
Tomato-fruited eggplant	Solanum naumannii	makêkê	Aubergine amère
Vanilla (orchid)	Vanila planifolia	Baunilha	Vanille
Watercress	Rorippa nasturtium-aquaticum/Lepidium sativum	Fiá-guinhom Agrião	Cresson
White mangrove	Avicennia nitida	mangue de praia	Palétuvier blanc
Wild cinnamon	Cinnamomum zeylanicum	Pau canela Caneleira	Canelle sauvage
Wild ginger	Zingiber officinalis	Gengimple Gengibre	Gingembre
Wild strawberry	Rubus pinatus	Molanga Framboesa brava	Fraise sauvage
(Yellow-flowering endemic tree, Myristicaceae)	Staudtia pterocarpa	Pau vermelho	Arbre endémique/ Myristicacée aux fleurs jaunes
Ylang-Ylang	Cananga odorata	Árvore perfume	Ilangue-Ilangue

Appendix 2

LANGUAGE

Portuguese is the official language and is understood by everybody. French is taught in school and is much more likely to be understood than English, though on Príncipe even French is of little use. Visitors who have travelled in Spanish-speaking countries often speak 'Portunhol', a mix that will be understood by most people. However, in everyday situations some 85% of *Santomense* people use creole, or *forro* (see box on page 20).

PRONUNCIATION

The alphabet The difficulty in understanding Portuguese lies in the nasalisation, sh sounds, and the fact that words often run into one another.

- Vowels that carry a tilde (~) or that are followed by -m or -n are nasalised: São (saint), quem? (who?)
- Stress usually lies on the penultimate syllable. Exceptions are words ending in -l, -r, -z, nasalised -ã,
- Accents signify stress/emphasis : Tomé, Príncipe, água (water), português (Portuguese)

Português

a = as in car (*carro*)
a (on its own) = as in **a** (on its own)
ã/an/am = as in **a**ngle
b = as in **b**ig
c = as in **c**at
ch = as in **sh**ame: *chá* (tea)
ç = as in **s**un: *açúcar* (sugar)
d = as in **d**og: *dá-me!* (give me!)
e = as in p**e**t: *esperar* (to wait)
f = as in **f**it: *fogo* (fire)
g = as in **g**od: *grande* (big)
h (at beginning) = dropped
h (after 'l' or 'n') = as in **y**oga: *molho* (sauce)
i = as in t**ea**: *livro* (book)
j = as in Ra**j**: *jantar* (have dinner)
l = as in **l**et: *léve-léve* (easy, relaxed)
m = as in **m**e: *maçâ* (apple)
n = as in **n**o: *noite* (night)
o (stressed) = open, as in **o**live: *porta* (door) or closed, as in Scottish 'no'
o (unstressed, on its own) = as in r**oo**t: *carro* (car)
p = as in **p**ig: Portugal
qu = before -a/-o as in **qu**est, before -e/-i as in **k**ettle: *quem?* (who?)
r = articulate strongly: *rua* (street)

rr = rolled: *carro* (car)

s (at beginning of word/syllable after consonant, and when spelt 'ss') = as in **s**un: *sábado* (Saturday)

s (between vowels and at end when following word begins with vowel) = as in **z**ealous: *casa* (house), *seis euros* (six euros)

s (at end and before unvoiced consonants: c,f,k,p,s,t,x) = as in **sh**ower: *festa* (party)

ss = as in **s**treet: *isso* (this)

t = as in **t**ea: *toma!* (take!)

u = as in n**oo**n: *tudo* (all)

v = as in **v**ery: *vamos!* (let's go!)

x = as in **sh**ort: *peixe* (fish) or *táxi* (taxi)

z = at beginning/between vowels: as in **z**en: *azul* (blue); at end: as in Ra**j**: *dez* (ten)

Basic grammar Most common verb conjugation: *falar* (to speak) *fal-o*: I speak, *fal-as*: you speak, *fal-a*: he/she/it speaks, *fal-amos*: we speak, *fal-am* (you/plural speak, they speak)

Common compound verbs *ser* (to be – permanently): *sou*: I am, *és*: you are; *é*: he/she/it is, *somos*: we are; *são*: you/plural, they are

Common past forms

fui: I was, *foi*: he/she/it was, *fomos*: we were; *foram*: you/pl, they were

estar: (to be – temporarily/location): *estou, estás, está, estámos, estão*

estive: I was, *esteve*: he/she/it was, *estivemos*: we were, *estiveram*: you/pl., they were

ter: (to have): *tenho, tens, tem, temos, têm*

tive: I had, *teve*: he/she/it had, *tivemos*: we had, *tiveram*: you/pl., they had

ir: (to go): *vou, vais, vai, vamos, vão*

fui: I went, *fomos*: we went, *foram*: they went

Useful verbs

to be	ser /estar	sa
to speak	falar	fla
to buy	comprar	kopla
to get, catch	apanhar	pega/koyê/ panha
to send	enviar, mandar	manda
to organise	arranjar	luma/ lanja/golo
to give	dar	da/ tanda/
to pick up	pegar	pega/toma/
to have	ter	tê/ sa ku
to leave, go away	ir-se embora	be dê/ lanka xê/
to like something/somebody	gostar de algo/alguem	ngosta di kwa
to work	trabalhar	tlaba
to see	ver	pya
to wander around/hang out	passear	paxa
to reach, arrive	chegar	xiga
to rent, hire	alugar	luga

Lungwa Santome sounds

a = as a in 'father'

e = as e in 'yet'

ê = as a in 'place'

i = as ea in 'meat' but shorter

o = as o in 'not'

ô = as oa in 'boat'

GESTURES

OK – thumbs up	OK/fixe
Hello/goodbye – wave hand, palm out, from side to side	olá/adeus
Ask for a lift (hitch-hiking)	boleia

u = as oo in 'moon'
tx = as ch in 'chess'
dj = as j in 'joke'
x = as sh in 'shame'

Vocabulary

(Note: *sun* is formal masculine, *san* is formal feminine and *bô* is informal for both masculine and feminine)

English	Portuguese	Creole
Essentials		
Good morning	*Bom dia*	*Bondja ô/abensa ô*
Good afternoon	*Boa tarde*	*Bwas tadji ê*
Good evening	*Boa noite*	*Bwa notxi ê*
Hello	*Olá, oi!*	*Bondja (ô)/abensa ô*
Goodbye	*Adeus*	*Adêsu ê*
What is your name?	*Como é que se chama?*	*Kê aglasa sun/san/bô ê?*
		Kê nomi sun/san/bô ê?
My name is…	*O meu nome é…*	*Aglasa/Nomi mu sa…*
Where are you from?	*De onde é?*	*Bô sa ngê d'andji?*
		Andji ku tê bô?
I am from…England/	*Sou … Inglês (Inglesa)/*	*N sa … nglêji*
America/	*Americano (Americana)*	*Amerikanu*
France/	*Francês (Francesa)/*	*Flansêji*
Germany	*Alemão (Alemã)*	*Alemon*
How are you?	*Como está?*	*Sun/San/Bô sa bwa?*
	Que ha de nova?	*Ki nova ê?/Kuma bô sa?/*
		Kuma vida sa ê?
		Kuma kwa ska dêsê ê?
How are you? (polite version)	*Como vai a saúde?*	*Ki nova saôdji ê?*
All OK (with you)? (very common)	*Tudo bem (contigo)?*	*Sun/san/bô sa bwa?*
All OK	*Tudo, obrigado/a*	*N sa bwa/Bwa so*
Are you OK?	*Está bom/boa?*	*Sun/san/bô sa bwa?*
Fine thanks	*(Estou bem) obrigado/a*	*N sa bwa/Bwa so*
Easy, with calm… (Santomean motto)	*Lévé-lévé*	*Leve-leve (tan)*
OK	*Normal*	*Axi-axi*
So-so	*Mais ou menos*	*Mê txibi*
Pleased to meet you	*Gosto em conhecê-lo/a/prazer*	
Thank you	*Kbrigado(a)*	*Dêsu ka paga sun/san/bô*
Don't mention it	*De nada*	*Kwa desu paga ê?*
Cheers!	*Saúde!*	*Saôdji*
Yes	*Sim/pois*	*Efan/E*
No	*Não*	*Inô/Nô ô*

It's OK/All right then	Kstá bem/está bom	Muntu ben/non sa fladu
I don't understand	Não compreendo	N na ska tendê fa
I didn't understand	Kão percebi	N na tendê fa
Please would you speak more slowly	Kor favor pode falar mais devagar?	Fla maxi momoli fan
Excuse me?	Diga?	Poda mu?
Calm down	(Com) calma	Kaluma fan
Do you understand?	Está a perceber?	Sun/San/Bô têndê an?
I don't know	Não sei	N na sêbê fa
I would like...	Queria…	N mêsê …

Questions

how?	como?	Kuma?
what?	o quê?	Kê kwa?
where?	onde?	Andji?
what is it?	o que é?	Sa kê kwa?
which?	qual	Kali dinen? (which one?)
when?	quando?	Kê dja?
why?	porquê?	Punda kamanda?/ Punda kê kwa?
who?	quem?	Kê ngê?
how much?	quanto é?	Kantu ku ê sa...?

Numbers

1	um	a
2	dois	dôsu
3	três	tlêxi
4	quatro	kwatlu
5	cinco	xinku
6	seis	sêxi
7	sete	sete
8	oito	wôtô
9	nove	nove
10	dez	dexi
11	onze	dexi ku a
12	doze	dexi ku dôsu
13	treze	dexi ku tlêxi
14	quatorze	dexi ku kwatlu
15	quinze	dexi ku xinku
16	dezasseis	dexi ku sêxi
17	dezassete	dexi ku sete
18	dezoito	dexi ku wôtô
19	dezanove	dexi ku nove
20	vinte	vintxi/dôsu dexi
21	vinte e um/a	vintxi/dôsu dexi ku a
30	trinta	tlinta/tlêxi dexi
40	quarenta	kolenta/kwatlu dexi
50	cinquenta	xinkwenta/xinku dexi
60	sessenta	sesenta/sêxi dexi
70	settenta	stenta/sete dexi
80	oitenta	wôtenta/wôtô dexi
90	noventa	noventa/nove dexi
100	cem	sem

| 101 | *cent e um/a* | *sem ku a* |
| 1,000 | *mil* | *mili* |

Time

What time is it?	*Que horas são?*	*Kê minda d'ola kwa sa ê?*
It's … am/pm	*São … da manhã/tarde*	*Sa … plaman/tadji*
now	*agora*	*miole/wele*
today	*hoje*	*oze*
tonight	*hoje à noite*	*oze nôtxi*
tomorrow	*amanhã*	*amanha*
tomorrow morning	*amanhã de manhã*	*amanha plaman*
yesterday	*ontem*	*onten*
morning	*manhã*	*plaman*
evening	*noite*	*nôtxi*

Days

Monday	*segunda-feira*	*segunda fela*
Tuesday	*terça-feira*	*tesa fela*
Wednesday	*quarta-feira*	*kwata fela*
Thursday	*quinta-feira*	*kinta fela*
Friday	*sexta-feira*	*sesta fela*
Saturday	*sábado*	*sabadu*
Sunday	*domingo*	*dja djingu*

Months

January	*Janeiro*	*janêlu*
February	*Fevereiro*	*fêvêlêlu*
March	*Março*	*masu*
April	*Abril*	*abli*
May	*Maio*	*mayu*
June	*Junho*	*junhu*
July	*Julho*	*julhu*
August	*Agosto*	*agôstô*
September	*Setembro*	*setemblu*
October	*Outubro*	*ôtublu*
November	*Novembro*	*novemblu*
December	*Dezembro*	*dezemblu*

Getting around

public transport	*transportes públicos*	*karu praça*
a one-way ticket	*um bilhete de ida*	*bilhêtê di be*
a return ticket	*um bilhete de ida e volta*	*bilhêtê di bi*
I want to go to…	*Quero ir para…*	*N mêsê ba…*
How much is it?	*Quanto é que é?*	*Kantu ku ê sa?*
What time does it leave?	*A que horas sai?*	*Kê mind'ola ê ka xê?*
What time is it now?	*Que horas são?*	*Kê mind 'ola kwa sa ê?*
The plane has been…	*O vôo está…*	*avion sa …*
…delayed …	*atrasado*	*trasadu*
…cancelled …	*cancelado*	*avion na bila ska bi fa*
first class	*primeira classe*	*primêra klasi*
second class	*segunda classe*	*sêgunda klasi*
ticket office	*bilheteira*	*luge di kopla bilhêtê*
timetable	*horário*	*ola d'avion*

from	de	djina
to	para	antê
airport	aeroporto	kampu d'aviason/kampu d'avion
port	porto	pôntxi
plane	avião	avion
dug-out canoe	canoa	kanwa
boat	barco	vapô
car	carro	karu
4x4	quatro vezes quatro/jeep	jipi
taxi	taxi	karu praça
minibus	minibus	atukaru txoko
motorbike/moped	moto	moto
bicycle	bicicleta	bixketa
arrival/departure	chegada/partida	ola xiga/ola xê
here	aqui	nai
there	ali	nala
Bon voyage!	Boa viagem	Be ku Dêsu! (go with God)

Private transport

Is this the road to...?	Esta é a estrada para...?	Stlada se sa stlada di ba...?
Where is the service station?	Aonde fica a bomba de combustível?	Bomba gasolina sa andji ê
Please fill it up	Por favor é para atestar/encher	Fen favôlô, xa mutoru
I'd like … litres	Queria … litros	N mêsê…litlu
diesel	gasóleo	gasolho
petrol	gasolina	gasolina
lift	boleia	bolêa
I have broken down	Tenho o carro avariado/empanado	Karu mu dana/karu mundja dê
jack	macaco (lit. 'monkey')	makaku

Road signs

give way	desistir	
danger	perigo	Pligu
entry	entrada	Lentla
detour	desvio	Bila nai
one way	sentido único	Ka be so
no entry	proibida a entrada	Na lentla fa
exit	saída	Xê

Directions

Where is it?	Onde fica?	Andji ku ... sa nê?
Go straight ahead	Sempre em frente	Ka be so
Turn left	Virar à esquerda	Toma mon xkedu
Turn right	Virar à direita	Toma mon glêtu
…at the roundabout	…na rotunda	
north	norte	notxi
south	sul	sulu
east	leste	
west	oeste	
behind	atrás	ni tlaxi
in front of	à frente	ni wê
near	perto	petu/ ni bodo/n zuntu
opposite	oposto	biladu wê da

Other useful words/expressions

money	*dinheiro*	*djêlu*
nothing	*nada*	*nadaxi*
open	*aberto*	*betu*
closed	*fechado*	*fisadu*
toilets – men/women	*casa de banho -*	*ke banhu d'ome/mwala letreti d'ome/letreti mwala*
information	*informação*	*informason*
Do you speak English/French?	*Fala inglês/francês?*	*Sun/san/bô sêbê fla/ inglêji/flansêji?*
He/she went out	*Ele/ela saiu*	*Ê xê*
He/she will be back at...	*Ele/ela volta às...*	*Ê ka bila bi ...ora*

Accommodation

Where is a cheap/good hotel?	*Onde fica um hotel barato/bom?*	*Andji ku tê a hotelu/penson blatu ê?*
Could you please write the address?	*Pode-me escrever a morada por favor?*	*Sun/San ka pô fe mu favôlô di sklêvê direson?*
Do you have any rooms available?	*Tem quartos disponíveis?*	*kwartu sen?*
I'd like...	*Queria...*	*N tava mêsê/ N mêsê*
...a single room ...	*um quarto com uma cama*	*...a kwartu k' a kama*
...a double room ...	*um quarto de casal*	*...a kwartu ku kama kasal/ ...ku kama pla dôsu ngê*
...a room with two beds ...	*um quarto com duas camas*	*...a kwartu ku dôsu kama*
...a room with a bathroom ...	*um quarto com casa de banho*	*...a kwartu ku ke banhu*
How much is it per night/person?	*Quanto é por cada noite/pessoa?*	*Kantu plô nôtxi?*
Where is the toilet?	*Onde é a casa de banho?*	*Ke banhu sa andji?/ Letreti sa andji?*
Where is the bathroom?	*Onde é a casa de banho?*	*Ke banhu sa andji?*
Is there hot water?	*Tem água quente?*	*Awa kêntxi sen?/ A tê awa kêntxi?*
Is there electricity?	*Tem energia?*	*Kandja/letrisidadi sen?*
There's been a power cut; the power will come back at...	*Houve um corte de energia; a energia vai voltar...*	*Kandja bê dê A kota kandja Kandja ka bi ... ora*
Is breakfast included?	*O pequeno almoço está incluido?*	*Ku matabisu ô?*
Can you make up a packed lunch?	*Pode preparar uma refeição para levar?*	*A ka pô fe mina kwa kume pa n be ku ê ô?*
I'd like to speak to the manager, please	*Faz favor, queria falar com o gerente*	*N mêsê fla ku patlon, xefi, jerenti*
I am leaving today	*Vou-me embora hoje*	*N ga be mu oze/n ga xê oze*

Food

Do you have a table for ... people?	*Tem uma mesa para ... pessoas?*	*Meza pla ....ngê sen?*
...a children's menu?	*...um menu para crianças?*	*kume pla mina pikina sen?*
I am a vegetarian	*Sou vegetariano/a*	*Na ka kume kani nê pixi fa*
Do you have any vegetarian dishes?	*Tem pratos vegetarianos?*	*Kume fya sen?*
Waiter! (informal)	*Moço/a! / Rapaz!* (but NOT *Rapariga!*)	*Sungê ê!/Sangê ê!*
Please bring me...	*Por favor traga-me...*	*Fe mu favôlô bi ku...*
...a fork/knife/spoon/glass/	*...um garfo/faca/colher/copo/*	*...galufu/ faka/kwiê/ kopu*

205

napkin	...guardanapo	gwadanapu
Can I have the bill please?	Traga a conta por favor	Fe mu favôlô bi ku konta
meal	refeição	kume
packed lunch	refeição para levar	kume di be ku ê
Can you heat this up for me, please?	Faz favor, pode-se aquecer?	Sun/san ka pô fe mu favôlô di kenta kwa se da mu?

Basics

bread	pão	mpon
biscuits/cookies	bolachas	bôlô
butter	manteiga	mantêga
cheese	queijo	kêzu
oil/olive oil/palm oil	óleo/azeite/óleo de palma	olho/zêtê doxi/zêtê (pema)
chilli	piri-piri	magita/
pepper	pimento	pimenton
salt	sal	salu
sugar	açucar	sukli
eggs	ovos	ovu
pasta	esparguete	spalageti

Fruit

papaya	mamão	mamon
bananas	bananas	bôbô, kitxiba, klete, bana (bana ôlô, bana mpon, bana plata, bana plata, bana manson)
pineapple	ananàs	nanaji
mango	manga	manga
orange	laranja	lanza
lime	lima	limon
lemon	limão	limon flansêji
safu (local fruit)	safú	safu
izaquente (local fruit)	izaquente	zêkêntxi
jack fruit	jaca	jaka
bread fruit	frutapão	fluta/ flupa mpon
cocoa	cacao	kakaw
(fruit from the spondias dulcis king's fruit, ambarella)	cajamanga	kajamanga
coco	coco	kokonja
passion fruit	maracujá	mlakunja
guava	goiaba	ngweva
tomato	tomate	tomatu

Vegetables

yam	inhame	nhami
mandioc	mandioca	mandjoka
spring greens	couve	kôvi
cabbage	repolho	rôpôlhu
(green) beans	feijão (verde)	fezon vêdê
carrots	cenoura	sinôra
garlic	alho	ayu
onion	cebola	sabola
potato/sweet	batata inglesa/doce	batata/batata doxi
beans	feijão	fezon

Fish

fish	*peixe*	*pixi*
barracuda	*barracuda*	*bakuda*
shark	*tubarão*	*ngandu*
flying fish	*peixe voador*	*vadô*
mackerel	*cavala*	*kavala*
mussels	*mexilhão*	
salmon	*salmão*	*salmon*
tuna	*atum*	*atun*

Meat

beef	*carne de vaca*	*kani bwê*
chicken	*galinha/frango*	*nganha*
goat	*cabra*	*kabla*
monkey	*macaco*	*makaku*
bat	*morcego*	*ngembu*
pork	*porco*	*plôkô*
lamb	*borrego*	*karnêru*
sausage	*salsicha*	*salsixa*

Drinks

beer	*cerveja*	*sêlêvêja*
coffee	*café*	*kafe*
tea	*chá*	*xa*
fruit juice	*sumo de fruta*	*sumu*
fizzy drink (coke, lemonade…)	'Sumol' (brand name)	'Sumol'
milk	*leite*	*lêtê*
water	*água*	*awa/awa galafa* (bottled water)
wine	*vinho*	*vin*

Shopping

I'd like to buy…	*Queria comprar…*	*N mêsê kopla*
How much is it?	*Quanto é?*	*Kantu kwa se sa?*
Have you got any…?	*Tem...?*	*Sun/San tê…?*
I don't like it	*Não gosto*	*N na ngosta fa*
I'm just looking	*Estou só a ver*	*N ska pya so*
It's too expensive	*É muito caro*	*Sa djêlu muntu fan*
I'll take it	*Eu compro*	*N ga kopla/N ga be ku ê*
Please may I have?	*Por favor queria?*	*N mêsê?*
There's no more	*…Acabou*	*Ê kaba za/Ê na bila sen fa*
Do you accept … ?	*Aceita-se … ?*	*Sun/ san ka toma … ?*
credit cards	*cartão de crédito*	*karton kreditu*
shop	*loja*	*vêndê*
change	*troco*	*tloku*
small change/coins	*moeda*	*tloku wini-wini*
more	*mais*	*maxi*
less	*menos*	*menu*
smaller	*mais pequeno*	*maxi pikina*
bigger	*maior*	*maxi nglandji*

Communications

I am looking for…	*Estou à procura de…*	*N ska golo*
bank	*banco*	*banku*

post office	*correios*	*korêyu*
stamps	*selos*	*sêlu*
church, cathedral	*igreja,catedral*	*glêza, ase*
embassy	*embaixada*	*embaxada*
exchange office	*câmbio*	*ke tloka djêlu*
public telephone	*telefone público*	*telefoni*
mobile/cell phone	*telemóvel*	*telemovel*
tourist office	*posto de turismo*	*sentru di turismu*

Health

diarrhoea	*diarreia*	*bega kôlê*
nausea	*náusea*	*bega uxi*
doctor	*doutor*	*dôtôlô*
I'd like to make an appointment with...	*Queria marcar consulta com...*	*N mêsê pa dôtôlô kunsuta mu*
prescription	*prescrição*	*papelu mindjan*
pharmacy	*farmácia*	*butxika*
paracetamol	*paracetamol*	*parasetamol*
antibiotics	*antibióticos*	*antibiotiku*
antiseptic	*anti-sépticos –*	*kwa di vita infeson*
tampons	*tampões –*	
condoms	*preservativos*	*kamisinha*
contraceptives	*contraceptivos*	*kumprimidu di na toma bega*
sunblock	*protector solar*	*pumada pa solo na kema ngê*
It hurts here	*Dói-me aquí*	*Ai ska dwê mu*
My head/teeth/stomach hurts	*Dói-me a cabeça/os dentes/a barriga*	*Kabesa/dêntxi/bega ska dwê mu*
I am...	*Sou...*	*N sa ...*
asthmatic	*asmático/a*	*n ga sufli d'asma*
epileptic	*epilético/a*	*n ga toma taki*
diabetic	*diabético/a*	*n ga sufli diabeti*
I'm allergic to...	*sou alérgico/a a...*	*n ga sufli d'alergia*
penicillin	*penicilina*	*pinisilina*

Travel with children

Is there a ... ?	*Tem ... ?*	*Ai tê ... ?*
...baby changing room? ..	*...quarto para mudar fraldas ao bébé?*	*...xitu di muda mina anzu fralda ô?*
...a children's menu? ...	*...menu para crianças?*	*...kume pla mina pikina ô?*
Do you have ... ?	*Tem ... ?*	*Sun/san tê?*
...infant milk formula?	*...leite em pó para bébés?*	*...lêtê en po pla mina anzu ô?*
nappies	*fraldas*	*fralda*
potty	*penico/bacio*	*baxa/piniku*
babysitter	*babysitter*	*ngê toma konta d'anzu*
highchair	*cadeira para bébé*	*banku pa mina anzu*
How old is he/she?	*Quantos anos tem?*	*Kantu anu ê tê?*

In the forest/woods

hike	*caminhada*	*skurson/ ba matu ba paxa*
slippery	*escorregadio*	*Kwa ka kloga*
plantation	*roça*	*losa*
tree	*árvore*	*po madêra*
floresta	*floresta*	*ôbô/matu*
wood	*madeira*	*madela /madêra*

Help!	Socorro!	Kidalê!
Call a doctor!	Chamem um médico!	sama dôtôlô
There's been an accident	Houve um acidente	a asidenti da
Careful!	Cuidado!	kwidadu!
I'm lost	Estou perdido	n plêdê
Go away!	Và-se embora!	Fô dai
police	polícia	sode (the corps)
		polisya (policeman)
fire	fogo	fôgô
ambulance	ambulância	ambulansia
thief	ladrão	ladlon
They took…	Roubaram-me…	A futa mu…
hospital	hospital	xipitali
I am ill	estou doente	n ska dwêntxi

tent	tenda	tenda
rain	chuva	suba
How long to get to … ?	Quanto tempo para chegar a … ?	Kantu nda antê ala … ?
How far is it to … ?	A que distancia fica … ?	Ê tê nda montxi … ?

In the club

Are you on your own?	Está sozinho/a?	Sun/san/bô tan ô?
Would you like a drink?	Quer beber alguma coisa?	Bô mêsê bêbê kwakwali kwa?
Would you like to dance?	Quer dançar?	Bô mêsê dansa?/bô mêsê sagudji
		tumbu?
Where is your husband/wife?	Onde é que está o seu marido/ a sua esposa?	Ome/mwala bô s'andji?
Do you have children?	Tem filhos?	Sun/San/Bô tê mina?
How many children do you have?	Quantos filhos?	Kantu mina sun/san/bô tê?
Where are you staying?	Onde mora/está hospedado/a?	Andji sun/san bô ska ta nê?
good-looking	bonito/bonita	glavi
I like you	Gosto de tí	N ngosta bô/N gôgô ku bô
party	festa	fesa
nothing happening	está fraco	kwa sa flakexidu

Other

my/mine/ours/yours	meu(s)/minha(s)/nosso(s)/vosso(s)	dji mu/dji non/dinansê
and/but	e/mas	ku/maji
some	algum(a)	a-a
this/that	isto/aquilo	ise/isala
with	com	ku
like that	assim	mo kwa se
expensive/cheap	caro/barato	karu/blatu
beautiful/awful	lindo/horrível	glavi/fê
pretty/ugly	bonito/feio	glavi/fê
old/new	velho/novo	ve/novu
good/bad	bom/mau	bwa, bon/ma,mau, bluku
early/late	cedo/tarde	sedu/tadji
hot/cold	quente/frio	kentxi/fiô

difficult/easy	difícil/fácil	kwa tê matxi/kwa na tê matxi fa
boring/interesting	chato/interessante	sê aglasa/ka da sun vonte
fast/slow	rápido/devagar	djandjan/momoli
excellent!	optimo!	fina leke-leke!
nice	giro/a	glavi
smart	esperto/a	supetu
exactly!	exactamente	efan/axen mé
funny	engraçado/a	ka fe sun li
black	preto, negro	pletu
white	branco (colomba, derog.)	blanku/kolomba
mixed race	mulato,	mulatu
foreigner	estrangeiro/a	strangêru
So? What are you up to?	Então?	Kuma?
Isn't it/isn't that so?	Não e?	Na sa axen me fa?
It's in poor condition/ not fit for use	Não tem condiçoes na sa buadu fa	Ê na ka da fa
problems, mess	confusão	tlomentu/kunfuson
Hello (on the telephone)	Estou (sim)	Alô
Do you see what I mean?	…Ouviu?	Sun/san/bô têndê?
Look!	Olhe! (formal)/Olha!(informal)	Pya!
There is?	há?	Ê sen?
…happened/there was…	…houve?	…kontêsê?/Tava sen?
That's enough!	Já chega!	Ê xiga za!
Damn!	Bolas!	Djanga!
(Son of a) bitch	(Filho da) puta	Fidaputa!
Well then, eh! (common exclamation)	Epá!	Êy kompa ê!
Thingy (filler word) ...	coiso...	kwa
a lot	bastante	a data/lumadu/muntu/ ku pasa
Excuse me (eg: pushing through a crowd)	Com licença	Da mu lisensa

Appendix 3

FURTHER INFORMATION

BOOKS Most books on São Tomé and Príncipe are in Portuguese, but increasingly titles are appearing in English. For reasons of space, this section includes only a selection of the most important titles in Portuguese (P), French (F) and German (G). For a more detailed bibliography, check www.usuarios.lycos.es/antropogeo/saotomebib/saotomebib.htm.

There are no bookshops on the archipelago. On São Tomé island, some publications may be consulted at the **National Archives**, the **National Library** or the **Writers' Union** UNEAS. The **Alliance Française** library is quite well stocked with books on STP, and the Instituto Camões occasionally sells volumes of local poetry. Most titles listed here you can only get outside the country, most easily online (for instance, on Amazon). Another good source are second-hand booksellers in Portugal; Lisbon has 90 *alfarrabistas* who often stock STP titles. (The dialling code for Portugal is +351.) The Lisbon-based **Instituto de Investigação Tropical** publishes many STP-related books (*IICT, Rua da Junqueira, n° 86 - 1°, 1300-344 Lisbon;* ✆ *21 3616340;* e *iict@iict.pt; www.iict.pt*). The Institute's publications are available from three booksellers, the most central of which is Livraria Portugal (*Rua do Carmo 70-74, 1200–094 Lisbon;* ✆ *21 3474982;* e *direccao@livrariaportugal.pt*). They will mail books abroad and also sell other STP-related titles. The IICT's library, CDI (*Centro de Documentação e Informação; Rua Gen. João de Almeida, 15, 1300-266 Lisbon;* ✆ *21 3619730;* e *cdi@iict.pt; www.iict.pt*), is open to the public 09.00–12.30 and 14.00–17.30 Mon–Fri, but you can't borrow. The **National Library** is at Campo Grande 83, 1749-081 Lisbon (✆ *21 7982000; www.bn.pt*). The British Library Direct service (*www.direct.bl.uk*) offers expensive direct downloads of some 40 catalogue items on São Tomé and Príncipe and the option to order some 250 more.

Fiction

Bragança, Albertino, *Rosa do Riboque* Caminho, 1998. Tales from the famous São Tomé neighbourhood (P).

Cohn, Paul D, *São Tomé – Journey to the Abyss: Portugal's Stolen Children* Burns-Cole Publications, 2005. Page-turning self-published historical novel following the fate of two Portuguese Jewish children kidnapped and brought to São Tomé.

Espírito Santo, Alda Graça, *E Nosso o Solo Sagrado da Terra* Ulmeiro, 1978, and *O Coral das Ilhas* UNEAS, 2006. Poetry by the *grande dame* of Santomean culture and politics.

Guisti, Emilio and Massa, Jean-Michel (eds): *Fablier de São Tomé* Edicef Fleuve et Flamme, 1984. 14 *Santomense* tales, in a P/F bilingual edition.

Marky, Sum, *Crónica de Una Guerra Inventada* Vega, 1999. Exploration of the 1953 massacre.

Rosa Mendes, Pedro, *Lenin Oil* Dom Quixote, 2006. What happens when oil hits a small island republic on the equator? Challenging ironic exploration (P) of this issue by a young award-winning Portuguese author – using a first-person narrative of an American oil executive and dramatic elements of the *tchiloli*. Beautiful illustrations by Alain Corbel.

Sousa Tavares, Miguel *Equador* (see page 27 for an extract) Bloomsbury, 2008; translation by Peter Bush. Hugely atmospheric novel charting the progress of young dandy Luis Bernardo Valença, sent from Lisbon to be governor of the islands and defeat the impending boycott of Santomean cocoa – only to find himself in hot political waters and a love triangle. The novel has sold over 250,000 copies in Portugal and been translated into a dozen languages and made into a television series for TV1 – filmed, however, in Brazil. The Portuguese publisher also brought out a large-format hardback version, beautifully illustrated with period postcards. Oficina do Livro, 2003.

Teles, Manuel Neto, *Retalhes do Massacre de Batepá* União dos Escritores Angolanos 2008. Historical novel on the 1953 massacre.

Poetry

Lima, Conceição, *A Dolorosa Raíz do Micondó* Caminho, 2006. Second collection (P) by acclaimed London-based poet, born and bred in Santana and former BBC World Service producer. (For one of her poems, see box, page 24.)

Mata, Inocência (ed), *Bendenxa: 25 poemas de São Tomé e Príncipe para os 25 anos de Independência* Caminho, 2000. Inspired selection of past and present Santomean poetry by 11 poets, including previously unpublished work (P).

Travel guides

Auzias, Dominique/Labourdette, Jean-Paul, *Gabon/São Tomé et Príncipe* Le Petit Futé, 2008

Gallet, Dominique, *São Tomé and Príncipe - Iles du milieu du monde* Karthala, 2001. Lively and detailed cultural guide, though a lot of the travel information is now out of date.

Iwainsky, Thomas/Weck, Karl Alexander, *Reiseführer São Tomé e Príncipe* Cosmoglobe Communications, 2003. Compact, nicely produced and personal travel guide (G).

Schweinberger, Bernd, *São Tomé and Príncipe – Trauminseln auf dem Äquator* 1995. Engaging travel narrative (G), plus tourism tips (now mostly out of date), by the first non-Portuguese tour operator to offer trips to São Tomé and Príncipe. Available from www.schweinberger.de.

Various, *São Tomé e Príncipe 2008*. Portuguese/English brochure-style guide, with lots of information and colour pictures; available from the tourist office in São Tomé.

Travel health

Wilson-Howarth, Dr Jane, *Bugs, Bites & Bowels* Cadogan/Globe Pequot, 2006. In-depth and entertaining advice, with case studies.

Wilson-Howarth, Dr Jane, and Ellis, Dr Matthew *Your Child Abroad: A Travel Health Guide* Bradt Travel Guides, 2005

General

Espírito Santo, Carlos, *Encyclopédia Fundamental de São Tomé and Príncipe* Cooperação Portuguesa, 2001. Illustrated, extensive if now a bit outdated overview of all aspects of São Tomé and Príncipe life – people, plants, politics, literature, history, local words, customs, etc.

Espírito Santo, Carlos, *Coração ao mar* Cooperação Portuguesa, 1998. Engaging study of *forro* culture, from birth to death, touching on language, rituals, religion, culture, crafts, medicine, with colour photographs.

Tournadre, Michel, *São Tomé and Príncipe* Editions Regards, 2000. Coffee-table book with excellent photography.

Arts/Culture

Burness, Donald, *Ossobó – Essays on the Literature of São Tomé and Príncipe* Africa World Press, 2005. The US-American expert on lusophone African literatures explores the themes of Santomean literature: the mythic Ossobó bird, the massacre of 1953 and Angolar culture. Includes 23 English translations of poetry by ten poets (Marcelo da Veiga, Francisco José Tenreiro, Fernando de Macedo, Alda Espírito Santo, Carlos Espírito Santo). Also available in P: *Ossobó: Ensaios sobre a literatura de São Tomé e Príncipe* Câmara Municipal de Lagos, 2007.

Espírito Santo, Carlos, *Tipologias do Conto Maravilhoso Africano* Cooperação Portuguesa, 2000. Analysis of African fairytales with focus on São Tomé and Príncipe, reprinting some local examples (P).

Ferraz, Luiz Ivens, *The Creole of São Tomé* Witwatersrand University Press, 1979. The first monograph on the local Creole language.

Gründ, Françoise, *Tchiloli – Charlemagne à São Tomé sur l'île du milieu du monde* Magellan & Cie, 2006. Beautifully illustrated study (F) on this unique dramatic cultural expression.

Günther, Wilfried, *Das portugiesische Kreolisch der Jlha do Príncipe* author's ed/Marburger Studien zur Afrika- und Asienkunde, Marburg, 1973. Detailed study (G) of the *lung'iye* language spoken on Príncipe, with glossary.

Kalewska, Anna, *Baltasar Dias e as metamorfoses do discurso dramatúrgico em Portugal e nas ilhas de São Tomé and Príncipe* Warsaw University, 2005. Study (P) on the sources of the *tchiloli*.

Laban, Michel, *Encontros com Escritores* Funcação António de Almeida, 2002. Interviews with Santomean writers (P).

Loude, Jean-Yves, *Coup de théâtre à São Tomé: Carnet d'enquête aux îles du milieu du monde* Actes du Sud, 2007. An ethnologist's travelogue (F), with illustrations by Alain Corbel.

Loureiro, João, *Postais Antigos de S. Tomé e Príncipe* Postais Ultramar, 2005. Over 200 views of São Tomé and Príncipe in the 19th and 20th centuries, some of them used for the illustrated edition of Miguel Sousa Tavares' *Equador* (see above); *www.postaisultramar.com.pt*.

Massa, Françoise and Jean-Michel, *Dictionnaire bilingue portugais-français des particularités de la langue portugaise à Saint-Thomas et Prince* CNRS, 1998. Portuguese-French dictionary with emphasis on the islands' linguistic particularities.

Mata, Inocência, *Diálogo Com as Ilhas: Sobre Cultura e Literatura de São Tomé e Príncipe* Edições Colibri, 1998. Overview of Santomean culture and literature, by Príncipe-born academic.

Maurer, Philippe, *L'angolar. Un créole afro-portugais parlé à São Tomé* Helmut Buske Verlag, 1995. A grammar of Angolar.

Pereira, Paulo Alves, *Das Tchiloli von São Tomé – Die Wege des karolingischen Universums* IKO Verlag, 2002. Thesis (G) placing the island's unique dramatic expression in its cultural context.

Reis, Fernando: *Pôvô Flogà, O Povo brinca. Folclore de São Tomé e Príncipe* Câmara Municipal de São Tomé, 1969. Seminal exploration of Santomean folklore (P), including the Tchiloli text.

Rizzo, Nora/Rocha, Luis: *Arquitectura colonial de São Tomé and Príncipe?* 2008/9. Forthcoming photographic inventory of São Tomé and Príncipe 's colonial architecture and plantations.

Soulié, Tony, *São Tomé – Le rêve africain* Au Même Titre, 2003. Glossy reproductions of French artist's collage paintings, with an excellent foreword by Bernard Carayon.

History/Society

Caixa Geral de Depósitos / SGE Mediateca, *Olhar O Futuro* 2006. Illustrated overview of contemporary São Tomé and Príncipe society, with data on living conditions, health, education (P).

Deus Lima, José: *História do Massacre de 1953 em São Tomé and Príncipe* 2002. History of the colonial 'massacre' and rallying call for Santomean nationalism (P), including many oral testimonies. Available from the Tourist Information in São Tomé and the National Archives/National Library.

Henriques, Isabel Castro, *São Tomé and Príncipe – A Invenção de uma Sociedade* Vega, 2000. Small but heavily illustrated study by Lisbon-based historian specialised in Africa and decolonialisation (P).

Nascimento, Augusto, *Poderes e Quotidiano nas Roças São Tomé e Príncipe de finais de oilocentos a meados de novecentos* Lisbon 2002. The Portuguese historian on the Santomean plantation system's heyday.

Ramos, João, *Quem é Quem em S. Tomé e Príncipe* Vitor Rosa, 2007. A Who's Who (P) of São Tomé and Príncipe's parliamentary, judiciary, military, diplomatic and NGO representatives, with pictures and contact information, invaluable for anybody who wants to do business on the islands. 300,000$ from the Mediateca, São Tomé.

Satre, Lowell J: *Chocolate on Trial: Slavery, Politics, and the Ethics of Business* Ohio University Press, 2005. The story of slavery in West Africa, and São Tomé and Príncipe in particular, and the intervention of William Cadbury, leading to the 1909 boycott of Santomean cocoa.

Seibert, Gerhard, *Comrades, Clients and Cousins – Colonialism, Socialism and Democratization in São Tomé and Príncipe* Brill, 2006. The 'bible' of São Tomé and Príncipe: an in-depth (over 600pp) and up-to-date analysis of history, society and party politics by Lisbon-based researcher and authority on São Tomé and Príncipe.

Valverde, Paulo *Máscara, Mato e Morte em São Tomé* Celta Editora, 2000. Study (P) of Santomean drama, rituals and beliefs.

Natural history Many books may be ordered through the British Natural History Book Store wildlife specialist (☏ *+44 (0)1803 865913;* e *customer.services@nhbs.co.uk; www.nhbs.com*), who offer an excellent customer service, including a no-quibble refund.

Atkinson, P W/Dutton, J S et al (eds), *A Study of the Birds, Small Mammals, Turtles and Medicinal Plants of São Tomé, with Notes on Príncipe* BirdLife International Study Report No 56, 1992. For a copy of the only available English-language round-up of the islands' flora and fauna, check www.africanbirdclub.org/sales/sales.2.html. At £10 it's worth getting, even if a few things are out of date.

Billes, Alexis, *On the tracks of sea turtles in Central Africa* Ecofac, 2005. Useful illustrated booklet describing the different species, their life cycle, identification guide, etc. Available from the Marapa NGO in São Tomé town, also in F and P.

Borrow, Nik & Demey, Ron, *Birds of Western Africa* Princeton Field Guides, new ed 2005. The gold standard, especially if you're combining your trip to São Tomé and Príncipe with Gabon. If you don't want to carry this weighty illustrated tome, just photocopy the back pages with the Gulf of Guinea endemics. Nik Borrow guides with the Birdquest tour operator (see page 43).

Christy, Patrice/Clarke, William V, *Les oiseaux de São Tomé and Príncipe*. Ecofac, 1998. The best bird guide to get, with 32 pages of excellent colour drawings illustrating the French text (introduction in P, too), and the creole names for many common birds.

De Naurois, René, *Les Oiseaux des Îles du Golfe de Guinée: São Tomé, Prince et Annobon/As Aves das Ilhas Do Golfo da Guinée: São Tomé, Príncipe e Ano Bom* IICT, 1994. This illustrated bird guide (F/P), the fruit of 20 years' ornithological research, is recommended by birders, but at a cover price of around $100 you're probably better off with the Christy book (see above).

Do Céu, Maria Madureira (ed), *Estudo Etnofarmacológico de Plantas Medicinais de São Tomé e Príncipe* Ministerio da Saúde de STP, 2008

Exell, A W, *Catalogue of the vascular plants of São Tome* British Museum of Natural History, 1944. Still the reference work.

Figueiredo, Estrela, *Nomes vulgares da flora de São Tomé e Príncipe* IICT, 1998. A list of the common names for many of the local plants and trees.

Jones, Peter/Tye, Alan, *The Birds of São Tomé and Príncipe with Annobon* British Ornithologists' Union, 2006. A professional checklist with no illustrations and few photographs, this bird book is only for hard-core birders.

Oliveira, Faustino/Stévart, Tariq, *As Orchídeas de São Tomé and Príncipe/Guide des Orchidées de São Tomé and Príncipe*. Ecofac, 1998 (P/F). Orchid guide,, fruit of the work of local botanist, Faustino Oliveira and Belgian colleague Tariq Stévart (e *tstevart@yahoo.com; www.geocities.com/tstevart*). Save a lot of money by downloading relevant pages (*www.ecofac.org/Biblio/Download/Guides/GuideOrchideesSTP.pdf*)

Roseira, Luís Lopes, *Plantas úteis da flora de São Tomé e Príncipe* new ed 2007. Fascinating local study (P) of the medicinal, industrial and ornamental uses of the islands' plants, with some drawings/photos. Available from the capital's Livraria de São Tomé opposite the cathedral.

Sargeant, David E, *A Birders' Guide to the Gulf of Guinea Islands of São Tomé and Príncipe* (Birders' Guides and Checklists, 1992). Slim A4 checklist by the ornithologist who first sighted São Tomé's rarest bird in recent times, with detailed diaries from his birdwatching trips in 1989 and 1991 and hands-on advice on how to explore the remote southwest.

Wilme, Lucienne, *São Tomé and Príncipe – balade sur deux jeunes îles du plus vieux continent* Ecofac, 2000. Handy illustrated overview of São Tomé and Príncipe's natural beauty, inc an extensive Latin/E/F glossary. Download it for free from www.ecofac.org/Biblio/TelechargementSommaire.htm.

Cookery

Aguiar, Sandra/Kilcher, Frédéric et al, *Receitas com Produtos da Terra* Alisei, 2006. Collection of recipes (P), from coconut cake to banana croquetes and orange wine. Available from the Alisei (see page 93) or Ossobô (see page 111) shops.

Corallo, Claudio/Rovira, *Eric, KKO – Esencia de Cacao* (Spanish). A homage to cocoa and chocolate.

Silva, João Carlos, *A Roça com os Tachos* Oficina do Livro, 2005. Beautifully produced illustrated cookery book based on an RTP Africa TV programme, featuring traditional recipes and presenting local fruit, herbs and vegetables. Photos by Adriana Freire. Also available as a DVD set, showing the charismatic chef cooking his way around the plantations. The 2006 follow-up, *Façam o Favor de Ser Felices*, contains further recipes and reflections on São Tomé and Príncipe.

Valério, Conceição, *Cozinha Tradicional de São Tomé e Príncipe* Centro Culturel Português, 2002

ARTICLES

Tügel, Hanne/Maitre, Pascal 'Warten auf den Ölrausch' (GEO magazine, July 2005, pp 84–104). Photo reportage (G).

Jary, Emmanuelle/Mallet, Jean-François 'São Tomé et Príncipe – Les îles du milieu du monde' (Saveurs Magazine Dec 2005/Jan 2006) Reportage and recipes (F).

Shaxson, Nicholas, in: *Poisoned Wells – The Dirty Politics of African Oil* (Palgrave 2007). In this analysis of the volatile African oil sector, this respected journalist devotes a whole chapter to São Tomé and Príncipe.

Various, ABP – Zeitschrift zur portugiesischsprachigen Welt, No. 1 (IKO, 1995) Articles (G/P) from a STP symposium at Cologne University.

Various, Maison des Cultures du monde International de l'Imaginaire No 14, 1990. Tchiloli and *Santomense* culture in general (F).

Various *Biodiversity and conservation in Sao Tomé* (journal articles on birds, medicinal plants, ferns and introduced mammals) Springer, Biodiversity and conservation, vol 3, no 9, December, 2004. Download from www.springerlink.com; US$30.

MAPS There are few maps available; it's probably best to just get whichever one you can find, as it is very difficult to find São Tomé and Príncipe maps outside the country. In São Tomé and Príncipe, you will see topographical maps and maritime charts from the 1960s hanging on office walls, but these are not available for sale. A good starting point is the one you can print off the Navetur website. A São Tomé town map should be for sale at Hotel Pestana and free from Hotel Phenicia; or print out the one available on the tourism office website. **GPS** (Global Positioning System) works better in São Tomé than in Príncipe, unless there is too much tree cover or other interference, such as clouds, blocking the satellite signal; the signal quality also depends on the quality of the receiver.

Burkina Faso-based Marcelin Ouangraoua spent two years putting together detailed 1:45,000 road maps of both São Tomé and Príncipe: **Rede Nacional das Stradas** (2005). These are the best and most-up-to-date maps, though as they are not topographical and don't feature small tracks, they won't help you much if you want to go trekking on your own. The maps should be available from Navetur; the agency is also planning a tourist version of this map. The safest option is to email Marcelin and order them from him direct, paying via electronic money transfer (expect to pay €25 in bank charges though!). Marcelin is very reliable, and can also email you pdf files. Contact Marcelin Ouangraoua, 01 BP 1517 Ougadougou 01, Burkina Faso; ✆ +226 70604650; e ouangraoua_marcelin@yahoo.fr. The most commonly available and cheapest map is the rather schematic **Alphita** map (no year) for €5. Fernando Lima da Trindades' **Carta Técnica** (1:100,000) of 1992 is a more user-friendly and colourful map of both islands, indicating different types of beaches, but you will look in vain for major points of interest, and there is no map of Santo António town. Amara Gaudêncio Mendes' **Carta Turistica** (€15, 1996, 1:75,000) has a lot of detail and good town maps for both capitals, but an irritating purple tinge makes it hard to use. The Lisbon-based **Instituto Geográfico do Exército** has STP 1:25,000 topographical maps published by the Portuguese military in the 1930s (São Tomé sheets 1–5, Príncipe 1–2, each sheet €50, €280/£190/US$383 for the set). Available as paper copies and digital files, they date from colonial times, and you need to request advance permission from the STP Embassy in Lisbon to obtain them (*Instituto Geográfico do Exército, Av Dr Alfredo Bensaúde, 1849-014 Lisbon; tel. +351 21 8505300;* e *igeoe@igeoe.pt; www igeoe.pt*). For an electronic version, check www.ggcg.st/maps/mapsintro.html. The first of four geological 1:25.000 maps, **Cartas Geológicas (CEAG)**, with an explanatory booklet, was published in 2006 by Lígia Barros of the Ministry for Natural Resources in Rua Soldado Paulo Ferreira, São Tomé (✆ *225272*). Ecofac (see page 101) can email you a 2MB map of the Obô National Park The free-to-download **Google Earth** aerial survey of the world only covers the northeastern part (not even half) of São Tomé island only. The images seem to date a few years back and there is no detail for Príncipe, but still: you can look at the president's swimming pool if you like…

MUSIC In São Tomé and Príncipe, music CDs and DVDs are on sale at *estudios de gravação*, music stores. If you know what you like, you can ask them to make up a mixed CD (60,000$) or simply even a current chart mix. The German-language site www.alewand.de/musik/saotome_music.html is the most-detailed I've seen, and www.kizomba.eu (with English-language option) has over 110 Santomean albums listed for purchase, some with audio clips. Also check www.sonsdafricapt.com.

Da Motta, José Vianna, Piano concerto in A major/Fantasia Dramatica/Ballada (Hyperion, 1999). A flavour of the São Tomé-born late-romantic composer, with the Gulbenkian Orchestra and pianist Artur Pizarro.

Domingos, Camilo: *The best of Camilo Domingos* (Sons d'Africa, 2003, CD/DVD). Available in São Tomé and Príncipe and Lisbon music stores. Other albums: *Maninha my love, Nova Onda, Dor de Mundo.*

Gapa (Álvaro Lima): *Regresso* (Sons d'Africa, 2006). Latest solo album by the former frontman of Sangazuza (1983–96) and ambassador of Santomean music.

Africa Negra: Best of Africa Negra 1 and 2 (Sons d'Africa, 2005). Popular traditional São Tomé and Príncipe band. *www.sonsdafricapt.com.*

Batuque da Ilha: *Bulaue Belezina.*

Juka, *Coração deseja-te* (Sons d'Afrique). Popular Santomean zouk/kizomba singer based in Lisbon. Latest albums: Amiga (Sons d'Afrique, 2006) and Lágrimas por Amor (ibid, 2007).

Os MA's: *Bligá* (available from Oswaldo Santos, page 81) (Os MA's/Grupo HB 2001). Bligá is a local martial art and the 'Associated Musicians' Oswaldo Santos and Nezó were mixed by Kalú Mendes for a fusion of traditional *Santomense* styles.

Sangazuza: *Conjunto Sangazuza – Na Voz de Helder Camblé – Ana Plata* (2004)

Sebastiana: *Em nome do pai.* Solos and duets by the islands' most famous female singer.

Trio Tempo: *L'île Chocolat … en chansons!* (AEFSTP, 2006). Oswaldo Santos, Nezó and Guillerme Carvalho fuse traditional Santomean styles. Download tracks from www.sao-tome.st/article/articleview/201/1/74.

Umbelina, Gilberto Gil: *Vôa Papagaio, Vôa!* (Mélodie, 1985). Lisbon-based award-winning popular singer from Príncipe, singing in *lung'iye*. Latest album out 2008. For copies, contact him direct on ☎ +351 968466605 (Portugal)/919918 (São Tomé and Príncipe); e umbelinagilberto@yahoo.fr. He speaks English and French.

Various: *A Viagem dos Sons – Tchiloli São Tomé* (Tradisom, 1999). With information in P/E.

Various: Primeiro Explosão Banda da Ilha, Mualá Tatalugua Sá Cú Beg (2002). Artists include Príncipe-born singer João Seria, ex-front man of Africa Negra 1977–2003.

Various: *Quê Santomé*. Sons d'Africa, 2006 (CD & DVD). Gapa, Camilo Domingos, Sebastiana, Africa Negra, etc. A good start to your collection. Available from www.lojadamusica.com.

Various/Gomes, Manuel (ed): *São Tomé and Príncipe - Musique de l'Île du Milieu*. Paris, Buda Musique, 2005. 17 tracks of traditional Santomean music, with E/F booklet. Available from www.amazon.fr (where you can listen to extracts and purchase a second-hand CD from €8) or www.budamusique.com.

Various/Gomes, Manuel (ed.): *São Tomé et Príncipe perdues dans l'océan: São Tomé e Príncipe perdidas no oceano*. 109-page booklet F/P, including above CD (E-dite, 2006), €30 from www.amazon.fr.

Various: *Socopé – Raiz de noz – Sons de São Tomé e Príncipe* (no year). Compilation including eight songs by the famous Os Úntues.

Viegas, Bill Lima: *Hirondina* (2007). Latest album by young, local kizomba singer.

FILMS

Berda, Virginie, *São Tomé, cent-pour-cent cacao* (Vodeo TV, 2004). Portrait of an island at the crossroads (F). Download from www.vodeo.tv-2-27-1629-sao-tome-cent-pour-cent-cacao.html.

Brödl, Helmut, *Frutinho do Equador* (1998). Wacky story of a giant breadfruit's travels around the island of São Tomé, beautifully shot. Not available commercially.

Torres, Ângelo, Mionga ki ôbo (Lx Filmes, 2005) 52-min documentary on the Angolares fishing community.

Vertongen, Derek, *Extra Bitter: The Legacy of the Chocolate Islands* (2000). 52-minute video film (VHS format) telling the story of *Santomense* slavery through interviews with historians, writers and locals, plus archive material. Available through www.filmakers.com.

Witte, Susanne, *São Tomé and Príncipe* (SWR, 2005). 45min reportage (G) focusing on the people of the archipelago.

WEBSITES
Culture
www.africultures.com
www.artafrica.gulbenkian.pt has an extensive list of Santomean artists, with visual samples of their work
www.bienal-stp.org Information on the cultural festival held every other summer (even years) in São Tomé
www.canalsantola.info Information and video clips with music you will hear in São Tomé and Príncipe : kizomba, zouk, etc
www.instituto-camoes.pt Portuguese Cultural Institute, with details of language courses all over the world, including their cultural activities in São Tomé and Príncipe
http://lrocha.mef.googlepages.com/projectos_fotograficos Beautiful b/w photographic diary of a Portuguese photographer's 2006 visit to São Tomé and Príncipe, with blog (P)
www.everyculture.com/Sa-Th/S-o-Tom-e-Pr-ncipe.html Excellent overview

Development
www.earthinstitute.columbia.edu/cgsd/STP/index_photos.htm Columbia University's Center on Globalization and Sustainable Development site charting the São Tomé e Príncipe Advisory Project, co-ordinated by Jan Hartman and led by globalisation guru Jeffrey Sachs, as well as a wealth of development-relevant links

www.indexmundi.com/sao_tome_and_principe Edited version of CIA World Factbook, with Millennium Development Goals

www.international-alert.org/our_work/regional/west_africa/sao_tome_principe.php Non-profit mediation agency pilot project on the challenges of oil wealth coming to São Tomé and Príncipe: conflict-resolution workshops, educational/media work

www.irinnews.org Humanitarian news agency site

www.saotomeproject.wordpress.com University of Illinois and São Tomé and Príncipe Partnership site, with blog

www.saotome.ch Dr Gian Meyer's Foundation Waldhaus (G/E, see page 93)

www.unicef.org/saotome/www.unicef.org/infobycountry/stp.html The UN's children's agency

www.uns.st New site of PNUD, the United Nations' representation in São Tomé and Príncipe

www.who.int/country/stp São Tomé and Príncipe data from the World Health Organisation

General

www.africa.upenn.edu Run by Pennsylvania University, with links to other sites

www.cia.gov/library/publications/the-world-factbook/geos/tp.html Regularly updated country profile, which, give or take a couple of inaccuracies, is a good place to start.

www.groups.yahoo.com/group/saotome/messages São Tomé and Príncipe newsgroup, with open access (after registering with your Yahoo ID and password) to members' messages on anything from houses for sale and special offers at restaurants, to the environment and the oil issue. Mainly Portuguese, but postings can be made in English or any Latin language. Becoming a member is the best way to stay abreast of developments on the islands.

www.library.stanford.edu/africa/saotome.html Links to organisations, radio programme transcripts, music labels, etc

www.mega.ist.utl.pt/~mles/SaoTome/FotografiasAntigas Photos of turn-of-the-20th-century São Tomé

www.principe.st Useful regional government site, with tourism information, a discussion forum, etc

www.tvciencia.pt/tvcicn/pagicn/tvcicn01.asp?cmb_pesq=loc&txt_pesq=S%E3o+Tom%E9&offset=0 Nearly 300 historical images

www.youtube.com Hundreds of São Tomé videos of music, sharks, camping tales, carnival, etc

Media

www.correiodasemana.info Current affairs (P)

www.jornaltropical.st Current affairs (P)

www.jornal.st Online news, updated daily, with searchable archive (P)

www.macauhub.com.mo Breaking news from the lusophone world (P/E)

www.voanews.com/engl São Tomé and Príncipe news/archive reports (E) by Voice of America

Politics/Economy

www.anp-stp.gov.st National Petroleum Agency (P/E)

www.gov.st Official government site

www.imf.org/external/country/stp The International Monetary Fund's site has a wealth of up-to-date documents and statistics on São Tomé and Príncipe poverty reduction programmes

www.parlamento.st National Parliament (P/E/F)

www.worldbank.org/st Country brief

Tourism

www.africadetodosossonhos.blogspot.com Information/blog on sustainable tourism in São Tomé and Príncipe provided by São Tomé and Príncipe expert Brígida Rocha Brito

www.banknotes.com/st65.htm Has pictures of all STP notes and sells them too, including older versions.

www.bcstp.st Central Bank site, with daily exchange rate for the dobra

wwwn.cdc.gov/travel/default.aspx Latest heath and immunisation advice

www.casaamarelacasavermelha.blogspot.com São Tomé guesthouse/responsible tourism

www.cstome.net Telecommunications provider site, with links to São Tomé and Príncipe online journals, and much more (P)

http://es.geocities.com/caueass/caue_cat.htm Barcelona-based Caué Association Friends of São Tomé

www.fotoscaminhadasedescobertastp.blogspot.com Large selection of beautiful photos

www.ilovestp.com New portal for tourism and investment, run by Swiss business consultant Reto Scherraus; try also www.visitstp.com

www.mistralvoyages.com Local tour operator, with French connections (see page 100)

www.navetur-equatour.st Local tour operator, best point of contact for English-speakers (see page 100)

www.saotome.st Site run by Swedish internet services provider behind worthy projects training local students to use the net etc. Good hotel advice and more

www.sao-tome.com E/G/P introduction to the islands, linked to Miramar Hotel

www.stome.net Detailed information (P)

www.travel.state.gov US Department of State's up-to-date travel information

www.turismo-stp.org Useful tourist board's official website, in E/F/P

Wildlife

www.bigmarinefish.com Pictures and general information on the big species: blue marlin, swordfish, yellowfin tuna

www.birdlife.org In-depth up-to-date information on the islands' threatened bird species

www.bird-stamps.org/country/stthom.htm Stamps with São Tomé and Príncipe's bird species for sale

www.calacademy.org/science_now/sao_tome 2001 expedition of California Academy of Sciences, hunting trap door spiders, tree frogs, scorpions, algae, etc. Entertaining dispatches, including an ascent report of Pico de Príncipe; excellent pics

www.ecofac.org Information (if currently fairly out-of-date) on Obô National Park and marine turtles, mainly in French, but with some English sections

www.env-impact.geo.uu.se/84Fahlman.pdf Grey parrot conservation on Príncipe

www.fatbirder.com Detailed information on endemic birds and useful links

www.fco.gov.uk The Foreign Office's official up-to-date travel information for UK citizens; however, don't take it as gospel. For instance, there are no 'frequent outbreaks of cholera' and cash advances on foreign cards are available

www.flickr.com Photo-sharing site with superb close-ups of STP's flora and fauna and other great shots

www.ggcg.st Excellent (if not regularly updated) site on biodiversity in the Gulf of Guinea. The webmaster is Angus Gascoigne, a Basque-Scottish naturalist who has spent a dozen years living on the islands and works for Voice of America

www.iucn.org World Conservation Union for Nature

www.montepico.blogspot.com Blog of the Monte Pico guides' association, with useful links and information about ongoing research and conservation projects

www.seaturtle.org Marine turtle protection

www.stellarium.org Free high-quality planetarium software showing you constellations anywhere in the world, in real time. Also try the new Sky feature in Google Earth

Bradt Travel Guides

www.bradtguides.com

Africa

Africa Overland	£15.99
Algeria	£15.99
Benin	£14.99
Botswana: Okavango, Chobe, Northern Kalahari	£15.99
Burkina Faso	£14.99
Cape Verde Islands	£13.99
Canary Islands	£13.95
Cameroon	£13.95
Congo	£14.99
Eritrea	£15.99
Ethiopia	£15.99
Gabon, São Tomé, Príncipe	£13.95
Gambia, The	£13.99
Ghana	£15.99
Johannesburg	£6.99
Kenya	£14.95
Madagascar	£15.99
Malawi	£13.99
Mali	£13.95
Mauritius, Rodrigues & Réunion	£13.99
Mozambique	£13.99
Namibia	£15.99
Niger	£14.99
Nigeria	£15.99
Rwanda	£14.99
São Tomé & Principe	£14.99
Seychelles	£14.99
Sudan	£13.95
Tanzania, Northern	£13.99
Tanzania	£16.99
Uganda	£15.99
Zambia	£17.99
Zanzibar	£12.99

Britain and Europe

Albania	£13.99
Armenia, Nagorno Karabagh	£14.99
Azores	£12.99
Baltic Capitals: Tallinn, Riga, Vilnius, Kaliningrad	£12.99
Belarus	£14.99
Belgrade	£6.99
Bosnia & Herzegovina	£13.99
Bratislava	£6.99
Budapest	£8.99
Bulgaria	£13.99
Cork	£6.99
Croatia	£13.99

Cyprus see North Cyprus

Czech Republic	£13.99
Dresden	£7.99
Dubrovnik	£6.99
Estonia	£13.99
Faroe Islands	£13.95
Georgia	£14.99
Helsinki	£7.99
Hungary	£14.99
Iceland	£14.99
Kiev	£7.95
Kosovo	£14.99
Krakow	£7.99
Lapland	£13.99
Latvia	£13.99
Lille	£6.99
Lithuania	£13.99
Ljubljana	£7.99
Macedonia	£14.99
Montenegro	£13.99
North Cyprus	£12.99
Paris, Lille & Brussels	£11.95
Riga	£6.99
River Thames, In the Footsteps of the Famous	£10.95
Serbia	£14.99
Slovakia	£14.99
Slovenia	£12.99
Spitsbergen	£14.99
Switzerland: Rail, Road, Lake	£13.99
Tallinn	£6.99
Ukraine	£14.99
Vilnius	£6.99
Zagreb	£6.99

Middle East, Asia and Australasia

China: Yunnan Province	£13.99
Great Wall of China	£13.99
Iran	£14.99
Iraq	£14.95
Iraq: Then & Now	£15.99
Kyrgyzstan	£15.99
Maldives	£13.99
Mongolia	£14.95
North Korea	£13.95
Oman	£13.99
Sri Lanka	£13.99
Syria	£14.99
Tibet	£13.99
Turkmenistan	£14.99
Yemen	£14.99

The Americas and the Caribbean

Amazon, The	£14.99
Argentina	£15.99
Bolivia	£14.99
Cayman Islands	£14.99
Colombia	£15.99
Costa Rica	£13.99
Chile	£16.95
Dominica	£14.99
Falkland Islands	£13.95
Guyana	£14.99
Panama	£13.95
Peru & Bolivia: The Bradt Trekking Guide	£12.95
St Helena	£14.99
USA by Rail	£13.99

Wildlife

100 Animals to See Before They Die	£16.99
Antarctica: Guide to the Wildlife	£14.95
Arctic: Guide to the Wildlife	£15.99
Central & Eastern European Wildlife	£15.99
Chinese Wildlife	£16.99
East African Wildlife	£19.99
Galápagos Wildlife	£15.99
Madagascar Wildlife	£15.99
North Atlantic Wildlife	£16.99
Peruvian Wildlife	£15.99
Southern African Wildlife	£18.95
Sri Lankan Wildlife	£15.99

Eccentric Guides

Eccentric America	£13.95
Eccentric Australia	£12.99
Eccentric Britain	£13.99
Eccentric California	£13.99
Eccentric Cambridge	£6.99
Eccentric Edinburgh	£5.95
Eccentric France	£12.95
Eccentric London	£13.99
Eccentric Oxford	£5.95

Others

Your Child Abroad: A Travel Health Guide	£10.95
Something Different for the Weekend	£9.99

WIN £100 CASH!
READER QUESTIONNAIRE

**Send in your completed questionnaire for the chance to win
£100 cash in our regular draw**

All respondents may order a Bradt guide at half the UK retail price – please
complete the order form overleaf.

(Entries may be posted or faxed to us, or scanned and emailed.)

We are interested in getting feedback from our readers to help us plan future Bradt
guides. Please answer ALL the questions below and return the form to us in order
to qualify for an entry in our regular draw.

Have you used any other Bradt guides? If so, which titles? . . . .
. . . .

What other publishers' travel guides do you use regularly? . . . .
. . . .

Where did you buy this guidebook? . . . .

What was the main purpose of your trip to São Tomé and Príncipe (or for what
other reason did you read our guide)? eg: holiday/business/charity etc. . . . .
. . . .

What other destinations would you like to see covered by a Bradt guide?
. . . .

Age (circle relevant category) 16–25   26–45   46–60   60+

Male/Female (delete as appropriate)

Home country . . . .

Please send us any comments about our guide to São Tomé and Príncipe or other
Bradt Travel Guides. . . . .
. . . .
. . . .
. . . .

Bradt Travel Guides
23 High Street, Chalfont St Peter, Bucks SL9 9QE, UK
☎ +44 (0)1753 893444 **f** +44 (0)1753 892333
e info@bradtguides.com
www.bradtguides.com

CLAIM YOUR HALF-PRICE BRADT GUIDE!

Order Form

To order your half-price copy of a Bradt guide, and to enter our prize draw to win £100 (see overleaf), please fill in the order form below, complete the questionnaire overleaf, and send it to Bradt Travel Guides by post, fax or email.

Please send me one copy of the following guide at half the UK retail price

Title	Retail price	Half price
... .	....	....

Please send the following additional guides at full UK retail price

No	Title	Retail price	Total
...	....	....	....
...	....	....	....
...	....	....	....

	Sub total	....
	Post & packing	....

(£2 per book UK; £4 per book Europe; £6 per book rest of world)

	Total	....

Name ....

Address...

Tel .... Email ....

☐ I enclose a cheque for £ .... made payable to Bradt Travel Guides Ltd

☐ I would like to pay by credit card. Number: ....

Expiry date: ... / ...   3-digit security code (on reverse of card) .....

Issue no (debit cards only) .....

☐ I would like to subscribe to Bradt's monthly enewsletter.

☐ I would be happy for you to use my name and comments in Bradt marketing material.

Send your order on this form, with the completed questionnaire, to:

Bradt Travel Guides STP1
23 High Street, Chalfont St Peter, Bucks SL9 9QE
↘ +44 (0)1753 893444   **f** +44 (0)1753 892333
e info@bradtguides.com   www.bradtguides.com

Index

Page numbers in **bold** indicate major entries; those in *italics* indicate maps.

223